AN INTRODUCTION TO PROGRAMMING AND PROBLEM SOLVING WITH PASCAL

G. MICHAEL SCHNEIDER
Department of Computer Science
University of Minnesota

STEVEN W. WEINGART
Compiler Development
Sperry Univac
and
Department of Computer Science
University of Minnesota

DAVID M. PERLMAN
Department of Computer Science
University of Minnesota

JOHN WILEY & SONS
New York   Chichester   Brisbane   Toronto

Library of Congress Cataloging in Publication Data:

Schneider, G Michael.
  An introduction to programming and problem solving with PASCAL.

  Bibliography: p. 373
  Includes indexes.
  1. PASCAL (Computer program language)
  2. Electronic digital computers—Programming.
I. Weingart, Steven W., joint author. II. Perlman,
David M., joint author. III. Title.
QA76.73.P2S36   001.6'424   77-12014
ISBN 0-471-02542-9

Printed in the United States of America

10 9 8

To Ruthann, Benjamin and Rebecca;
Ellen and David; Shelly, Staci and Nicki

PREFACE

This textbook represents the culmination of our efforts to develop an introductory programming course at the University of Minnesota that would reflect the growing concern for teaching the design and development of good, reliable software. Too often a student's introduction to programming has been through a service course where the major concern is the syntax of some elementary programming language, and the programs are graded solely on whether they did or did not produce correct results. Unfortunately, these service courses often instill and reinforce bad habits, and later attempts to "unlearn" them are usually futile. (In this respect it is interesting to note that the students who usually encounter some difficulty in our course are *not* the ones without prior programming experience but, instead, are those who have already had a low-level exposure to FORTRAN or BASIC. These students are forced into rethinking their approach to programming.)

We have found it incorrect to assume that beginning programming students are unable to handle "higher-level" concepts. We have found it both reasonable and worthwhile to present the topics of algorithm development, stepwise refinement, recursion, and topdown modular programming along with details of a particular language. When these topics are discussed during the *initial* stages of learning, they tend to instill good programming habits immediately. The results are solutions that are well thought out, programs that are well-structured, and documentation of high quality. This is simply because our students have not been taught any other way. To them, it is the normal way of doing things.

This book has three goals that, in order of importance, are:

1. Introducing *all* aspects of the programming and problem-solving process, including problem specification and organization, algorithms, coding, debugging, testing, documentation, and maintenance.
2. Teaching what constitutes *good* programming style and how to produce a high-quality finished product. These points are brought out in numerous style clinics throughout the text.
3. Teaching the syntax of the PASCAL programming language.

We have chosen to use PASCAL as our programming language because it is an excellent language for introducing these concepts. However, we did not wish merely to replace a FORTRAN-based service course with a PASCAL service course. Instead, we wanted to develop a textbook that utilizes PASCAL as a *vehicle* to introduce a range of programming concepts. Although, of necessity, a large portion of the book is dedicated to our third goal, this should be viewed in its proper perspective.

Chapters 1 and 2 introduce the student to the preparatory work that must be done prior to the coding phase—problem specification and algorithm development. Chapters 3, 4, and 5 introduce the basic elements of the PASCAL language. In class we treat the syntactic details of these chapters quickly and prefer to concentrate on the stylistic aspects discussed in the text and in the style clinics. Chapter 6 discusses the topics of debugging, program testing, documentation, and maintenance. Chapters 7 and 8 discuss additional data structures and the subprogram facilities available in the language. Again, in class the syntactic rules are covered quickly, and the conceptual and stylistic details are considered at greater length. Chapter 9, one of the most important chapters in the book, discusses techniques for developing and managing large "real-world" problems and writing quality programs. Sufficient time should be allowed to insure that the material in that chapter is treated adequately.

We are currently using this text in a one-quarter, introductory, undergraduate computer science course at the University of Minnesota. The students include both computer science and noncomputer science majors. This textbook assumes no prior programming experience or extensive mathematical background on the part of the student. The programming examples have been chosen to span a wide range of both numeric and nonnumeric applications.

We have carefully tried to avoid aspects of PASCAL that might be specific to a particular computer system. Where machine-dependent details are required (e.g., control cards), we have referred the student to his or her instructor for the necessary information.

Finally, we would like to thank the people whose names do not appear on the front cover but who contributed significantly to the production of the book. Among them are Sara Graffunder who edited the final manuscript, Michael Meissner and Brad Blasing who helped to test the numerous programming examples in the book, and Judy Matheson who typed both the first draft and the final manuscript. We also thank the many referees whose excellent suggestions were so liberally used. Special thanks must go to Andy Mickel of the University of Minnesota Computer Center who not only reviewed the manuscript but initiated and encouraged our interest in PASCAL as a language tool for teaching programming. Without the help of all these people, this project would still be merely an idea.

We sincerely hope that this book will contribute to an improvement in the quality of programming instruction as well as to the view of computer programming as a rational and organized discipline.

Minneapolis, Minnesota   **G. Michael Schneider**
                                                            Steven W. Weingart
                                                            David M. Perlman

FOREWORD

The maturation of programming into an art or a science is characterized by our ability to abstract essential principles from particular cases. As fundamental concepts emerge, a notation is needed to express them. We have become accustomed to calling such a formal notation a "language." The better it is tailored toward expressing the essential abstractions, the better it is suited to introduce the subject of programming, because the more it can recede into the background. Ideally, the language presents itself as the natural notation to express the basic concepts of programming, and it should hardly need further attention and explanation.

Yet, in the design and analysis of algorithms, we are forced to express ourselves unusually exactly. This implies that we need a thorough mastery and precision in understanding our language. Is it therefore surprising that its details still consume a considerable amount of time in teaching the art of programming?

The language PASCAL was developed in the late 1960s in recognition of the fact that the language used is of paramount importance in programming. The authors of this book have chosen PASCAL as a vehicle, and they are able to concentrate on the fundamental principles of programming and problem solving. Nevertheless, the details of the language are given due attention, and they are clearly motivated. Consequently, they appear as rules that can be understood instead of merely being memorized. The book explains the style of programming that was the guiding idea in the design of PASCAL. By explicitly motivating the principles of structured programming and the corresponding features of PASCAL, it provides insight instead of merely coverage.

Zürich, August 1977   N. Wirth

CONTENTS

STYLE CLINICS

CHAPTER 1

AN OVERVIEW

1.1 INTRODUCTION

This book is about programming. However, that statement is not as simple as it may first appear. What we mean when we use that term, and what others mean may be quite different. What we imply by the term *computer programming* is "the entire series of steps involved in solving a problem on a computer." Too often, however, the word *programming* has been used as a synonym for the word *coding*—the process of writing statements in some existing computer language. Classes that have purported to teach computer programming have frequently been nothing more than long litanies of syntactic do's and don'ts for some specific language. The worst part of this approach is that it tends to reinforce the mistaken idea that the best technique for solving problems on a computer is to take a pencil and a piece of paper, begin writing a program, and keep writing until you are done. You

1

then hope that you have produced a valid solution. Nothing could be further from the truth. An enormous amount of preparatory work must precede the actual coding of any potential solution. This preparation involves steps such as defining exactly what is wanted, clearing up any ambiguities or uncertainties in the statement of the problem, deciding how to solve it, and roughing out the outline of the solution in some convenient notation. In fact, if this preparatory work has been done well, the coding phase, which seems the most important to many people, becomes relatively straightforward and uncreative. It becomes simply the mechanical translation of the solution for a problem into grammatically correct statements of some particular language.

In addition, just as we must spend much time and effort before we code, we still have much to do after we have finished coding. We must then grapple with the problems of detecting errors, correcting them, polishing the documentation, and testing, validating, and maintaining the program.

The point we are trying to make is that computer programming is an extremely complex task made up of many individual phases, all of which are important and all of which contribute to the solution of a problem. Do not confuse the concept of programming with any single phase, for example, coding, to the exclusion of all others. We hope this explains why the first complete PASCAL program does not appear until the end of Chapter 4. In constructing your own programs, the PASCAL coding should be preceded by a great deal of preparatory work clarifying, organizing, structuring, and representing your solution. Failing to understand this principle is the first and greatest mistake you can make when learning computer programming.

1.2 THE STEPS INVOLVED IN COMPUTER PROGRAMMING

In the introduction to this chapter we repeatedly stressed that programming involves many steps. Let us be a little more specific and describe the actual steps involved.

1. *Defining the problem.* The inclusion of this step seems trivial. It is obvious that we must know exactly what we want to do before we can begin to do it. But this "obvious" phase is too often overlooked or omitted by programmers who begin their work on problems fraught with ambiguities and uncertainties. A clear understanding of exactly what is needed is absolutely necessary for creating a workable solution. The task of defining the problem will be discussed in the remaining sections of this chapter.

2. *Outlining the solution.* Except for the very simplest of problems, a program will not be composed of a single task, but of many interrelated tasks. For example, a computerized payroll system would most certainly not be viewed as a single program. Instead, it will probably contain several programs that validate input data, sort files, merge files, compute and print

paychecks, print various reports, print error logs, and keep year-to-date information. On large projects that involve a number of programs and a number of programmers, it becomes extremely important to specify both the responsibilities of each task and how these individual tasks interrelate and interact. This is to insure that the pieces being developed separately are designed in the context of the whole.

Of necessity, the early programs in this textbook are short and simple and are composed of single tasks. For these programs the outlining phase can probably be neglected without severe complications. However, they should be viewed as "toys" being used for teaching purposes only. In Chapter 9 we will be devoting a great deal of time to the topics of program development, program structure, and the management of large, real-world programming projects.

3. *Selecting and representing algorithms.* We have now specified the various tasks and subtasks required to solve our problem. For each task we know what information we will provide and what results we want to produce. But we have not as yet specified *how* the program is to accomplish its stated purpose. An *algorithm* is the specific method used to solve a problem. The algorithm may be one already developed and published in the literature or, alternately, one of our own creation and design. For reasons that we will discuss later, it is not a good idea to begin immediately coding the informal specifications of an algorithm directly into some existing programming language. Instead, it is extremely advantageous to describe the details of the proposed solution in an algorithmic representation that is independent of any computer language or machine. In the next chapter we will discuss algorithms and their development. In addition, we will describe in detail one specific method of representing algorithms.

4. *Coding.* Only after unambiguously defining the problem, organizing a solution, and sketching out the step-by-step details of the algorithm can we consider beginning to code.

Your choice of which computer language to use will probably be dictated by three considerations.
   a. The nature of the problem.
   b. The languages available on your computer.
   c. The dictates and limitations of your particular computer installation.

Some programming languages are general purpose; others are very specific for certain classes of problems. Some languages are very widely available; others can be run only on a very few computers. Figure 1-1 lists a few of the more common programming languages that you may encounter.

In this textbook we will employ the language called PASCAL. It is a very elegant language, complex enough to introduce important concepts in computer programming but simple enough to be a good teaching tool in

LANGUAGE	APPROXIMATE DATE OF INTRODUCTION	GENERAL APPLICATION AREAS
FORTRAN	1957	Numerically oriented language. Most applicable to scientific, mathematical, and statistical problem areas. Very widely used and very widely available.
ALGOL	1960	Also a numerically oriented language but with new language features. Widely used in Europe.
COBOL	1960	The most widely used business oriented computer language.
LISP	1961	Special-purpose language developed primarily for list processing and symbolic manipulation. Widely used in the area of artificial intelligence.
SNOBOL	1962	Special-purpose language used primarily for character string processing. This includes applications such as text editors, language processors, and bibliographic work.
BASIC	1965	A simple interactive programming language widely used to teach programming in high schools and colleges.
PL/1	1965	An extremely complex, general-purpose language designed to incorporate the numeric capabilities of FORTRAN, the business capabilities of COBOL, and many other features into a single language.
APL	1967	An interactive language that introduced a wide range of new operations and language features.
PASCAL	1971	A general-purpose language designed specifically to teach the concepts of computer programming and allow the efficient implementation of large programs.

FIGURE 1-1   Survey of Some Widely Used Computer Languages.

a course in computer programming. Chapters 3, 4, 5, 7, and 8 discuss and describe correct usage of the PASCAL language. However, our concern is not merely to teach you how to use PASCAL correctly but to use it well. We will devote a great deal of effort to developing a set of guidelines to aid you in writing "good" programs. These guidelines taken together constitute a *programming style* and will be presented both in the text and in numerous style clinics.

5. *Debugging.* The novice programmer quickly learns that a problem is far from solved once the program has been coded and run. We must still locate and correct all the inevitable errors. This is a time-consuming and

often agonizing task. Section 6.3 tries to provide some tips and guidelines to make debugging a little more manageable and a little less painful.

6. *Testing and validating.* Getting results from a program is not enough. We must guarantee that they are the correct results. Furthermore, we must try to convince ourselves that the program will, indeed, produce correct results in all cases, even those that have not been explicitly tested. Section 6.4 addresses the topics of testing and validating computer programs.

7. *Documenting.* The documentation of a program is a continuous and on-going process. The program specifications from step 1, the algorithmic representation from step 3, and the program itself from step 4 can all be considered as part of the documentation of a program. However, following the successful completion of the program, we must insure that our documentation is complete and in a finished, usable form. This includes both *technical documentation* for the programmers who may be working with and modifying the completed program and *user-level documentation* for the users of the program. Section 6.5 contains guidelines and standards for both levels of documentation.

8. *Program maintenance.* As you will be discovering, this textbook is concerned with effective communication between persons, not just communication between a person and a computer. This will be evident from our treatment of topics such as program clarity, program readability, and documentation. This concern is caused by the fact that programs are not static entities. They frequently become outdated as errors are discovered, new problems need to be solved, or new equipment becomes available. Programs written weeks, months, or even years ago will almost always need to be reviewed, understood, and then modified by someone else. Unless we are quite careful to document clearly what we have done and write our programs in a clear, systematic, and legible fashion, this step can be frustrating or even impossible. Even if we always maintain our own programs we may find that time has dimmed our memories and that we require the same high-quality documentation as anyone else. Because the best documentation possible is simply a clearly written, well-organized, and well-structured program, we can in a sense say that this entire textbook is devoted to facilitating the continuing task of program maintenance.

Finally, we should stress that the programming process described above is not as linear as these eight steps may lead you to believe. Most of these steps overlap each other; for example, documentation will be written continually during program development. Many of these steps will need to be repeated; for example, as debugging uncovers errors, we will go back to recode portions of our program or to rethink the solution. The point of this discussion was simply to show that programming is truly a complex job. It is easy to become a good *coder*—reading this textbook and learning the rules of PASCAL should accomplish that. Your goal should be a higher one: to become a good *programmer,* someone who understands and can manage the entire spectrum of programming responsibilities. However, programming, in this fuller sense of the word, cannot be passively taught but must be actively learned through practice and experience. When accomplished, though, it leads to a much more creative and rewarding experience.

1.3 THE PROBLEM DEFINITION PHASE

The *problem definition phase* involves developing and clarifying the exact specifications of the problem. In short, we must find out exactly what we are supposed to do. Because this is such an obvious step, many programmers skip it entirely and neglect to think about and understand the problem they are attempting to solve. As a result, they frequently begin to develop a program with an ill-defined and ill-conceived statement of the problem. This can lead to confusion, uncertainty and, worst of all, an incorrect solution.

Another reason why the problem definition phase is frequently handled poorly by programmers is that this topic tends to be slighted both in programming textbooks and in classroom instruction. This slighting becomes obvious when we view the way that programming assignments are usually presented in a learning environment. The problem definition phase is done separate from and independent of the student, either by the teacher or the author. A well-defined problem is neatly typed onto a sheet of paper, copied, and presented to the student. It states quite explicitly something such as the following: "You are to input values for A, B, and C, perform operations I, J, and K, and produce results X, Y, and Z." The student is rarely bothered by or concerned with nagging questions such as "Where did we get the values A, B, and C?" "Why did I pick operations I, J, and K over the alternatives L, M, and N?" "What if it should become impossible for me to successfully complete operation I?" "Don't you think we should also present the user with the value of W?" If these questions are important they will have already been addressed and answered by others. Students do not get to treat them as part of the programming assignment. They do what the handout specifies. Period.

Of course, in "real life" (a term we will use frequently to refer to the way things happen outside a classroom environment), problems are rarely so well-defined and unambiguous. On the contrary, it is not at all uncommon for people to describe problems in terms that are quite ill-defined, horribly ambiguous, and virtually useless in their initial form. Frequently the originator of the problem is not a programmer and has had little or no experience working with computers and understanding their capabilities and limitations. From that point of view it would be perfectly natural and understandable for a person in the business world to pose problems in the following loose forms.

Can your computer help us with our inventory control problem?
I sure would like to automate our payroll and accounting system. We have six secretaries who do nothing all day but type paychecks and produce federal and state tax reports.
Can we put computer terminals in all our warehouses so that order processing can be automated?

Likewise, the scientist might suggest the following problems.

Can your computer reduce this mountain of experimental data to something I can manage?
Could we write a program to look at X rays and automatically locate malignancies?
I would like to create a simulation model of the ecosystem of a freshwater Minnesota lake.

To the experienced programmer, all of these represent valid application areas of computers, but all are much too vague to form the basis of a potential solution. How do we proceed?

We need a dialog with the problem originator to work mutually toward a clearer understanding of exactly what is wanted. By thinking and rethinking the problem and by discussing the capabilities of a computer, we will clarify the problem and make it take shape. Where options exist, the alternatives must be presented and a rational choice made.

What will ultimately result from these interactions is a set of written *problem specifications* that spell out in clear, unambiguous language the exact problem we are attempting to solve. These problem specifications will contain three important classes of information. Although these classes need not be itemized and discussed separately, all the following must be included.

1. *Input specifications.* This section describes the input to the program. This should include answers to the following questions.
   a. What specific values will be provided to the program?
   b. What format will the values be in (order, spacing, accuracy)?
   c. For each input item, what is the valid range of values that the input may assume?
   d. What restrictions (if any) are placed on the use of these values? May we modify the input? May we discard the input when we are done?

e. How will we know when we have exhausted the input? Will there be a special symbol or will we have to determine that for ourselves?

2. *Output specifications*. Just as we needed to specify the input provided to the program, we must describe in detail the output that will be produced. The output specifications must include answers to the following types of questions.

a. What values will be produced?

b. What is the format of these values (significant digits, decimal accuracy, and location on the page)?

c. What specific annotation, headers, or titles are required in the finished report?

d. Is there any indication as to the amount of output that will be produced? (This will guide us in making intelligent choices among alternative methods. A technique satisfactory for handling 10 items may be quite useless when used with 10 million items.)

Typically, one of the most effective ways to present output specifications is simply to show a detailed example of the output reports that the program will be producing.

3. *Special processing*. If everything were to progress smoothly we probably would have all the information we need to go on to the next phase of programming. However, as you are probably aware, that rarely happens. As Murphy's law states, "If something can go wrong, it will!" In the problem specifications it is imperative that we itemize special conditions that must be checked and that we specify the recovery action to take if such a condition does occur. These special conditions could be considered as either unusual circumstances that require unique handling or as errors that require correction and recovery. In either case, any possible variations from the norm should be included in the written specifications of the problem.

The input, output, and special processing specifications represent the most important information collected during the problem definition phase. However, you may be wondering why we have omitted one of the most fundamental parts of any problem solving process—the *method* of solution. We have been very careful to specify in detail what we have to start with and what we wish to end up with, but we have given no indication whatever about *how* we are to accomplish this task.

This omission was done quite consciously. The detailed step-by-step specification of the algorithms used to solve a problem is usually not part of the written specifications. There is good reason for this. If we specify too early the low-level details of how an operation must be performed, we lock the programmer into the use of that specific technique. He or she now lacks the flexibility to pick and choose what may be the best technique for solving a particular problem within some particular environment. For example, some techniques work quite well on very large problems, while others do not. Some techniques may be very easy to implement but are inherently inefficient. The programmer should be relatively free to evaluate the needs of the user and choose the most appropriate technique.

This clear separation between problem definition and algorithms may not always exist in a classroom environment. There the problem definition will frequently contain both the problem specifications and a requirement of which algorithm must be used to solve the problem. Usually this choice has been made to teach the student a particular programming concept or because it is the only technique the instructor feels the student will be able to manage.

In real life this is rarely the case. The problem originator is concerned only with getting the desired results and not with how we achieve them, as long as the finished program is not grossly inefficient. Once we have produced a mutually satisfactory written problem specification, we are free to choose the algorithm that best solves the stated problem. Methods for choosing and representing computer algorithms and criteria for comparing their efficiency comprise the second phase of the problem-solving process and will be discussed in the next chapter.

To give you some experience in program development, some of the later programming exercises in this book have intentionally been left incomplete. These exercises can be recognized by the parenthesized comments following the problem statement. These comments hint at important details purposely omitted. For these omissions there are no single right answers or correct approaches. You will have to list and evaluate whatever alternatives there seem to be and choose what you feel is the most reasonable solution.

STYLE CLINIC 1-1

Think First, Code Later

Henry Ledgard, in his book *Programming Proverbs* (Hayden Book Co. Inc., 1975), stated an interesting corollary to Murphy's law that he called Murphy's Law of Programming. Stated simply, it says: "The sooner you start coding your program the longer it is going to take." Although the truth of this maxim has not been formally proved, personal experiences have more than borne out its correctness. Trying to write anything but the simplest of programs without a well-organized solution outline is akin to building a house with hammer, nails, and lumber but no blueprints! Chaos soon follows.

Think first, think second, think some more, and only then begin to write your program.

1.4 EXAMPLES

1.4.1 TABLE LOOK-UP

Let us use as our first example a very simple, yet very important problem in computer programming—*table look-up*. This particular application does not usually occur as a separate and complete problem in its own right but, instead, as a single task within a much larger programming project. For example, in a payroll system we may need to look up an employee's pay rate in a pay rate table; in a language translation program we may need to look up a word in a dictionary list to find its equivalent in another language; finally, in a typical criminal justice application, we might need to look up a license plate in a list of stolen automobiles.

The problem is usually phrased in a form something like the following.

> Given a list of values, along with one special value that we wish to find, look through the list and print out whether or not that special value occurs anywhere in the list.

That simple problem statement might seem fairly clear. However, if we apply the criteria discussed in the preceding section, we find that it is actually an extremely poor and quite unacceptable description of the table look-up problem. All of the following questions have been left unanswered:

Given a list of values, along with one special value . . .

1. What specific type(s) of values are contained in the list?
2. Do we know how many elements are in the list?
3. What type of value is the special value?
4. What is the range of values that the items in the list may assume?
5. Can there be duplicates in the list?

. . . print out whether or not that special value occurs anywhere within the list.

6. Exactly what message do we want to produce if the value is found?
7. Exactly what message do we want to produce if the value is not found?
8. Do we want any other information printed in addition to one of the two messages above?

The answers to all of these questions will have to be provided.

If we use the stolen automobile problem as a specific example, we might find that discussions with knowledgeable authorities have led us to a problem statement of the following type.

> You will be given a variable length table of six-character license plate identifiers in the following form.

Characters 1, 2:   A–Z
Characters 3, 4, 5, 6:   0–9

The last license plate in the list will be the special value "AA0000" and is used solely to mark the end of the list.

You will also be given one single key value that will be of the same format as the table entries.

Develop a program that determines whether the key value occurs anywhere within the table. If it does occur, print the following message.

PLATE NO. "ccnnnn" REPORTED STOLEN

If it does not occur, produce the following message.

PLATE NO. "ccnnnn" NOT REPORTED STOLEN

This problem statement is considerably more formal than the previous one and represents a significant improvement. However, even this problem statement is far from complete. It is quite ambiguous about certain situations. Reread the previous specifications and you will see that it neglects to specify what we should do in the following circumstances.

1. The special key value we search for is in incorrect format. For example, a license plate ABC123.
2. The key value occurs more than once in the table. Do we find just the first occurrence? All occurrences?
3. Do we stop after processing a single key value or will there be a number of different keys?
4. Will the table be directly available or must we read it from some input device?

(There are numerous other questions we would need to address in an actual system. How do new numbers get added to the list, how do we remove numbers once the automobiles are found, and what about the other information that we would need such as names, date, and places? We will not bother with all these questions now.)

Valid answers to the above questions must be determined in discussions of the valid alternatives. For example, the problem of handling invalid data could be resolved simply by adding the following statement.

If the key value does not conform to the specified format for license plate entries, produce the following message.

cccccc
INVALID FORMAT—PLEASE CHECK AND RE-ENTER

Skip the remainder of the processing phase for this data case.

The second problem, that of multiple entries, has a greater number of alternatives. The correct one would simply be the one that gives the police the information they wanted. One possibility would be to modify the previous specification to read as follows.

> Write a program to find *every* occurrence of the key value within the list. If there has been at least one such occurrence, produce the following message.
>
> ### PLATE NO. "ccnnnn" REPORTED STOLEN "nn" TIMES
>
> where "nn" is the total number of occurrrences of the designated license plate in the list.

The complete specifications for this problem are shown in Figure 1-2.

> You will be given a data set in two distinct parts. The first part is a master list of license plate numbers of stolen automobiles. Each data item contains one six-character license plate identifier in the following format.
>
> >   Columns 1, 2:   A–Z
> >   Columns 3–6:   0–9
>
> The last license plate number in the list is the special value "AA0000" and is used solely to mark the end of the list. The entire list is currently stored on a magnetic tape file labeled PLATES.
>
> The second part of the data set is on punch cards and contains license plates in the same format as the list described above. If this data set contains an entry in an improper format, produce the following message:
>
> >   cccccc
> > ### IMPROPER FORMAT—PLEASE CHECK AND RE-ENTER
>
> and omit the processing of that item.
>
> Develop a program that will input a license plate number from a punch card and locate *all* occurrences of that number in the master list. If the license plate never occurs in the master list, produce the following message.
>
> ### PLATE NO. "ccnnnn" NOT REPORTED STOLEN
>
> If the number appears at least once in the master list, produce the following message:
>
> ### PLATE NO. "ccnnnn" REPORTED STOLEN "nn" TIMES
>
> where "nn" is the total number of occurrences of the license plate in the master list.
>
> Repeat this process for every data card provided.

FIGURE 1-2   Program Specifications for the Table Look-Up Problem.

Contrast this final problem statement with the initial one given a few pages earlier. What has resulted from this development is a clear, unambiguous statement of the problem that we will be solving. The input that is required and the output that will be produced are clearly stated. If the statement as written in Figure 1-2 is not acceptable, it is very easy to change at this stage. If the statement is acceptable, it will form the basis for the next stages of program design. In either case it is extremely useful to have such a complete specification.

The development of a computer algorithm for actually performing the table look-up operation described here will be shown in the next chapter.

1.4.2 STATISTICAL COMPARISONS

Assume that we were approached by an English instructor with the following problem. The instructor would like to know if the students who do well on the midterm examination always do well on the final exam, or if there are some students who have learned significantly more (or less) and whose performance on the final differs markedly from the first exam. The scores on both exams are available in the instructor's record book but, because there are over 200 students in the class, it will be difficult to do the operations manually. The instructor would like some type of comparison between the performances on the two examinations to use as a guide to plan for the next semester. When we inquire further about this "measure" and what it should be, the instructor claims to be totally unfamiliar with and untrained in the area of statistics and cannot help us. If we are also not trained in statistics, we must seek out a third party—a competent statistician.

After we describe our problem, the statistician states that it sounds like we want a *correlation*—a statistical measure of the relationship between pairs of values. Furthermore, the statistician states that we can either correlate the raw scores themselves in which case we end up with what is called a *correlation coefficient,* or we can correlate the rankings of the scores (e.g., third best on the midterm, fifth best on the final) and get a *rank correlation coefficient.* In simple terms, the implications of using each measure are described to us.

We can now go back to the problem originator with a choice of techniques and the criteria needed to make an intelligent choice. Assume that, after listening to the alternatives, the instructor decides the rank correlation coefficient is what is really wanted. We explain that this coefficient is a numerical value that will range between -1 and $+1$. Values at the extremes represent a very high degree of relationship between the two sets of scores, and values near zero represent little or no relationship. For a more specific interpretation of the meaning of this coefficient, the instructor will need to go to a handbook on statistics and look at charts that give levels of significance as functions of the amount of data used. We plan to provide only the numerical coefficient.

This initially seems unacceptable to the instructor who does not want to be bothered doing statistical interpretations. The instructor had originally thought that our program would not only produce a numerical measure, but would also interpret its meaning by producing one of the following messages.

EXTREMELY SIGNIFICANT RELATIONSHIP
VERY SIGNIFICANT RELATIONSHIP
SIGNIFICANT RELATIONSHIP
LITTLE RELATIONSHIP
NO RELATIONSHIP
CANNOT DETERMINE

Our own experience with computers and programming, however, warns us that this type of qualitative decision making will not be easy. It might require as much programming effort as all the rest of our work combined. If the interpretation of the results is performed manually, we can save a great deal of programming effort, and the instructor can maintain greater control over the interpretation process. After numerous discussions about this, the instructor (reluctantly) agrees to a program producing a single rank correlation coefficient, which the instructor will interpret.

At this point in the problem specification we can also get detailed formats on the exam scores in the instructor's grade book and begin writing the input specifications for the problem. After looking in the grade book, we realize that we have encountered another problem—some students were excused from taking one or both of the examinations. We cannot merely leave the score blank or enter a 0 because 0 represents a valid (although poor!) score and could ruin the computations. We could simply omit from the data any student not taking both exams. However, the instructor tells us that a listing of all students who did not take both examinations is also needed. We decide to use the special value -1 to indicate that a student did not take an examination. Since a -1 cannot possibly be a valid examination score, we can distinguish between a student taking or not taking an examination. This should allow us to correctly produce the information desired.

We now trudge back one last time to the statistician to say that we have chosen one of the suggested techniques. The statistician gives us a good formula for computing this value and, in addition, warns us about a potential pitfall—the problem of ties. We will be assigning ranks to scores. We will need a policy on how to assign ranks to tie scores. There are three ways to handle this.

SCORE	RANK	SCORE	RANK	SCORE	RANK
100	1	100	1	100	1
95	2	95	2	95	2.5
95	3	95	2	95	2.5
85	4	85	4	85	4
(a)		(b)		(c)	

Our own experience with ties (primarily in sports, not statistics) would probably have led us to choose method b, assigning the highest rank to all tie scores. However, the statistician warns us that to get the best result we must use method c, assigning the average of all tie rankings to the tie scores. We agree to do that.

We are finally in a position to draw up a formal set of written problem specifications that defines the problem we will be solving. They are shown in Figure 1-3.

This example, much more so than the previous one, illustrates the time and effort involved in developing adequate problem specifications. In this example we utilized the services of three persons—the problem originator and the programmer as before but, in addition, a specialist in a particular application area. We had numerous conferences and extracted compromises when difficult decisions had to be made. But, again, it was worth it because we have ended up with a clear, concise, and unambiguous problem specification statement that is acceptable to all parties concerned. How much better to spend the time now to make sure that what we are doing is what is actually wanted than to find out after additional work has been done. It is easy to make changes now but much more difficult once the program has begun to be "cast."

Remember that while you are in a learning environment all problems will probably be presented in a well-defined form. However, the problem definition phase has not been omitted or neglected. Instead, it has been done for you. It is still a crucially important phase in the overall programming and problem-solving process.

We will be given a series of data cards, each containing three values separated by one or more blank spaces. The first value is a student identification number. It will be a six-digit integer. The next two values are examination scores. They correspond to the scores of that student on the midterm and final examinations. Both values must be integers in the range 0 to 100. If a student did not take either examination, a value of −1 is entered in the proper place. If either (or both) of the scores is invalid or missing, discard both scores and do not use those values in the following computation.

The last data card will be denoted by a student identification number of 000000.

We will develop a program to input the above values and compute a rank correlation coefficient between all valid scores. Ties will be handled by assigning to
the tie scores the average of all tie rankings. The program will produce as
output the following reports.

REPORT 1—CORRELATION REPORT

THE FOLLOWING STUDENTS HAD TWO LEGAL SCORES
AND WERE INCLUDED IN THE COMPUTATION.

STUDENT ID.	MIDTERM SCORE	RANK	FINAL SCORE	RANK
nnnnnn	xxx	xx.x	xxx	xx.x
nnnnnn	xxx	xx.x	xxx	xx.x
.	.	.	.	.
.	.	.	.	.
.	.	.	.	.
nnnnnn	xxx	xx.x	xxx	xx.x

nnn   LEGAL SCORES
±n.nnn   RANK CORRELATION COEFFICIENT

The program will also produce an error report with the '*' character used to
indicate a score is missing or in error:

REPORT 2—ERROR LOG

THE FOLLOWING STUDENTS HAD ONE OR MORE SCORES
MISSING OR IN ERROR AND INDICATED BY '*'. THEY WERE
NOT USED IN THE PRECEDING COMPUTATION.

STUDENT ID.	MIDTERM SCORE	FINAL SCORE
nnnnnn	xxx *	xxx
nnnnnn	xxx	xxx *
.	.	.
.	.	.
.	.	.
nnnnnn	xxx *	xxx *

mm   IMPROPER SCORES
nn   STUDENTS OMITTED

FIGURE 1-3 Problem Specification for the Statistical Correlation Program.

EXERCISES

1. For each of the following general problem areas state what questions need to be answered to make the problem statement unambiguous. Then make whatever assumptions are necessary and produce an acceptable set of problem specifications.

    *a. Find the first N prime numbers.
    b. Produce a frequency table of all letters in some English language text.
    c. Compute the average score on a final examination.
    d. Sort a list of numbers into numerical sequence.
    e. Compute weekly take-home pay from a daily time card.

2. A hardware store would like to computerize its inventory control system. The store owner would like to have a computer program that keeps track of the quantity on hand of each of the 3000 items sold by the store, the wholesale and retail price of each of them, and other relevant information. Analyze this situation and present possible input specifications and output specifications for this program. Try to consider these aspects.

    a. Information that would be needed by the hardware store owner.
    b. Information required by the suppliers.
    c. Cumulative year-to-date information that may be needed for either stockholders or the government.
    d. How the necessary data can be collected and prepared.

---

* Asterisks preceding an exercise number or letter indicate that the exercise answer appears in the Selected Answers Section.

CHAPTER 2

ALGORITHMS

2.1 INTRODUCTION

A fundamental concept in computer science is that of an *algorithm*. Informally, we can view an algorithm simply as a way to solve a problem, or a set of directions, or a recipe that tells exactly how to go about getting desired results. We work with algorithms all the time, although we are not often so formal as to call them algorithms. The set of instructions that tells us how to put a tricycle together from its component parts, the procedures for going through college registration, and the recipe for making an apple pie are all probably examples of valid algorithms. Even the following directions taken from a shampoo label could be called a "shampooing algorithm."

1. Wet hair.
2. Lather.
3. Rinse.
4. Repeat.

Because it does not conform to the definition of an algorithm in some respects, as we will see later, it actually is invalid.

More formally, we will define an *algorithm* as "a sequence of operations that, when executed, will always produce a result and terminate in a finite amount of time."

By "sequence of operations," we mean that for each step within the algorithm, a next step is unambiguously defined. That is, upon completing one step we must always know where to look for the next step. The ordering could, for example, be specified by numbering the steps with the positive integers and following the sequencing rule:

> Unless told to do otherwise or unless we are at the last step, upon completion of step (i) go on to step (i+1); i = 1, 2, . . .

Alternatively, the ordering could be implied by position: Upon completing the operation on line (i), we must execute the operation written on the line just below—(i+1). Since we will sometimes not wish to follow the assumed sequence of steps, some steps in our algorithms may say, in effect, "Do not go on to step (i+1); instead, do step (k)." Regardless of how we phrase the instruction, our identification of the next step must be completely unambiguous. One problem with the "shampooing algorithm" above is that Step 4 defines the next step ambiguously. We cannot tell which of the preceding steps are to be repeated.

Inherent in the concept of a sequence of operations is the idea of a beginning and an end. An algorithm must always have one clearly understood starting point and one or more clearly understood ending points. The starting point can be implied—we usually assume that we are to start at step 1—or it can be stated explicitly—one step may be labeled START. More than one starting point would create ambiguity about where to start, violating the ordering condition stated above. However, it is perfectly acceptable, even desirable, to identify one or more of the steps in the algorithms as *terminators*—steps that, when executed, terminate execution of the entire algorithm. The reason for this is that frequently a problem can be divided into two or more disjoint sections, depending on the particular value being processed. However, regardless of which section we execute, we wish to stop after completing that section.

1. START

2. Make a decision that divides the
   problem into three possible cases.

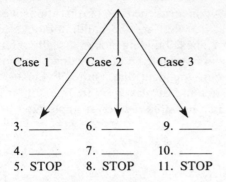

<pre>
3. _____   6. _____   9. _____
4. _____   7. _____   10. _____
5. STOP   8. STOP   11. STOP
</pre>

This skeletal outline contains a single clearly identified starting point and three clearly defined terminators. The set of steps executed will always be either (1, 2, 3, 4, 5), (1, 2, 6, 7, 8), or (1, 2, 9, 10, 11).

The existence of one or more terminators, however, is insufficient to guarantee that execution will actually stop. This trivial (and, from a programming point of view, awful) set of operations

.
.
.

    5. go to step 7
    6. STOP
    7. go to step 5

.
.
.

makes that fact quite obvious. To have a valid algorithm, we must guarantee that executing the algorithm will eventually cause us to execute one of the terminators and thereby come to a halt. We should not, however, confuse the term "eventually" with terms such as "quickly" or "efficiently." All we are saying is that the algorithm will terminate after a finite number of steps. It is theoretically unimportant whether that number is 1 or 10^{10000}. Practically, of course, we may reject a valid algorithm that takes too much time because it is impractical or inefficient. For example, an exhaustive search algorithm of all chess games possible from a given board position can be formally specified, but it would take about 10^{40} years to work through a game at current machine speeds. Furthermore, the algorithm must terminate in a finite time for any arbitrary set of data, regardless of how pathological.

A basic question about algorithms concerns the type of operations we are allowed to write at each step. That is, what are the building blocks from which we can compose an algorithm? These building blocks, usually referred to as *primitives,* must be clearly understandable and totally unambiguous to the person or machine that will execute the algorithm. Quite obviously, this will change with the level of sophistication displayed by that person or machine. For example, the following is a possible recipe for apple pie.

1. Make the crust.
2. Make the apple filling.
3. Place the filling inside the crust.
4. Bake at 375° for 30 minutes.

This might be acceptable to a person quite familiar with pie making. However, steps 1 and 2 would probably be unclear and ambiguous for the great majority of people without baking experience. For these people those two steps would not be considered acceptable baking primitives. Operations such as

MIX x INTO y
MEASURE x units OF ingredient
STIR x
COOK x AT y° for z minutes/hours
COOK x UNTIL condition

whose meaning is more nearly unambiguous to the great majority of persons would be more realistic examples of cooking primitives. However, even these simple statements may not be acceptable primitives if there is any ambiguity or uncertainty about their meaning. For example, does COOK mean bake, broil, fry, or grill?

We can now define *primitive operations* in a more formal way. They are the most sophisticated and complex operations that the person or machine executing the algorithm is capable of directly understanding and performing and that do not have to be broken down into more basic steps. One of the major purposes of the next section will be to develop an acceptable and adequate set of primitive commands that we can use in developing computer algorithms.

In summary, an algorithm is a procedure for performing a particular task. The procedure must have the following characteristics.

1. Upon completing the execution of each step, we will always know the identity of the step to be executed next.
2. There is a single clearly defined starting point and one or more clearly defined stopping points.

3. In all cases, the algorithm will terminate after a finite number of steps.
4. The algorithm is composed of primitives whose meaning is clear and unambiguous to the person or machine executing it.

Looking back at the shampooing algorithm, we can now see that it is invalid for two reasons. The identity of the steps to be repeated at step 4 is ambiguous—do we go back to step 1, 2, or 3? Second, there is no provision to terminate this algorithm. It would repeat forever, or at least until we ran out of shampoo, hot water, or patience! In the next section we will provide the necessary tools for rewriting this algorithm to conform to the requirements listed above.

2.2 DEVELOPING ALGORITHMS

The process of developing an algorithm to solve a specific problem can be a trial-and-error process requiring numerous attempts, much the same as the process of developing the outline of a story. Programmers will make some initial attempt at a solution and review it to test its correctness. The errors they discover will usually lead to insertions, deletions, or modifications in the existing algorithm or possibly to scrapping that attempt and beginning anew. This refining continues until the author is satisfied that the algorithm is essentially correct and is ready to be executed. The more experience we gain in developing algorithms, the closer our first attempt will be to a correct solution and the less revision will be required. However, under no circumstances should a beginning programmer view developing an algorithm as a single-step operation. This point needs to be stressed very early, since many of the algorithms contained in this textbook are presented simply as correct solutions. They represent, however, the final stage, either for the authors or others, in the development of suitable algorithms. That development is usually complicated by false starts and dead ends and obstructed by innumerable errors—errors obvious to everyone except their creators. In fact, the final version of the algorithm itself will often still contain errors that will not be discovered until the algorithm is actually run as a computer program.

2.2.1 EXAMPLE ONE—TABLE LOOK-UP

The best way to introduce the algorithmic process is to work through an example. In Chapter 1 we developed the specifications for a very common programming problem called table look-up (see Figure 1-2). Our problem now will be to develop an algorithm to solve that problem correctly. The technique we will use in this example will be the simplest and most obvious —sequential search. We will look at the first element, the second element, the third, and so on, until we either find the item we are looking for or we come to the end of the list. If the list is in no particular order (e.g., numerical or alphabetical) the sequential search is actually the best technique available. However, if the list has already been organized in some fashion, then the sequential search, which does not take advantage of any such organization, is usually the most inefficient technique. This is an important point and one that we will develop more fully later.

For this example, assume that the list contains n items called a_1, a_2, . . . , a_n, and the special value we are searching for is termed the "key."

First Attempt
> Is a_1 equal to the key?
> Is a_2 equal to the key?
>
> .
>
> .
>
> .
>
> Is a_n equal to the key?

This would seem to be the most straightforward and logical solution to the problem, but it is a totally unacceptable algorithm for a number of reasons. The number of steps it takes to write out the algorithm is directly proportional to the size of the problem. As the size of the list grows very large, the number of statements becomes intolerable. We are not using the power of the computer and are missing a most fundamental concept in programming—*iteration*. Instead of writing an operation n distinct times, we should strive to write it only once and successively execute it as many times as needed. This way, the representation of the algorithm is relatively independent of the specific data set we are working with.

In this problem, for example, we could use a variable i as a pointer or an index into the list in place of the constants 1, 2, ... As we change the value of i, the expression a_i would successively refer to each of the values a_1, a_2, . . . , a_n.

When looking at the initial attempt, you probably assumed that the first line was the starting point of the algorithm. This is the convention we always use in interpreting recipes or instructions. Since an unambiguous starting point is an absolute necessity, we must now formally adopt this convention. In order to gain the maximum clarity when writing algorithms we will assume that there exists an algorithmic primitive called START that must appear exactly once as the first line of the algorithm. The first executable primitive is the one immediately following the START command. Since the algorithm must also eventually terminate, we will similarly adopt the convention that there will exist a primitive called Stop that may appear one or more times anywhere within the algorithm. When we come to a Stop, execution of the algorithm is terminated. In addition, we will include a primitive called END OF THE ALGORITHM that must physically be the last line. (Remember, a

Stop can appear anywhere within an algorithm, not just at the end.) The START and END primitives will always be capitalized to help us visually identify the beginning and end of the algorithm.

```
START
    statement-1
    statement-2
        .
        .
    statement-n
END OF THE ALGORITHM
```

Next let us look closely at each of the lines of the initial attempt. They each say "Is a specific element of the list equal to the key?" That is a troublesome statement. What are we supposed to do if they are equal and what do we do if they are not? It is not clear. What we need is a formal way to represent a question being asked or a condition being tested with the answer to the question affecting what we do next. The most common way to implement this is by using the If/Then/Else primitive.

If *condition* Then *operations*
Else *operations*

The condition specified in the If primitive represents any condition that can be understood and evaluated by the person or machine executing the algorithm and that produces a value of true or false. If the indicated condition is true the entire set of operations contained in the Then clause is executed and the Else clause is skipped. If the condition is false the operations contained in the Then clause are skipped and the Else clause is executed. Thus there will never be any ambiguity about exactly what operations are to be performed. If the set of operations in either clause is quite lengthy then to avoid confusion we may use a bracket, [, to group logically all primitives belonging to the same clause.

$$
\text{If } \textit{condition} \text{ Then} \quad \begin{bmatrix} s_1 \\ \cdot \\ \cdot \\ \cdot \\ s_n \end{bmatrix}
$$

$$
\text{Else} \quad \begin{bmatrix} s_1 \\ \cdot \\ \cdot \\ \cdot \\ s_m \end{bmatrix}
$$

The following is an example of the use of this primitive.

$$\text{If } x < 0 \quad \text{Then compute } \sqrt{-x}$$
$$\text{Else compute } \sqrt{x}$$

If the condition $x < 0$ is true we will execute the Then clause and take the square root of $-x$ (since the negative of a negative value is positive). If the condition $x < 0$ is false we will skip the Then clause and execute the Else clause, which computes the square root of x.

A useful variant of the If/Then/Else primitive is the If/Then form.

$$\text{If } \textit{condition} \text{ Then } \textit{operations}$$

If the condition is false we do not execute any operations but simply go on to the next step in the algorithm. The If/Then/Else and If/Then constructs are the basic "question asking" or "condition testing" primitives used in constructing computer algorithms.

Another obvious primitive is needed: a way to print the results produced by our algorithm. Our output primitive will be simply.

$$\text{Write } \textit{values}$$

We will adopt the convention that a value within double quotes, " ", is a message to be printed exactly as is. A letter or word not in quotes represents an item whose current value is to be printed. If r is a computed radius that we wish to print, we would say

$$\text{Write "The radius is", r}$$

Finally, we will assume that our computer has all the arithmetic capabilities of any sophisticated electronic calculator. Therefore, the following commands

    Add a to b
    Subtract a from b
    Multiply a times b
    Divide a into b
    Increment a
    Decrement a

        .
        .
        .

or anything similar will all be considered valid algorithmic primitives.

Let us now apply what we have discussed and rewrite our algorithm:

Second Attempt
       START
           If a_i equals the key
               Then ⌈Write "found at location", i
                    ⌊Stop
               Else ⌈Increment i
                    ⌊Repeat
       END OF THE ALGORITHM

This begins to take on the form of a computer algorithm in the sense that we are iterating—repeatedly executing a group of statements. However, the algorithm is not yet correct.

If we look at the second line of the algorithm we will see that it refers to the ith element of the list a. However, neither the value of the index i nor the values in the list have been explicitly specified. We have committed an *initialization error*. We are trying to use a variable or item (add it, print it, test it) before we have given it a value. Every algorithm must explicitly specify how a value will be assigned to an item before attempting to use that item. The two most common ways to assign values are by using internal and external data. *Internal data* means values created within the algorithm itself. *External data* means that the specific values reside on some external input device separate from the person or machine executing the algorithm. The values are made available to that person or machine by "reading in" the data from this device.

We will assume the existence of two algorithmic primitives for these two approaches.

Internal data: Set *variable* to *a value*
    For example: Set x to 1
                        Set the index to the sum of a and b (of course, a and b
                                                    must already be defined)

External data: Read *values*
    For example: Read the values of x, y, and z
                        Read the elements $a_1, a_2, \ldots, a_n$

If we take a look at the last line of the algorithm we also find that the command "Repeat" is unacceptable. Like the shampooing algorithm, it states neither what to repeat nor how often to repeat it.

One of the characteristics of algorithms starting to become obvious is the frequent use of iteration. Virtually every algorithm we write will have a group of statements repeated some large number of times. When developing algorithms it would be nice to think specifically in terms of *looping primitives* —constructs that specify both a block of statements to be executed and criteria for determining exactly how many times they are to be executed. The most natural ways to think of iteration are as repetition some fixed number of times or repetition until some event occurs. We should provide primitives for both of these cases.

a) While *condition* do
s_1
s_2
.
.
.
s_n
End of the loop

The While primitive allows us to repeat a group of primitives s_1, s_2, . . . , s_n as long as some condition is true. The condition specified in the While clause is any condition that can be evaluated by the person or machine executing the algorithm and that is either true or false. The condition is checked initially and, if it is true, all statements s_1, . . . , s_n are performed. This process is repeated continually until the condition becomes false. If the condition is false to begin with, none of the statements is executed.

b) Repeat the following *count* times
s_1
s_2
.
.
.
s_n
End of the loop

Count represents any constant or variable that has a nonnegative whole number as its value. The primitives s_1, . . . , s_n are executed as many times as specified by the current value of *count*. If the count is initially zero, the primitives s_1, . . . , s_n are not executed.

We can now begin to construct iterative algorithms using the above two primitives as building blocks.

Third Attempt
START
Read in the size of the list, n
Read in the list a_1, . . . , a_n and the key

```
           Set i to 1
           Set found to false
           While the key has not been found and i < n do
               If aᵢ equals the key
                   Then Set found to true
                   Else Increment i
           End of the While loop
           If the key was found
               Then Write "The value was found at location", i
               Else Write "The value was not found"
           Stop
       END OF THE ALGORITHM
```

The algorithm now looks sufficiently correct to begin checking it by trying out sample cases. We must be very careful to check its performance not only on simple, valid cases but also on the following.

1. *The limiting cases.* How does the algorithm perform at the extremes of the valid cases, for example, finding elements at the very beginning or end of a list, or setting the list size to the smallest or largest allowable value?
2. *The unusual cases.* What happens when we input data that violate the normal conditions of the problem or represent an unusual condition? For example, what happens if the key cannot be found in the list?
3. *The invalid cases.* How does the algorithm react for data that is patently illegal or completely meaningless, such as a list of length −1? Such meaningless data occur frequently in programming environments and can be caused, for example, by pressing the wrong key when creating the data. A cardinal rule of computer programming and one that we will attempt to follow throughout this book is that an algorithm should work correctly and produce meaningful results for any data whatsoever, regardless how pathological or absurd. We call this concept *foolproof programming*.

Let us look at how the algorithm as it now stands works under this set of requirements. We will take as a sample data set the following values.

$$n = 4 \qquad \begin{aligned} a_1 &= 13 \\ a_2 &= 5 \\ a_3 &= 21 \\ a_4 &= 22 \end{aligned}$$

For the sample cases of key = 13, 5, or 21 the algorithm works correctly. (You should validate this and all other assertions by working through the

algorithm with paper, pencil, and the designated data.) For the value key =
35 the algorithm also produces the expected result—the message "The value
was not found." However, for the value key = 22, the algorithm incorrectly
produces the same message. The problem arises in the fifth line of the
algorithm, which tests for termination. In effect it is asking if we have come
to the end of the list. However, it is asking that question before we have
actually tested the last item. The correct condition to test is actually i ≤ n.
This mistake is representative of a very common class of programming mistakes called *off-by-one errors*—performing an iteration either one time too
few or one time too often. It is extremely important when developing algorithms to insure that your iterations terminate at the correct step by testing
and evaluating these boundary conditions.

What if the value of n is equal to or less than 0? Of course, this is meaningless but, as we said before, you should be able to state that your algorithm
still operates properly. In this case it does not. The third line of the algorithm
will attempt to read data that do not actually exist. One simple test will allow
us to catch this invalid situation.

The finished version of the algorithm is shown in Figure 2-1.

We have spent a great deal of time developing this simple algorithm,
probably more than it deserves. However, this problem has introduced some
very important concepts that will recur throughout this book: iteration, the
structure and organization of algorithms, programming errors, and primitives. Most important, we have developed a set of primitives to use in representing and writing algorithms. This set of primitives, which we will call an

---

```
START
    Read in the size of the list, n
    If n ≤ 0
        Then Write "Invalid list size—cannot process"
        Else  Read values for a₁, a₂, . . . , aₙ and the key
              Set i to 1 and set found to false
              While the key has not been found and i ≤ n do
                  If aᵢ equals the key
                      Then Set found to true
                      Else Increment i by 1
              End of the While loop
              If the key was found
                      Then Write "The value was found at location", i
                      Else Write "The value was not found"
    Stop
END OF THE ALGORITHM
```

FIGURE 2-1   Table Look-Up Algorithm Using Sequential Search.

algorithmic language, is summarized in Figure 2-2. However, algorithmic languages are quite informal and contain few, if any, strict rules of grammar or syntax. The primitives we developed are merely examples of primitive statements that are typically used. Feel free to modify them or to add others that may seem more natural or convenient to you.

One question you are probably now asking is why did we choose to develop and use an algorithmic language as the vehicle for presenting algorithms? Is this the only way to represent algorithms or are there alternate, and better, techniques?

The answer to this question is that we are using an algorithmic language because it represents an ideal compromise between the representational extremes of natural language (the language we speak and write) and the PASCAL programming language. We could write algorithms directly in English text. For example, the table look-up algorithm in Figure 2-1 would start out something like the following.

Let's first read in the data. If there are no items in the list, we will want to write

START
Stop
If *condition* Then *operations* Else *operations*
If *condition* Then *operations*
Set *variable* to *a value*
Read *values*
Write *values*
Add x to y
Subtract x from y
Multiply x times y
Divide x into y
Increment x
Decrement x
While *condition* do
    .
    .

End of the loop
Repeat the following *count* times
    .

    .

End of the loop
END OF THE ALGORITHM

FIGURE 2-2 Representative Algorithmic Primitives.

out an error message. Now we are going to start looking through the list by asking. . . .

This approach has some obvious limitations. It is enormously wordy. The sentences that we write are not limited to any particular form or vocabulary. They might be totally unrelated to the statements available in the programming language we will eventually use. This could make the actual programming phase very difficult. Finally, the sentences themselves would not give us any clues as to the relationship between parts of the algorithm or any indication of general organization. It would simply appear as a single, large, unstructured paragraph.

Given the above arguments, a natural first reaction is to go to the opposite extreme—forget about any intermediate representations and develop the algorithms directly in a programming language which, in our case, is PASCAL. A portion of the table look-up algorithm might now appear as follows.

```
PROGRAM TABLELOOKUP(INPUT,OUTPUT);
VAR I,N: INTEGER;
   A: ARRAY[1 . . 100] OF REAL;
   KEY: REAL;
BEGIN
   READLN(N); I:=1;
   WHILE I <=N DO
      BEGIN
         READLN (A[I]); I:=I+1
      END;
         .
         .
         .
```

and again the disadvantages become immediately apparent. By writing directly in PASCAL we necessarily become concerned with syntactic considerations that are not really part of the algorithmic process—considerations such as the location of semicolons, the delimiting of reserved words, type declarations for variables, and the declaration of specific external files. These concerns have no place in this development phase and can, in fact, clutter up and slow this process by inundating us with extraneous detail. They should be relegated to the *coding phase,* where we are specifically concerned with translating algorithmic primitives into the syntax of some specific programming language.

Therefore, an algorithmic language such as the one described in Figure 2-2 is a reasonable compromise for the following reasons.

1. By a judicious choice of algorithmic language primitives, we can insure that our final algorithms will be closely related to our desired programming language, thus facilitating the next step of translation into that language. You will soon discover that the algorithmic language used in this textbook is closely related to the PASCAL programming language.
2. We will not, however, be bogged down in the restrictive syntax of a specific language. An algorithmic language should be viewed as a set of guidelines for building algorithms, not as a rigid set of rules. There will not be any rules for punctuation, spelling, vocabulary, or use of synonyms.
3. The representation of algorithms in our algorithmic language, along with a judicious use of indentation, will quite clearly indicate the relationships between various statements and allow us to gain a better picture of their overall organization.

We should stress that not all programmers use algorithmic languages like ours. There are many other representational techniques, with one of particular importance. We will mention it for the sake of completeness but will not use it very frequently in this book. The other technique in widespread use is the *flowchart*. Essentially, a flowchart is a blueprint or a logical diagram of the solution to a problem. The algorithm is constructed out of boxes, with the shape of each box indicating the kind of operation being performed. Figure 2-3 shows some of the generally accepted flowcharting symbols. The actual operation to be performed is written inside the symbol. The arrow (or arrows) coming out of the symbol indicates which operation to perform next. The algorithm is executed by starting at the oval symbol labeled START, following the arrows and performing all indicated operations, and continuing until we reach the oval symbol labeled STOP. The table look-up algorithm that we first developed would probably look something like the flowchart in Figure 2-4.

A comparison of Figures 2-1 and 2-4, two representations of the same algorithm, shows quite clearly what we feel is the biggest drawback to flowcharts—they do not clearly indicate the hierarchical structure of the algorithm. Using boxes and arrows instead of algorithmic primitives prevents certain structural aspects of the problem from becoming immediately apparent—aspects such as loops, nested tests, or disjoint clauses. However, the use of flowcharts is very widespread. In Chapter 9 we will present some rules for writing a specific type of flowchart, called a *segmented flowchart,* which attempts to make the diagrams we write as clear and as well organized as possible. These will eliminate much of the "spaghetti" tangle of lines and boxes exemplified by Figure 2-4 and so typical of most flowcharts today.

The flowcharting technique is useful primarily for macrolevel or system flowcharts where we are concerned with the most general level of operations needed to solve a large problem. Each element of a system flowchart would

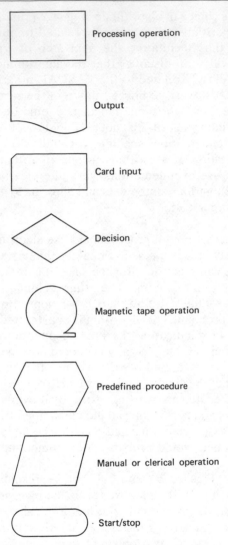

Processing operation

Output

Card input

Decision

Magnetic tape operation

Predefined procedure

Manual or clerical operation

Start/stop

FIGURE 2-3   Some Standard Flowchart Symbols.

typically represent a fairly large and complex manual, clerical, or computer procedure for which an algorithm must be developed and implemented. These individual procedures could be developed and represented using an algorithmic language similar to the one described in this chapter. Figure 2-5 is a macrolevel flowchart for the implementation of a file merge—combining an old master file with updating information to produce a new master file and other reports. This specific example shows a payroll file containing salary information on every employee. The update information could be the list of

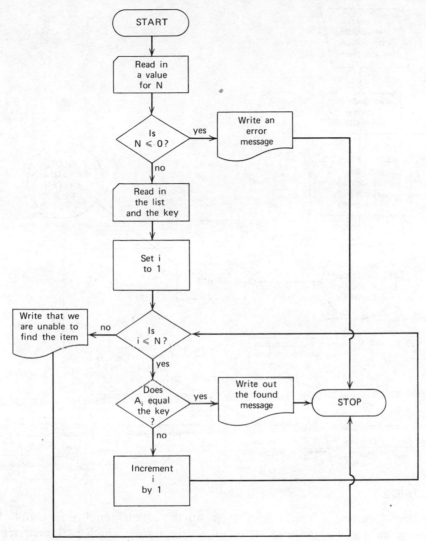

FIGURE 2-4 A Flowchart of the Table Look-Up Algorithms.

all employees who have been hired, fired, promoted, or demoted during the past week. The output may be both a new payroll file incorporating all the new information as well as the various reports required by the company. Most of the broad operations on that flowchart would become distinct problems that would need to be defined, developed, and solved individually, and then combined into a single system.

After viewing the same algorithm represented in a number of different ways, you may have a strong opinion about which representation is "best"

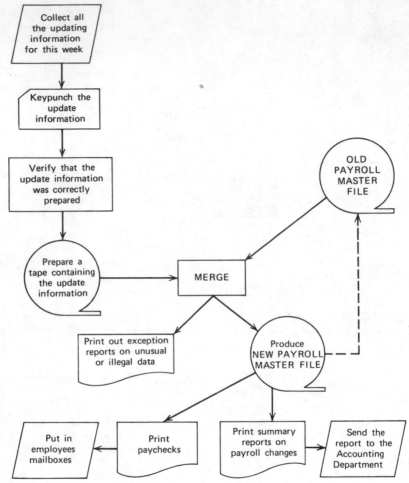

FIGURE 2-5   Example of a System Level Flowchart.

or most "natural." This brings us to an important conclusion about the representation of algorithms. It is not so important which particular technique you use, as long as you use something that you can work with comfortably and that allows you to develop correct algorithms independent of and unencumbered by the syntactic limitations of any specific programming language.

2.2.2 EXAMPLE TWO—A BETTER TABLE LOOK-UP

In the first example in this chapter we developed an algorithm for searching a list sequentially from beginning to end. However, if the list we are searching is already organized in some fashion (e.g., names listed alphabetically), then that technique is foolish. Imagine searching for SMITH, JOHN J. in the New York City telephone directory by beginning with AARDVARK, ALAN A. and continuing sequentially! Instead, we quite naturally enter the book somewhere in the middle and move rapidly toward the desired name. Let us develop an algorithm that efficiently searches an alphabetized list of names either to locate a particular one or discover that it is not in the book. It is essentially the same problem as before, but the data are organized in a different manner.

The main purpose of this example will not be to show how to represent the algorithm but to show how to *find* it. In the previous example we were primarily concerned with developing an algorithmic language. The algorithm itself, that is, the actual sequence of steps, just "happened." However, what do we do when we have no idea of how to proceed in solving a problem? Is there any technique or guideline for aiding a programmer in this *algorithm discovery* or problem-solving process?

As in any creative process, there is no foolproof method for developing good or even correct algorithms. Just as with a poem, an essay, or the plot for a novel, nothing, other than experience, can guarantee results every time. But that does not mean that discovering an algorithm is a completely unstructured, trial-and-error process. There are techniques, guidelines, and aids to help a programmer develop reasonable solutions to complex problems.

Probably the single most important design aid is the technique called *top-down development;* it is also known as *modular development* or *stepwise refinement.* In top-down development, we initially describe the problem we are working on at the highest, most general levels. Typically the description of the problem at this level will be concerned with what must be done—not with how it must be done. Usually this description will not be given in the algorithmic language primitives that we developed in the previous section. Instead, it will be described in terms of complex, higher-level operations. We need to take each of the operations individually at this level and break them down into simpler steps that begin to describe how to accomplish the tasks. If these simpler steps can be represented as acceptable algorithmic primitives, we need not refine them any further. If not, we refine each of those second-level operations individually into yet simpler steps. This stepwise refinement continues until each of the original top-level operations has been described in terms of acceptable primitive statements.

This top-down approach to developing algorithms offers a number of significant advantages over trying to develop solutions in a random, unorganized fashion. First, and most important, it allows the programmer to keep "on top of" a problem and be able to view the developing solution in its context. The solution is always proceeding from the highest levels down. With other techniques we may find ourselves bogged down with very low-level decisions at a very early stage. It will be difficult to make these decisions if it is not clear how our decision may affect the remainder of the problem. For example, it would probably be difficult to decide what type of table look-up technique to choose if we do not yet know how the table will be used, what it will look like, or what values it will contain.

Also, top-down development is a very good way to delay decisions for problems whose solution may not be readily apparent. At each stage in the development, the individual operation will be refined into a number of more elementary steps. (Figure 2-6). If we are not sure how to proceed with step a_2 we can still work on step a_1. If the best methods to use with a_{11} and a_{12} are not obvious, we could proceed with steps a_{13} and a_{14} and, later on, come back and finish the problem.

Finally, by subdividing the problem into a number of subproblems, we have made it easier to share problem development and to work in teams. For example, one person could be responsible for step a_1, while another individual handles step a_2. The person in charge of a_1 could either handle it personally or farm out steps a_{11}, a_{12}, a_{13}, a_{14} to four other programmers and merely manage and coordinate their efforts. On large problems (certainly larger than the little problems we are developing here!) this latter advantage takes on extraordinary importance.

In school, students are usually discouraged from trying to solve assigned problems together. Competition among individuals is much preferred, even encouraged. While realizing that you may be asked to solve programming problems alone for class, we want to emphasize that, in the real world, people are becoming more and more concerned with how to manage and use teams of programmers to solve problems most effectively. We will say more about team efforts in Chapter 9, where we discuss large, real-world problems.

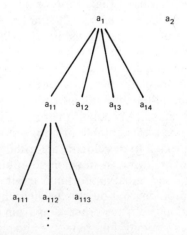

FIGURE 2-6   Example of Stepwise Refinement.

1. Input the list and the key we are searching for
2. See if the key is in the list
3. If it was found
4.   Then Write an appropriate message
5.   Else Write some other appropriate message

FIGURE 2-7   Top-Level Description of the Table Look-Up Algorithm.

We will now use the top-down technique just discussed to develop a better table look-up algorithm. The very highest level of the algorithm is shown in Figure 2-7 (the steps are numbered for reference in the text).

Figure 2-7 describes the problem only at the level of the highest and most general operations. Each step will need to be refined quite extensively until it is expressed in terms of algorithmic primitives. For example, we can initially concern ourselves with statement 1 above: How do we do the input operation and what checking is necessary? The refinement of statement 1 is shown in Figure 2-8.

If the steps shown in Figure 2-8 are all acceptable primitives, we are done. If not, we can refine them even further. For example, in step 1.3 the appropriate recovery action could be described in more detail.

1.31   Then Write an error message that says
             the list is of incorrect size
1.32   Stop

If, however, we were not sure what recovery procedure we would need to initiate, we would merely leave step 1.3 as it is and continue with another part of the algorithm. Eventually we would need to come back to this point and fill in the missing details. This is a good example of how top-down methods allow us to delay decisions on low-level implementation details.

We can now begin refining and describing the main part of the algorithm—step 2 of Figure 2-7. When we open a telephone directory to search for a name, we do not, as we did in Example 1, begin looking on page 1. We usually open the book somewhere in the middle and see whether we are too far or not far enough; that is, we see whether to continue our search in the first or second half. We can repeat the halving until we reach the desired

1.1 Read in the list size, n
1.2 If the list size is less than 1
1.3   Then take the appropriate recovery action
1.4   Else Read in the list $a_1, a_2, \ldots, a_n$
1.5   Read in the special key we are searching for

FIGURE 2-8   Refinement of the Input Section of the Algorithm.

2.1 Repeat the following steps until we find what we want or we have looked
    at the entire list
2.2   Look at the "middle" item of what is left of the list
2.3   If it is the special key
2.4   Then we have found the name
2.5   Else If the key is in the top half
2.6   Then throw away the bottom half of the list
2.7   Else throw away the top half of the list

FIGURE 2-9 First Refinement of the Searching Section of the Algorithm.

page and name. This idea of looking somewhere in the middle and discarding
the half that is not needed will form the basis for the first refinement of
step 2. Figure 2-9 shows the refinement.

Figure 2-9 gives an excellent high-level view of this search technique but
leaves a number of questions unanswered. For example, what is this
"middle" item we are referring to? Obviously it will be the item halfway
between the top and bottom of whatever part of the list we are looking at.
Therefore, somewhere in the algorithm we must include a definition of the
items at the top and bottom of the list.

2.01 Initialize top to 1, the index of the first item in the list
2.02 Initialize bottom to n, the index of the last item in the list

We can now say:

2.21 Set middle to $\dfrac{\text{top} + \text{bottom}}{2}$ (rounded to an integer)
2.31 If the item at position "middle" of the list equals the key

Now that we have defined the top and bottom of the list, we explain what it
means to "throw away" half the list as we directed in steps 2.6 and 2.7.
We can discard a portion of the list merely by calling the middle item the new
top or new bottom. That is, we reset "top" or "bottom" to "middle." Figure 2-10a shows the current situation. If we reset the top pointer to the value
of middle, we discard the top half, as shown in Figure 2-10b, and if we reset
the bottom pointer to the value of middle, we discard the bottom half, as in
Figure 2-10c.
We can represent this in our algorithm as follows.

2.51 Else If the value of the middle item of the list comes alphabetically after
    the special key

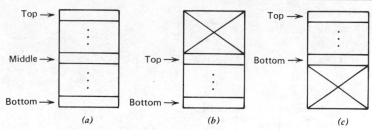

FIGURE 2-10   Discarding Half the List.

2.61   Then Set bottom to the current value of middle
2.71   Else Set top to the current value of middle

This entire process will continue until either we find the desired item (the value of the middle item equals the key) or the list is exhausted (top and bottom have the same value).

The technique we have just developed is called the *binary search* algorithm. The complete algorithm is shown in Figure 2-11. Before coding it into PASCAL, we should apply the testing criteria discussed earlier to see whether or not the algorithm as written does indeed operate correctly on all data cases and find the desired name. We must be sure to include the limiting, unusual, and illegal cases, as well as valid data sets.

This example has made two important points concerning algorithms. The first is the point that we started out to make: the top-down approach is an excellent design aid for producing computer algorithms. Look back at Figure 2-11 and imagine trying to develop the finished algorithm in one step. Even if that project does not seem too difficult, imagine trying to design algorithms that are 10, 100, or even 1000 times more complex. Without some strategy for organizing we would soon become lost.

The other point to notice is that we have developed two different algorithms for two different types of lists, one unalphabetized, one alphabetized. A simple change in the way the data was organized allowed us to develop an improved method for searching. The point we are making is that the purpose of an algorithm is to process data and the way the data are represented will usually strongly influence the algorithm that finally results. Although they frequently may be discussed separately, you should always consider the topics of data organization and algorithm development as inextricably related. Although some lower-level decisions concerning the data may be postponed (e.g., Should values be integers or real numbers? Should names be limited to 20 characters?), the higher-level decisions (e.g., Should the data be stored in a list, and should it be sorted?) will usually need to be made at the time the algorithm is being developed.

START
    Read in the list size, n
    If $n \leq 0$
        Then Write an error message that the list is of incorrect size
            Stop
        Else Read in the list $a_1, a_2, a_3, \ldots, a_n$
            Read in the special key
            Set top to 1
            Set bottom to n
            Set found to false
            While the key has not been found and top $\leq$ bottom do

$$\text{Set middle to } \frac{\text{top + bottom}}{2} \text{ (rounded to the nearest integer)}$$

                If $a_{middle} = $ key
                    Then Set found to true
                    Else If a_{middle} is alphabetically greater than key
                        Then Set bottom to middle $-$ 1
                        Else Set top to middle $+$ 1
            End of the While loop
            If the item was found
                Then Write "The item was found at position", middle
                Else Write "We have searched the entire list and could not
                        find the key"
        Stop
END OF THE ALGORITHM
FIGURE 2-11   The Binary Search Algorithm.

As an example of this latter point, consider the problem of computing the average of a set of examination scores using the well-known formula

$$\text{Average} = \frac{\text{Sum of all scores}}{\text{Number of scores}}$$

Before we can even begin to design the algorithm, we must make an important decision about the organization of the data. Computing an average does not require us to have read all the data values in advance. We could, if we wished, read one data item at a time. We would bring in that value, add it to a running total, keep track of how many scores we have processed, and then bring in the next value. This would require only a single storage location for all the scores. This strategy would probably result in an algorithm like that of Figure 2-12. Alternately, we could decide to use a list and immediately read all examination scores into this list. We would now compute the average by working through the list, from beginning to end, summing up

START
    Set the running-total to 0
    Set the score-counter to 0
    While there are still scores to process do
        Read a single score
        Add that score to the running-total
        Increment score-counter by 1
    End of the loop
    If score-counter is 0
        Then Write a message that there were no scores
        Else Set average to running-total divided by score-counter
            Write out the average
    Stop
    END OF THE ALGORITHM

FIGURE 2-12 Averaging Algorithm Without Lists.

the scores as we go. We would now end up with something similar to Figure 2-13. We have produced two quite different algorithms, not because the problem is different but because the data have been organized differently. Notice that while we were concerned about the structure of the data, we never cared about the actual format of the examination scores—whether they were integers 0 to 100, or decimal values 200.0 to 800.0. That decision can probably be postponed until we actually begin encoding the algorithm into a specific programming language.

START
    Set the running-total to 0
    Read in the list size, n
    If n is 0
        Then Write a message that there were no scores
        Else Read in the entire list $e_1, e_2, \ldots, e_n$
            Set i to 1
            While i $\leq$ n do
                Add e_i to the running total
                Increment i by 1
            End of the loop
            Set average to running-total divided by n
            Write out the average
    Stop
    END OF THE ALGORITHM

FIGURE 2-13 Averaging Algorithm Using a List.

STYLE CLINIC 2-1

Don't Reinvent the Wheel

The preceding discussion may have given you the mistaken impression that all algorithms are designed by the programmer from scratch. That is completely false. In most cases, all or part of an algorithm needed to solve a problem can be found in the published literature of computer science or related disciplines. There is an almost limitless number of well-documented and well-analyzed algorithms for performing virtually any task. For certain common problems—sorting, searching, merging, root finding, matrix operations, simple statistics—there may be as many as a dozen different methods to choose from. So before you begin your task, first see if someone has already done the work for you. It may save a lot of time and effort.

2.3 THE EFFICIENCY OF ALGORITHMS

The previous two sections have been concerned solely with techniques for finding and representing algorithms. However, as our discussion of the two methods of searching showed, some correct solutions are better than others. Pragmatic considerations require that the algorithms we design not only be formally correct but that they be reasonably efficient. That will require us to develop both the criteria for defining "efficiency" and the procedures for comparing and evaluating alternative techniques.

The most obvious measure would be simply to take an algorithm, supply it with a specific set of data, and count either the number of steps or the amount of time it takes to produce the desired solution. What this would produce, however, is merely a measure of efficiency for a very specific case that may have no relationship to the performance of the algorithm for a completely different set of data. An algorithm for finding a name in a telephone book by sequentially searching all names from A to Z would probably provide acceptable performance for all telephone books with less than 50 entries. Its performance on the New York City directory would be totally unacceptable. What we need is a way to formulate a general guideline that says that for any arbitrary set of data, one particular algorithm will probably be better than another. Specifically, we would like to associate a value n, called the size of the problem, with a value t, the computer time needed to produce the answer. The association would be in the form of a formula, $t = f(n)$, where the function is usually called the *time complexity* of the algorithm.

What is the meaning of this value n? It is simply a measure of the size of the problem we are attempting to solve. For example, if we are sorting a list into alphabetic order, a natural measure of the size would be the number of elements in the list. If we are inverting a matrix we would probably choose the dimensions (i.e., the number of rows and columns) of the matrix. Finally, if we are building a data base, the number of individual entries in the files could measure the size.

We will examine the examples we developed earlier—the table look-up algorithms shown in Figures 2-1 and 2-11. A natural choice for the size of this problem would be the size of the list we are searching. With the sequential search method we may, in the worst case, need to look at all n items in the list to find the desired one or determine that the value is not there. Thus the relationship between t and n would be given by

$$t = c * n \qquad \text{(for the worst case)}$$

where c is some constant based on the internal speed of the machine we are working with and thc number of machine instructions it takes to look at an item in the list. Formulas like this one are rarely used for computing exact timings, because the constant c is frequently quite difficult to obtain. However, that was not what we wanted, anyway. What we really want from a formula is a general guideline to aid us in evaluating and choosing algorithms. We can get this information by using what is called *0-notation*.

$$t \cong 0(f(n))$$

Formally, the 0-notation concept says that there exist constants M and n* such that if $t \cong 0(f(n))$, then $t \leq Mf(n)$ for all $n > n*$.

This imposing-looking definition is not really that difficult to understand. Informally, the definition says that the computing time of the algorithm grows no faster than the order of f(n)—as n increases (i.e., the problem gets bigger), the time to solve it increases at a rate bounded by the function f(n).

So, for example, assuming the order of an algorithm were $0(n^2)$, then if n, the size of the problem, doubled, the time to solve the problem would increase about fourfold. If n tripled the new solution would take about nine times as long as the old one. The concept of the *order* of an algorithm is then an approximate measure of the amount of resources it uses when solving a problem. (In this section the only resource we will look at will be time, but there are others.) Quite obviously, then, our goal will be to develop algorithms of the *smallest order possible*. We cannot state explicitly how much time the algorithm will require for a particular data set, but we can, in general, say that as the size of the problem increases, the time needed to compute a result will not increase as rapidly as with other techniques. This is the general guideline we have been looking for and this is why 0-notation has become the fundamental technique for describing the efficiency properties of algorithms.

Looking again at the sequential search algorithm, we can see quite clearly that it is 0(n). If the list were to double in size, the time to search the entire list would also double. We now analyze the binary search algorithm.

With each comparison we halve the size of the list still under consideration. Therefore the list will be ½, ¼, ⅛, $^1/_{16}$, . . . its original size. In the worst possible case this process will continue until the list is empty. We can represent that by saying that the greatest possible number of comparisons will be k, where k is defined as the first integer value such that

$$2^k \geq n \qquad \text{(the length of the list)}$$

If we now take the logarithm of both sides we get

$$k \geq \log_2 n$$

and the order of the binary search algorithm can be given as $0(\log_2 n)$. This is a lower-order algorithm than the sequential search, because its order grows more slowly as n gets larger (see Figure 2-14). Thus, the larger a list, the more time we save by using a binary search instead of a sequential search. For a list of 50,000 items the sequential search would, in the worst case, require 50,000 comparisons, while the binary search would never require more than $\log_2 (50,000)$ or about 16. This represents an improvement factor of about 3000!

The statement that the binary search is more efficient than the sequential search is somewhat misleading, however. For the binary search to work correctly, the list we are searching must be sorted. The sequential search works for sorted and unsorted lists. To compare the efficiency of each, we must assume that every list we search is sorted, or we must add the time it takes to sort a list to the time required for the binary search. Many real-world problems that require searching also require sorting and, in these cases, the binary search will be more efficient than the sequential search, once sorting has been done.

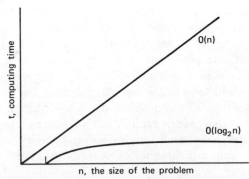

FIGURE 2-14 Comparison of O(n) and O(log₂n) Algorithm.

Since sorting—putting a list into an ordered sequence—is such a common process, we now look at algorithms for sorting as a second example of finding time-efficient algorithms. One of the most common techniques for sorting is called the *selection sort*. With this method we search the list to find the largest element. We interchange that element with the element currently in the first position. We now find the largest item remaining in the list, beginning our search at position 2. When we find it, we interchange it with the element currently in the second position of the list. After repeating this operation n − 1 times, where n is the size of the list, the entire list will be sorted. The entire algorithm is shown in Figure 2-15.

To find the largest element the first time through the list will require us to look at all n values in the list. Finding the second largest, however, will require looking at only n − 1 values, and so forth. Therefore a measure of the total number of operations required to perform the selection sort is:

$$n + (n - 1) + (n - 2) + \ldots + 2 = \sum_{i=2}^{n} i$$

$$= \frac{n(n + 1)}{2} - 1$$

$$= \frac{1}{2}n^2 + \frac{1}{2}n - 1$$

For large problems (i.e., for large values of n) the term containing the n^2 completely overwhelms the other terms. In general, when analyzing algo-

---

START
　　Read in n, the size of the list
　　If n ≤ 0 Then Write "Illegal size list, cannot sort"
　　　　Stop
　　Read in all n items $l_1, l_2, \ldots, l_n$
　　If n=1 Then the list is already sorted. Nothing need be done.
　　　　Else Set i to 1
　　　　　　Repeat the following (n−1) times
　　　　　　　　Find the largest item in the list beginning with position i
　　　　　　　　Interchange the largest item just found and the item at
　　　　　　　　　　position i in the list 1
　　　　　　　　Increment i by 1
　　　　　　　　End of the loop
　　　　Write out the values $l_1, l_2, \ldots, l_n$
　　Stop
　　END OF THE ALGORITHM
FIGURE 2-15　Algorithm for the Selection Sort.

rithms, we consider all lower-order terms unimportant and discard them. Furthermore, the coefficient 1/2 is also unimportant, in comparison with n^2, and we can discard it. The complexity of the selection sort can thus be written as $0(n^2)$.

There are literally dozens of other sorting algorithms. If, after actually writing and running an selection sort program, we were not satisfied with its performance, we could either attempt to improve that program or choose a different algorithm. A fundamental concept in the study of algorithms follows.

> The true problem in the choice of algorithms is not to simply find a better algorithm of the same order but to find one of a lower order. The efficiency gains to be made by the latter will exceed the former by orders of magnitude.

Thus we would gain most by choosing a new sorting algorithm with a lower order than the n^2 characteristic of the previous method.

Let us look at one more sorting procedure—the *merge sort*—to see if we can find one of a lower order. The merge sort is the way that people tend to operate when sorting manually. Instead of sorting the entire list directly, we first break the original list into m smaller piles or sublists and then sort each pile individually.

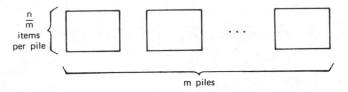

After each of the piles is sorted, we merge them back into a single sorted list.

To sort each individual pile, we can use any $0(n^2)$ sorting technique (e.g., the selection sort just discussed). Since there will be n/m items in each little sublist, the approximate time to sort each one will be $0(n^2/m^2)$. There are m of these lists, so the total sorting time will be $0((n^2/m^2)*m) = 0(n^2/m)$. After sorting, we must merge all m sublists. This will involve looking at the top item in each of the m piles to find the largest. This requires m comparisons. This process must be repeated n times, so the approximate time for the merge is $0(m*n)$. The overall time for a merge sort is thus given by

$$0\left(\frac{n^2}{m} + mn\right)$$

Now, by choosing as the value of m the optimum number of piles, we can gain enormously. [Notice, by the way, that if m = 1 or m = n, the merge sort again becomes an $0(n^2)$ algorithm, and we have gained nothing.] The optimum number of piles is m $\cong \sqrt{n}$.* So if we are sorting a list of 50 items we would use about 7 piles, and for a list of 10,000 items we would have 100. If we use the optimum value for m in the above formula, the order of the merge sort becomes:

$$\frac{n^2}{m} + mn$$

$$\frac{n^2}{\sqrt{n}} + \sqrt{n} \cdot n =$$

$$n^{3/2} + n^{3/2} =$$

$$2n^{3/2} =$$

$$0(n^{3/2})$$

The merge sort, with $\sqrt{n}$ piles, becomes an $0(n^{3/2})$ technique. For very small lists the computing time difference between $0(n^2)$ and $0(n^{3/2})$ is not great and the choice of techniques does not matter greatly. But, as n becomes quite large, the difference becomes extremely significant and the merge sort becomes a much more attractive algorithm. In fact, if n becomes enormously large, we will not be able to solve certain problems using the $0(n^2)$ technique because the computing time, t, has become so excessive.

To illustrate this last point numerically, assume that we have six different algorithms A_1 through A_6 that solve some arbitrary problem P with the following complexities.

$$
\begin{array}{lll}
A_1 & : & 0(n) \\
A_2 & : & 0(n \log_2 n) \\
A_3 & : & 0(n^{3/2}) \\
A_4 & : & 0(n^2) \\
A_5 & : & 0(n^3) \\
A_6 & : & 0(2^n)
\end{array}
$$

Assume that the constant of proportionality, c, is approximately the same for all six and is 1 millisecond/operation (rather large for today's machines). We can now ask the following question. Given 2 minutes of computing time (t), what is the largest problem that we are able to solve in that 2 minutes, using each of the six algorithms? This is an important way to phrase this type of question, since the limiting factor in solving problems is usually the pragmatic consideration of how much computer time we can afford. The results are shown in Figure 2-16.

---

* For those with some knowledge of calculus, the optimum is discovered by taking the derivative with respect to m, setting it to 0, and solving for m. However, this is not necessary for understanding the discussion that follows.

ALGORITHM	COMPLEXITY	LARGEST PROBLEM THAT CAN BE SOLVED IN $t = 2$ MINUTES (120 SECONDS)
A_1	$0(n)$	$n = 120,000$
A_2	$0(n \log_2 n)$	9,000
A_3	$0(n^{3/2})$	2,400
A_4	$0(n^2)$	350
A_5	$0(n^3)$	50
A_6	$0(2^n)$	17

FIGURE 2-16   Comparison of Computing Times for $t = 2$ minutes.

Figure 2-16 shows clearly the enormous difference in efficiency. If we used the merge sort algorithm, which is $0(n^{3/2})$ then, for the conditions stated above, we could solve a problem about 7 times larger than with the $0(n^2)$ algorithms developed earlier. If we could find and develop an $0(n \log_2 n)$ sorting algorithm we would solve a problem 25 times larger than before in the same time. These order-of-magnitude differences are typical of what can be expected when we use algorithms of lower orders on large problems. This contrasts sharply with the 10, 20, or 30% improvements that are usually achieved by trying to improve an existing algorithm. Finding an algorithm of a lower order should always be our first consideration, although these other improvements can be meaningful if still more time efficiency is important.

A more thorough treatment of the complexity of algorithms is well beyond the scope of this textbook. What we have tried to do in this section is merely introduce certain fundamental concepts concerning the analysis of algorithms. Even though your knowledge and understanding of these methods of analysis may currently be quite limited, we hope we have made you aware of some extremely important points concerning algorithms and problem solving.

1. There do exist quantitative methods for measuring the "goodness" of algorithms.

2. There are guidelines to help us choose the best algorithms where alternatives are available.

3. The truly significant gains in efficiency are realized not by trying to make minor changes in the current algorithm but by choosing a better algorithm entirely.

In your future course work in computer science you will investigate this subject in much greater detail.

2.4 RECURSIVE ALGORITHMS

Our discussion so far has dealt with the single class of techniques called *iterative algorithms*—those that move toward a solution a step at a time. We will now briefly examine a totally different kind of algorithm called a *recursive algorithm*.

An algorithm is termed *recursive* if it is defined in terms of itself. In an iterative algorithm a portion of the solution may be repeatedly executed (e.g., a WHILE loop), but a recursive algorithm calls for the reexecution of the entire algorithm from the beginning.

The fundamental idea behind a recursive solution is to define a problem in terms of a similar version of itself. If we do this repeatedly we will ultimately end up with the simplest or most trivial case, for which a direct answer is already known. We can now use this value to back up through the various subproblems that were generated until we have arrived back at the original problem and produced the desired answer.

STYLE CLINIC 2-2

What Is Efficiency?

Programmers (and programming textbooks!) used to treat the topic of efficiency solely in terms of shaving every possible statement and microsecond from a program or algorithm. They would spend hours on arcane considerations such as whether it was faster to use

$$A - B + B + B + B$$

or

$$A = B * 4$$

and whether they could save a few milliseconds by using integer values instead of decimal ones. They were quite proud of the resulting program, which now ran a few seconds faster than before.

This section should make you realize that this is not the proper way to view program efficiency. If minimum computing time is an important factor, worry first about choosing the best possible algorithm. Once that is done, develop the clearest, most straightforward, and most easily understood version of that algorithm. The excessive modification of an algorithm to save a fraction of a second is usually a losing proposition. First, you may find that it usually costs you more money, in terms of the hourly wage of the programmer, than was saved in reduced machine costs. Second, if the tricks that were played to save time were extremely complex, you may find that at some point in the future you are no longer able to decipher what you did! You would have been penny wise and pound foolish.

This discussion does not imply that we tolerate gross inefficiency or total neglect for the concerns of time. It is simply to make you aware of where the real gains in efficiency are made—in the algorithm, not in the coding.

The computation of factorials is a classic example of recursion. We all know what factorial means:

$$4! = 4 \times 3 \times 2 \times 1$$

and, in general,

$$n! = n \times (n - 1) \times \ldots \times 3 \times 2 \times 1$$

If we wished to develop a recursive algorithm for computing factorials, our first problem would be to redefine the meaning of the factorial function in terms of itself. We can do this easily by observing the following fact.

$$6! = 6 \times 5!$$

and, in general,

$$n! = n \times (n - 1)!$$

We have defined n! in terms of a simpler version of the same problem, $(n - 1)!$. We could likewise redefine $(n - 1)!$ in terms of $(n - 2)!$, and so forth. This would continue until we come to the trivial case, 0!, which is defined to be 1. A complete recursive algorithm for computing factorials is shown in Figure 2-17.

The value n following the name of the algorithm is called a *parameter* or an *argument;* it represents a value we pass to the algorithm when it is executed. The algorithm works as follows when we compute Factorial(2). At line 2 we test the value for n (which is currently 2) and see that it is not 0, so we execute the Else clause on line 4. This asks us to multiply 2 × the result produced by executing Factorial(1). We must reexecute the algorithm. However, we must remember where we left off in the current execution so that we can eventually return. Imagine a marker left at the end of line 4 that says "Come back to this point to finish computing Factorial(2)." After leaving this marker, we can begin evaluating Factorial(1). All this does is ask us to

Line
1   START Factorial (n)
2   If n = 0
3   Then Set result to 1
4   Else Set result to n × Factorial (n − 1)
5   Stop
6   END OF THE ALGORITHM

FIGURE 2-17   Recursive Algorithm for Computing Factorials.

multiply 1 × Factorial(0). We must leave another marker saying, in effect, "Come back to this point to finish evaluating Factorial(1)." Now we can work on Factorial(0). For this case the algorithm produces the value 1 directly and ends. We now check if there are any outstanding markers and, if so, begin finishing those incomplete cases. We return to the markers in the reverse order they were put down—the last marker left is the first one we return to. Thus we begin computing Factorial(1), which was defined as 1 × Factorial(0). Since Factorial(0) produced a result of 1, this pass produces a result of 1 and also ends. The next marker now says return to computing Factorial(2), which was defined as 2 × Factorial(1), which we can now say is 2. The algorithm has now ended because there are no more markers outstanding. The result of executing Factorial(2) is 2.

We have spent a great deal of time explaining in detail how recursive algorithms work. This understanding is very important, because those who do not understand them clearly tend to feel that recursive algorithms are "complicated," "unusual," or "higher level" than iterative algorithms. This is not true; recursion offers a very useful and powerful programming tool. It frequently allows us to solve problems with just a few steps that, iteratively, would be extremely complex.

Unfortunately, the factorial example was not the best illustration of this latter point. An iterative algorithm for computing factorials is quite obvious and just as easy to write. Another example will make this point better.

Figure 2-18 shows a *binary tree,* a very common data structure in computer science. It has *nodes,* represented by the circles, with the name of the node written inside and, at most, two pointers coming from each node. These pointers are called the *left pointer* and the *right pointer* of the node. The very top node of the tree is called the *root.* You are probably familiar with this type of data structure from charts that show the chain of command in corporations, although we would probably allow more than two pointers coming from each node in such charts (otherwise they would be top-heavy with management!).

Assume we are given the problem of developing an algorithm to go through this tree and print out the name of every node in the tree. An itera-

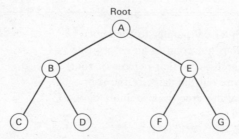

FIGURE 2-18   Example of a Binary Tree.

tive algorithm for this is certainly a nontrivial problem, and the answer is not immediately obvious.

If we wish to solve the problem recursively our first step would be to attempt to define the problem in terms of itself. A tree has one very nice property that allows us to do this quite easily: if we follow a pointer from one node to another, what we are left with is still a tree. For example, in Figure 2-18, if we follow the left pointer from node *A*, we are left with the following tree.

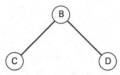

If we follow the left pointer of *B,* we are left with the following one-node tree.

Finally, if we attempt to follow the left pointer of this tree, we have come to the trivial case—an empty tree.

This characteristic allows us to write the recursive algorithm "Search-a-tree," which is shown in Figure 2-19. The parameter to this algorithm is a pointer to the root of the tree we are currently searching. Initially, it will point to the root of the entire tree.

The recursive approach has led us to an elegant five-line solution to a quite complex problem. You should apply the algorithm, using the marker technique discussed earlier, to the tree shown in Figure 2-18. The algorithm should produce the following output.

C
B
D
A
F
E
G

START Search-a-tree (pointer to the root)
   If pointer does not point to an empty tree
      Then Search-a-tree (left pointer of root)
         Write out the name of the root
         Search-a-tree (right pointer of root)
  Stop
END OF THE ALGORITHM
FIGURE 2-19 Recursive Algorithm for Searching a Binary Tree.

Recursion should be viewed as another tool in a programmer's problem-solving kit. It can frequently lead to very concise and very elegant algorithms that would be hard to visualize or develop iteratively. PASCAL allows the writing of recursive programs; numerous examples of these will be discussed in Chapter 8.

2.5 CONCLUSION

This chapter has provided an overview of algorithms, including their development, representation, and efficiency. Some of the important points we have tried to highlight are:

1. An algorithm is a procedure for solving a problem. It is composed of unambiguous commands whose order of execution is known, and it is always guaranteed to stop in a finite amount of time.
2. There are many formats for representing and developing algorithms, and the specific one used by a programmer is not important except as it affects the difficulty of thinking about the algorithm and coding the solution. The ideal format is the one with which the programmer feels most comfortable and that can be converted into the desired programming language with relative ease.
3. The truly creative part of programming is the design and development of correct and efficient algorithms. The coding phase, which will occupy much of the remainder of this book, can be viewed simply as the process of translating an algorithm into the syntax of a particular programming language.
4. There exists a measure, called the order of the algorithm, that allows us to compare the relative efficiency of one algorithm with other algorithms that solve the same or similar problems.

The next three chapters will introduce you to a specific programming language—the language called PASCAL.

EXERCISES

*1. Rewrite the shampoo algorithm on page 19 so that it is valid.

    a. Use the While primitive.
    b. Use the Repeat primitive.

2. Write an algorithm that specifies the procedures followed in registering for courses at your school.

3. Write an algorithm that describes how to place a telephone call. Be

sure to include the possibilities of not knowing the phone number,
lack of a dial tone, getting a busy signal, or no answer.

*4.   a. Each of the following represents an attempt to write an algorithm
         that computes the sum of the first 10 integers. State why each is
         either poor or invalid.

      i. START
            Set sum to 1+2+3+4+5+6+7+8+9+10
            Write sum
         END OF ALGORITHM
      ii. START
            Set n to 10 and sum to 0
            Add n to sum
            Decrement n by 1
            See if n > 0
            Go back and repeat
            Write sum
         END OF THE ALGORITHM
      iii. START
            Set i to 0 and sum to 0
            Repeat the following 10 times
               Add i to sum
            End of the loop
            Write sum
         END OF THE ALGORITHM
      iv. START
            Set i to 0 and sum to 0
            While i <= 10 do the following
               Add i to sum
            End of loop
            Write sum
         END OF THE ALGORITHM

      b. Write a valid algorithm to sum the first 10 integers.
      c. Write a valid algorithm to sum the first k integers 'where k is a
         value read from a data card. (Be sure to allow for the pathological
         case of k <= 0.)

5.   Modify the sequential search algorithm shown in Figure 2-1 so that it
      counts the total number of occurrences of the key value in the list.

6.   Assume that in addition to the information wanted to problem 5, we
      also want to obtain the location of every occurrence of the key value

in the list. For example, if our key were 'Z' and the list contained the following items:

'A' 'Z' 'M' 'N' 'Z' 'P' 'B' 'Z'

then the algorithm should produce the value 3 (the total number of occurrences of the character 'Z') and a list containing the numbers

2   5   8

since 'Z' occurs in the second, fifth, and eighth positions.

*7. A *palindrome* is a word or phase that reads the same both forward and backward without regard to spaces. For example:

RADAR
A MAN A PLAN A CANAL PANAMA

Write an algorithm to read in a k-character string and determine whether it is or is not a palindrome.

8. a. Design an algorithm to find and output both the value and the position of the largest item in a list. What is the order of your algorithm? (*Consider.* What should we do if there is a tie for the largest?)
b. If the list you were given is already sorted, what is the order of the most efficient algorithm for finding the largest value?

9. a. Assume that we have two lists that are sorted into ascending sequence. List A contains M items and list B contains N. Design a merge algorithm that will produce a single sorted list C containing all the elements of A and B.
b. Modify the algorithm from part a so that we eliminate any items that may be duplicated in both lists A and B.

10. Write an algorithm that finds all the possible ways of making change from a dollar bill when the items purchased cost c cents ($c \leq 100$).

11. Develop an algorithm to solve quadratic equations of the form: $ax^2 + bx + c = 0$ using the quadratic formula

$$\frac{-b \pm \sqrt{b^2 - 4ac}}{2a}$$

Be sure to check for:

a. Complex roots ($b^2 - 4ac < 0$).
b. Double roots ($b^2 - 4ac = 0$).
c. Nonquadratic equations ($a = 0$).

*12. Given k distinct characters, construct an algorithm to print all possible strings of length k that contain each character exactly once.

13. a. What is the output if we apply the recursive tree-searching algorithm of Figure 2-19 to the following tree.

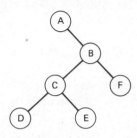

b. What is the output of the following variation of the tree-searching algorithm when applied to the tree from part a?

> START Search-a-tree (pointer to the root)
> If pointer does not point to an empty tree
> Then Search-a-tree (left pointer of root)
> Search-a-tree (right pointer of root)
> Write out the name of the root
> END OF THE ALGORITHM

*14. Construct a *recursive* binary search algorithm (*Hint.* View the algorithm as having three inputs—the number being searched for, the bottom of the list, and the top of the list.)

*15. Assume that we have two lists, x_i and y_i, both containing n items. The *rank correlation coefficient*, r, between the lists x and y is defined as follows.

$$r = 1 - \frac{6 * \sum\limits_{i=1}^{n} (a_i - b_i)^2}{n * (n^2 - 1)}$$

where a_i and b_i are the ordinal rankings of the raw scores contained in x and y, respectively. For example, if n = 4, and x and y are:

$$x_1 = 52 \qquad y_1 = 17$$
$$x_2 = 30 \qquad y_2 = 93$$
$$x_3 = 79 \qquad y_3 = 62$$
$$x_4 = 60 \qquad y_4 = 77$$

then a and b are:

$$a_1 = 3 \qquad b_1 = 4$$
$$a_2 = 4 \qquad b_2 = 1$$

$$a_3 = 1 \qquad b_3 = 3$$
$$a_4 = 2 \qquad b_4 = 2$$

Assume also that there already exists an algorithm called:

Rank (x, a)

which takes a set of raw scores in x, determines the proper rankings, and stores those ranking in a. Rank (y, b) will do the same for y and b, respectively. If Rank encounters a raw score of -1, implying a missed examination, it assigns a rank of -1.

Without worrying about how Rank is implemented, write an algorithm to solve the problem whose specifications are contained in Figure 1-3.

16. Develop the algorithm Rank that was used in the correlation assignment in problem 15. Rank should assign to a raw score of -1 a ranking of -1, and should handle ties by assigning the average of all the ranks to the scores.

CHAPTER 3

BASIC **PASCAL** CONCEPTS

3.1 INTRODUCTION

This chapter begins our introduction to the programming language called PASCAL. This language was developed by Professor Niklaus Wirth at the Eidgenössische Technische Hochschule (ETH) in Zurich, Switzerland. The initial report on the language appeared in the literature in 1971,* and revised reports describing language improvements appeared during 1972† and 1973.‡

---

* N. Wirth, "The Programming Language PASCAL," *Acta Informatica, 1* (1), 1971, pp. 34–65.

† N. Wirth, "The Programming Language PASCAL" (Revised Report), ETH Tech. Report 5, Zurich, Switzerland, 1972.

‡ C. Hoare and N. Wirth, "An Axiomatic Definition of the Prog ming Language PASCAL," *Acta Informatica, 3*, 1973.

The first reference manual intended for use by PASCAL programmers was produced in 1974.§

Some of the primary motivations behind the development of PASCAL were to develop a programming language that would:

1. Be efficient to implement and run on today's computers.
2. Be interesting enough to teach the important concepts of computer programming.
3. Allow the development of well-structured and well-organized programs.

We feel that, taken together, these characteristics make PASCAL an outstanding introductory programming language. It will allow us to present the topic of computer programming as a systematic discipline, not as a hit-or-miss art.

PASCAL is a general-purpose language that is applicable to a wide range of numeric and nonnumeric problems. To place the language in some relation to other well-known and widely used general-purpose programming languages with which you may be familiar, we could say that PASCAL has a very loose similarity to both FORTRAN and BASIC except that it has a much richer set of available statements and data types. PASCAL is somewhat more similar to PL/1 and its variant PL/C, but it is most closely related to the language called ALGOL, since it is a descendant of ALGOL 60.

3.2 THE CONCEPT OF DATA TYPES

One of the most important contributions of the PASCAL language and one of its most fundamental ideas is the formalization of the concept of a *data type*. A data type is described by a set of rules that gives the specific format for elements of that type. Stated another way, a data type is simply a set of data objects, such as whole numbers, that are alike in some way.

The most basic data types in PASCAL are called *scalar data types,* in which one simply defines or enumerates all the possible constants of that type. This enumeration is always assumed to be ordered. Each constant has exactly one of the following relationships—greater than, less than, or equal to any other constant of that type. The scalar data types themselves are divided into two classes, the *standard* scalar data types and the *user-defined* scalar data types. The standard scalar data types are the classes of data that are provided automatically by the PASCAL language. There are four of these—integer, real, character, and boolean—and they will be discussed in

---

§ K. Jensen and N. Wirth, "PASCAL User Manual and Report," Springer-Verlag, Heidelburg, 1974.

the following section. The user-defined scalar data types represent new data types that a user can create to aid in solving a specific problem. They will be described in Chapter 7.

The scalar data types just mentioned can be combined to form highly complex *structured data types*. The way in which the scalars are combined and the type of relationship they have to each other determine the particular structured type. Furthermore, the structured types themselves can be combined to form even more sophisticated data structures with exceedingly complex interrelationships. However, regardless of their complexity, all data structures can ultimately be viewed as being composed of the basic building blocks of the language—the simple scalar data types. The structured data types will be introduced and discussed in Chapter 7.

Figure 3-1 summarizes the various data types available in PASCAL. One of our goals in this text is to convey an appreciation of the richness of the data structuring capabilities of PASCAL. It is primarily this characteristic that distinguishes PASCAL from most popular programming languages.

3.3 THE STANDARD SCALAR DATA TYPES

3.3.1 INTEGERS

The constants of the standard data type INTEGER are the whole numbers between some implementation-defined limits. In order to avoid having to know these limits for a specific computer there exists a predefined PASCAL constant called MAXINT. The value of MAXINT is the largest integer constant available on that computer system. For example, on both the UNIVAC 1100 series computers and the PDP-10, MAXINT is $2^{35}-1$. This would allow

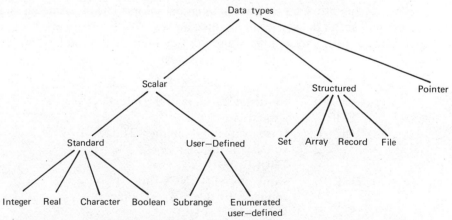

FIGURE 3-1   The Hierarchy of Data Types in PASCAL.

us to write integers with about 11 significant digits. However, be aware that this value will probably be different on other machines.

Some examples of valid PASCAL integers are:

                27500   (not 27,500)
                −123
                   1
                   0
                MAXINT
                 +20

Note that a comma cannot be used in an integer.

The standard PASCAL operators defined for the integers are:

+	addition
−	subtraction (or unary negation)
*	multiplication
DIV	integer division (divide and truncate)
MOD	modulus (A MOD B = the remainder after dividing B into A)
>	greater than
>=	greater than or equal
<	less than
<=	less than or equal
=	equal
<>	not equal

The last six operators are called relational operators. They operate on any of the standard scalar data types to produce a result that has the value TRUE or FALSE. There are also four standard functions that produce integer results.

ABS(I)	the absolute value of the integer I
SQR(I)	I squared
TRUNC(R)	R is any decimal number. The result is the integer portion of R TRUNC(2.61) is 2
ROUND(R)	same as TRUNC but R is rounded to the nearest integer. ROUND(2.61) is 3

3.3.2 REALS

The *real numbers* are the set of implementation-defined decimal values. There are two methods of representing real constants. In *decimal notation* we represent the number with an optional sign, a whole number part, a decimal point, and a fractional part. There must be at least one digit on each side of the decimal point. An alternate shorthand notation permits easy representation of very large or very small real values. This representation is *scientific notation*. The real number is written as a value, called the *characteristic,* multiplied by the appropriate power of 10. Because key-punches and computer terminals cannot type above the line, we cannot use standard algebraic notation for exponents in PASCAL. Therefore, to indicate the exponent in scientific notation, we use the letter E. When encountered within a number, this letter should be read as "times 10 to the power of." There may or may not be a decimal point in the characteristic part, but any number in scientific notation is always of type REAL. As we will see, scientific notation may significantly reduce the keystrokes needed for representing very large or small constants and is a very convenient notation. The following are examples of valid real constants in PASCAL.

$$3.1415927$$
$$-25.0$$
$$+0.198$$

5E6	(5000000)
−6.0E−8	(0.00000006)
+6.08E+27	

The following are all invalid REAL constants.

31	(a valid integer but not a REAL value)
3.	(no digit to the right of the decimal point)
.00215	(no digit to the left of the decimal point)
−2.4E7.2	(only whole number exponents allowed)

As the above examples indicate, the rules for forming REAL values differ slightly from standard mathematical notation. When translating an algorithm into the PASCAL language, we must be aware of and adhere to those rules.

Each installation will define its own limits on the *range* (the largest and smallest allowable values) and *precision* (maximum number of significant digits) of real numbers. If the real numbers are viewed as a continuous line, then four sections of that line will always be unavailable on a computer (Figure 3-2).

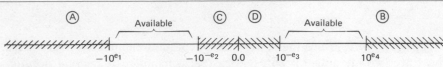

FIGURE 3-2   The Set of Available Real Numbers.

The shaded areas A and B represent areas with real values too large (either positive or negative) to represent on the computer. Areas C and D represent areas with values too small, that is, numbers too close to zero, to represent on the computer. The unshaded areas in Figure 3-2 are the set of real numbers that will be available to you in PASCAL. Specific values for the exponents e_1, e_2, e_3, and e_4 will vary from machine to machine and will have to be provided locally. As one example, on the Control Data 6000 Series computers,

$$e_1 = 322$$
$$e_2 = 294$$
$$e_3 = 294$$
$$e_4 = 322$$

The operators and functions available for the REAL data type are listed below.

+	addition
−	subtraction (or unary negation)
*	multiplication
/	real division (the fractional part is not truncated)
ABS(R)	the absolute value of the real number R
SQR(R)	R squared
SIN(R)	the sine of R
COS(R)	the cosine of R
ARCTAN(R)	the arctangent of R
LN(R)	the natural logarithm of R
EXP(R)	exponential function (e^R)
SQRT(R)	the square root of R

In addition the relational operators discussed earlier are defined and available for real values.

3.3.3 CHARACTERS

The elements of the data type *character* (abbreviated CHAR in PASCAL) are all the individual characters that can be represented on a specific machine. Unfortunately, there is currently no single, industry-wide standard character set.* Therefore character processing can become a highly machine-dependent function for many different reasons.

1. The number of different characters available may vary from one computer to another. Character sets of 64, 128, or 256 distinct characters are not uncommon.

2. The specific characters available on a particular system may differ from the characters available on a different system. The only minimal assumption we can make in PASCAL is that, regardless of the implementation, we will always have available the 26 capital letters A, . . . , Z, the 10 digits 0, . . . , 9, and the blank character. In practice, the available character set will always be quite a bit larger. Appendix C contains a listing of the characters used in standard PASCAL. Your installation may make some changes in this standard set because of local limitations.

3. Internally, the characters are represented by the nonnegative integers 0, 1, 2, . . . , n − 1, where n is the number of distinct characters available. The mapping of the characters onto their corresponding internal integers is called the *collating sequence*. The specific sequence has not been standardized and may be different on different machines. Appendix C lists internal character representations for a number of widely used character sets.

To indicate an element of the data type CHAR we surround the character with two apostrophes (single quotes). To indicate the apostrophe character we simply write it twice.

‘A’

‘<’

‘1’

‘,’

‘’’’   (The apostrophe character)

You should be careful to realize that the elements of the scalar data type CHAR are always single characters. Constructs such as ‘HELLO’ or ‘***’ are not elements of this type, but are elements of a more complex data type composed of sequences of characters. That data type, the *string,* will be described later.

There are four standard PASCAL functions particularly useful for processing character data.

---

* There is currently a widespread attempt to make the *ASCII* code (*A*merican *S*tandard *C*ode for *I*nformation *I*nterchange) a universal standard; however, many machines are not currently using it, and it cannot now be treated as a standard. The ASCII code is shown in Appendix C.

STYLE CLINIC 3-1

Accuracy of Real Numbers

It is not always possible to store real numbers exactly in the internal representation of a computer. Some values just cannot be represented in a finite number of digits. For example, in decimal:

$$\tfrac{1}{3} = .3333333 \ldots$$

Regardless of where we stop, we will not have the exact representation of $\tfrac{1}{3}$. Our representation will have introduced a small, but distinct, *truncation error*. If we now perform computations using this truncated value the results will also be slightly in error. Most computers perform their computation in binary (base 2), not decimal (base 10). However, since binary is also a positional numbering system, it also suffers from the same problem.

The impact of these truncation errors is that

1. Real values computed by your programs may be off slightly in the last decimal places. The analysis of these errors and the methods for approximating their size are complex mathematical problems and are beyond our scope.

2. More important, from our point of view, you should never expect a real value to be *exactly* equal to any particular value. You should never test REAL constants for exact equality. For example, given the truncation error inherent in representing $\tfrac{1}{3}$, the apparent relationship

$$\tfrac{1}{3} + \tfrac{1}{3} + \tfrac{1}{3} = 1$$

would actually be false. If you must test a real value for equality check instead to see if it is "very close" to the desired value and accept that closeness in place of equality. The following comparison,

If Abs(value − x) ⩽ ε
Then Write that x is equal to value

where ε is an appropriately small value, solves the problem mentioned above.

ORD(C)	The *ordinal function*. C represents any character in our character set. ORD(C) is the internal integer representation of that character. For example, referring to Appendix C, in the ASCII character set ORD('L') = 76.
CHR(I)	The *character function*. I is a nonnegative integer.

CHR(I) is the external character corresponding to that integer. Again, for the ASCII character set CHR(35) = '#'.

PRED(C) The *predecessor function*. If C is any character, PRED(C) is the "previous" character in the character set; that is, CHR(ORD(C)−1), except that if C is the first character, CHR(0), the predecessor function is undefined.

SUCC(C) The *successor function*. If C is any character, SUCC(C) is the "next" character; that is, CHR(ORD(C)+1), except that if C is the last element of the character set, CHR(N − 1) where N is the size of our character set, the successor function is undefined.

The PRED and SUCC functions also apply to any scalar data type except REAL. For example:

PRED(7) is 6
SUCC(9) is 10

Because of the lack of standardization in the ordering of characters, we should realize when applying the relational operators >, <, >=, <=, =, <> to character data that a relationship that is true on one machine [e.g., 'A' < '5' or '0' = SUCC('Z')] may not be true on all others, thus making it difficult to run the program correctly at other installations. One of the characteristics we will strive for in our examples in this text is *portability*—the ability to transfer a program from one computer to another and successfully execute the program without modification or with only minor modifications.

3.3.4 BOOLEAN

The elements of the scalar data type BOOLEAN are simply the two constants TRUE and FALSE ordered so that FALSE < TRUE.

The relational operators operate on the INTEGER, REAL, CHAR, or BOOLEAN data types and produce a boolean result. In addition, there are three operators that can be applied only to boolean values to produce a boolean result.

AND logical conjunction (binary operator)
OR logical disjunction (binary operator)
NOT logical negation (unary operator)

They are defined by the tables shown in Figure 3-3.

Although these are the only three logical operators provided as a standard part of the PASCAL language, all other common logical operations can be implemented by using the standard relational operators and the knowledge that FALSE < TRUE. For example, if P and Q are boolean values,

P	Q	P AND Q
F	F	F
F	T	F
T	F	F
T	T	T

P	Q	P OR Q
F	F	F
F	T	T
T	F	T
T	T	T

P	NOT P
F	T
T	F

FIGURE 3-3 Definition of the Boolean Operators.

P <= Q

is exactly equivalent to P ⊃ Q (P implies Q).

Finally, there are boolean functions in standard PASCAL, called *predicates,* that return a value of either TRUE or FALSE. The only one we will mention now is:

ODD(I)   This function is TRUE if the integer I is odd and FALSE otherwise

3.3.5 THE CONST DECLARATION

The problem with the use of a constant within the body of a program is that it carries no mnemonic value [except for well-known ones such as 3.14 (π) or 2.71 (e)]. Looking at an individual constant rarely gives us a clue to its function or purpose. Frequently it becomes attractive to associate a name with some specific constant and then use the name throughout the program to improve legibility. In PASCAL this can be done by using the CONST declaration.

To describe the formation of this declaration and all the other statements contained in PASCAL, we will be using the following informal notation.

1. Words written in capital letters (e.g., CONST) are PASCAL identifiers that should be written as is.
2. Words in lowercase letters will describe a generic class of objects. In an actual PASCAL statement, that name is to be replaced by a valid object of the appropriate class.
3. The ellipsis, . . . , will be used to indicate that an object can be repeated as many times as desired.

This notation is quite informal and not very rigorous. For a formal definition of the syntax of all valid PASCAL statements, refer to the syntax charts in Appendix A.

We can now describe the form of the CONST declaration.

CONST   name = constant; name = constant; . . .

The indicated name can now be used in place of its corresponding constant throughout the entire program. However, remember that the name still represents a constant value and cannot be changed by any other part of the program, any more than the constant itself could be changed.

CONST   PI = 3.1415927;
         MINIMUMTAXRATE = 0.14;
         BLANK = ' ';

In addition to providing increased legibility, the CONST declaration makes it easier to change a program. If we had a dozen occurrences of the same constant in a program, each would have to be located and modified if a change became necessary. With symbolic constants, only the single CONST declaration need be modified.

STYLE CLINIC 3-2

Symbolic Constants

Any constant that either:

1. Is used frequently within a program.
2. Could possibly be changed in future versions of the program.
3. Is important to an understanding of the logic of a program.

should be defined symbolically using a CONST declaration.

3.4 NAMES IN PASCAL

The previous sections have indicated at least two situations in which we may wish to use a symbolic name in PASCAL. In Section 3.2 we indicated that you may define and name a new data type. In Section 3.3.5 we showed why you may want to substitute a symbolic name for a scalar constant. In this section we will talk about a third use—choosing names for PASCAL variables. The use of these symbolic names, or more properly *identifiers*, is fundamental to all aspects of the language.

There are three distinct classes of names in PASCAL.

1. *Reserved keywords.* These are names reserved by PASCAL for a specific purpose; they cannot be used by a programmer in any other way. These keywords must be delimited by one or more blank characters. The ones we have encountered so far are:

CONST   AND   OR   MOD   DIV   NOT

Appendix B contains a list of all the reserved keywords in standard PASCAL.

2. *Standard keywords.* These are names that have a predefined meaning in PASCAL but that may, if necessary, be redefined by the user for another purpose. However, if they are redefined, they cannot be used for the original purpose in the remainder of the program. For example, a user may create and use a symbolic constant named ABS. Then, however, the

STYLE CLINIC 3-3

Portable Programs

The earlier discussion of the character data type raised an extremely important point—the idea of *portable programs*. It is frustrating to have a program work well on one computer but, when the inevitable new machine comes in, have it fail completely. It is also very nice to be able to share programs developed by other people at other sites. This requires that a program that was written for one computer be easily movable to another.

To achieve portability, we must adhere to writing programs in the standard version of the language—those language elements that, by agreement or convention, have been adopted for use on all machines. Local language modifications or extensions may be cute and helpful, but using them guarantees that your program will not be easily moved to any other site. In this book we have attempted to adhere to a description of standard PASCAL and have avoided mentioning any nonstandard PASCAL extensions. Your site no doubt will support some nonstandard features, but use them carefully and with an awareness of what you are doing to your program.

Another limit to writing portable programs is the inclusion of machine-dependent information directly in your program. The use of such information can occasionally be avoided—such as by using MAXINT in place of 34359738367, or by ascertaining that ORD('Z') = ORD('A')+25 instead of automatically assuming that the letters of the alphabet are in proper sequence on all machines.

When the use of a particular piece of locally dependent datum absolutely cannot be avoided, organize your program so that this information is easy to locate and easy to change. Do not bury this detail in the depths of your program. A good way is through the use of the CONST declaration. For example:

```
CONST NUMBEROFTERMINALS = 2 ;

          { This value represents the number of terminals on this
            machine. You must change this declaration if the num-
            ber available at your installation is different.   }
```

user would no longer be able to use the absolute value function, ABS, which is automatically provided as part of the language. Examples of some standard keywords encountered so far include:

MAXINT   TRUE   FALSE   INTEGER   SUCC   ABS

A complete list of standard keywords in PASCAL is also given in Appendix B.

3. *User identifiers.* These are names created by the user that have no other predefined meaning. They may be used to name a wide range of different objects such as new data types, constants, variables, or even entire programs.

The rules for forming a user identifier specify that the identifier must start with an alphabetic character 'A', . . . , 'Z' or 'a', . . . , 'z' (if lowercase is available on your computer) and that it be composed only of alphabetic and numeric characters. No special characters (e.g., +, $, *, ;) are allowed. The user identifier may be as long as desired, but standard PASCAL only looks at the first eight characters to determine uniqueness. (Different installations may enlarge that figure somewhat but will never decrease it.) Some examples of valid identifiers in PASCAL are:

X
A500
RESULT
THEFIRSTROOT
THEFIRSTATTEMPT (although it may be treated as
equivalent to the one above)
THISISANEXTREMELYLONGIDENTIFIER

Some examples of invalid user identifiers are:

BEGIN   (a reserved keyword)
1C   (begins with a digit)
STOCK#   (contains the special character #)

3.5 SCALAR VARIABLES

A *variable* is simply an object that can assume different values during the execution of a program. Alternatively, a variable can be thought of as a location inside the computer that has a name and that can store a value. In PASCAL, variable names can be any valid user identifier.

It is very important to recognize and remember the distinction between the *name* associated with a variable and the *current value* of that variable.

X | 1.5 |

In the above example the name of the variable is X; its current value is 1.5. The name of a variable is permanent (with one exception that will be mentioned in Chapter 8). It is specified only once at the beginning of a program in a declaration we will discuss shortly. The value, however, is quite volatile and may change often during the program's execution. In the algorithmic notation of the previous chapter, any of the following commands:

Set x to 2.5
Add 10 to the current value of x
Read in a new value for x

would leave the name of the variable unchanged but produce a new current value.

In some languages there are no restrictions on what specific values we may assign to a variable. For example, in some languages a variable could have the integer value 6 at one point but then be changed to the real value −2.71. Such languages are usually called *weakly typed* or *typeless*. In these languages the concept of data type is not fundamental, and there are few or no explicit rules associated with data typing. PASCAL represents the opposite approach and is termed a *strongly typed* language. This means that:

1. Each scalar variable must be explicitly associated with a single scalar data type.
2. The variable may assume values of only that data type for the duration of its existence.
3. Most operators and functions are defined only for specific data types. Applying them to any other data type is treated as an error.
4. Mixing data types (e.g., adding a character variable to an integer constant) is usually an error.

The beginning PASCAL programmer frequently finds the explicit typing requirement awkward and time consuming. However, it has many advantages for both the user and the computer. It enhances the legibility and organization of the program by collecting in a single location, almost as in a table of contents, all the variables used in the program and their associated data types. In addition, these required declarations allow the computer to perform extensive error checking during program execution.

To declare the variables contained in the program, we use the VAR declaration.

```
VAR  name, . . . , name: data-type;
     name, . . . , name: data-type;
               .
               .
               .
     name, . . . , name: data-type;
```

In this chapter, "data-type" will mean the scalar data types we have discussed: INTEGER, REAL, CHAR, and BOOLEAN. Later, we will use the term to refer to a larger number of other data types.

Here is an example of a valid VAR declaration.

```
VAR  DEPENDENTS: INTEGER;
     ROOT1,ROOT2: REAL;
     SWITCH: BOOLEAN;
     CH1,CH2,CH3: CHAR;
```

Once we have specified a data type for a variable, we have automatically defined the range of values it may assume, the set of operations that can be performed on it, and the class of standard procedures and functions that may be used on it.

We are now in a position to distinguish among the three classes of operations that are performed on PASCAL variables.

1. *Declaring* a variable. This operation is done only once. It assigns a name to a variable and permanently associates the variable with a data type. It typically does not assign a current value to that variable and no specific initial value (e.g., zero) should be assumed. By making the following declaration

```
VAR K: INTEGER;
```

we reserve a location in memory called K but give K no current value.

K | ? |

STYLE CLINIC 3-4

Variable Names

All variables used in programs you write should be given mnemonic names that give a clear and obvious indication of their exact purpose within the program.

A variable used to store the computed value for daily receipts could be given any of the following names within the program.

```
        X
       DR
     RECEIPTS
  DAILYRECEIPTS (assuming no other variable begins with the char-
                 acters DAILYREC)
```

However, the clarity of the name increases dramatically as we go down the list and certainly the first two (and possibly the third) should be considered totally inadequate. The use of obscure, nonmnemonic names is a major obstacle to understanding a program. Avoid such names at all costs.

The values that may eventually be put into K will be limited to the valid PASCAL integers.

2. *Defining* a variable. This is the process of either creating a value for or changing the current value of a variable. A variable must be declared prior to being defined. When a variable is redefined, the new value will replace the old value, and the old value will be lost. All of the following algorithmic commands are valid ways to define the variable K declared above.

	Current value
Set K to 3	3
Increment K by 1	4
Read in a value for K	whatever was on the data card just read

An attempt to do something such as

Set K to 123.456

is invalid. In the declaration, we stated that K was a variable of type INTEGER. Therefore, when defining K, we must limit it to that class of values.

3. *Referencing* a variable. This is the process of using the current value of a variable in some way.

Write out the current value of K
If K is equal to 3 then Stop
Set L to the current value of K

It should be obvious that a variable must be defined before it can be referenced. Failure to define it will lead to an error. It is also the rule in PASCAL (and almost all other programming languages) that the process of referencing a variable never changes the current value of that variable. In a sense, we can imagine we are making a copy of a variable each time we wish to look at or use its value. We do not change the value by copying it. So, for example, none of the three algorithmic statements written above would cause a change to the current value of the variable K.

3.6 THE SHELL OF A PASCAL PROGRAM

So far we have only described a few of the individual statements which comprise a PASCAL program. We have not really seen how they fit together into a single unit. All PASCAL programs will look something like the example in Figure 3-4.

```
PROGRAM name(file₁,file₂, . . . , fileₙ);
    LABEL declaration; {Discussed in Chapter 5}
    CONST declaration;
    TYPE declaration; {Discussed in Chapter 7}
    VAR declaration;
    PROCEDURE declarations; {Discussed in Chapter 8}
    FUNCTION declarations; {Discussed in Chapter 8}
BEGIN
    statement;
    statement;


        .
        .
        .

    statement
END.
```

FIGURE 3-4   Shell of a PASCAL Program.

A PASCAL program is divided into three distinct parts. The *program heading* is a single statement beginning with the reserved word PROGRAM. The heading assigns a name to the entire program. Additionally, it lists the specific external data files that will be used by the program to communicate with the outside world. These files will be introduced in Chapter 4.

The *declaration section* of the program contains declarations that describe the data objects that we will be using in the program. We have described two of these, the CONST and VAR declarations. There may be up to six different kinds of declarations in this section. They are illustrated in Figure 3-4.

The *executable section,* which is delimited by the reserved keywords BEGIN . . . END, contains statements that perform explicit actions on the data we have just described. These actions can take many forms, such as initializing, changing, testing, or outputting values. The description of the PASCAL statements will begin in the next chapter.

Figure 3-4 illustrates some other points about a PASCAL program that should be mentioned.

1. A *comment* is any explanatory information that is added to the program to help a reader understand what is happening. In PASCAL comments can appear anywhere in the program. They are delimited by the characters { }. On many machines, the brace characters are not available, so PASCAL also allows comments to be delimited by the symbol pairs (* *).

2. The semicolon ';' is used in PASCAL as a statement separator, not a statement terminator. That is, it is used to separate statements from each other, not to end a statement. Careless use of the semicolon can cause

serious programming errors. This point will be discussed fully in Chapter 5.

3. PASCAL statements are completely free format and may appear anywhere on a line. More than one statement may be placed on a single line. A name or a number may not be divided between lines, however. If there is not enough remaining space on a line for the whole name or number, leave blanks at the end of that line and begin on the next line.

4. A PASCAL program ends with the character period ('.').

STYLE CLINIC 3-5

Indentation

PASCAL allows the use of free formatting and multiple statements per line. The excessive misuse of this, however, can lead to a program that is difficult to read. You should quickly adopt good habits of indentation to enhance the readability of your programs and to highlight their logical structure.

For example, the following program fragment:

```
PROGRAM SAMPLE(INPUT,OUTPUT); CONST SINGLE=1;
DOUBLE=2; TRIPLE=3; VAR ROOT1,ROOT2:REAL;DELTA:
INTEGER;GOODFLAG,BADFLAG:BOOLEAN;
```

is syntactically equivalent to:

```
PROGRAM SAMPLE(INPUT,OUTPUT);
{
        An example of much better
        identation habits
                                }
CONST  SINGLE=1;
        DOUBLE=2;
        TRIPLE=3;
VAR  ROOT1, ROOT2        : REAL;
        DELTA                 : INTEGER;
        GOODFLAG, BADFLAG: BOOLEAN;
```

but the second example is obviously much more legible than the first. The need for a good indentation scheme will become even more crucial when you begin writing programs with multiple levels of nested logic. So develop the habit early of preparing your program so that it clearly and succinctly reflects the operations you are performing. The specific rules for indenting will, of course, be a matter of personal style but, once chosen, they should be used consistently and should result in a clear and readable program.

STYLE CLINIC 3-6

Comments

Comments are helpful explanatory notes within the program itself that explain what the program is doing. Good comments can aid enormously in understanding the purpose of a program or a section of code. Unfortunately, good commenting habits are usually the exception and not the rule. For example, when helping a student with a long complex program, an instructor mentioned that it was a difficult program to work with because it did not contain a single comment. The student was quite taken aback and said "Of course it isn't commented yet; I'm not ready to hand it in!" The student was incorrectly viewing comments only as something the instructor required and that were needed to get full credit on a programming assignment.

Try to learn good commenting habits immediately. Although specific rules for commenting may again be viewed as a matter of personal style, there are some basic don'ts and do's of fundamental importance.

DON'T

1. *Undercomment.* Consider the comment as another type of PASCAL statement. Use them judiciously and wisely when *first* writing the program. Don't forget about them because they are never actually required, and don't add them later merely because the instructor requests them. Comments can help others to understand your program and even help you to remember what you meant by something you wrote long ago.

2. *Overcomment.* It is a natural human tendency to go to extremes. "If the instructor asked us to include comments, that's what I'll give." The program may become 90% comments, and the actual statements of the program become difficult to even find, let alone correct. If this is the case, some of the comments could probably be eliminated or put into a report separate from the program listing.

3. *Rehash obvious program logic.* Don't use comments to restate the obvious purpose of a PASCAL statement.

```
READ(NUMBER);   {Read in a value for number}
IF NUMBER<0   {If number is negative print out an error message}
  THEN WRITELN (' ERROR');
```

DO

1. Include an extensive comment block right at the top of your program that describes in simple English the general purpose of the program, who wrote it, and the date it was written. You may want to include some other helpful information here, depending on how the program will be used.

```
PROGRAM COLUMNALIGN (TEXT, INPUT, OUTPUT);
  {
```

This program takes a character string
from a file called TEXT, and produces
36 character lines formatted so that
the first and last character of each
line are nonblank.

```
          Author:    J. Hustiford Quimby
          Address:   Section 4, Bldg. B,
                     Ext. 1013
          Date:      7/4/77
                                    }
```

2. Use comments to *paragraph* your PASCAL program—visually set off
and identify logically related segments of a program.

```
     {
          This is the data input and validation section
                                                      }
          READLN(NUMBER);
          READLN(X1,X2);
          IF X1<X2
               THEN WRITELN (' ERROR IN INPUT DATA ')
               ELSE BEGIN
     {
          Here we begin to process class 1 data sets
                                                   }
```

3. Use comments that tell *what* something is or *why* something is being
done, not *how* it is being done. Comments should be in simple English and
be directed at explaining the higher-level algorithmic functions being
performed.

```
     {   Search for the octal pattern 63   }
```

is a poor comment unless you are truly intimate with the problem. It is much
clearer to read:

```
     {   Look for the end of the data set   }
```

even though in the end they may mean the same thing.

EXERCISES

*1. Show the PASCAL representation of the following constants:

a. π.

b. e (the base of the natural logarithms).

c. 16/32.

    d. $6.02 * 10^{23}$.
    e. The number 7.
    f. The character 7.

*2.   Which of the following are valid PASCAL CONST declarations? Identify the error(s) in each of the invalid declarations.

    a. CONST HIGHVALUE = 200;
    b. CONST LOWVALUE = 0 OR 1 OR 2;
    c. CONST FIRSTCHAR : 'A';
    d. CONST GREATEST = 200.0;
              LEAST   = −100.0;

*3.   Write a single CONST declaration for the following values:

    a. The terminator character, '.'.
    b. The integer constant 80 representing the maximum length of a line.
    c. The real constants 0 and 100 representing the range of scores on an examination.

*4.   Which of the following are valid PASCAL VAR declarations? Identify the error(s) in each of the invalid declarations.

    a. VAR   1A,2A,3A: CHAR;
    b. VAR   A1,A2,A3: CHAR;
                B1   : REAL;
                A3   : INTEGER;
    c. VAR   A: INTEGER;
                B: INTEGER;
                C: INTEGER;
           ABC: REAL;
    d. VAR   RESULTA,RESULTB: REAL;
                   COUNT   : INTEGER;
                   CI   : CHAR;
                   X,Y   : REAL;

*5.   Choose reasonable names and write a single VAR declaration for the following values.

    a. The three real coefficients of a quadratic equation.
    b. The two real roots of that equation.
    c. A value indicating whether there was or was not a solution.
    d. An integer value which indicates the data set number.

6.   Choose reasonable names and write a single VAR declaration for the following values.

a. Six-digit student identification number.
b. One-digit code specifying the year in school (1 = Freshman, . . .)
c. Year of graduation.
d. Grade point average (A = 4.0).
e. A variable indicating whether all current fees have been paid or not.

7. What is the purpose of a *comment* in a PASCAL program? How is a comment written? Add appropriate helpful comments to the VAR declarations of problems 5 and 6 so that someone unfamiliar with the problem would understand the purpose of each variable.

*8. Classify each of the following character strings as a reserved keyword, standard keyword, user identifier, constant, or invalid.

a. BEGIN	h. 1E1
b. REAL	i. 1E
c. START	j. 234
d. SQR	k. TRUNCATE
e. MAXINT	l. CHARACTER
f. XYZ	m. .7
g. E1	n. 3.

9. State what the result of each of the following expressions would be on your computer.

a. SUCC('Z')
b. PRED(ORD('#'))
c. CHR(TRUNC(SQRT(517)))

*10. Using the relational operators and the knowledge that

TRUE > FALSE

implement the following logical operators as defined by the given truth tables.

a. P ≡ Q (equivalence)

P	Q	P ≡ Q
F	F	T
F	T	F
T	F	F
T	T	T

b. $P \oplus Q$ (exclusive $-$ OR)

P	Q	$P \oplus Q$
F	F	F
F	T	T
T	F	T
T	T	F

c. $P \not\subset Q$ (negative implication)

P	Q	$P \not\subset Q$
F	F	F
F	T	F
T	F	T
T	T	F

CHAPTER 4

ELEMENTARY
PASCAL PROGRAMMING

We have considered some of the fundamental aspects of the PASCAL programming language: data types, constants, variables, and declarations. We will now add to this framework the additional concepts needed to write complete PASCAL programs. This will include arithmetic and boolean expressions, the assignment of values to variables, and techniques for performing input and output operations. We will end this chapter with some simple, but complete, PASCAL programs and some general information on how to run those programs.

4.1 ARITHMETIC EXPRESSIONS

We listed earlier the various arithmetic operators of PASCAL. Forming arithmetic expressions with them is a very simple matter. We must, however, pay close attention to the data types we use and to the order in which the arithmetic operations are performed.

We will begin with some very simple examples. Suppose that A and B have been declared INTEGER, and C and D have been declared REAL. Each of the following is an acceptable arithmetic expression in PASCAL.

Integer expressions: A+B
                          A−5
                          B*312
                          A DIV 3 {integer division—the remainder is discarded. If A has the value 8 the value of the expression is 2}
                          A MOD 3 {The remainder after dividing A by 3. If A is 7 the value of the expression is 1; if A is 9 the value of the expression is 0}

Each of the above expressions produces an integer result.

Real expressions: C+1.51
                          C−D
                          C*D
                          D/2.0 {Real division—the result is a real quantity. If D has the value 9.0 the value of the expression is 4.5}

Each of the above expressions produces a real result.

Note that in each of these expressions, we have used two operands of the same type. That is, regardless of whether the operands were variables or constants, both were REAL or both were INTEGER. Performing an operation on operands of different data types is called mixing data types. Mixing types in an arithmetic expression is not always strictly invalid. In some cases the PASCAL system will perform automatic type conversions and carry out the computation without any ill effects. For example, if C is declared a real variable, and we write C+1, PASCAL will treat the second operand as 1.0 (a real quantity) and compute a real result. However, these automatic conversions are not always performed. For example, the operators DIV and MOD require both operands to be integers. Thus, A DIV 2.0 is invalid, even though the intent seems clear. It is important not to lose sight of the fact that there *is* a difference between integers and reals: 1 and 1.0 may superficially seem identical, but the computer represents them differently and treats them differently. It is a good idea to exercise a bit of care in formulating arithmetic expressions and not rely on PASCAL to interpret correctly the intent of a mixed type expression. The habit of consistently using a single data type throughout a given expression will provide an increased sensitivity to data types and also avoid certain kinds of programming errors.

Things would be dull if our arithmetic expressions were limited to precisely the sort of examples just presented: a binary operator and two operands. Fortunately, PASCAL permits us to construct arithmetic expressions of arbitrary complexity, as in:

A * 7 + B DIV 2 − A MOD 3

or

C / 1.51 * D − 3.001

It should be obvious that there is a very essential consideration in more complex arithmetic expressions such as the last two. In what order are the arithmetic operations performed? For example, consider the second of the two examples above. It is not immediately clear what the denominator of the division operation is. It might be 1.51, 1.51*D, or it might be the entire expression to the right of the division operator, 1.51*D−3.001. Clearly, the result of the computation will be different for each case.

In this particular case the denominator is simply 1.51. That is, the division is performed as if we had written

(C / 1.51) * D − 3.001

There is more to be said about this example. What will be the multiplier of the quotient obtained from the division? Will it be D or the quantity D−3.001? We can use parentheses to obtain either effect but, in the absence of parentheses, PASCAL will use just D. That is, evaluation will proceed as if we had written

((C / 1.51) * D) − 3.001

PASCAL utilizes a hierarchy of operators. Certain operators are said to have higher *precedence* than other operators. In the absence of any other information (i.e., parentheses that would explicitly indicate an ordering), PASCAL will evaluate arithmetic expressions so that operators with higher precedence are evaluated before operators of lower precedence. For the operators that we have been considering so far, the precedence rules are:

1. Subexpressions in parentheses are evaluated first.
2. *, /, DIV, MOD operations are evaluated next.
3. +, − are evaluated last.

Thus, parentheses have the highest precedence, the multiplication and division operations next highest, and the addition and subtraction operations lowest. If we write R+S*T, the evaluation will proceed as if we had written R+(S*T), because the multiplication operator has higher precedence than the addition operator.

However, our hierarchy of operators has not resolved all of the uncertainty concerning how expressions are evaluated, since we may have more than one operator of the same precedence. In the expression R/S*T, is the division or the multiplication performed first?

To resolve this situation, there is another precedence rule. When there are no parentheses and there is more than one operator of the same precedence, evaluation proceeds from left to right in an expression. Thus, R/S*T behaves as (R/S)*T.

We now have all the rules we need to evaluate arithmetic expressions. Consider these examples.

EXPRESSION	MEANING
A*7+B DIV 2−A MOD 3	((A*7) + (B DIV 2)) − (A MOD 3)
U−11.3*V−W+X	((U−(11.3*V)) − W) + X
E+F−G*H/K	(E+F) − ((G*H)/K)

In each of these cases we could have originally written the expression with some or all of the parentheses as indicated on the right without changing the order of evaluation. Alternatively, we could have used parentheses to change the interpretation of the expression. For example:

$$((A * (7 + B)) \text{ DIV } (2 - A)) \text{ MOD } 3$$

is a perfectly legitimate arithmetic expression (as long as A does not have the value 2) with a meaning that is obviously different from the meaning of the first example above.

4.2 USE OF STANDARD FUNCTIONS

The PASCAL language automatically includes a set of *standard functions* that perform common and useful operations.* These functions have already been listed in Chapter 3.

---

* In Chapter 8 we will discuss the techniques for writing our own functions to deal with the cases in which the built-in functions are inadequate. This is a very important aspect of programming in PASCAL (or any language). However, now we will limit ourselves to those provided for us by the language itself.

To use a function, we simply write the name of the function followed by an *argument* enclosed in parentheses. The argument is simply the particular value that we want the function to use when performing its computation. For example, SQRT(3.26) would compute the square root of 3.26. In this case, 3.26 is the argument of the function named SQRT.

If we want to make use of the square root that was just computed we would incorporate the function reference into an arithmetic expression. Now the function reference is acting exactly as a simple variable or constant. For example:

SQRT(3.26) * 7.0 + 3.6

is an acceptable PASCAL expression. First the square root is computed, then that value is multiplied by 7.0 and, finally, that result is added to 3.6.

In the above example we used a constant as the argument of the function SQRT. That is actually a very special case. In general, the argument of a standard function can be an arithmetic expression of arbitrary complexity. We can say not only SQRT(3.26), but also:

SQRT(X)
SQRT(X+1.76)
SQRT((X+Y) − (X*Y)/2.0)
SQRT(SIN(X))

as long as the variables X and Y have all been defined and the argument has a nonnegative real value. The order of evaluation of the argument expression will follow the same precedence rules we have already described.

When using a standard function, we must again pay particular attention to the concept of data type. It is essential to recognize that there are two data types involved. We must concern ourselves with both the data type of the function's argument as well as the data type of the function itself (i.e., the data type of the result the function produces). We cannot emphasize too strongly that these two types need not be the same. A function can take a real argument and yet produce an integer result (TRUNC(2.61) is 2), or it may take an integer argument but produce a result of type CHAR (on a Burroughs B6700 computer, CHR(76) is '<'.) In addition, some of the standard functions will accept arguments of more than one type. For example, the argument to SQR can be either real or integer. When using a PASCAL function, we must always provide an argument of the proper type.

After making sure that the argument for a function is of the proper type, we are only half done. We must also be concerned with the data type of the result produced by the function. This means that when we incorporate a function reference into an arithmetic expression, we should still have an expression in which all the data types are consistent. For example, the

STYLE CLINIC 4-1

Parentheses

After spending a great deal of time describing the precedence rules of PASCAL, we will add a new rule of our own. Parenthesize an expression to improve the readability of your program.

When writing an expression such as

A/ B+C / D+E /F

the reader must remember the rules of precedence to interpret the meaning correctly. If that person has forgotten these rules, then the formula could be misinterpreted. It would have been much easier to have written simply

(A/B) + (C/D) + (E/F)

Nothing has been actually changed but we no longer need rely on someone's (possibly faulty) memory.

However, use your common sense to avoid using so many parentheses that you confuse instead of clarify.

((((A/B) + (C/D)) + ((E/F))))

A single expression of extreme complexity with many adjacent parentheses should be broken into a number of separate expressions for clarity. After four or five levels of parentheses, it becomes difficult for your reader to comprehend what an expression means.

SQRT function produces a real result. If A and B are real variables we could correctly write:

A + SQRT(B+3.5) / 2.0

Our expression deals consistently with real quantities and does not mix types. Likewise, if M and N are integer quantities,

M + (1−N) DIV TRUNC(2.73)

is a consistent integer expression.

In summary, when using a standard PASCAL function, we must be aware of the two data types involved: that of the function's argument and that of the function's result. Figure 4-1 summarizes this information for the functions mentioned in Chapter 3. These functions are standardized and are guaranteed to be part of every PASCAL implementation. However, individual installations may have some additional functions not on this list. That information can be provided by the local computing facility.

4.3 BOOLEAN EXPRESSIONS

Just as we used arithmetic operators to construct arithmetic expressions, we use relational and boolean operators to construct boolean expressions of arbitrary complexity. A *boolean expression* is any expression that has the value TRUE or FALSE.

As with arithmetic operators, we must pay close attention to data types. The relational operators ($<$, $<=$, $=$, $<>$, $>$, $>=$) can be used to compare either REAL, INTEGER, CHAR, or BOOLEAN quantities but, in any given comparison, both operands should be of the same type. The result of the comparison is a boolean quantity, TRUE or FALSE.

As indicated earlier, the logical operators (AND, OR, NOT) operate only on boolean values to produce a boolean result.

If we wish to construct a complicated boolean expression, the syntax of PASCAL requires us to parenthesize all elementary subconditions except

FUNCTION NAME	DESCRIPTION	TYPE OF ARGUMENT	TYPE OF RESULT
ABS	Absolute value	Integer	Integer
		Real	Real
ARCTAN	Arctangent	Real or integer	Real
CHR	Character that corresponds to an integer	Integer	Char
COS	Cosine	Real or integer	Real
EXP	Exponential	Real or integer	Real
LN	Natural logarithm	Real or integer	Real
ODD	Tests for odd value	Integer	Boolean
ORD	Integer representation of a character	Char	Integer
PRED	Predecessor	Any scalar type but real	Same type as argument
ROUND	Rounding	Real	Integer
SIN	Sine	Real or integer	Real
SQR	Square of argument	Integer	Integer
		Real	Real
SQRT	Square root	Real or integer	Real
SUCC	Successor	Any scalar type but real	Same type as argument
TRUNC	Truncation	Real	Integer

FIGURE 4-1 Standard PASCAL Functions.

those involving the NOT operation. This might appear to be a rather awkward requirement, but it is actually a worthwhile programming technique to follow since, as we mentioned before, it greatly improves the clarity and intent of the expression. For example.

$$(A<B) \text{ AND } (C=D) \text{ OR } (E=O)$$

is a boolean expression. It would be invalid if the parentheses were omitted. Even with the parentheses as indicated, the expression could be invalid if the data types of the operands were inappropriate. A and B must be of the same type, C and D must be of the same type, and E must be INTEGER. It is important to recognize that not *all* of the variables need be of the same type. Each subcondition will produce a valid boolean value if its operands are of compatible types.

We might very well want to perform a comparison that involves an arithmetic expression, such as $A<B+1$. We once again have the question of the order in which the operators are to be applied. A moment's reflection will reveal that the only reasonable interpretation for this example is $A<(B+1)$. The grouping $(A<B)+1$ would call for the integer value 1 to be added to the boolean constant TRUE or FALSE, a meaningless operation. We will always want the comparison operation performed after the arithmetic operation. This means that in PASCAL the relational operators should have a lower precedence than the arithmetic operators.

Of course the operators AND, OR, and NOT must also have a place in the hierarchy of operators. Figure 4-2 depicts the precedence levels for all of the operators discussed so far. When there are several operations at the same level of precedence, the operations are performed from left to right, and the precedence of any operation can be overridden through the use of parentheses.

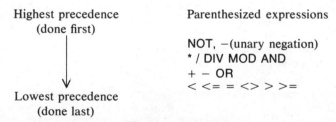

Highest precedence
(done first)

Lowest precedence
(done last)

Parenthesized expressions

NOT, −(unary negation)
*/ DIV MOD AND
+ − OR
$< <= = <> > >=$

FIGURE 4-2   Precedence of Operators in PASCAL.

4.4 THE ASSIGNMENT STATEMENT

The *assignment statement* is a PASCAL statement that assigns a value to a variable. The form of the statement is:

variable := expression

We sometimes speak of the symbol := as the *assignment operator*. The expression on the righthand side of the assignment operator is evaluated, and that value becomes the current value of the variable on the lefthand side of the assignment operator. Note that this requires all variables occurring in the expression to have been already defined, perhaps by earlier assignment statements. If the variables were not defined, it would be impossible to evaluate the expression, and the assignment statement would be meaningless.

If we have made the following declarations in our program

```
VAR   ROOT1,ROOT2   :  REAL;
      VOWEL         :  CHAR;
      COUNT,NUMBER  :  INTEGER;
      FLAG1,FLAG2   :  BOOLEAN;
```

and if ROOT2 has already been defined, then each of the following is a valid assignment statement.

```
        VOWEL:='E'
        COUNT:=153
        ROOT1:=ROOT2*6.71
        FLAG2:=ROOT2<100.0
NUMBER:=(TRUNC(ROOT2)-4)*302 MOD 7
    FLAG2:=ODD(ROUND(SQRT(ROOT2+1.5)))
```

In each case, the type of the result produced by evaluating the expression is the same as the type of the variable being assigned a value. This is a requirement of the assignment operation. (There is one exception to this—an integer value can be assigned to a real variable. However, taking advantage of this special exception is likely to lead to too casual an attitude toward data types. In all other cases the data types on either side of the assignment operator must be the same.) Thus, if A is a real variable and L is an integer variable, the following is invalid.

L := A

We could formulate this as a valid assignment statement by writing either L:=TRUNC(A) or L:=ROUND(A). In either case, the result of evaluating the function is an integer.

There is one very important point to keep in mind concerning the assignment statement. Do not confuse the assignment operation with the notion of mathematical equality. They are not at all the same!

To make this point clear, consider the perfectly acceptable assignment statement K:=K+1. Some people will commonly read this as "K equals K+1." Unfortunately, the use of the word "equals" connotes the mathematical concept of equality, and this example would appear to be asserting the impossible. This leads some people to think that such an assignment statement is invalid. That is not the case. It is essential to remember that the assignment operation is providing a value for the variable that appears to the left of the := symbol. This suggests a more illuminating way in which the := symbol can be read: K "is given the value of" K+1. Although it is a bit more verbose than "equals," it is an alternative that clearly conveys the meaning of the assignment statement.

4.5 INPUT AND OUTPUT

The concepts of input and output are of crucial importance in computer programming. Computers are very adept at performing calculations, but they will do precisely what they are told and no more. We can write a program to perform an intricate calculation flawlessly. However, and this should seem obvious, the results will remain in the computer's memory, hidden from the outside world, unless we include an instruction to display those results. This is the role of the output statements in PASCAL. We will also find it helpful to use the output statements to print headers and identifying text along with the output so that it can be more readily understood. In any event, there should always be at least one output statement in every program we write so that we can see the final results.

An input statement allows a program to obtain data values from an external input device such as a card reader or a terminal (see Figures 4-5 and 4-6). As the computer executes the program, these data values are input and assigned to certain variables in the program. This allows a computation to be carried out for a number of different data values without changing the program itself. Only the data cards* must be changed.

To illustrate, let us assume we wish to write a program that computes and prints out the square root of a real number. If the program is written so that the particular number is specified within the program, it will not be terribly interesting. Once we execute the program and obtain the square root, the program is of no further value unless we make an explicit change to the program itself. A better technique is to write the program so that it computes the square root of a variable whose value is obtained by an input statement.

---

* Throughout this section we will use the phrase "data cards" when referring to the external input device. We do not in any way imply that the PASCAL input statements apply only to the classical input medium of punched cards. In reality, these "data cards" may be lines typed on a computer terminal or input from some other external device.

This means that the same program can be meaningfully executed many times simply by using a different data card each time. Defining a variable by bringing its value in from an external source is termed using *external data*. Defining variables directly in the program itself is usually termed using *internal data*.

4.5.1 READ AND READLN STATEMENTS

One form of the READ statement is

READ(variable, variable, . . . , variable)

One or more variable names may appear inside the parentheses with commas separating successive names. Each of the following is a legitimate READ statement, as long as every variable has appeared in a valid PASCAL declaration.

READ(COEFFICIENT)
READ(SOCSEC, GROSSPAY, DEPENDENTS)
READ(BIRTHRATE, DEATHRATE)

There is no limit to the number of variables that can appear in a READ statement although, as a practical matter, a READ statement with many variables can be too complex to be clear. There is also no limit to the number of READ statements that may appear in a program.

The READ statement causes the program to examine as many data cards as necessary until a data value has been found for each variable in the READ list. The association of a data value with a variable is done entirely on the basis of position. The first value found on the data card is associated with the first variable name in the list, the second value with the second variable, and so on. The values provided by the input data must be consistent with the declared data types of the variables. For example, if our program contains three real variables, A, B, and C, and the statement READ(A, B, C) we might set up data cards as follows (each line represents an individual data card or line).

1.573   2.0
          − 1.9E6

The result would be that A is assigned the value 1.573, B is assigned the value 2.0, and C is assigned the value −1900000.0. Note that the data cards contain no indication whatsoever of the variable names to be associated with the given values. It is essential to remember that the association of values with variables is done entirely by position. If the two data cards above were inadvertently reversed, the result of the READ would be:

A: −1900000.0
B: 1.573
C: 2.0

We actually have a great deal of flexibility when setting up our data cards. We can place as many numbers as we like on a card, and we can use as many cards as we wish. The only specific requirements are:

1. Data values must conform to legitimate PASCAL syntax. Thus, no commas can appear in numbers and if a decimal point appears it must be preceded and followed by at least one digit.
2. A data value must have a type consistent with the type of the variable that occurs in the corresponding position in the READ statement.
3. Successive data values are separated by one or more spaces. The only exception to this is type CHAR. Since we know that values of this type will always be of length 1, we do not need to separate them by spaces. As a matter of fact, the space itself is a valid character and can be input as data.
4. A data value must reside completely on one card (i.e., a value cannot start on one card and be continued on the next one).

As long as these requirements are met, data values can span any number of cards and can be prepared in whatever format is most natural. The computer will continue to read cards until it has found a value for each variable in the READ statement.

What happens if there is not an exact correspondence between data values and variables? If there are more data values than variables, there really is no problem. The extra data values are simply not used. Ignoring or skipping data values is never considered an error condition and could be a perfectly valid situation. The values may be read by the next READ command, or they may not be used at all. However, a mismatch might signify a logical error in the program—perhaps the omission of some variable names in the READ statement or too few executions of statements in a loop. The computer will not provide an error message in this situation. It will have to be detected by careful checking of the output produced.

The situation is different if too few data values to satisfy the READ statement are on the data cards. In this case the computer tries to read another data card where none exists. We say that we have an *end-of-file* condition.*

---

* We will discuss the notion of a *file* more fully later on. For now we will simply view a file as a collection of items that are somehow related to one another. When we have exhausted all the items, we have reached the end of the file.

PASCAL includes a standard boolean function that allows us to test for exactly this situation. We can test whether we have reached the end of any particular file with the standard function EOF(filename). This function returns the value TRUE if an end-of-file condition exists for the specified filename and FALSE otherwise.

In this chapter, we will always be dealing with the special file named INPUT that contains the data cards that we provide with our program or the lines that we enter at a terminal. We can therefore use EOF(INPUT) to determine whether all of the data has been read. Because the particular file INPUT plays such a special role in PASCAL, it is used as the default file name in many contexts. Thus, we can also write simply EOF without an argument when we mean EOF(INPUT).

In the next chapter we will see an example of how this EOF test can be used within a program to control how data is input. The basic idea will be to set up the program so that particular instructions (i.e., the READ commands) are executed only if the function EOF is FALSE, implying that more data cards are available. If we do not do this test for an end-of-file condition, then we must be absolutely certain to provide enough data values to satisfy all the READ statements that the program will attempt to execute. If we do not, the computer will terminate execution because of an error (often with a cryptic and not too helpful error message) when it attempts to input data where none exists.

Another standard boolean function that is useful for inputting data is EOLN(filename) or simply EOLN when using the standard file INPUT. This predicate tests for an *end-of-line* condition. It is TRUE if we are currently at the end of a card or line and FALSE otherwise. This function is particularly useful for working with character-oriented information where the data is organized into lines, paragraphs, and pages. We will see numerous examples of this predicate in later programs.

One final detail about the READ command is the READLN variant. Both the READ and READLN commands operate in exactly the same manner with respect to inputting data values. The only difference occurs at the end of the input operation. If we imagine a "pointer" moving along the data card looking for values, we can say that the READ command leaves the pointer at the position it was when the READ instruction was completed. The READLN command advances the pointer to position 1 of the next card or line.

Assume we had the following two data cards.

```
1   2   3
4   5   6
```

If the pointer were positioned at the beginning of the first card, then the commands

READ(A, B); READ(C, D)

would first assign the following values:

A:=1
B:=2

and leave the input pointer where it was when the input operations were completed: just past the integer value 2. The second read operation will begin from that position and assign the following values.

C:=3
D:=4

However, the following two statements:

READLN(A, B); READLN(C, D)

would result in first assigning

A:=1
B:=2

and then resetting the "pointer" to the beginning of the second line. This will, in effect, discard the remainder of the first line. The second command will result in the values:

C:=4
D:=5

4.5.2 WRITE AND WRITELN STATEMENTS

The WRITE statement permits a program to write the values of expressions and text directly onto the output listing. The form of the statement is similar to the READ statement.

WRITE(item, item, . . . , item)

There may be any number of items (including zero), and commas are used to separate consecutive items in the list. An item in the list is either an expression of arbitrary complexity or a character string enclosed in apostrophes ('). If the item is an expression, it is evaluated, and its value is printed. If the item is a character string, it is printed exactly as it appears but without the delimiting ' characters. To print an apostrophe within the character string, write two successive ' characters. For example, if A and B are integers having the values 5 and 20 respectively, the statement:

　　WRITE(' A=', A, ', THE SUM OF A AND B IS', A+B)

will produce the output:

　　A=　　　　　5, THE SUM OF A AND B IS　　　　25

The statement:

　　WRITE(' THIS ' ' IS THE QUOTE CHARACTER')

will produce:

THIS　　' IS THE QUOTE CHARACTER

If a variable (or an expression) is specified in a WRITE statement, the value written will be in accordance with the data type of the expression or variable. Boolean values will be written as TRUE or FALSE and real values will be written in scientific (power-of-10) notation. A value will usually be printed with a particular "field width," or number of columns, that depends on the data type and on the conventions of each local installation. The field widths used in our examples follow.

DATA TYPE	NUMBER OF COLUMNS
Integer	10
Real	22 (exponent is of the form E±dd)
Boolean	10
Character	1
'text string'	length of text string

These default values may not apply on every computer, so inquire about the values on a particular machine. (Or, write a simple program that will determine this information.)

In our previous example, the values of A and A+B were each allocated 10 character positions (or columns) for printing. Although neither number required 10 characters, the computer utilized the entire field by inserting an appropriate number of blanks to the left of the number. We say that such a number has been *right-justified,* and that there is *blank fill* on the left. Thus, we have nine blanks preceding the number 5 and eight blanks preceding the number 25. The computer will automatically adjust the number of blanks for the particular data type being printed and the number of characters required for printing each value.

We might at times find that the default field widths are inconvenient. For example, perhaps we want to arrange the output in the form of a chart or a table and the default field widths will not achieve the effect we desire. It is a relatively simple matter to override the defaults and specify whatever field widths we need. We simply follow any item in the WRITE statement with a colon and an integer constant or variable that specifies how many columns we wish to use when printing this value. (Remember to allow enough columns for a negative sign, decimal point, and exponent—if appropriate—as well as the actual digits to be printed.) For example, the statement

WRITE(' A=', A:3, ', THE SUM OF A AND B IS', A+B:5)

will produce

A=   5, THE SUM OF A AND B IS   25

As in the default case, if there are not enough characters to fill in the requested field, blanks are inserted to the left. Furthermore, if the field is too small to contain the value being printed, PASCAL will automatically extend the field to a sufficient size.

There is another option that applies to the printing of real values. For a real quantity we can specify two "field widths." The first value is the true field width, which specifies the total number of columns to be occupied by the value being printed. The second "field width" (if present) invokes decimal representation for a real value in which the number is written with a decimal point and the specified number of places after the decimal point. For example, if R, S, and T are real variables with values 1.234, −8000.76, and 63.123, the WRITE statement

WRITE(R:6:2, S, T:12)

will produce the following.

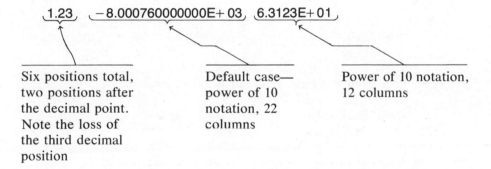

Six positions total, two positions after the decimal point. Note the loss of the third decimal position

Default case— power of 10 notation, 22 columns

Power of 10 notation, 12 columns

There is one additional issue we must consider in dealing with WRITE statements. In order to provide the greatest flexibility in formatting program output, the PASCAL WRITE statement has been designed so that successive WRITE statements put their output on one continuous print line. The programmer can (and, in fact, must) specifically indicate the termination of each print line. A line is not printed until this termination point is specified. Then any subsequent WRITE statements are used to construct the next print line which, in turn, is printed after its termination has been explicitly specified.

A print line is terminated (and actually printed) by the WRITELN command. If we have the statements

```
WRITE(A, B);
WRITELN;
WRITE(C);
WRITELN
```

we will print the values of A and B on one line of output and the value of C
on the next line. Contrast this with

        WRITE(A, B, C);
        WRITELN

which will place the values of A, B, and C all on one line.

    There is a shorthand notation that is often convenient. All we have to do
is replace the word "WRITE" with "WRITELN." In other words, the
statement

        WRITELN(R, S)

will add the values of R and S to the print line under construction and then
terminate and print that line. The single statement given above replaces the
two statements

        WRITE(R, S);
        WRITELN

We could have used this form in all our previous examples.

        WRITELN(A, B);
        WRITELN(C)

will print A and B on one line and C on the next line, while

        WRITELN(A, B, C)

will print A, B, and C all on one line.

    Remember to use WRITELN to terminate and print each output line be-
fore it gets too long to fit on one line of the printed page. The length of an
output line depends on the particular type of printing device attached to the
computer. Typical values for line lengths might be 72, 80, 120, or 132 characters, but other lengths are possible. Find out how many character positions per line there are on your particular printing device.

STYLE CLINIC 4-3

Output with Style

    The output of your program is its entire reason for being. Most users of a
program will be unconcerned with the programmer's programming ability,

cleverness, or ingenunity. They want answers that are correct and presented in a clear, easily understood, highly legible format. Even though a program produces correct answers, if it is difficult to interpret the output listing, the program will be used very little or not at all.

Your first concern should, of course, be making the program correct. As long as it is legible, no one else really cares what the output of a program looks like during its development. But once the program is working, spend some time making the output pretty. Always avoid writing programs that produce output that looks like this.

```
              378245621
     .28735E03    3    .4725E2
          208.07
```

Always annotate your output with helpful text and place values in groups for increased readability.

```
SOCIAL SECURITY NO:  378-24-5621  DEPENDENTS:  3
              GROSS PAY      =   $287.35
              FED TAX        =   $ 47.25
              STATE TAX      =   $ 32.03
                                 - - - -
                                 $208.07
```

The numbers are exactly the same, but the output is much more meaningful. Output like the latter case can be produced in PASCAL without a great deal more effort than that required for the former case.

4.6 EXAMPLES OF PROGRAMS

We are now in a position to write some simple, but complete, PASCAL programs.

Example 1

```
PROGRAM SQUAREROOT(INPUT, OUTPUT);
{Read a data card that contains a nonnegative real number.
 Compute and print the square root of that value}
VAR INPUTVALUE, SQROOT: REAL;
BEGIN
  READ(INPUTVALUE);
  SQROOT:=SQRT(INPUTVALUE);
  {Note. Before invoking the square root function we
    should really check INPUTVALUE to be sure the argument
    is nonnegative. This can be done with a conditional
    statement, which we will discuss in the next chapter}
```

```
        WRITELN(' X=', INPUTVALUE:10:3, ' SQUARE ROOT OF
        X=', SQROOT:10:3)
    END.
```

Note that our WRITELN statement prints not only the result of the computation, but also the data value that was used in the computation. Furthermore, we are printing not only the numerical values but also some identifying text. It is good to use both of these techniques wherever possible because they substantially improve the readability of the output. It might occasionally be impractical to print out all the data values that were input, but there is *never* any excuse for printing results without any identifying text.

Because the program contains several statements, we have separated consecutive statements with semicolons. In the next chapter we will discuss the details of where semicolons do and do not belong.

Example 2

```
        PROGRAM CHARCODE(INPUT, OUTPUT);
        {Read a data card that contains a single character.
         Print the character and its numerical representation
         (its character code). The character should be punched
         in the first column of the first data card}
        VAR CHARACTER: CHAR;
                CODE: INTEGER;
        BEGIN
            READ(CHARACTER);
            CODE:=ORD(CHARACTER);
            WRITELN(' CHARACTER ''', CHARACTER, ''' HAS THE
            CODE ', CODE:5)
        END.
```

If this program is executed on an IBM 360/370 series computer with the character 'A' punched in the first column of the first data card, the output will be:

CHARACTER 'A' HAS THE CODE   193

Try it on your computer to see what it produces.

Example 3

```
        PROGRAM COMPARE(INPUT, OUTPUT);
        {Read a data card that contains two integers.
         Compare the first number with the second and
         indicate whether each of the tests LESS THAN,
```

```
                   EQUALS, and GREATER THAN is true or false}
VAR                               A, B:INTEGER;
        LESS, EQUALS, GREATER:BOOLEAN;
BEGIN
{Input and echo print the data}
    READ(A,B);
    WRITELN(' A=', A, ' AND B=', B);
{Perform the three relational comparisons}
        LESS:= A<B; EQUALS:= A=B; GREATER:= A>B;
{Write out the results of the comparisons}
    WRITELN(' A<B IS', LESS);
    WRITELN(' A=B IS', EQUALS);
    WRITELN(' A>B IS', GREATER)
END.
```

If this program were executed with the following data card,

5   9

what would the output look like?

4.7 RUNNING A PROGRAM

In the previous section, we developed some examples of complete PASCAL programs. We are now in a position actually to execute these programs on a computer and produce the desired results.

Quite obviously the first step in running a PASCAL program on a computer is getting it into a *machine-readable form* that can be input to the computer. The specific form used will depend on which of two quite different methods are used to access the computing resources available.

Batch processing was historically one of the first techniques for running programs, and is still a widely used method for running typical student jobs. In batch processing, the program is first converted to machine readable form *off-line*—that is, not linked to the computer. This preparation is usually done on 80-column punch cards (Figure 4-3). It is the function of the keypunch (Figure 4-4) to translate a keystroke made by the programmer at the keyboard into the combination of punched holes that represent that character and that can later be read by a device called a card reader. The relationship between the printed characters and the punch code can be seen in Figure 4-3.

After the program has been prepared and any obvious mistakes corrected, the program deck, as it is called, is brought to an Input/Output station. There it may either be entered directly into the machine or collected together with

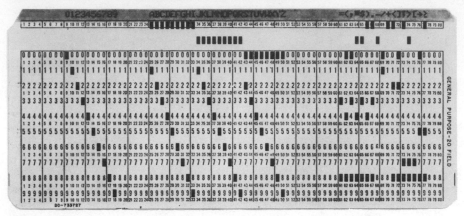

FIGURE 4-3   Standard 80-Column Punch Card.

other programs into a single batch that is processed as a single unit. Some time later (the exact time typically depends on factors over which you have little or no control, such as the current workload of the computer) results are returned in the form of a listing containing either the desired answers or, more typically, error messages.

FIGURE 4-4   Keypunch.

The most important characteristic of batch processing is that it is impossible to interact with a program while it is being executed. All data must be presented to the machine at the time the job is run. Using batch processing, we could not, for example, run a program with a single data set, view the results, choose the next data set based on those results, and continue running the program from that point.

This type of interaction requires a quite different technique for accessing computing resources. This other approach goes by many names—*time-sharing, interactive processing,* or *demand processing.* In this environment, the conversion to machine readable form is done *on-line*—by communicating directly with the computer. Typically, the student sits at a terminal containing a keyboard and printing mechanism (Figure 4-5). Alternatively, the

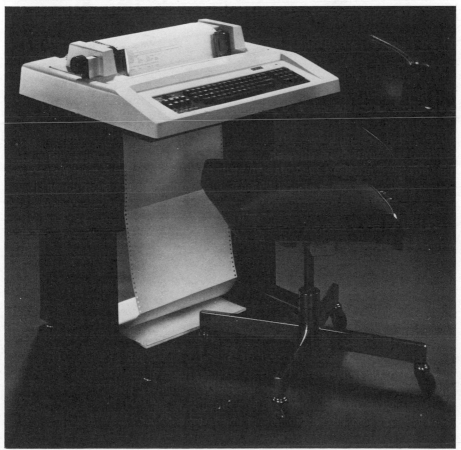

FIGURE 4-5   Keyboard/Printer Computer Terminal.

FIGURE 4-6   Keyboard/CRT Computer Terminal.

printer may be replaced by a cathode-ray tube (usually abbreviated CRT), which looks much like a TV screen (Figure 4-6). Regardless of which type of terminal is available, a keyboard is used to type and edit the program. When the program is complete, a request is entered to execute the program, and it is usually run immediately. Input may be requested during execution, and any output produced by the program (results, error messages) is displayed on the printer or the screen. After viewing the output, we may make changes in the program or the data. Both program development and execution are done in a give-and-take fashion.

Regardless of the approach, there will be three distinct components to the completed program deck. The first component is, of course, the program itself, punched or typed according to the rules of the language. The second component is the external data that will be read in by the program. Some programs may not require any external data, so this component should be considered optional. Remember that these data are not in any way part of the PASCAL program. They represent values to be presented to the program at the time it is executed. In batch processing, the data cards usually are separate from and follow the program cards. In a time-sharing environment, the input data is usually keyed in by the user when the program requests it. The request is typically in the form of a prompt—a character (e.g., '?') typed out before the program stops to wait for the input data.

The third component of the program deck is a set of *control cards*. These cards provide important information about who you are and what you want to do. The specific format of these cards varies from one site to another, but the same general information is usually provided.

1. *Personal identification.* Name, department, course, semester, year.
2. *Accounting information.* Account numbers, billing numbers, budget limits.
3. *Security information.* Passwords, privacy codes.
4. *Language information.* What computer language is to be used (PASCAL in our case).
5. *Delimiters.* Identifying the beginning and end of programs and/or data.
6. *Other resources.* Other computer resources to be used, such as a filing system or a text editor.

Figures 4-7 and 4-8 show the first example program of Section 4.6 prepared for batch processing and time-sharing, respectively, for a hypothetical computer. These figures are merely examples to illustrate the points we have been discussing. The actual control card format at your installation will almost certainly differ. The information needed for the control cards of PASCAL programs on a particular computer will usually be supplied by instructors or by the local computer center.

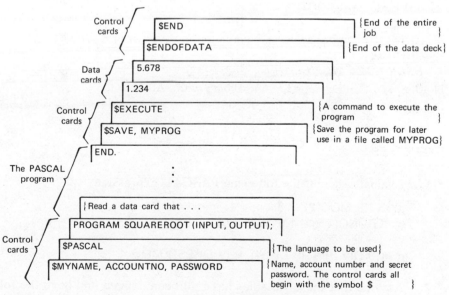

FIGURE 4-7   Sample Batch Processing PASCAL Program Deck.

(Information produced by the computer is in *italics*. Information typed by the programmer is in the normal typeface.)

ACCOUNT NUMBER: 123456
PASSWORD:
■■■■■■■   (blacked out for security reasons)
LANGUAGE: PASCAL   (the language we will be using)
OLD OR NEW: NEW   (this will be a new program)
NAME: SQUAREROOT   (the file name)
READY   (we now type in the program)
00100   PROGRAM SQUAREROOT(INPUT, OUTPUT);
00200   {Program to compute square roots}
00300   VAR INPUTVALUE, SQROOT: REAL;
00400   BEGIN

                .

                .
                .
01200   END.
RUN   (request to execute this program)
MM/DD/YY HH.MM.SS   (date and time)
PASCAL SYSTEM
? 2.0   (a prompt for input)
1.41421356E+00   (the answer)
RUN COMPLETE
SAVE,SQUAREROOT
READY
(Here there can be additional requests to the computer or a sign-off)
GOODBY
USER 123456 SIGNED OFF

FIGURE 4-8   Sample Time-Sharing Dialog with PASCAL.

EXERCISES

* 1.   Evaluate each of the following PASCAL expressions.

   a. 3 *(9 MOD 2) − 5
   b. TRUNC(1.6 + 1.9/2.0 +3.0)
   c. 1 − 2 − 3 − 4 − 5
   d. ((9 DIV 3) + (9 DIV 4) + (9 DIV 5)) MOD 4

* 2.   Assume that these variables have all been defined and have the following values. (*Note.* The choice of names could be greatly improved if we had specific knowledge of the purpose of each variable.)

A is 7
B is −6
C is 30
D is 10.8600
E is 1E3
F is '*'
G is TRUE

What is the value of each of the following expressions?

a. A + B DIV TRUNC(D) + 3
b. D − 0.75/(E + 140.0) * 70.0
c. SQRT(ABS(B − A) + SUCC(ORD(F)))
d. CHR(10 * A MOD SQR(B))
e. NOT((A >= B) AND G)
f. (ODD(B) OR (SQR(B) >C)) AND (G AND NOT (ABS(B) <> 6))

3. A, B, and C are boolean variables that have been given these values.

A is TRUE
B is FALSE
C is TRUE

Evaluate each of these expressions.

a. A AND (B OR C)
b. (A AND B) OR (A AND C)
c. (NOT A) OR (NOT C)
d. A AND NOT B OR NOT C

* 4. Determine whether the PASCAL expressions are a correct translation of the corresponding mathematical expression. If a PASCAL expression is incorrect, correct it.

	MATHEMATICAL EXPRESSION	PASCAL EXPRESSION
a.	$\sqrt{\dfrac{a+b}{c}}$	SQRT(A + B/C)
b.	$ax^2 + bx + c$	A * X * X + B * X + C
c.	$(6.02 \times 10^{27})(\ln(1 + e^{(x-1.)}))$	6.02E27(LN(1 + EXP(X) − 1.))

* 5. Translate the following expressions into proper PASCAL assignment statements.

a. Taxable pay is gross pay − $11 × number of dependents − $14
b. Contingency is $\sqrt{\chi^2/(N + \chi^2)}$

c. Capacity is WT $\ln(1 + \frac{S}{N})$

d. Weighted average is (k * sum of scores)/(N − invalidated values)

e. Amplitude is A/2 $\sin[2\pi(fc + fm)t - \frac{\pi}{2}]$

f. TEST is TRUE if VALUE is between 1 and 10 (inclusive), otherwise FALSE.

* 6. Assume we have three data cards with the following values:

```
53      78*    6
   110      Z
59     −8
```

and the following declarations:

```
VAR  X, Y, Z : INTEGER;
     CH    : CHAR;
```

What values will be assigned to the variables by the following input operations?

a. READ(X); READ(Y); READ(CH)
b. READLN(X); READLN(Y); READLN(CH)
c. READLN(X); READLN(Y, CH); READ(Z)
d. READ(CH); READLN; READ(X)

7. Write the input commands to read in the following data.

a. A master payroll card containing a social security number and a department identification number (integers). This is followed by a time card containing total hours worked this week (real).

b. A student grade card containing a student identification number and four letter grades all separated by one blank space.

* 8. A calculation has been done with two REAL variables, WPRICE (wholesale price) and MARKUP (percentage markup), to produce a value for a third REAL variable, RPRICE (retail price). Prepare WRITELN statements that clearly convey the computation that was done.

9. Let X be 1.0, Y be 2, and Z be 3.0. What will be printed by these statements?

a. WRITELN(X, Y, Z)
b. WRITE(X:10); WRITELN(Y:10); WRITELN(Z:10:3)
c. WRITELN(X,Y:3); WRITELN(Z:10)

*10. Prepare the statements needed to produce the following output. Assume the necessary values have already been computed and stored in the variables.

a. Variables are GROSS, DEDUC, NETPAY.

GROSS PAY	$xxx.xx
DEDUCTIONS	$xxx.xx
NET	$xxx.xx

b. Variables are NUMBER, AVG, HIGH, LOW.

TOTAL NUMBER	AVERAGE	RANGE
xxx	xx.x	xx–xx

*11. Write a complete PASCAL program that inputs three values corresponding to the coefficients of a quadratic equation and computes and prints the two real roots. Disregard (for now only!) the possibility of negative square roots and divisions by 0. Use the quadratic formula.

$$\text{Roots} = \frac{-b \pm \sqrt{b^2 - 4ac}}{2a}$$

12. Write a complete PASCAL program that first reads a real value corresponding to the dollar amount of a purchase and then computes and prints the 4% sales tax on that purchase to the nearest penny. The program should then print the total amount of the bill, including both the purchase amount and the tax.

CHAPTER 5

FLOW OF CONTROL

5.1 INTRODUCTION

At the end of Chapter 4 we wrote some complete but simple programs. We view those programs as simple not so much because of their limited length, but because of their structure: they are what we would term straight-line programs. That is, they reflect operations that are simply sequential in nature. The general model of these straight-line programs is:

Read a data value;
Compute an intermediate result;
Use the intermediate result to compute the desired answer;
Print the answer;
Stop.

Although we might occasionally need to solve a real problem of this kind, more often than not we will find that our problem is not susceptible to such a simple analysis.

In our discussion of algorithms, we saw that most algorithms utilize the techniques of *repetition* (perhaps through iteration or recursion) and *decision making*. Since most real-world problems require these techniques, we will find that most computer programs make abundant use of these ideas.

The *control statements* of a programming language allow us to alter the normal, sequential flow of instructions within our programs and allow us to accomplish these repetitive and decision-making operations. PASCAL contains an extensive set of control statements, and we are now in a position to examine them in some detail. In addition to the extensive range of data structures available in PASCAL (as we mentioned earlier), it is the wide range of control structures that most sharply distinguishes PASCAL from other high-level programming languages.

5.2 THE COMPOUND STATEMENT

The *compound statement* is used in PASCAL to indicate that a sequence of statements is to be executed in sequential order. The general form of the compound statement is:

```
BEGIN
    S₁;
    .
    .
    .
    Sₙ
END
```

Notice that the reserved delimiters BEGIN and END surround the statements that make up the compound statement. For example,

```
BEGIN
    READLN(NUM1,NUM2); SUM:=NUM1+NUM2;
    WRITELN(' THE SUM IS', SUM)
END
```

is a valid compound statement. Note that we have written more than one PASCAL statement on a single line. The computer will process all statements on a given line before proceeding to the next.

Observe the use of semicolons (';') to separate successive PASCAL statements. This is important. A semicolon is not part of a PASCAL statement.

It simply serves as a statement separator. It is also important to recognize that BEGIN and END are not PASCAL statements. They are merely markers that designate the beginning and the end of a compound statement. Thus, in our example we used a semicolon between the READLN statement and the assignment statement, and another semicolon between the assignment and the WRITELN statement. We do not have a semicolon after BEGIN or before END because there is nothing to separate. (Remember, BEGIN and END are not statements.)

What would happen if we placed a semicolon between the WRITELN statement and END? This would appear to be an error, because the semicolon would not be separating two statements. However, PASCAL includes an interesting construct, the *empty statement,* that will come to our rescue in this particular case. What is the empty statement and what does it do? The answer to both questions is, nothing at all! It is simply a syntactic construct that PASCAL uses, at times, to try to make sense of a program or statement that might not be strictly correct. We will now look at a particular example— a compound statement with an extra semicolon. Try to find the empty statement that will permit a correct interpretation of our compound statement. (Of course, being invisible, the empty statement can be difficult to spot!)

```
BEGIN
    READLN(NUM1,NUM2); SUM:=NUM1+NUM2;
    WRITELN(' THE SUM IS', SUM);
END
```
                        The empty statement is right here

In this example the idea of an empty statement permits a proper interpretation of our compound statement, despite what appears to be a violation of the rule for the use of semicolons. The extra semicolon is viewed as separating the WRITELN statement from the empty statement. However, this discussion does not mean we should become casual in our use of semicolons. The empty statement will not always be able to undo the damage caused by misplaced separators. We should still be careful and use these statement separators only where they belong.

So we see that the idea behind a compound statement is really quite simple: a group of PASCAL statements, separated from one another by semicolons, and bracketed by the reserved delimiters BEGIN and END. Since a compound statement will be processed in the obvious order (sequentially), why do we need it? In our upcoming discussions of some of the more sophisticated control statements in PASCAL, we will see that in several places the syntactic description will call for a single "statement." This indicates that any individual PASCAL statement is permissible. But what if we want to use several statements at that point in our program, instead of being restricted to just one? There is no problem if we simply group the statements together as a compound statement (i.e., bracket the statements with BEGIN and END) because of a fundamental rule—PASCAL will always accept a compound statement wherever any individual statement is allowed. We will see some examples of this in the next few pages.

5.3 REPETITIVE STATEMENTS

It is usually the case that one part, and perhaps several parts, of an algorithm needs to be executed repetitively. In our discussion of algorithms we represented this notion by means of the WHILE and REPEAT constructs. We can now examine three different statements that allow us to accomplish repetition in PASCAL.

5.3.1 THE WHILE STATEMENT

The PASCAL WHILE statement permits a program segment to be repeatedly executed as long as a specified condition is true. The statement has the form

WHILE   boolean expression   DO   statement

A boolean expression is, of course, an expression that produces a value of TRUE or FALSE. The boolean expression is initially evaluated. If it is TRUE the statement (which may be any statement, including a compound statement) is executed. The cycle then repeats as the boolean expression is again evaluated and a decision about whether to execute the statement is made. The execution of the WHILE statement is complete when the boolean expression is evaluated in the WHILE clause and found to be FALSE.

As a simple example, consider the following program (Figure 5-1), which computes the sum of the first 10 integers.

```
PROGRAM TOT(INPUT, OUTPUT);
{Find the sum of the first 10 integers}
VAR NUMBER, SUM: INTEGER;
BEGIN
SUM:=0; NUMBER:=10;
WHILE NUMBER>0 DO
   BEGIN
   SUM:=SUM+NUMBER;
   NUMBER:=NUMBER−1
   END;
WRITELN(' SUM OF THE FIRST 10 INTEGERS=', SUM)
END.
```

FIGURE 5-1   Program to Compute the Sum of the First 10 Integers.

It should be clear that this program computes the sum $10+9+8+ \ldots +1$ and then prints out the sum. Note the use of the compound statement to designate that we wish to have two statements executed if NUMBER>0. The first of these statements adds another number to the sum, while the second statement modifies NUMBER so that it will have the value needed for the next cycle. Observe that the last number added to the sum is 1. Once NUMBER reaches 0, the condition NUMBER>0 is no longer true and the compound statement after the DO is not executed.

As another example, we consider a program (Figure 5-2) that deals with character data. We will read one character at a time, keeping a running total of characters until either a period is reached or we come to the end of the current line of text.

```
PROGRAM COUNTCHARS(INPUT, OUTPUT);
{Read characters until either a period is reached or
  we come to the end of the input line. Count the
  number of characters read, excluding the period}
CONST PERIOD='.';
VAR        COUNT: INTEGER;
    CURRENTCHAR: CHAR;
BEGIN
    COUNT:=0;
    READ(CURRENTCHAR);
    WHILE (CURRENTCHAR<>PERIOD) AND (NOT EOLN) DO
        BEGIN
        COUNT:=COUNT+1;
        READ(CURRENTCHAR)
        END;
    WRITELN (' THE NUMBER OF CHARACTERS IS ', COUNT)
END.
```

FIGURE 5-2   Program to Count Characters.

Note that two READ statements appear in this program. The first one, before the WHILE, provides an initial value for the variable CURRENTCHAR so that the test specified by the WHILE can be performed the first time. (Otherwise CURRENTCHAR would be undefined.) The second READ statement provides a new value of CURRENTCHAR for the next iteration of the WHILE. You should verify that the program does not include the period in the count of characters.

It is important to realize that the statement(s) after the DO may never be executed at all. If the specified boolean condition is FALSE from the beginning, then the body of the WHILE statement will be skipped. Consider this program fragment.

```
        READLN(K);
        WHILE K>0 DO
          BEGIN
                .
                .
                .
          END
```

The statements between the BEGIN and END will be executed only if a positive data value is provided for K.

In the above fragment we have left unspecified the nature of the statements contained between the BEGIN and END. Do we know anything at all about those statements? In this particular case we do. Let us suppose a positive data value has been provided for K so that the statements after the DO will, indeed, be executed. These statements will be executed repeatedly as long as K remains greater than zero. It should be apparent that the statements after the DO must include changing the value of K; otherwise, they will be executed forever! We can conclude that among the statements after the DO there ought to be at least another READLN(K) to provide a new value of K, or an assignment statement that changes the value of K. Of course, there might be several such statements but, unless there is at least one, we will be trapped "inside" the WHILE forever. We never want to write a program that calls for an infinite number of iterations!

There is one more thing we should keep in mind. Even if we do alter the value of K, that does not guarantee the iteration will terminate. For example, if the above loop contained the assignment statement $K := K + 1$, we will add 1 to K during each cycle. Since K was positive at the start of the loop, it should be clear that in this case the loop will never terminate. So merely altering K is not enough. The alteration must be such that at some time K will become nonpositive. We have been looking at a simple example. However, keep in mind the general idea that no matter what boolean condition we are testing, the loop must modify the variables in such a way that the condition eventually becomes FALSE and the loop terminates.

5.3.2 THE REPEAT STATEMENT

The REPEAT statement involves the same basic idea as the WHILE statement: an indicated statement (or group of statements) is repeatedly executed and a specified test is performed to determine when the repetition is to stop. But there are two principal differences between WHILE and REPEAT.

1. WHILE performs the test *before* each cycle; REPEAT performs the test *after* each cycle.

2. These two statements consider the test to be performed from opposite points of view. One statement performs repetition WHILE a certain condition is true; the other statement performs repetition UNTIL (i.e., it REPEATs . . . UNTIL) a certain condition becomes true.

Pictorially the difference can be represented this way.

STYLE CLINIC 5-1

Too Low a Time Limit?

Suppose you submit a program for execution and find that the output contains a message similar to

TIME LIMIT EXCEEDED — EXECUTION TERMINATED

Apparently your program was using too much computer time and did not conclude normally. When you originally submitted your program, you specified a time limit (one that was probably supplied by your instructor). This limit prevents any one program for monopolizing the computer for too long, thereby providing a reasonable level of service for all users. But your program did not finish, so apparently the time limit you provided was too low. You should resubmit the program, this time with a higher time limit. Right? Wrong!

Although a mistaken time limit is a possibility, it is most unlikely to be your problem. (Do not be fooled by what appears to be a ridiculously low time limit—computers are fast! On a large computer system a time limit of 2 to 5 seconds might be ample for a class assignment. On a smaller system 10 or 15 seconds might be appropriate. In any case, for class assignments in a beginning course, you will always be dealing in seconds, not minutes.) You should first proceed on the assumption that the time limit provided by your instructor is an appropriate one.

What, then, is the problem? Your program undoubtedly contains an error! Your program is probably caught in an *infinite loop*—it is performing a repetitive operation (perhaps a WHILE statement or one of the other repetitive statements that we will discuss), and the condition for terminating the repetition has not become true. You probably forgot to alter one or more variables inside the loop, and it is impossible for the boolean condition ever to achieve the necessary value.

You should not run your program again with a higher time limit. Nothing will change, and you will only be wasting time—yours as well as the computer's. Find the mistake in your program. Carefully examine every repetitive section of the program and notice the conditions under which each repetitive statement terminates. What data values are you using in this execution of the program? Will the repetitive statements terminate?

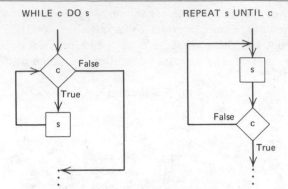

The specific form of a REPEAT statement is:

REPEAT statement; statement . . . UNTIL boolean expression

It is interesting to note that the syntax explicitly permits a sequence of statements and we do not have to use a compound statement to achieve this. This comes about because the statements to be repeatedly executed are bracketed by the two reserved words REPEAT and UNTIL. Therefore there is never any uncertainty about which statements are to be repeated. Of course, if we wish, we could still bracket our statement sequence with BEGIN and END, as in:

REPEAT

    BEGIN
    S_1 ;
    S_2 ;

    .

    .

    .

    S_n
    END

UNTIL boolean expression

This is not wrong but it is redundant.

When using a REPEAT statement, there will always be at least one execution of the statement sequence, because the test for completion is performed at the end of the cycle, not at the beginning. For example, if we were to write:

```
READLN(K);
REPEAT
   statement 1;
   statement 2
UNTIL K<0
```

statement 1 and statement 2 would always be executed once, even when a negative data value has been given to K. Things can actually get quite tricky. Even if a negative value has been given to K initially, if either statement 1 or statement 2 alters K so as to make it nonnegative, the loop will still continue. The iteration will terminate only when K is left with a negative value after all the statements in the body of the loop have been executed.

We will now use a REPEAT statement in a program fragment that computes the average of a set of 20 numbers read from data cards.

```
SUM:=0.0; COUNT:=0;
REPEAT
   READLN(VALUE); WRITELN(' DATA VALUE= ', VALUE);
   COUNT:=COUNT+1; SUM:=SUM+VALUE
UNTIL COUNT=20;
AVERAGE:= SUM/COUNT
```

We have set up the program to read a data value and add it to the sum, performing each step 20 times. The variable named COUNT is used to keep track of how many repetitions there have been. When COUNT reaches 20, the loop ends and the average is computed. Note that when we use a REPEAT statement, we specify the condition that will terminate the repetition. Contrast this with the WHILE statement, in which we specify the condition for continuing the repetition.

You may be wondering why we wrote the last statement as AVERAGE:=SUM/COUNT instead of AVERAGE:=SUM/20.0. We certainly could have used the second form. However, by using the variable COUNT instead of the constant 20, we will find it easier to modify our program in the future. For example, suppose we wanted to compute the average of 100 numbers instead of 20. We only need to make one change to our program. We would write

```
UNTIL COUNT=100;
```

(Of course, we would also have to provide 100 data values instead of 20, but that is a change to the data and not a change to the program.) Clearly we would have had to make a second change if we had used the constant 20 in the division operation.

This may seem like a small point, but it does illustrate a very important principle of computer programming. Even if the specific problem does not demand it, it is usually a good idea to write programs with as much generality as possible as long as the increased generality is not at the cost of an overly complicated program. It should be possible to take a program that computes an average of 20 values and convert it to a program that works for any number of values with a minimal amount of work. We use the term *program generality* to mean a computer program that will work correctly on variations of a problem with little or no modification to the program itself. The fewer the changes, the less opportunity there is for introducing errors.

In this particular example we can carry the idea even further. By using a CONST declaration to specify how many numbers we are dealing with, we can localize the only change that must be made. We know that to change the program we need only change the CONST declaration near the beginning of the program. We don't have to search our program for all of the references to the constant 20, 100, or whatever. For example, we might write our program this way (Figure 5-3).

```
PROGRAM AVER(INPUT,OUTPUT);
{Program to compute the average of "HOWMANY" real
  values. "HOWMANY" is defined in a CONST declaration}
CONST HOWMANY=20;
VAR SUM,VALUE,AVERAGE: REAL;
                    COUNT: INTEGER;
BEGIN
   SUM:=0.0; COUNT:=0;
   REPEAT {Find the sum}
      READLN(VALUE); WRITELN(' DATA VALUE= ', VALUE);
      COUNT:=COUNT+1;
      SUM:=SUM+VALUE
   UNTIL COUNT=HOWMANY;
   AVERAGE:= SUM/HOWMANY;
   WRITELN(' THE AVERAGE IS ', AVERAGE)
END.
```

FIGURE 5-3 Program to Compute Averages.

It is obviously a simple matter to change the second line of the program to read, for example,

CONST HOWMANY = 100;

Now our program will compute the average of 100 numbers. (Remember, we would still need to provide the 100 required data values.)

We can carry this concept of generality still further. We can actually write a program that will work for any number of data values without requiring any modifications to the program. How do we do it? Simply by agreeing to provide one additional piece of data: the number of values we will be using during that particular program run. For example, if we want the average of 20 numbers, our first line of data would contain the number 20. We would then provide the 20 numbers whose average we seek. If we want to run our program again to find the average of 100 numbers, our first data value would be 100 and, of course, we would follow that with the 100 required values. One program would work for both cases without change. Our program would look like the one in Figure 5-4.

It is interesting to note that this version of the program is not very different from the one in Figure 5-3. Instead of being a constant, HOWMANY has become a variable whose value is set by reading a line of data each time the program is run. The only changes are to the data; the program need not be touched.

This is an interesting programming technique, but we should note that it is appropriate only if the number of data values is relatively small. Experience has shown that if the number of data values is large, the user of the pro-

```
PROGRAM AVER(INPUT,OUTPUT);
{Find the average of a set of real data values. The
 number of values Is specified by an integer on the
 first data card}
VAR   SUM, VALUE, AVERAGE: REAL;
        HOWMANY, COUNT    : INTEGER;
BEGIN
READLN(HOWMANY);   }Find out how many data values there will
                     be. After getting this number, we should
                     check to make sure that it is a positive
                     number. We will learn how to do this later
                     in this chapter}
WRITELN(' THERE ARE ', HOWMANY, ' DATA VALUES');
SUM:=0.0; COUNT:=0;
REPEAT {Find the sum of the values}
    READLN(VALUE); WRITELN(' DATA VALUE= ', VALUE);
    COUNT:=COUNT+1;
    SUM:=SUM+VALUE
UNTIL   COUNT=HOWMANY;
AVERAGE:=SUM/HOWMANY;
WRITELN(' THE AVERAGE IS ', AVERAGE)
END.
```

FIGURE 5-4   Modified Program to Compute Averages.

gram might very well count incorrectly and provide the wrong data value for the variable HOWMANY. Computers can count more reliably than people can.

It is usually a much better idea to set up a program so that it simply continues to read data values until there are no more, regardless of how many that might be. There are two techniques for doing this.

The first technique uses a construct called the *signal card*. This is a data card that contains a value that could not validly appear on any other data card. The user adds this card to the end of the data set, and the program is written to test for the appearance of this card. For example, if the values to be averaged were exam scores in the range 0 to 100, then a value of -1 could be used to signal the end of the data. The program would look like the one in Figure 5-5.

The second technique utilizes the idea of *end-of-file* (usually designated EOF) that we introduced in Chapter 4. We can continue to execute a loop until the boolean predicate EOF becomes TRUE. This would indicate that no more data values are available. If we were to revise our program along these lines, the program would appear as in Figure 5-6.

```
PROGRAM AVER(INPUT,OUTPUT);
{Find the average of a set of real data values. A data card
  with a value of −1 will signify the end of the data}
CONST   ENDOFDATA=−1.0;
VAR     SUM, VALUE, AVERAGE: REAL;
                          COUNT: INTEGER;
BEGIN
SUM:=0.0; COUNT:=0;
READLN(VALUE); WRITELN(' FIRST VALUE IS ', VALUE);
WHILE VALUE<>ENDOFDATA DO
    BEGIN {Compute the sum and count the number of values}
    SUM:=SUM+VALUE;
    COUNT:=COUNT+1;
    READLN(VALUE); WRITELN(' NEXT VALUE IS ', VALUE)
    END;
AVERAGE:=SUM/COUNT; {Later we will learn how to guard against
                          division by 0}
WRITELN(' THERE ARE ', COUNT, ' VALUES');
WRITELN(' THE AVERAGE IS ', AVERAGE)
END.
```

FIGURE 5-5   Use of a Signal Card for End-of-Data Indication.

```
PROGRAM AVER(INPUT,OUTPUT);
{Find the average of a set of real data values. Data values
 will be processed until EOF is reached}
VAR   SUM, VALUE, AVERAGE: REAL;
                         COUNT: INTEGER;
BEGIN
SUM:=0.0; COUNT:=0;
REPEAT {Find the sum and count the number of values}
   READLN(VALUE); WRITELN(' DATA VALUE= ', VALUE);
   SUM:=SUM+VALUE;
   COUNT:=COUNT+1
UNTIL EOF(INPUT); {EOF would be sufficient (INPUT is assumed)}
AVERAGE:=SUM/COUNT;
WRITELN(' THERE ARE ', COUNT, ' VALUES');
WRITELN(' THE AVERAGE IS ', AVERAGE)
END.
```
FIGURE 5-6   Use of EOF for End-of-Data Indication.

Now our data values can consist only of the numbers that are actually used in computing the average. We do not have to count these values and punch an additional data card for HOWMANY, and we do not have to remember to place a signal card at the end of the data values. The program will continue reading data values until none are left.

5.3.3 THE FOR STATEMENT

In our discussion of the WHILE statement we looked at a program that computed the sum of the first 10 integers. We now rewrite that example, making some relatively trivial changes.

```
SUM:=0; N:=1;
WHILE N<= 10   DO
   BEGIN
   SUM:=SUM+N;
   N:=N+1
   END;
WRITELN(' SUM= ', SUM)
```

In this version we are performing the computation $1+2+ \ldots +10$ instead of $10+9+ \ldots +1$ as before. This requires a different initialization for N as well as a different condition for the WHILE.

If we look at this example, we observe that we are repeatedly executing the assignment statement SUM:=SUM+N under circumstances in which the variable N is one greater with each iteration. We also know exactly how many repetitions there will be. These facts allow us to rewrite this program segment with a bit less effort by using a FOR statement, another kind of iterative statement. However, it does more than the WHILE or REPEAT because it automatically includes the following.

1. An initialization of a special variable called the *control variable*, which will be used for counting iterations.
2. A test of the control variable before each iteration to determine if enough iterations have been performed.
3. An automatic incrementing of the control variable after each iteration.

If we rewrite our most recent example using a FOR statement instead of a WHILE to control the repetition, we would have the following.

```
SUM:=0;
FOR N:=1 TO 10 DO SUM:=SUM+N;
WRITELN(' SUM = ', SUM)
```

In addition to replacing the WHILE with the FOR, we have eliminated the two statements, N:=1 and N:=N+1. Both of these operations are performed by the FOR statement itself.

The FOR statement repeatedly executes the statement SUM:=SUM+N as N varies from 1 to 10. But let us examine, step by step, exactly what happens.

1. The control variable N is initialized to 1 (the *initial value*).
2. N is compared to 10 (the *final value*). Since N is *less than or equal to* this value, the statement after the DO is executed. This statement constitutes the *body* of the loop.
3. N is incremented by 1.
4. Steps 2 and 3 are repeated until N exceeds 10, the *final value*. When N reaches a value greater than the final value, the statement after the DO is no longer executed. The computer has completed executing the FOR statement, and the program continues with the statement following the FOR.

Of course, a FOR statement gives us more flexibility than this example displays. The general form of the FOR statement is:

STYLE CLINIC 5-2

End of Data Indicators

We have discussed several ways in which a program can be made aware of the number of data values to be processed.

1. The number can be built directly into the program through an explicit constant, as in

WHILE COUNT<20 DO
.
.
.

2. The number can be referred to through a CONST declaration, as in

CONST LIMIT=20;
.
.
.

WHILE COUNT<LIMIT DO

3. The count can be read from the input data.
4. Data can be read until a signal value is encountered
5. Data can be read until end-of-file is encountered

We can make some very worthwhile observations. Alternatives 1 and 2 should rarely, if ever, be used, because they needlessly restrict the usefulness of the program. We must change the program even for trivial changes in the problem statement.

Alternatives 3, 4, and 5 provide the generality we seek, but alternative 3 is very error-prone. There is simply too great a chance that at some time a user will count data values incorrectly and the program will produce incorrect results.

Alternatives 4 and 5 are the methods of choice. They provide the desired generality, and they are easy to use. Of course, the user must always remember to add the signal card to the set of data values, so alternative 5 is probably the very best technique, since it requires no action whatsoever by the user. (Note that alternative 4 would be appropriate if the program is to process several sets of data during a single program run. The signal value would represent an "end-of-file" condition for each set of data.)

FOR control-variable := initial-value TO final-value DO statement

Pictorially, we might represent the operation of this statement as follows.

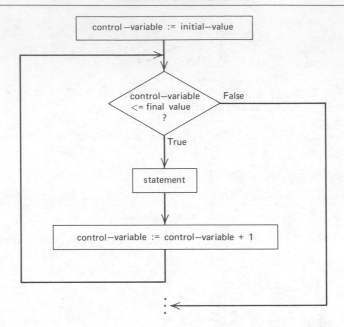

The body of the loop, which may, of course, be a compound statement, is repeatedly executed, while the control variable ranges from the initial value up to the final value in increments of 1. For now we will say that the control variable, initial value, and final value must all be of type INTEGER. Later, when we discuss user-defined types, we will generalize this rule a bit. The initial value and final value need not be constants. Any expression of the proper type (INTEGER, for now) is acceptable. However, we must be careful. These expressions are evaluated only once, when the FOR statement is first encountered. It is therefore meaningless to use an expression that will in any way depend on the repetitive execution of the statement that follows the DO. For example, we can write

FOR I:=K+1 TO K+(J*2) DO statement

Since the two expressions will be evaluated only when the FOR is first encountered, K must already be defined. Otherwise, there would be no initial value to assign to I. J must also be defined, since the final value will also be established at this time. Note that any changes made by the statement to K or J will not be reflected in the final value, since that has already been fixed.

There are some important points to keep in mind concerning the control variable. First, this variable must never be altered by the body of the FOR. The control variable will be automatically updated by the built-in mechanism of the FOR statement, and that is the only way it may be changed. We may use the value of the control variable, for example, in an arithmetic computation, but we may not change it. This means that it cannot appear on the left side of an assignment statement or in a READ or READLN statement. Consider this example.

```
SUM:=0;
FOR  I:= FIRSTVALUE TO LASTVALUE DO
   BEGIN
      SUM:=SUM+I;
      I:=I+5   {This is invalid}
   END
```

The body of the FOR is a compound statement that consists of two assignment statements. The first is perfectly legitimate. It merely uses the value of I, the control variable. The second assignment statement is invalid because it seeks to change I. That is something we are not allowed to do.

You may be wondering about what happens to the control variable after the FOR statement has completed its processing. Strangely enough, the control variable, in a sense, disappears! More precisely, we say that upon completion of the FOR statement, the control variable is *undefined*. This may appear strange, since we would normally expect its value to be 1 greater than the final value. This is not the case. If for any reason we wish to reuse that variable, we must reestablish a value for it. Of course, a READLN or an assignment statement would suffice for this purpose. But as an interesting special case, you might note that the variable could reappear as a control variable in another FOR statement (recall that the first operation done by a FOR is to set the control variable to the indicated initial value).

If we look back at our example program, which computes the average of a set of numbers, we might note that a FOR statement would be a good statement to use in place of the REPEAT. The FOR statement could automatically replace the variable COUNT, which was used to count the number of repetitions. Our program would look like Figure 5-7.

Suppose the data values for the variable HOWMANY were mispunched— suppose a negative value was erroneously specified. What would the program do? (*Hint.* Consider exactly when the FOR statement performs the test to determine when enough repetitions have been performed.) Regardless of what the FOR statement actually does, we should never allow the program even to reach the FOR loop when the program has read such meaningless data. In the next section we will introduce a statement that will allow us to test specifically for this possibility.

Before we leave our discussion of repetitive statements, we should mention an alternative form of the FOR statement.

```
FOR control-variable:=initial-value DOWNTO final-value DO
statement
```

```
PROGRAM AVER(INPUT,OUTPUT);
{Find the average of a set of real data values. The
  number of values is specified by an integer on the
  first data card. We are using this technique so that
  a FOR statement can be illustrated—we again caution
  against its general use}
VAR    SUM, VALUE, AVERAGE: REAL;
              HOWMANY, COUNT: INTEGER;
BEGIN
  READLN(HOWMANY); {Find out how many data values}
  SUM:=0.0;
  FOR   COUNT:=1  TO  HOWMANY  DO   {Find the sum of the
                                           values}
    BEGIN
      READLN(VALUE); WRITELN(' DATA VALUE= ', VALUE);
      SUM:=SUM+VALUE
    END;
    AVERAGE:=SUM/HOWMANY;
    WRITELN(' THE AVERAGE IS ', AVERAGE)
END.
```

FIGURE 5-7   Use of FOR Statement to Compute Averages.

This statement is similar to the FOR statement we have already discussed, except that it counts "down" instead of "up." That is, the control variable is checked to see if it is *greater than or equal to* the final value; if it is, the statement is executed, the control variable is *decremented* by one, and the cycle is repeated. In all other respects it is the same as the previous version of the FOR statement.

As an example, note that the sum of the integers from 1 to L could be computed using either form of the FOR statement.

```
SUM:=0;                          SUM:=0;
FOR K:=1 TO L DO                 FOR K:=L DOWNTO 1 DO
    SUM:=SUM+K                       SUM:=SUM+K
```

5.4 CONDITIONAL STATEMENTS

In our discussion of algorithms, we made use of two primitives for the selection of alternative courses of action: IF-THEN and IF-THEN-ELSE. As we will now see, these two primitives correspond to two statements available in PASCAL. Although we could view these as just two different forms of a single statement—with the IF-THEN being a special case of the IF-THEN-ELSE—we will, for now, discuss them as two separate statements. These statements, along with a third called the CASE statement, allow us to write PASCAL programs that execute sections of code only if certain conditions are satisfied.

STYLE CLINIC 5-3

Off-by-One Errors

A common programming error is to pay too little attention to the exact number of times a loop will be executed. We often set up a loop that is correct in its basic structure but produces incorrect results. This is frequently because the loop is executed once too often or once too seldom. We say there is an *off-by-one error*.

Consider this simple attempt to find the sum of the first N positive integers.

```
SUM:=0; NUMBER:=1;
WHILE NUMBER<N DO
    BEGIN
    SUM:=SUM+NUMBER;
    NUMBER:=NUMBER+1
    END
```

This loop will produce an incorrect result. It is actually computing the sum of the first $N-1$ positive integers, and we should have written

```
WHILE NUMBER <= N DO
    .
    .
    .
```

The nasty thing about off-by-one errors is that they usually do not generate error messages—they just generate wrong answers. To make things worse, we may not even recognize that the results are incorrect. An error of this kind can be difficult to detect once a program has proceeded to the testing stage. Obviously, a good set of test cases with known answers will be a tremendous help. We may not always have such handy test cases, however.

What can we do about off-by-one errors? We can prevent these errors by carefully examining every program loop we write as soon as we write it. If we wait until the entire program is written and we begin to check out the program by running test cases, it is possible we will never be aware of a mistake. As soon as we write a loop, we should examine the conditions for the first and last cycles of the loop and ask how many times the loop will be executed. These assessments should be made automatically for every loop in every program. Developing this habit will save an untold amount of grief.

STYLE CLINIC 5-4

More on Semicolons

In our discussion of the compound statement we mentioned that the existence of the empty statement can sometimes allow PASCAL to accept semicolons in places that would otherwise be incorrect. Some experienced programmers like to exploit this by making it a habit to use a semicolon before UNTIL or END. This makes it possible to insert one or more statements at a later time without having to remember to add a semicolon. For example, consider this program fragment.

```
WHILE  N <= 10  DO
    BEGIN
    SUM := SUM + N;
    N := N + 1
    END
```

If we find it necessary to add another statement after the assignment to N, we must remember to include a semicolon as a separator. Instead, we might have written this as:

```
WHILE  N <= 10  DO
    BEGIN
    SUM := SUM + N;
    N := N + 1;
    END
```

We know that the semicolon after the 1 will not result in an error message because of the empty statement. Now we can add a statement before the END without backing up to the previous line to add a semicolon.

As we have said, some experienced programmers like to use this technique, but it is not one that we recommend to a beginning programmer because it leads to too casual an attitude toward semicolons, and there are places where an extra semicolon can be disastrous. For example:

```
FOR  I := FIRST  TO  LAST  DO;
    SUM := SUM + I;
WRITELN(' THE SUM IS', SUM)
```

Note the semicolon after DO—this one is not at all harmless! The semicolon indicates that an empty statement follows the DO, and it is the empty statement (not the assignment statement!) that is repeatedly executed as the variable I takes on values from FIRST to LAST. The point that is especially noteworthy is that this construct will not result in an error message because it is a perfectly valid statement. However, since it is apparently not the construct that was intended, it will cause the program to produce incorrect results. It is a programming error, but it is one that will not usually be detected by PASCAL. This kind of error can be extremely difficult to find.

In any case, you should find it reassuring to know that PASCAL will detect

If you are concerned about the possibility of forgetting to add a semicolon, you may find it helpful to get in the habit of including the semicolon on the new line instead of the previous one.

```
N := N + 1
; new-statement
```

Although this may look a bit strange at first, it is perfectly valid.

In any case, you should find it reassuring to know that PASCAL will detect an omitted semicolon and provide an error message. On the other hand, PASCAL will, in some cases, accept an "extra" semicolon and provide an interpretation that is quite different from the one the programmer had in mind, and no error message will be printed. If you want to use extra semicolons, do so with care.

5.4.1 IF-THEN

We know that there are occasions when we want to perform an operation only if a certain condition is satisfied. This can be accomplished by writing:

IF boolean expression THEN statement

The meaning of this should be apparent. The statement (which may, of course, be a compound statement) will be executed if and only if the boolean expression has the value TRUE. The statement will not be executed if the boolean expression is false. Pictorially, we might view the situation like this.

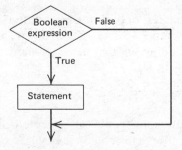

For example, we might use

IF A>0 THEN WRITELN(' A= ', A)

to write the value of A only if A is positive.

We can use the logical operators AND, OR, and NOT to construct more complicated boolean expressions. For example, to execute statement S when all of the conditions $C_1, C_2, \ldots, C_i$ are true, we would write:

IF (C_1) AND (C_2) AND . . . AND (C_i) THEN S

To execute statement S when any one condition is true, we would write:

IF (C_1) OR (C_2) OR . . . OR (C_i) THEN S

These compound conditions can be built up to any desired complexity. From our discussion of boolean expressions we recall that in complex expressions each of the elementary subconditions must be parenthesized. Additional parentheses may be needed to enforce the correct order of evaluation. For example,

IF (($A>B$) OR ($A=10$)) AND ($C<0$) THEN statement

Here is an instance in which the use of parentheses is not merely good form; these parentheses are required for proper precedence and correct evaluation.

In setting up compound conditions we must be careful to write out exactly the test that we want to perform. A fairly common error is to attempt to apply a type of distributive law to the test and write:

IF $A<B$ AND C THEN $A:=A+1$

in which the intention is to test for the two conditions $A<B$ and $A<C$. If that is what we want, then we must write it explicitly.

IF ($A<B$) AND ($A<C$) THEN $A:=A+1$

Now A will be incremented only if both conditions are satisfied.

Note that we allow any PASCAL statement to be the one that is conditionally executed, including another IF statement. This would lead to the construct

IF condition-1 THEN IF condition-2 THEN statement

Now the indicated statement would be executed only if both condition-1 and condition-2 were true. This could clearly be extended to any number of conditions. Compare these two constructs:

(1)   IF ($A<B$) AND ($A<C$) THEN $A:=A+1$
(2)   IF $A<B$ THEN IF $A<C$ THEN $A:=A+1$

Both are legitimate PASCAL statements and both have the same ultimate effect—increment A only if A is less than both B and C. But there is a subtle difference between them, and we should be aware of what the difference is. In construct (1) the tests are done at the same level; in construct (2) one test is subordinate to the other. Thus, in the first case both tests are always performed.* In the second case A is compared to C only if it has already been determined that A is less than B.

Since both constructs lead to the same result, which one should we use? There are situations in which each is appropriate. Since the first method (using a compound condition) is a bit shorter and easier to write, we should probably use it most of the time. Our programs will then be a bit neater and easier to read. However, we might have a situation in which one test can be performed only if another condition has already been found to be true; this clearly requires alternative (2), subordinate conditions. We might also want to use this scheme if we are very concerned about the efficiency of our program. Suppose we want to perform two tests, test-1 and test-2, which are fairly complicated (perhaps they involve a large amount of computation and not just simple comparisons). Suppose also that these tests could be performed in either order, but we know that more often than not, one of them (say test-2) will be false. If we are concerned about the efficiency of our program, we would write

> IF test-2 THEN IF test-1 THEN statement

instead of

> IF (test-2) AND (test-1) THEN statement

or even

> IF test-1 THEN IF test-2 THEN statement

Since we know that test-2 is usually not true, the first construct will usually avoid the evaluation of test-1. In the second construct both tests will (in general) be carried out; the performance of the third construct will depend on the frequency with which test-1 is true. If we have a situation in which program efficiency is of great importance, the tests are fairly complicated, and we know something about the probability of success for each of the tests, then we might find it advantageous to use the subordinate testing scheme. But it is rare for all these factors to exist simultaneously, so more

---

* We might note that some implementations might perform only as many tests as necessary to ascertain that the entire expression is true or false (thus if A were not less than B, A might not be compared to C), but this sort of optimization would vary from one system to another. As programmers, we cannot make any assumptions about this.

often than not we will merely choose the approach that improves the clarity of our programs.

One of the obvious ways to use an IF statement is in checking data values for validity. It is not at all uncommon to use a computer program that is "correct" and yet obtain incorrect or meaningless results because incorrect data values were provided. In almost every program there are certain checks that can be made to guarantee that data values fall into an allowable range. If the data values are outside this range, the program should print an informative message instead of trying to carry out the computation with meaningless values. Of course, the data values might well be in the allowable range and still not be the values we intended, but that is why we should always echo-print the input data. That way a simple inspection of the computer output will disclose data values that were "valid" but still not "correct." These topics will be pursued in Chapter 6.

The particular tests for validity that have to be performed will depend on the problem to be solved. We will consider a particular example so that we can discuss several alternative ways to structure these tests.

Suppose we have three integer variables, X, Y, and Z, whose values will be read from data cards. Suppose further that the values must fall within the following ranges if the computation is to be meaningful.

> X: must be positive
> Y: must be greater than 10
> Z: must be between 50 and 100, inclusive

We might write the following PASCAL statements.

```
{Read and print data values}
READLN(X,Y,Z); WRITELN(' X=', X, ' Y=', Y, ' Z=', Z);
{Perform the computation if the data values are valid}
IF (X>0) AND (Y>10) AND (Z>=50) AND (Z<=100) THEN
   BEGIN
   {Carry out the computation}
   END
```

That is one way to handle the situation. However, suppose we wanted to print out an informative message if any of the data values are invalid. We could make the printing of the message contingent on the data being invalid, as indicated by this conditional statement.

```
IF (X<=0) OR (Y<=10) OR (Z>100) OR (Z < 50) THEN
WRITELN(' INVALID DATA')
```

Note that each test has been changed to test for invalid data, and OR has been used instead of AND. The overall condition will now be satisfied if any one of the subconditions is satisfied.

This will take care of printing the informative message, but we still need a mechanism to prevent the program from continuing with the computation. We might want to introduce a boolean variable for this purpose. If we begin the program with this variable being false and set it to true if the data values are invalid, we can easily accomplish our objective.

```
{Read and print data values}
ERROR:=FALSE;
READLN(X, Y, Z); WRITELN(' X=', X, ' Y=', Y, ' Z=', Z);
{Check for invalid data}
IF (X<=0) OR (Y<=10) OR (Z<50) OR (Z>100) THEN
    BEGIN
    ERROR:=TRUE;
    WRITELN(' INVALID DATA')
    END;
{Perform computation if data is valid}
IF NOT ERROR THEN
    BEGIN
    {Carry out the computation here}
    END
```

FIGURE 5-8   Checking for Valid Data with IF-THEN.

If we analyze this situation carefully, we see that there are two actions that are to be conditionally performed: the printing of an error message and the computation, which is the principal objective of the program. Interestingly, these two actions arise from complementary conditions. If the data are invalid we want to print the message and not do the computation; if the data are valid we want to do the computation and not print the message. In either case we want to do one action but not the other. Figure 5-8 has shown how this can be accomplished using IF-THEN and an auxiliary boolean variable. In the next section we will discuss the IF-THEN-ELSE statement, which will allow us to achieve these results without using this additional variable.

5.4.2 IF-THEN-ELSE

The IF-THEN-ELSE statement is a construct that allows us to select one of two statements by evaluating a specified condition. The form of the statement is:

IF boolean expression THEN statement-1 ELSE statement-2

If the boolean expression is true, statement-1 is executed and statement-2 is skipped. If the boolean expression is false, statement-1 is skipped and statement-2 is executed. Thus, one and only one of the two statements will always be executed. Pictorially, we have

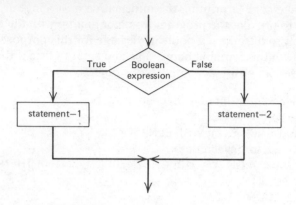

For example, if we write

IF A>B THEN LARGE:=A ELSE LARGE:=B

we would assign the greater of A and B to LARGE. What happens if A=B? Since the condition tests specifically for A greater than B, the boolean expression would be false and the second statement (the one following ELSE) would be executed. It is important to remember that one of the two statements will always be executed.

The IF-THEN-ELSE mechanism is perfectly suited for the task we illustrated in Figure 5-8. Since we have alternative courses of action and we always want to perform one of them, but never both, the IF-THEN-ELSE is ideal (Figure 5-9).

```
{Read and print data values}
READLN(X,Y,Z); WRITELN(' X=', X, ' Y=', Y, ' Z=', Z);
{Check for invalid data}
IF (X<=0) OR (Y<=10) OR (Z<50) OR (Z>100)
    THEN WRITELN(' INVALID DATA')
    ELSE BEGIN {The data values are OK}
        .
        .
        .
        {Carry out the computation}
        .
        .
        .
    END
```

FIGURE 5-9 Checking for Valid Data with IF-THEN-ELSE.

When either (or both) of the conditionally executed statements are compound statements, it becomes especially important to exercise some care in positioning the various parts of the IF-THEN-ELSE so that the intent of the entire construct can be readily grasped. It is quite possible to have a nested sequence of IF-THEN-ELSE statements. Such a sequence can be readily understood by the reader of a program only if some consistent indentation scheme is followed. (Of course, the program will be understood by PASCAL no matter how it is laid out, but it is important to write programs that can be readily understood by humans.) There are many different indentation schemes that can be used, and the specific details are not important as long as you pick a reasonable scheme and use it. Figure 5-10 shows two particular schemes that we find useful, but we emphasize that any approach that clearly depicts the flow of control is acceptable.

```
IF condition THEN              IF condition
    BEGIN                          THEN BEGIN
       .                                   .
       .                                   .
       .                                   .
    END                            END
ELSE                           ELSE BEGIN
    BEGIN                              .
       .
       .                                   .
       .                          END
    END
        (a)                                    (b)
```

FIGURE 5-10   Indentation Schemes for Conditional Statements.

Either of the above layouts allows our eyes to find either statement quickly and mentally skip the one that will not be executed. This matter of indentation and program layout may seem like a small mechanical point but, in a large program with several nested conditional statements, it can be a tremendous aid to comprehension.

Consider this PASCAL statement.

```
IF A>0 THEN IF B>0 THEN B:=B+1 ELSE A:=A+1
```

(We have deliberately written this on one line to make our point.) What is the meaning of this construct? If you think the answer is obvious, look again, because two different interpretations are possible. To which "IF" does the "ELSE" belong? In other words, does the construct mean

```
(1)   IF A>0 THEN
         BEGIN
         IF B>0 THEN B:=B+1 ELSE A:=A+1
         END
```

or does it mean

```
(2)   IF A>0 THEN
         BEGIN
         IF B>0 THEN B:=B+1
         END
      ELSE
         A:=A+1
```

FIGURE 5-11   The Dangling ELSE Problem.

We have inserted a BEGIN and END to indicate the two possible meanings and we have used indentation to highlight these meanings (Figure 5-11). Note that the difference in meaning is significant: in alternative 1, A is incremented only if A is positive and B is not positive; in alternative 2, A is incremented only if A is not positive. Which meaning is correct?

This well-known ambiguity is usually termed the *dangling ELSE* problem. To resolve this problem, PASCAL uses the first interpretation: an ELSE is associated with the most recent IF. There is a lesson to be learned here. Sometimes the addition of a redundant BEGIN and END can help to clarify the meaning of a construct. Just as it pays to use parentheses to make the meaning of an arithmetic expression obvious, it sometimes helps to use BEGIN and END to bracket parts of a control construct even if the BEGIN and END might not be technically necessary. Note also that there can never be a ';' before the reserved word ELSE, because ELSE is not a statement.

5.4.3 CASE

The CASE statement allows a program to select one statement for execution out of a set of statements. During any one execution of the CASE statement, only one of the possible statements will be executed; the remaining statements will be skipped. The selection of the statement to be executed is made by the selector expression in conjunction with a set of constants. Take a very simple example.

```
{Assume J is an integer variable}
CASE J OF
    1: A:=A+1;
  2, 3: B:=B+1;
    5: C:=C+1;
6, 8, 10: D:=D+1
  END
```

The CASE statement will execute one (and only one) of the assignment statements based on the value of J: if J is 1, A will be incremented; if J is 2 or 3, B will be incremented; if J is 5, C will be incremented; if J is 6, 8, or 10, D will be incremented. Only one statement will be executed and the rest will be ignored. The program will then continue with the statement following the END.

An obvious question has probably occurred to you. What happens if J does not have one of the values 1, 2, 3, 5, 6, 8, or 10? It might be nice if nothing at all happened—that is, the entire CASE statement would be ignored. However, that is not what happens. If the CASE statement is executed at a time when J does not have one of the indicated values, the effect of the CASE statement is *undefined*. We simply do not know what will happen, and we can make no assumptions whatsoever. This means that we can use a CASE statement only if we know in advance all the possible values that the selector expression can have. If we know all the values we can list them as possibilities, and the CASE statement will always do something meaningful. Of course, if the number of possible values is quite large, it would be impractical to list them all. In such a situation we would not use a CASE statement.

Let us look at the general form of the CASE statement.

```
CASE expression OF
    cll: statement;
    cll: statement;

          .
          .
          .

    cll: statement
  END
```

Each cll ("case label list") is a list of constants (separated by commas) of the same type as the selector expression (the type REAL is not allowed). The items in each list indicate the values of the selector expression for which the associated statement is to be executed. We can have as many items in a case label list as we like (in any order), and we can have as many lists as we like, although a given constant can appear in only one list. Also, any of the associated statements can be a compound statement. Note that an END

STYLE CLINIC 5-5

Clarifying the Flow of Control

Are you wondering if indentation alone can be used to convey the intended meaning of a construct like the one in Figure 5-11? Be careful—indentation can convey a meaning to the program reader, but it cannot force a meaning on the computer. For example, suppose we rewrite the second of our possible interpretations, using good indentation but omitting the BEGIN and END.

```
IF A>0 THEN
    IF B>0 THEN B:=B+1
ELSE
    A:=A+1
```

Things are not what they appear to be! The indentation suggests one meaning, but the computer is oblivious to the indentation. The actual meaning is that of alternative 1; the ELSE is associated with the nearest IF, regardless of how we choose to lay out the program on the printed page. If we want the meaning of alterative 2, we must state it explicitly, using BEGIN and END.

```
IF A>0 THEN
    BEGIN
    IF B>0 THEN B:=B+1
    END
ELSE
    A:=A+1
```

In summary, we must remember that a good indentation scheme is important because it can help the reader to understand the control flow of a program. But indentation cannot change the flow of control, and we never want the indentation to suggest a meaning that is not the proper one. Therefore, if there is ever any doubt as to the meaning of a particular construct, resolve that doubt with an explicit indication of intent, even if it means being somewhat redundant.

terminates the CASE statement. This is one of the few places in PASCAL where an END appears without a matching BEGIN. After writing a fairly lengthy program it is not uncommon to get an error message during the first run of the program, indicating an improper number of BEGINs and ENDs. In checking your program, remember that it is not required to have each END balanced by a BEGIN. If your program has CASE statements, each one will terminate with an END, which matches the CASE instead of a BEGIN.

Keep in mind that CASE statements are not restricted to situations in which the selection is based on integer values. Suppose that CURRENT-CHAR is a CHAR variable and at some point in a program we have ascertained that CURRENTCHAR represents one of the vowels. If we want to execute a different statement for each of the possible values of CURRENT-CHAR, we can write:

```
CASE CURRENTCHAR OF
    'A': statement-1;
    'E': statement-2;
    'I': statement-3;
    'O': statement-4;
    'U': statement-5
END
```

Note that this is a reasonable scheme only if we are certain that CURRENT-CHAR has one of the five indicated values. If the CASE statement is executed when the variable has any other value, the result will be unpredictable.

We now look at a specific example in which a CASE statement might be helpful. Suppose we consider a simplified version of a real estate tax computation. We will consider a situation in which the tax rate varies with the assessed value of the property, as follows:

ASSESSED VALUE	TAX RATE
< $20,000	3% of assessed value
$20,000–$29,999	4% of assessed value
$30,000–$59,999	5% of assessed value
≥ $60,000	6% of assessed value

Because we have four possible tax rates, we might want to use a CASE statement to select the appropriate rate each time. Since the assessed value could presumably be any positive number, we might at first glance think we would have to list a very large number of possibilities in the case label lists. Even if we had the patience, we could not list all the possibilities, since there is no upper bound.

A simple programming technique can solve our problem. Instead of using the assessed value as the selector expression, we will use a value computed from the assessed value. In particular, we can map 10,000 assessed values into a single integer if we divide the assessed value by 10,000. For example,

```
20000 DIV 10000     yields  2
20001 DIV 10000     yields  2
20500 DIV 10000     yields  2
29999 DIV 10000     yields  2
```

and so on. In this manner we can deal with the positive integers 1, 2, 3, . . .
instead of all the numbers in the 10,000s, 20,000s, 30,000s, . . . But we still
must be careful. Since there is no upper limit on the assessed value, there
is no upper limit on our integers. A value of $60,000 will yield 6 when divided
by 10,000, but a value of $100,000 will yield 10 when divided by 10,000.
Larger assessed values will result in still larger values for our selector expression. We will solve this problem by performing a special test before
executing the CASE statement: if the value of the selector expression exceeds 6, we will reset it to 6, since any assessed value greater than $60,000
is in the highest tax bracket.

Our CASE statement will look like this.

```
CATEGORY:=VALUE DIV 10000;
IF CATEGORY>6 THEN CATEGORY:=6;
CASE CATEGORY OF
    0,1  : RATE:=0.03;   {$0-$19,999}
    2    : RATE:=0.04;   {$20,000-$29,999}
    3,4,5: RATE:=0.05;   {$30,000-$59,999}
    6    : RATE:=0.06    {  ≥$60,000}
END;
TAX:=VALUE*RATE
```

Note that as long as the assessed value is a positive number, our CASE statement has dealt with all of the possibilities. The selector expression is guaranteed to have a value between 0 and 6.

Let's incorporate this into a complete program that will read an assessed
value (an integer) from a data card and compute the appropriate tax. The
program will continue processing data cards until a negative or zero value
is encountered for an assessed value. Note that the program will be set up to
process any positive data value; any nonpositive value will stop the program.
The program appears in Figure 5-12.

5.5 UNCONDITIONAL BRANCHING

We have seen how IF-THEN, IF-THEN-ELSE, and CASE statements
allow us to alter the execution flow of our program to execute a statement
conditionally. We will now discuss a mechanism that allows us to alter the
control flow unconditionally. An *unconditional branch* is a jump to another

```
PROGRAM TAX(INPUT, OUTPUT);
{Program to compute property tax from the assessed value}
VAR VALUE, CATEGORY: INTEGER;
              RATE, TAX: REAL;
BEGIN
READLN(VALUE);  {Input the assessed value of the property}
WHILE VALUE>0 DO  {Nonpositive value will stop program}
  BEGIN
  CATEGORY:=VALUE DIV 10000;
  IF CATEGORY>6 THEN CATEGORY:=6;  {Values ⩾ $60,000 are
                                     put into the same
                                     category}
  CASE CATEGORY OF
      0,1: RATE:=0.03;    {$0-$19,999}
        2: RATE:=0.04;    {$20,000-$29,999}
    3,4,5: RATE:=0.05;    {$30,000-$59,999}
        6: RATE:=0.06     { ⩾ $60,000}
  END;  {of CASE statement}
  TAX:=VALUE*RATE;
  WRITELN(' ASSESSED VALUE IS', VALUE,' TAX IS', TAX);
  READLN(VALUE)  {Get next data value}
  END  {of WHILE}
END.  {of program}
```

FIGURE 5-12   A Program for Computing Property Tax.

point in the program without making a test or satisfying any specific condition. The idea is fairly simple, but we will see that the need for this seldom arises in a program that has been well thought out.

There are two aspects to the mechanism of unconditional transfer of control. One is the statement that performs the actual transfer; the other is a labeling mechanism that uniquely identifies the place in the program to which the transfer is made.

5.5.1 STATEMENT LABELS

If we are interested in transferring to a particular point in a program, we must label that point with a *statement label,* an unsigned integer placed before any PASCAL statement and followed by a colon.* For example,

    150:   A:=A+1

---

* Each implementation defines a range of values for statement labels. For example, in many implementations labels can consist of up to 4 digits, so the possible labels range from 1 to 9999.

affixes the label 150 to the assignment statement. The number 150 has no real significance. We could use 3, 75, 910, or any other number that does not appear as a statement label elsewhere in the program. As a matter of programming style, however, if our program contains several labels we should select values for them so that the labels increase in magnitude as we proceed through the program. This will improve the readability of the program by making the labels easier to find.

We can attach labels to as many statements in a program as we like as long as each label is unique. However, the only reason for using a label is to indicate a place in the program to which an unconditional transfer will be made. Since we will see that the need for these unconditional transfers is rare, it follows that most programs should contain very few labels. In fact, most of the time there will be none.

There is one more aspect to defining a statement label. All statement labels must appear in a *label declaration* at the beginning of the program. This declaration appears before the VAR and CONST declarations. For example, if our program made use of 15 and 25 as statement labels, we would write:

```
LABEL  15, 25;
```

We should note that statement labels are not the same as integer constants that might appear in a CASE label list, despite the similarity in syntax. Statement labels appear in a label declaration, and they designate places to which a program can transfer; CASE labels appear in the context of a CASE statement, and they designate the values for which the associated statements will be executed. Thus, despite the apparent similarity in syntax, 10 and 15 are not being used as duplicate labels in this example.

```
LABEL 10, 15;
VAR    K: INTEGER;
       .
       .
       .
10: statement-1;
    CASE K OF
         5:  statement-2;
        10:  statement-3;
        15:  statement-4
    END;
15: statement-5
       .
       .
       .
```

IF statement to achieve the effect of a WHILE. We are actually using some primitive building blocks to construct a more interesting structure. Since the entire structure is available in the language as a WHILE statement, it makes more sense to use the structured statement. It is easier to write and provides a clearer indication of what is happening.

In a similar manner we could synthesize all the other control statements (REPEAT, FOR, IF-THEN-ELSE, CASE) using only IF-THEN and GOTO statements. This might be an interesting exercise, but it would not be a productive way to go about writing programs. Our programs will be easier to write (and read) and more apt to be correct if we utilize the higher-level structures that are built into the language. The rich set of control structures in PASCAL distinguishes it from many other programming languages.

Theoretically, we do not need the GOTO statement at all. Any PASCAL program can be written entirely without GOTO statements. Then why is it present in the language? In certain circumstances it can be awkward to achieve a certain effect without a GOTO statement. Thus, occasionally the use of a GOTO statement will allow us to write a program that is clearer than it would be without it. We need a bit of insight as to when the GOTO statement may be able to help us.

When we discussed the concept of algorithms, we introduced a number of constructs that served as convenient building blocks. We have seen that these constructs have direct analogs in our programming language, and it is convenient to think in terms of these constructs—WHILE, REPEAT, FOR, and so on—when we write computer programs. However, on rare occasions it happens that the natural structure of our algorithm has to be broken, usually to deal with some type of exceptional condition. These breaks in the overall algorithmic structure can often be handled quite naturally with GOTO statements.

It is not possible to catalog all of the situations in which a GOTO statement might properly be used, except to say that they almost always involve a special circumstance of one sort or another and usually involve a forward jump within the program. (A backward jump can almost always be better expressed by one of the structured statements.) For example, in the process of doing a lengthy calculation, we might find that an unacceptable intermediate result has occurred (e.g., a negative value where one was not permitted). This might make it meaningless to continue with the rest of the computation. It would be appropriate to print an error message and jump to the end of the program. Of course, if this action can be conveniently incorporated into the algorithm with a structured statement (e.g., IF-THEN-ELSE), it would make sense to do so. Sometimes, however, it is a bit awkward to use a structured statement to deal with this situation.

As a concrete example of what we are describing, let us look again at the issue of data verification. In Figure 5-9 we showed how an IF-THEN-ELSE can be used to handle this. The test would be constructed to look for invalid we are writing a loop that counts characters, it should count *all* the characters we are interested in. It is bad policy to design a loop that does most of the work followed by a separate statement that does the rest. Since we want all the counting to be done in the loop, we might be initially tempted to use a GOTO to leave the loop after the period has been counted.

```
COUNT := 0;
READ(CURRENTCHAR);
WHILE NOT EOLN DO
  BEGIN
  COUNT:= COUNT + 1;
  IF CURRENTCHAR = PERIOD THEN GOTO 15;
  READ(CURRENTCHAR)
  END;
15:
```

Note that we have altered the loop test so that it checks only for end of line. The other condition has been embedded in the loop. (If we had not made this alteration we would obtain the wrong answer when a period is the first character read. The count would be 0 instead of 1.)

The above example, however, is not a desirable use of the GOTO statement. If the loop is large we may not be able to see where the GOTO is taking us. More important, the intent of the loop is not clearly expressed by the boolean condition in the WHILE statement.

There is a much better way to handle the problem of an early exit from a loop. We can use a boolean variable in the loop expression to help control the execution of the loop. A conditional statement inside the loop can be used to set this variable to the appropriate value so that the loop is exited after the terminating condition occurs. In our example we might use a boolean variable called ENDOFSENTENCE, which is set true when a period is encountered. We can then write our loop as follows.

```
COUNT:= 0; ENDOFSENTENCE:= FALSE;
READ(CURRENTCHAR);
WHILE (NOT ENDOFSENTENCE) AND (NOT EOLN) DO
  BEGIN
  COUNT:=COUNT+1;
  IF CURRENTCHAR=PERIOD
    THEN   ENDOFSENTENCE:= TRUE
    ELSE   READ(CURRENTCHAR)
  END
```

In this loop it is clear that there are two distinct termination conditions. Note that the use of a suggestive name for the boolean variable greatly enhances the readability of the code.

The programming technique of using a boolean variable to terminate a loop in place of jumping out using a GOTO is a good one to become familiar with. It is another instance in which avoiding a GOTO statement can lead to a program that is much more readable.

Keep in mind that a GOTO statement will be helpful in a relatively small number of cases. We should always try to conceive our programs in terms of higher-level control constructs and use the GOTO only when the natural flow of the program must be broken. If you find yourself writing a PASCAL program that contains a large number of GOTO statements, you should stop and think. You have probably not thought out the program carefully enough. The excessive use of GOTO statements will result in a program that is difficult to comprehend.

STYLE CLINIC 5-6

The GOTO Controversy

You may be interested to know that this is an area of debate among computer scientists. The "GOTO controversy" has contributed to the development of an important movement called *structured programming*. Although structured programming does not yet have a fixed definition, one of its most important concerns is for the types of control statements needed in a programming language and the relationship between certain control structures and a program's clarity. As in any new movement, there are proponents of extreme positions. In the area of structured programming, one of these extreme positions is that the inclusion of *any* unconditional branch in a program is inherently bad. Our position is not related to the worth of a statement itself, but to the overall clarity of the resulting program. If a particular situation lends itself naturally to an unconditional branch, use it.

5.6 CASE STUDY

In this section we will go through the step by step development of a complete program to solve a real problem. The problem is to find the root of an equation. Although there are fairly sophisticated mathematical techniques that can be used, we will use a simple, straightforward approach. This will allow us to focus on the actual development of the program without getting distracted by the complexity of the mathematics. For relatively simple, well-behaved equations our technique will do a fairly good job, although there are classes of equations for which this simple technique will not work.

Our first step is to analyze the problem and decide on a basic approach for a solution. If we have an equation of one variable we can use the notation $f(x)$ to represent our equation. $f(x)$ could be $x^2 - 4$ or $\sqrt{x/(x-1)} - 3x$ or any other equation that involves a single variable named x. We seek a value of x for which f(x)=0; that is what we mean when we speak of the root of an equation. In graphical terms we might view the situation like this.

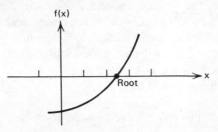

The root of the equation will be the point at which the graph of the equation crosses the x-axis. The graph suggests a fairly obvious technique for finding the root.

ALGORITHM FOR FINDING THE ROOT OF AN EQUATION

Beginning at some arbitrary starting point, we evaluate f(x) at a series of points that are a distance Δ apart. When we find that the sign of f(x) has changed from one evaluation to the next (i.e., the value at x compared with the value at x + Δ), we know that we have passed a root.

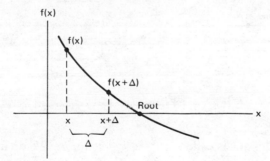

We have not passed the root.

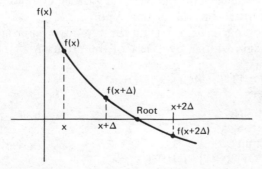

We have passed the root.

Once we have passed the root we can turn around and evaluate f(x) again, but moving in the opposite direction and with a sequence of points obtained by using a smaller Δ. We can continue this procedure, turning around each time we pass the root and evaluating with a finer and finer Δ, until we have used as small a Δ as we wish (that is |Δ| < accuracy desired). This technique can get us as close as we like to the root as long as our function is reasonably well-behaved. Our accuracy will be limited only by the limitation on significant digits imposed by our computer and the accumulation of round-off errors as we perform the computations.

In general our solution will proceed in the following way.

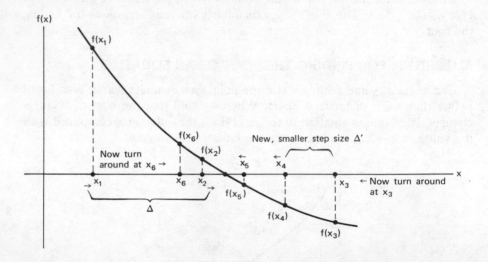

This type of technique is called an *iterative solution*. We do not get an exact answer but we proceed closer and closer to the answer and stop when we feel we have a sufficient level of accuracy. Most computer techniques for solving numerical problems are of this type.

We will develop our program using the top-down approach described in Chapter 2. We begin with an overview of the program.

ALGORITHM ROOTFINDER
START
    Initialize
    Getroot
    Output
END OF ROOTFINDER

We now look at each component of the algorithm and develop a representation in terms of PASCAL constructs and algorithmic primitives without concern about precise syntax.

The INITIALIZE section will read and validate the data values and perform an evaluation of the function at the starting point.

```
ALGORITHM INITIALIZE
START
   Read values for starting point, step size, accuracy desired
   If the data is invalid
      Then┌Write "Error in data"
           └Stop
      Else┌Set X to starting point
          └Evaluate the function at the starting point
END OF INITIALIZE
```

Our first attempt to sketch the GETROOT program segment might be:

```
ALGORITHM GETROOT
START
   While desired accuracy not yet obtained do
      ┌Take a step along the x-axis
      │PASSROOT   {Keep stepping until the root is passed}
      └Change to smaller step size, in opposite direction
END OF GETROOT
```

Our GETROOT algorithm invokes another algorithm, PASSROOT, which steps along the x-axis and evaluates the function at a series of points until the sign of the function has changed.

```
ALGORITHM PASSROOT
START
   While OLDVALUE and NEWVALUE have the same sign do
      ┌Set OLDVALUE to NEWVALUE
      │Set X to X + Δ
      └Set NEWVALUE to the value of the function at X
END OF PASSROOT
```

This would be acceptable if we were certain that we would always pass a root. But consider the following situation.

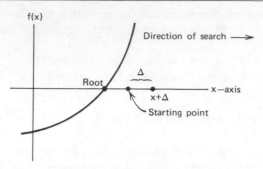

In this example we are starting at a point on the x-axis that is past the root, and each step that we take moves us further away from the root. Our PASSROOT algorithm will never terminate. To guard against this problem, we will ask the user of our program to specify an upper bound for our "walk" along the x-axis. Our PASSROOT algorithm will then terminate if we ever reach this upper bound. This will indicate to the user that there is no root of the function in that particular region of the x-axis. Our PASSROOT algorithm would look like this.

```
ALGORITHM PASSROOT
START
{OLDVALUE and NEWVALUE represent evaluations of f at
    different points}
    While OLDVALUE and NEWVALUE have the same sign do
        Set OLDVALUE to NEWVALUE
        Set X to X + Δ
        If X>UPPERBOUND
            Then  Write "Can't Find Root"
                  Stop
            Else  Set NEWVAL to F(X)
END OF PASSROOT
```

(We must remember to modify INITIALIZE, since there is now an additional variable to be read.) Now if there is not a root within the region of the x-axis that we are considering, the algorithm will print a message and stop. We might then want to run our program again starting at a different region of the x-axis.

Note that we have left unspecified what our function is. We have simply assigned F(X) to a variable when we wish to have the function evaluated. We will continue to use this notation throughout our solution. Everywhere that F(X) occurs, you can just substitute a particular function of X. In Chapter 8 we will discuss a technique that can be used to make this case study general enough to apply to any function at all without modification to the program itself.

Now we can represent GETROOT in a more detailed form by incorporating our latest version of PASSROOT and changing some of our English-like statements to a more precise notation.

> ALGORITHM GETROOT
> START
>   While desired accuracy not yet obtained do   {Take a step}
>   Set OLDVALUE to NEWVALUE
>   Set X to X + Δ {Δ is the step size}
>   Set NEWVALUE to F(X)
>   {Begin PASSROOT}
>   While OLDVALUE and NEWVALUE have the same sign do
>   Set OLDVALUE to NEWVALUE
>   Set X to X+Δ
>   IF X>UPPERBOUND
>   Then   Write "Can't Find Root"
>   Stop
>   Else   Set NEWVALUE to F(X)
>   {End of PASSROOT}
>   Set Δ to $-$(SCALEFACTOR * Δ)
>   {0 < SCALEFACTOR < 1}
> END OF GETROOT

Note that each time we pass the root we reduce the value of Δ so that we take smaller steps and we change the sign of Δ so that we move in the opposite direction.

    Now we need to describe the OUTPUT module. GETROOT will determine that the root exists within a certain interval. We will take the middle of the interval as the root and print the result.

> ALGORITHM OUTPUT
> START
>   Set ROOT to X $-$ (Δ/2)
>   Write ROOT
> END OF OUTPUT

    We can now put the pieces together to form a complete ROOTFINDER algorithm (Figure 5-14).

    We are now in a position to write our PASCAL program. Our algorithmic notation is actually so close to PASCAL that this will be relatively straightforward. Our only concerns will be the technical details of PASCAL syntax. We will have to select legitimate names for all our variables (Δ is not acceptable as a PASCAL identifier), and we will have to provide suitable declarations for all of our identifiers.

    We can now clearly see the advantage of working with an algorithmic

```
ALGORITHM ROOTFINDER
START
{Initialize}
   Read values for starting point, upper bound, Δ, accuracy
      desired
   If data invalid
      Then Write "Error in data"
            Stop
   Set X to the starting point
   Set NEWVALUE to F(X)
   {Getroot}
   While desired accuracy not yet obtained do   {Take a step}
         Set OLDVALUE to NEWVALUE
         Set X to X + Δ
         Set NEWVALUE to F(X)
         {Passroot}
         While OLDVALUE and NEWVALUE have the same sign
         do
             Set OLDVALUE to NEWVALUE
             Set X to X + Δ
             If X>UPPERBOUND
                Then  Write "Can't Find Root"
                      Stop
                Else    Set NEWVALUE to F(X)
         {End of Passroot}
         Set Δ to −(SCALEFACTOR * Δ)   {0 < SCALEFACTOR
             < 1}
   {End of Getroot}
   {Output}
   Set ROOT to X − (Δ/2)
   Write ROOT
   {End of output}
END OF ROOTFINDER
```
FIGURE 5-14 The Rootfinder Algorithm.

notation before writing the program in PASCAL. The details associated with a programming language need not concern us during the algorithm development phase. We do not want to be distracted by the details of semicolons, reserved identifiers, type declarations, and so on while we are working at this higher level. Only when we are generally satisfied with the algorithmic solution should we become involved with the constraints imposed by a particular programming language.

In Figure 5-15 we have written a complete program [except for substituting an actual formula for F(X)], but we are not done. We should check out our program for a few well-chosen test cases to see if it will perform correctly. Unfortunately, in all but the most trivial programs, testing will not guarantee that our program is perfect. We can find out if our program performs properly for a few test cases, but that will not usually insure that the program will work in all cases. In general, we will want to run a number of test cases, checking out the program for data values that are reasonable and unreasonable. Most of these tests can be made by simply letting the computer execute the program, but it is usually a good idea to test at least one case by *hand-simulating* the program. This can often uncover bugs in the program before it has even been prepared for execution, when corrections will be easier to make.

We will now hand-simulate one test case, using "reasonable" data values. This should provide some assurance that at least the basic concept underlying the program is valid. The next chapter will discuss more completely the topic of testing programs.

The key to hand-simulating a program is good organization. You should start with several clean sheets of paper (trying to work in an unused corner of some scrap paper can be disastrous!) and should have a scratch pad and an electronic calculator for computing intermediate results. It is important to start at the beginning of the program and faithfully carry out the steps exactly as they appear. It is all too easy to obtain false conclusions by doing several steps at a time because you "know what has to be done." What often happens is that you carry out the instructions that you were thinking about when you wrote the program, but not the actual instructions that you wrote down.

We present below the sequence of intermediate values obtained when the ROOTFINDER program was hand-simulated for a particular test case. We used an electronic calculator to compute values. The number of significant figures is small, because we intended only to verify the reasonableness of the program and not obtain a very precise answer—we will let the computer do that.

```
PROGRAM ROOTFINDER(INPUT, OUTPUT);
{A program to find a root of an equation using a simple iterative
  technique}
LABEL 100;   {For program termination}
CONST SCALEFACTOR=0.1;
VAR    OLDVAL, NEWVAL, DELTA, EPSILON,
       X, XSTART, XFINAL, ROOT, OLDDELTA  :   REAL;
BEGIN
{The data input section}
READLN(XSTART, XFINAL, DELTA, EPSILON);
WRITELN(' STARTING POINT=', XSTART, ' LIMIT POINT=', XFINAL,
```

```
                        ' STEP SIZE=', DELTA, ' DESIRED ACCURACY=',
                        EPSILON);
{Check for invalid data}
IF (XSTART>XFINAL) OR (DELTA>XFINAL−XSTART) OR
    (EPSILON>DELTA)
    THEN WRITELN(' ERROR IN INPUT DATA—CANNOT PROCESS')
    ELSE BEGIN   {Data are OK—do the computation}
            X:=XSTART; NEWVAL:=F(X);  {Replace F(X) with an
                                        actual function}
        WHILE ABS(DELTA)>=EPSILON DO  {Desired accuracy
                                        not yet obtained}
        BEGIN
        OLDVAL:=NEWVAL;
        X:=X+DELTA; NEWVAL:=F(X);  {Replace F(X) with an
                                        actual function}
        WHILE (OLDVAL*NEWVAL)>0.0 DO
            BEGIN  {Look for a root}
            OLDVAL:=NEWVAL;
            X:=X+DELTA;
            IF X>XFINAL
                THEN BEGIN
                        WRITELN(' CANNOT FIND ROOT IN THIS
                                INTERVAL');
                        GOTO 100   {Skip rest of program}
                        END
                ELSE NEWVAL:=F(X)   {Replace F(X) with an
                                    actual function}
            END;  {While signs are the same}
        {Have passed a root. Now try smaller step-size in
            opposite direction}
        OLDDELTA:=DELTA;
        DELTA:= −DELTA*SCALEFACTOR
        END;   {While accuracy not obtained}
        {Have localized root to the interval X, X+DELTA. We want
            to take the middle of this interval as the root. To accom-
            plish this we must restore DELTA to the value it had when
            the last step was taken}
        DELTA:=OLDDELTA;
        ROOT:= X−(DELTA/2.0);
        WRITELN(' THERE IS A ROOT AT', ROOT)
        END;  {Of computation}
100:  {Transfer here if root is not in the interval}
END.
```

FIGURE 5-15   The Rootfinder Program.

TEST OF ROOTFINDER

$F(X) = X^2 - 3.5$ (*Note*. Roots are $\approx \pm 1.871$)

XSTART : 0.0   (starting point)
XFINAL : 5.0   (upper bound)
DELTA   : 1.0   (initial step size)
EPSILON: 0.005 (desired accuracy)

Start
    Read data; Write data
    Data check out OK

DELTA	X	OLDVAL	NEWVAL	
1.0	0.0		−3.5	
	1.0	−3.5	−2.5	
	2.0	−2.5	0.5	Sign change
−0.1	1.9	0.5	0.11	
	1.8	0.11	−0.26	Sign change
0.01	1.81	0.26	−0.22	
	1.82	−0.22	−0.19	
	1.83	−0.19	−0.15	
	1.84	−0.15	−0.11	
	1.85	−0.11	−0.08	
	1.86	0.08	−0.04	
	1.87	−0.04	−0.003	
	1.88	−0.003	0.03	Sign change
−0.001				

    ABS(DELTA) is now less than EPSILON, so the iteration
      terminates

    Restore DELTA: DELTA:=OLDDELTA
                     DELTA is now 0.01

    Pinpoint ROOT: ROOT:= 1.88 − (0.01/2.0)
                     ROOT:= 1.875

Note that our answer, 1.875, differs from the true value, 1.871, by 0.004;
this is within the requested tolerance of 0.005 (the value of EPSILON).

You will probably find it worthwhile to hand-simulate ROOTFINDER with
a different set of data to gain experience with the technique.

EXERCISES

*1. For each of the problems listed below, write a PASCAL fragment first using a WHILE and then a REPEAT.

  a. Read in characters from a card until the occurrence of a '*' or EOLN.
  b. Read in integers from a card. Count the number of positive and negative values. Stop when you encounter a value of 0.
  c. Find the greatest integer whose square is less than 142,619.

2. Explain why it is difficult to do the exercises in problem 1 using a FOR statement.

*3. The following program fragment uses GOTO statements needlessly; a structured statement would be much clearer. Rewrite this fragment using a FOR statement.

```
    CURRENTVALUE:= 150; GOTO 20;
10: CURRENTVALUE:= CURRENTVALUE − 1;
20:    S₁;
    IF CURRENTVALUE > 15 THEN GOTO 10
```

4. Write a complete PASCAL program to find all integer solutions to the equation

$$3X + 2Y - 7Z = 5$$

for values of X, Y, and Z in the range 0 to 100.

*5. Let V1 and V2 represent boolean variables and let S1, S2, and S3 represent PASCAL statements. Suppose that one of the statements is to be executed based on the values of the boolean variables, as follows.

		V2	
		T	F
V1	T	S1	S2
	F	S3	S3

Set up a conditional statement to achieve this effect.

6. Write a complete PASCAL program to compute the average of all legal examination scores. A legal score is one in the range 0 to 150. Your program should read scores until an end-of-file condition occurs and then produce as output:

a. The average of all legal scores.
b. The number of legal scores.
c. The number of illegal scores.

7. The Fibonacci series is defined as

$$N_1 = 1, \; N_2 = 1$$
$$N_{i+2} = N_{i+1} + N_i \qquad i = 1,2,3 \ldots$$

Thus, the first seven Fibonacci numbers are

1, 1, 2, 3, 5, 8, 13

Write a program fragment to compute and print the first K Fibonacci numbers, where K is read from a data card.

*8. Temperatures on the Celsius (or centigrade) scale are related to those on the Fahrenheit scale by the formula

$$C = \frac{5}{9}\,(F - 32)$$

Write a complete program that prints the Celsius equivalent of Fahrenheit temperatures from -40 to 120 degrees.

9. Write a program that reads text and produces encoded text by replacing each character with the character that occurs five positions "later" in the character set. (Thus, considering the typical ordering for alphabetic characters, 'A' would be replaced by 'F', 'B' by 'G', and so on.) This replacement should "wrap-around" the end of the character set so that there is a well-defined replacement for each character. (That is, the character that occurs at the end of the character set should be replaced by the character in the fifth position. You will have to know how large the character set is on your computer.) Read text and print the encoded form until an end-of-file condition occurs.

10. Write a complete program that computes the minimum number of coins and bills needed to make change for a particular purchase. The cost of the item and the amount tendered should be read as data values. Your program should indicate how many coins and bills of each denomination are needed for change.
Make use of these denominations:

Coins: 1¢, 5¢, 10¢, 25¢
Bills: $1, $5, $10

11. Write a program to determine the frequency of each vowel in some English language text. The input will consist of sentences running over a number of lines. The end of the text is indicated by the special symbol '*'.

   The output of the program should be the input text and the percentage of characters that were equal to 'A', 'E', 'I', 'O', 'U'. Blanks should not be treated as characters and should not be included in the total.

*12. The area of a circle whose radius is 1 is π, and the area of a square that just contains the circle is 4. Therefore, if a large number of points are chosen randomly in the square, the fraction of those points that fall within the circle will be approximately $\pi/4$. Assuming the existence of a real-valued function called RANDOM that returns a random number between 0 and 1, write a program to compute an approximation to π.

*13. Assuming RANDOM is a real-valued function that returns a random number between 0 and 1, write a program that approximates the probabilities for rolling the values 2 to 12 with two dice. Use a CASE statement in the program.

14. Write a PASCAL program to process the weekly payroll of the Worldwide Widget Company. For each employee of WWC your program will compute the gross pay, deductions, and net pay. This information is to be clearly printed in the output along with certain summary information for the entire payroll.

   Each week WWC punches a data card for each employee that includes the following information.

Social security number	(9 digits)
Hourly pay rate	(xx.xx)
Number of exemptions	(0 to 19)
Health insurance code	(1, 2, 3, or 4)
Hours worked	(xx.x)

   Using this information, your program should carry out the following computations.

   a. *Gross pay.* Regular pay for the first 40 hours and time-and-a-half beyond that up to a limit of 54 hours in any given week.

   b. *Deductions.*

   Let G represent gross pay and T taxable pay
   Let E represent number of exemptions
   i. Federal income tax withholding is defined as

Let $T = G - \$14.00*E - \$11.00$
Withholding $= T*(0.14 + 2.3\text{x}10^{-4}*T)$

  ii. State income tax withholding
      State withholding is defined as 31% of the
      amount withheld for federal income tax.
 iii. Social security tax
      $16.70 or (7.7% of G) whichever is smaller.
  iv. Health Insurance
      1—No coverage
      2—Employee coverage ($2 per week)
      3—Family coverage ($7.50 per week)
      4—Major medical coverage ($13 per week)

c. *Net pay.*   Gross pay less all deductions.

For each employee your program should produce an output report in
a legible format with each item clearly labeled.

After the last employee has been processed, your program should
print a summary report that includes the number of employees
processed, total gross pay, total deductions of each type, and total
net pay.

Your program must be capable of processing an arbitrary number
of data cards and should perform reasonable operations for all data
sets regardless of how meaningless they are. (For example, what if
deductions exceed gross pay? What if taxable pay is negative? Be careful to check those and similar situations and decide the appropriate
action.)

15. Assume that another program has already computed the mean, M,
    and standard deviation, σ, on a homework assignment for our class.
    We now wish to write a program that assigns letter grades to the indi-
    vidual homework scores. The input to this program will be M and σ
    followed by student grade cards containing an identification number
    (integer) and a score, S. The rules for assigning letter grades are as
    follows.

IF S IS GREATER THAN	BUT NO MORE THAN	LETTER GRADE
$M + \frac{3}{2}\sigma$	100	A
$M + \sigma/2$	$M + \frac{3}{2}\sigma$	B
$M - \sigma/2$	$M + \sigma/2$	C
$M - \frac{3}{2}\sigma$	$M - \sigma/2$	D
0	$M - \frac{3}{2}\sigma$	F

For each student print out the identification number, examination score, and letter grade. Continue until an end-of-file condition exists. (What should be done for a student whose homework score is outside the range 0 to 100?) When you are all done, print out the number of students who received each of the five possible grades.

16. Another algorithm for root finding is called the "secant method." It is based on having two points on opposite sides of the root and drawing a line connecting them. If the formula is "well behaved," the point where that line crosses the axis will be closer to the root than either of the original ones.

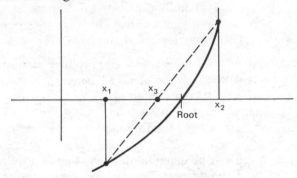

In the above figure, the new point is x_3. We now discard the old point which lies on the same side of the root as the new point—in this case x_1. We would now repeat the process using points x_2 and x_3 above. The formula for a new point x_3 given old points x_1 and x_2 is:

$$x_3 = \frac{x_2 f(x_1) - x_1 f(x_2)}{f(x_1) - f(x_2)}$$

a. Develop an algorithm to find roots of aribtrary equations using the secant method. Make any necessary assumptions about points not discussed in this problem statement (e.g., the number of roots to find, how to handle error conditions, or the specific output format).

b. Write a complete PASCAL program for this problem.

c. Test the program with the same equation used in the ROOT-FINDER case study—$x^2 - 3.5$. Set $x_1 = 0$, $x_2 = 5$ and accuracy = 0.001. Compare the number of iterations needed to get a solution by both methods. If we assume that each iteration required 0.0005 seconds of machine time (probably a good ballpark figure) compute the actual time savings of one method over the other. Compare this with the approximate total time it took you to write this program. If machine time costs $10 per minute and a programmer costs $10 per hour, how much time would a programmer have to spend to be equivalent in cost to the machine time savings gained with this new method?

CHAPTER 6

RUNNING, DEBUGGING, AND TESTING PROGRAMS

6.1 INTRODUCTION

At the end of Chapter 4 we introduced some simple, straight-line PASCAL programs, and we discussed how to prepare programs for computer processing. In Chapter 5 we added a sufficient number of PASCAL statement types to be able to write relatively interesting and nontrivial programs such as the case study on root finding.

You should now have sufficient knowledge of both algorithm development and the PASCAL language to attempt to solve some interesting problems on your own using these tools. This chapter will discuss the important aspects of programming that come into view after the program is written: interpreting error messages, debugging, testing, and maintaining programs.

Our discussion will be general enough to apply to any computer system. However, there are certain details (e.g., the format of error messages and the availability of debugging aids) that differ from one system to another, so you will probably want to obtain the specific information that applies to your particular computer system.

6.2 PROCESSING THE PROGRAM

One of the nice features of programming in a high-level language such as PASCAL is that it can be done with almost a total lack of understanding of what a computer is and how it actually operates. Machine-dependent details such as maximum integer size and internal character codes are few in number and can be learned easily without probing deeply into computer design. This is as it should be. There is no reason why someone who wants to write a computer program should have to understand the electronic circuitry of a computer.

Nevertheless, you will find it helpful to know something about what the computer is doing with your program. Our goal in this section is to look at the processing of a program from a macroscopic, not a microscopic, point of view. We will outline the general sequence of events that takes place when the computer begins to process your program. This knowledge can be particularly helpful to you as you try to understand error messages that the computer produces.

The PASCAL language or, for that matter, any of the high-level languages mentioned in Chapter 1, cannot be directly understood by any computer. That is, no known computer can execute the commands of those languages directly. Programmers write in these high-level languages because they are convenient. Their English-like words, their natural algebraic notation, and their use of the familiar decimal numbering system are helpful to the programmer. However, a program in one of the high-level languages, called a *source program,* must be translated into an equivalent program in the internal machine language of the computer. That program is called the *object program.* The process of translating a source program in some high-level language into an equivalent object program in machine language is called *compilation.* Compilation is done by a computer program called, naturally enough, a compiler. The input to the compiler program is a program (a source program) and the output of the compiler is another program (the object program) and a *program listing.* The program listing is simply a printed representation of the program that was presented to the compiler for translation. This listing may also include error messages and other information from the compiler about the translation process. Although using one program (the source) as data for another program (the compiler) to produce still another program as output (the object program) may seem strange, it is inherently no different from using alphanumeric data as input for an "ordinary" program to produce alphanumeric results.

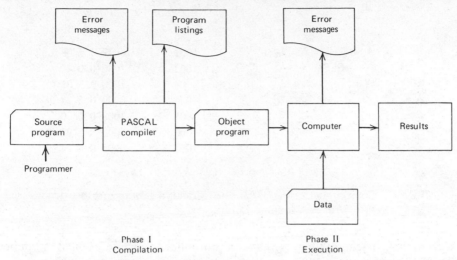

FIGURE 6-1 Overall Program Execution.

After compilation we begin the second phase of running a program on the computer: *execution*. During this step, the computer will sequentially execute the machine language commands contained in the object program. Any input data requested by the object program will now be read and any output produced will be printed. Figure 6-1 summarizes how a program is executed.

You might wonder why we bother going through the compilation phase at all. If we were to write directly in machine language, the computer could execute the program directly without wasting time performing a translation. The reason this is never done is quite obvious if one simply looks at a typical machine language translation of a PASCAL statement. The machine language used for this example is MIX*, which is frequently used to introduce students to topics in computer organization, but our conclusion would be the same regardless of the machine language we had chosen.

The example in Figure 6-2 should make it obvious that machine languages are completely devoid of any useful user-oriented features that are available in high-level languages like PASCAL. There are no symbolic variable names, there is no use of algebraic notation, and there are no high-level control statements (e.g., WHILE or CASE). There are not even any words to help us understand what is going on. The enormous difficulty of writing machine language programs makes it worthwhile to spend a few extra

---

* D. E. Knuth. *MIX: The Design of a Typical Computer and its Assembly Language, with Programming Problems and a Glossary of Basic Computer Terminology*, Addison-Wesley, 1970.

	Location	*Contents*
	1000	00001
IF A>0 THEN A:=A+1	1001	0999 0 5 08
ELSE A:=A−1	1002	1006 0 0 40
	1003	1000 0 5 01
	1004	0999 0 5 24
	1005	1008 0 0 39
	1006	1000 0 5 02
	1007	0999 0 5 24

(*a*)   (*b*)

FIGURE 6-2   Comparison of PASCAL and Machine Language Instructions. (*a*) PASCAL. (*b*) Machine Language.

seconds of machine time to have a compiler translate typical student PASCAL programs into the machine language of a particular computer.

In fact, we concern ourselves with the object program only if we have developed a program that will be run very often. It is foolish to translate such a program every time we wish to execute it, because the wasted time will eventually become significant. To avoid waste, we usually translate the program once and store the object program itself in a program library. When we wish to run the program, we may execute it directly without using the compiler to translate it. This use of an object program also explains why the concept of program generality is so important. In the previous chapter we talked about how to set up programs that handle, without being modified, variations in the original problem. We can now see why this is so important. In the "real world," we frequently do not have direct access to the PASCAL source program. We may be limited to working with the translated version that is stored in the program library. This version can be modified only with the greatest of difficulty.

Since student programs (once working) are rarely run more than once or twice, the need to store the object program is rare, and this feature may not be frequently used or even allowed. In most student programming environments, the computer proceeds directly from compilation to execution without any intermediate commands. You usually will be unaware of the existence of these two distinct phases in the running of your program.

6.3 DEBUGGING

The process of *debugging* involves discovering, locating, and correcting all errors that cause a program to produce either incorrect results or no results at all. A beginning programmer usually does not realize (but quickly becomes aware) that program debugging can be the single most time-

consuming phase in the overall program development process. Studies on
the development of large programming systems indicate that it is not uncommon for 50 to 75% of the overall programming time to be spent on finding and correcting errors. This percentage is probably accurate for student
jobs as well.

You should not feel that your job is almost done when you have written
the program and entered it into the machine. Instead, you have just begun.
In extreme cases, programs have been literally scrapped because they could
not effectively or economically be corrected. Sometimes *bugs* (i.e., programming errors) become so deeply ingrained in programs that programmers, in frustration, give up on ever being able to find the errors and,
instead, resort to issuing instructions on how to get around the problems!
These are the kinds of horrible habits and "almost-working" programs that
you should learn to avoid from the very beginning.

There are many reasons debugging can consume so much time, but two
are of primary importance. First, it should be obvious that the ease of finding
errors in a program is directly related to the clarity and lucidity of the structure of that program. Programs with complex, intricate, and "jumpy" logic
are much more difficult to work with and to debug. To understand what we
mean, see how much time it takes you to find and fix the following program
fragment, which was supposed to print out the largest of three unequal data
values X, Y, Z but which contains a bug.

```
       IF X>Y THEN GOTO 1;
       IF Y>Z THEN GOTO 5;
       GOTO 2;
   1:  IF X>Z THEN GOTO 2;
       GOTO 4;
   5:  WRITE(Y);
       GOTO 3;
   2:  WRITE(X);
       GOTO 3;
   4:  WRITE(Z);
   3:      remainder of the program
```

(In case you have not spotted it, the error is in the third line.) Program segments like the one above greatly complicate debugging. Unfortunately, programs like this have, in the past, been all too common.

When these programs are large (hundreds of thousands of lines long), it
becomes almost impossible to follow the flow of control through the program. The many GOTO statements create too many logical paths for the
mind to keep track of. It is much easier to find errors when structured statements (and indentation) delineate the control paths. For example, consider
the same program segment (with the same error) coded with IF-THEN-
ELSE.

```
IF X>Y THEN
   BEGIN
   IF X>Z THEN
      WRITE(X)
   ELSE
      WRITE(Z)
   END
ELSE
   BEGIN
   IF Y>Z THEN
      WRITE(Y)
   ELSE
      WRITE(X)
   END;
remainder of program
```

It is easier to find the error because it is easier to see the conditions that had to be met in order to reach a particular section of the program.

The second main reason that programmers encounter difficulty during debugging is that, unfortunately, debugging has usually not been taught with the same systematic approach that has characterized the teaching of algorithms and coding. These latter subjects are often presented quite formally with a great deal of organization, rules, and well thought out examples. However, debugging has been treated more as an ad hoc subject—almost as black magic. Students have rarely had formal instruction about what to do when their programs fail without giving error messages or other clues about what is wrong. This has usually led to a great deal of confusion, wasted time, frustration and, ultimately, incorrect and undebugged programs. This is totally unacceptable since in most application areas a partially debugged program is no better (and sometimes worse) than no program at all.

Our objective is to classify the approaches to debugging so that, when the inevitable errors do occur, you will have some logical, organized method for finding their causes—other than scratching your head and heading for the instructor's office.

STYLE CLINIC 6-1

Clear Programs and Software Engineering

It is a fundamental principle of debugging that the single most useful debugging aid is a well-written, well-organized, well-structured program. This fact is the reason for our overriding concern for teaching good programming habits and style. It is also one of the reasons for the recent increase of interest in languages like PASCAL that allow clear and natural expression of program structure. And, finally, it is the reason for the rapid growth of *software engineering,* a new area of computer science that deals with the tools and techniques needed for the efficient and systematic implementation of correct programs.

6.3.1 SYNTAX ERRORS

Syntax errors are among the most common errors made in programming and the easiest to find and correct. A *syntax error* is simply any violation of the grammatical rules of the language. For example, the PASCAL syntax for the IF-THEN-ELSE construct is:

IF boolean expression THEN statement ELSE statement

All statements of this type must adhere to this format without exception. Therefore, all of the following violate a syntactic rule of PASCAL (assume A and B are boolean values and X is real).

IF A AND B THEN WRITE(A);
    ELSE WRITE(B)

{Misplaced semicolon}

IF A AND B THEN WRITE(A); WRITE(B)
    ELSE WRITE(A)

{Two statements placed where only one should be}

IF X+1.3 THEN WRITE(X)
    ELSE WRITE(Y)

{A real expression placed where a boolean expression should be}

Syntax errors are easier to correct than most other kinds, because they usually produce an error message that gives a clue about what is wrong with that statement. These error messages are produced by the PASCAL compiler while it is attempting to translate a PASCAL program into an object program. Any grammatical mistake will cause problems when the translation is performed. The compiler will usually produce a message indicating where the mistake is and what PASCAL believed the mistake to be.

Figure 6-3 is a listing of a PASCAL program that contains numerous syntactic (as well as other) errors. This example shows the way in which errors are printed in a particular PASCAL system. You may be using a system that prints error messages in a different form, but the information provided should be comparable.

```
00100 PROGRAM AVERAGE(INPUT,OUTPUT);
00110 CONST   LOWRANGE=0;
00120          HIGHRANGE=100;
00130 VAR VALUE,NUMBER,SUM,AVG,ERROR: INTEGER;
00140 {    This program computes the sum of examination scores
00150      in the range 0 to 100. The number of exams is contained
00160      on the first card}
00170 BEGIN
00180    READLN(NUMBER);
00190    SUM:=0; WRITELN(NUMBER,' DATA SETS'); ERROR:=0;
00200    FOR I:=1,NUMBER DO
00210      READLN(VAL);
00220      IF VAL >=LOWRANGE AND VAL <= HIGHRANGE
00230         THEN SUM := SUM + VAL;
00240         ELSE ERROR := ERROR + 1
00250      END;  { The for loop }
00260    AVG := SUM DIV NUMBER - ERROR;
00270    WRITELN(' AVERAGE OF THE SCORES IS ',AVG)
00280 END.
READY
RUN
```

⎫
⎬ Program
⎭ listing

```
000041 00200   FOR I:=1,NUMBER DO
******                 ↑104,155↑6        ↑55
000042 00210   READLN(VAL);
******                          ↑104
000046 00220     IF VAL >=LOWRANGE AND VAL <= HIGHRANGE
******            ↑104                        ↑104↑59
000046 00230        THEN SUM := SUM + VAL;
******                                  ↑104
000046 00240        ELSE ERROR := ERROR + 1
******                 ↑6
000046 00250     END;  { The for loop }
******             ↑6
****** EOF ENCOUNTERED
```

⎫
⎬ Syntax
⎭ errors

COMPILER ERROR MESSAGES:

```
    6:  ILLEGAL SYMBOL
   55:  "TO" OR "DOWNTO" EXPECTED
   59:  ERROR IN VARIABLE
  104:  IDENTIFIER NOT DECLARED
  155:  CONTROL VARIABLE MUST NOT BE FORMAL
```

⎫
⎬ Explanation
⎬ of error
⎭ codes

FIGURE 6-3 Sample PASCAL Syntactic Error Messages.

Figure 6-3 highlights almost all the major points that you should be aware of when working with syntactic error messages.

1. Some of the error messages produced are quite clear and quite explicit as to the nature of the mistake. For example, on line 200 of the program, PASCAL gives error message 55—"TO" OR "DOWNTO" EXPECTED. A quick glance at the FOR loop shows that we did not adhere to the correct syntax.

> FOR control variable:=initial value [TO/DOWNTO] final value DO statement

On line 220 we get the error message "IDENTIFIER NOT DE-CLARED", with the pointer pointing at the variable VAL. Looking at the VAR declaration on line 130, we see that there is no variable declaration for VAL. There is a declaration for VALUE, however, and some simple checking would convince us that we mistakenly changed names in midstream.

2. Unfortunately, the meaning of many error messages is not always as clear, concise, and helpful as the first example might indicate. Some of the error messages we will get tell us nothing more than that an error occurred. It is left up to us to determine the cause. For cxample, on line 240 we get the cryptic message "ILLEGAL SYMBOL", and the pointer pointing at the reserved identifier ELSE. What is wrong and how arc we to find the problem? First, we should compare the statement from the program with the legal PASCAL syntax for that statement type. Element by element, we compare the IF statement on lines 220-240 with the allowable syntax of the IF-THEN-ELSE statement.

> IF boolean expression THEN statement ELSE statement

Usually the comparison will lead us to the error—in this case, the incorrect semicolon at the end of line 230—immediately. If a thorough check of the offending statement fails to identify the error, we should next check the statements immediately before and immediately after the one supposedly in error. Many syntax mistakes are caused either by the erroneous termination of statements or by statements that are accidentally run together and considered as one. Finally, we should check out all other statements related in any way to the one in error. For example, we should check the VAR declaration for all variables contained in the statement, matching BEGIN/END pairs, THEN and ELSE clauses of IF statements, or REPEAT/UNTIL pairs.

Line 250 also contains the cryptic message "ILLEGAL SYMBOL". Using your knowledge of the syntax of a FOR statement and some of the clues above, you might find it instructive to work through the program to determine what is causing that error message.

3. There is rarely a one-to-one relationship between error messages produced and corrections that need to be made. Frequently, a single error will generate numerous error messages. For example, our error in failing to declare the variable named VAL caused an error message to be produced every time VAL was referenced throughout the program—lines 210, 220, and 230. Be aware that many of the causes for the error messages you encounter will have already been corrected by earlier corrections of other mistakes. Another example of this are the two errors 104 and 155 on line 200, both caused by our single failure to include the control variable I in the VAR declaration.

4. You may require a second run to eliminate all syntactic mistakes. Frequently, a syntax error is missed by the compiler because of the presence of other mistakes on that same line. For example, line 220 will still cause syntactic problems after the error described in Figure 6-3 is corrected. After the second compilation, all, or nearly all, of the original syntax should be corrected.

6.3.2 RUN-TIME ERRORS

When your program is grammatically correct and produces no syntactic error messages, there is still no guarantee that it will produce correct results because of the possibility of a run-time error. A *run-time error* is any error that causes abnormal program behavior during execution. For example, the statement in line 260 of Figure 6-3,

$$\text{AVG := SUM DIV NUMBER } - \text{ ERROR}$$

is grammatically correct and will not produce any error messages. However, if NUMBER has the value 0, this statement will cause a division by 0 and lead to program termination. This fact will not be known until the program is actually executed, and that is why it is termed a run-time error.

In addition to division by zero, some of the most common run-time errors include:

1. Case statement expressions not corresponding to one of the case labels.
2. Real to integer conversion, where $ROUND(ABS(real)) >= MAXINT$
3. $SQRT(X)$ or $LN(X)$ when $X<0$.
4. Subrange out of bounds (this will be discussed in Chapter 7).
5. Array indices out of bounds (this will be discussed in Chapter 7).

As with syntactic errors, run-time errors also produce some type of error message. For example, unless the following feature is explicitly suppressed

STYLE CLINIC 6-2

Debugging Programs

There are many valid approaches to debugging programs. There is one approach that is utterly wrong—blindly trying something, anything, because you do not know what else to do. Too often, after a cursory glance at a program fails to reveal the cause of a problem, you start groping in the dark for any advice on how to proceed, whether good or bad. You start listening to and heeding worthless advice such as, "Hey, I think somebody once tried _____ and it might have worked," or "Throw in _____ , it probably won't hurt." The end result is that the error is still present, your program is getting needlessly confusing, and you have wasted valuable computer time.

That error is obviously being caused by some incorrect operation. Until you have an indication or a clue about what, specifically, that incorrect operation is or how to go about finding it logically, it makes no sense to change or rerun the program. Use the program listing and results along with a textbook, or reference book, the debugging aids discussed in this chapter, and your own experience to identify the likely cause of the error before you begin making changes. In the unlikely event that you still cannot isolate the problem and are unsure how to proceed, seek out competent, professional advice. Reject any advice that seems to leave you groping blindly and is not based on a rational plan for finding the problem. Suppress the urge to make a quick correction. Run-time errors can be symptomatic of serious flaws in your program.

One final comment: be extremely suspicious about suggestions to rerun the program without changes because the error may have been caused by a "machine mistake." Such hardware malfunctions are rare, and the rerun will more than likely produce the identical problems and leave you in the same predicament.

by the programmer, all of the above run-time errors would produce a *post-mortem dump*. This condensed history of the state of the machine at the time of abnormal termination is intended to help the programmer find out what happened. Although the format may vary from one system to another, this dump usually includes:

1. A message indicating what caused the termination.
2. Which program unit you were in. As we will see in Chapter 8, programs will typically be composed of more than one unit, each with its own name.
3. Where within that program unit the error occurred. (This information

might be given in terms of the object program and not your source program, so it might not be too helpful.)

4. The names and current values of all variables in that program unit.

If we were to correct the program in Figure 6-3 and run it for a data set where NUMBER was 0, the output might appear as in Figure 6-4.

The preceding discussion explained how PASCAL helps you to recover from abnormal terminations. However, it is wrong to expect PASCAL to help you recover; you should prevent abnormal termination by using the concept of foolproof programming that we introduced in Chapter 3. When you write and develop programs, you should insert checks for illegal or invalid operations wherever necessary.

The computation of the discriminant of the well-known quadratic formula is given by the following formula.

$$\sqrt{b^2 - 4ac}$$

This could be computed by the following PASCAL statement.

```
DISCRIMINANT:=SQRT(B*B - 4.0*A*C)
```

Since square roots are undefined for negative values, this statement runs the risk of abnormal termination if $(b^2 - 4ac) < 0$. A much better way to perform this computation would be:

```
DISCSQR:= B*B - 4.0*A*C;
IF DISCSQR < 0
    THEN WRITELN(' THE ROOTS ARE COMPLEX—
                  PROGRAM CANNOT CONTINUE')
    ELSE BEGIN
        DISCRIMINANT:=SQRT(DISCSQR)
```

.

.

.

By preventing run-time errors before they occur instead of waiting until they do, we gain the ability to recover in the program itself and continue processing instead of irrevocably stopping. Even if the program does nothing more than write an appropriate error message before stopping, it is usually easier to figure out what went wrong. This is because you are now interpreting a message that you produced instead of trying to interpret a message produced by the computer system that may or may not be clear.

```
00100 PROGRAM AVERAGE(INPUT,OUTPUT);
00110 CONST LOWRANGE = 0;
00120        HIGHRANGE = 100;
00130 VAR VAL, I, NUMBER, SUM, AVG, ERROR: INTEGER;
00140 {    This program computes the sum of examination scores in the range
00150      0 to 100. The number of exams is contained on the first
00160      card  }
00170 BEGIN
00180   READLN(NUMBER); WRITELN(NUMBER,' DATA ITEMS');
00190   SUM:=0; ERROR:=0;
00200   FOR I := 1 TO NUMBER DO
00210     BEGIN
00220     READLN(VAL);
00230     IF(VAL>=LOWRANGE) AND (VAL<=HIGHRANGE)
00240        THEN SUM := SUM + VAL
00250        ELSE ERROR := ERROR + 1
00260     END;  { The for loop }
00270   AVG := SUM DIV NUMBER − ERROR;
00280   WRITELN(' AVERAGE OF THE SCORES IS ', AVG)
00290 END.
READY

RUN

PASCAL   PROGRAM   AVERAGE
```

} Data value for
? 0   } NUMBER

      0 DATA ITEMS   } Run-time error
— PROGRAM TERMINATED AT: 000063 IN AVERAGE } message
— ATTEMPTED DIVISION BY ZERO   }

	AVERAGE	
ERROR	=	0
AVG	=	U
I	=	U
NUMBER	=	0
SUM	=	0
VAL	=	U

Postmortem dump
} U means undefined
value

(In this system the
location is given in
terms of the object
program.)

  * AT ADDRESS 000063 IN PROGRAM AVERAGE

FIGURE 6-4 Sample Output from a Run-Time Error.

6.3.3 LOGICAL ERRORS

By the time you have eliminated the syntax and run-time errors from your program, you have usually invested a fair amount of time and effort. You will have made a few computer runs and spent a great deal of time hand-simulating the program, interpreting error messages, and preparing corrections.

Therefore it is only natural for you to become overjoyed at the first run that actually produces meaningful results. However, you should realize that you have now reached the point where you are ready to begin locating and correcting the most difficult and time-consuming errors in the programming process—logical errors. A *logical error* is simply an incorrect translation of either the problem statement or the algorithm. An excellent example of a logical error is the following PASCAL translation of the well-known formula for computing the two roots of quadratic equations.

$$r = \frac{-b \pm \sqrt{b^2 - 4ac}}{2a}$$

```
DISCRIMINANT:= (B*B) − (4.0*A*C);
IF (DISCRIMINANT >= 0.0) AND (A <> 0.0) THEN
    BEGIN
    ROOT1 := −B + SQRT(DISCRIMINANT)/(2.0*A);
    ROOT2 := −B − SQRT(DISCRIMINANT)/(2.0*A)
    END
```

STYLE CLINIC 6-3

Get All the Information You Can

When you build tests into your program to guard against abnormal termination at run-time, you keep control of the situation. In addition to printing a meaningful message that will be easy to interpret, you might also want to reset any variables that have inappropriate values to values that will allow the program to continue.

For example, if a test indicated that your program was on the verge of trying to find the square root of a negative number, you might want the program to print a message and then replace the negative value with zero. This will allow your program to continue, and you may obtain useful information about the rest of the program. Perhaps there is an error further along that you will be able to find during this program run instead of during the next run.

You should always try to get as much information as possible out of each program run. Whenever possible, reset invalid values (always print a meaningful message when you do this!) and keep going.

The two assignment statements contained in the THEN clause are syntactically acceptable and would not cause any error messages. However, they would produce wrong answers. Those two lines are not a correct translation of the desired quadratic formula. Instead, they translate the following.

$$r = -b \pm \frac{\sqrt{b^2 - 4ac}}{2a}$$

The two assignment statements for ROOT1 and ROOT2 should have been written as follows.

```
ROOT1 := (−B + SQRT(DISCRIMINANT))/(2.0*A);
ROOT2 := (−B − SQRT(DISCRIMINANT))/(2.0*A)
```

Another example of a logical error is the following PASCAL fragment that seeks to find the sum of "COUNTFIELD" values. It is syntactically correct, but produces wrong answers.

```
READLN(COUNTFIELD);
IF COUNTFIELD > 0 THEN
    BEGIN
    FOR I:=1 TO COUNTFIELD DO
      BEGIN
      SUM:=0;
      READLN(NUMBER);
      SUM:=SUM+NUMBER
      END;
    WRITELN(' SUM OF ', COUNTFIELD, ' VALUES IS ',
            SUM)
    END
```

Do you see the error? The initialization of the variable SUM was mistakenly placed inside the FOR loop.

Both of these examples indicate why logical errors are so difficult to correct. You will typically have no clue about what is happening except that the program produces a wrong final value. There will usually be no indication about which section of the program is in error and no message to help determine what type of mistake you have made. Sitting down with a paper and pencil and hand-simulating the program (i.e., playing computer and doing step by step what the program says) may help. In the majority of cases, however, the program will be too complex or the mistake too subtle to be able to find the error in this way. Instead of allowing frustration to set in, you should begin to use your debugging tools.

By far the most powerful and useful debugging tool in PASCAL (aside from a well written program!) is simply the good old-fashioned output statement we introduced in Chapter 4.

WRITELN(values)   WRITE(values)

Too often we tend to think of the WRITE and WRITELN statements only as vehicles for writing out final answers. This is completely false. An output operation can be used to write out any values whatsoever—including intermediate results that may aid in locating mistakes. An important rule to remember is that there is (up to some point of diminishing returns) a direct relationship between the amount of output produced by a program and the ease of debugging that program. A 1000-line PASCAL program that should have produced a value of 1, but instead printed 2, would probably leave us

STYLE CLINIC 6-4

Instrumenting Your Program for Errors

Anyone who believes his or her program will run correctly the first time is either a fool, an optimist, or a novice programmer. Inevitably, there will be errors. You should anticipate their occurrence and prepare for them by having all necessary tools included in your program from the start. Always try to get the most information out of each computer run.

The most important tools to include from the beginning are well-placed output statements to produce intermediate results on the status of the computation. Avoid writing long, complex programs that contain only a single output statement as the last line. Include a sufficient number of well-placed WRITEs to facilitate finding the errors that may occur.

For convenience you may wish to mark these statements with comments to facilitate their removal when the program is running satisfactorily.

```
        .
        .
        .
    WRITELN(' A=', A);   {For debugging purposes only}
        .
        .
        .
```

Do not worry about the elegance of these WRITELN statements. Of course, you should always print some identifying information (never print numbers alone) but beyond this, do not waste too much time trying to make the debugging output "pretty." When the program is correct, you may want to remove these WRITELN statements or you may want to change them to produce fancier output.

wondering where even to begin to look for errors. If the same program included WRITELN statements that produced status reports on how the computations were proceeding, we would probably find the task considerably easier.

The primary concern is not whether to include statements to produce intermediate output, but simply where to put these statements. Although this is somewhat a matter of personal style and other considerations (size of the program, time available, and the cost of paper), there are certain general guidelines to follow.

Because PASCAL contains such a wide range of control statements (IF-THEN-ELSE, WHILE, REPEAT, CASE, FOR, BEGIN/END), most well-written PASCAL programs will be composed entirely of single-entry, single-exit program units that we will call *segments*. A well-structured segment is a group of statements that begins execution at the first line, performs some useful computation, and exits from the segment upon completion of its last line. There are no jumps into or out of the middle of the segment. A segment can be nested inside other segments, but each one should follow the single-entry, single-exit restriction. If we construct a program in this way, we will find that it is easy to read and debug because we can readily identify the control paths through the program. Examples of program segments might include those in Figure 6-5.

The first goal of debugging is to isolate an error to a specific segment of the program. We can accomplish this by initially bracketing a few of the outer program segments with WRITELN statements. Prior to entering the segment, we print the current value of all important variables that are referenced in the segment. After exiting, we print the current value of all variables defined or redefined within the segment. Since a well-structured segment should not have any jumps into or out of it, we should be able to determine whether the statements within that segment are correct or whether they contain an error. When we find that one segment contains an error, we can narrow our search even more. Since a segment may contain other segments nested inside, we bracket some inner segments with output statements to check if those segments are correct. We continue until the error becomes obvious or we have isolated the problem to a small enough area that we are able to trace it by hand.

There are two other general guidelines you should be aware of concerning the placement of output statements during debugging.

1. It is always a good idea to *echo-print* all input data immediately. Your program may be producing garbage not because it is wrong, but because you are feeding it garbarge. Although most of the output statements used for debugging will be removed when the program is completed, the echo-prints are quite useful and should probably remain. They will allow the user to associate any particular result with the data set that produced it.

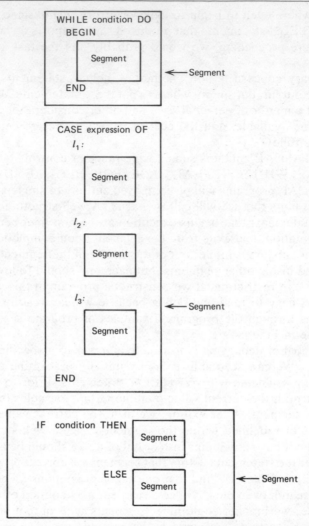

FIGURE 6-5   Examples of Program Segments.

2. Be very careful when placing an output statement within instead of around a highly repetitive loop. You may be flooded with output and meaningful values can be lost or overlooked. If you produce too much output you will be unable to find the specific information you need. If you must place a WRITE statement inside a highly repetitive loop, consider printing a value only every nth iteration.

```
FOR I := 1 TO 5000 DO
   BEGIN
```

IF (I MOD 50)=0 THEN WRITELN(. . . .)
{The WRITELN will be executed every 50th iteration}

As an example of what we have been discussing, let us assume that we ran the program in Figure 6-4 with the following data set.

```
  5   {The number of scores}
 70
 80
-50   {An invalid value}
 90
110   {An invalid value}
```

We would expect the program to produce an answer of 80, the average of the three valid scores, 70, 80, and 90. The actual output produced by the program would be:

```
5 DATA ITEMS
AVERAGE OF THE SCORES IS 46
```

Assuming that we have not already spotted the error, what would we do? We might insert the following lines in the program.

```
225  WRITELN(' VAL =', VAL);
255  ;WRITELN(' SUM=', SUM, ' ERROR =', ERROR)
```

With these lines included we now get:

```
5 DATA ITEMS
VAL =   70
SUM=   70   ERROR=0
VAL =   80
SUM= 150   ERROR=0
VAL =-50
SUM= 150   ERROR=1
VAL =   90
SUM= 240   ERROR=1
VAL = 110
SUM= 240   ERROR=2
AVERAGE OF THE SCORES IS 46
```

By comparing what the program produced with what was expected, we see that through line 255 everything is proceeding correctly. However, at line 280, we have produced an incorrect average. Therefore we now know that the problem must be with the single assignment statement at line 270. A careful check of that statement would show the problem to be a missing set of parentheses leading to an improperly evaluated expression. The statement should have been:

$$AVG := SUM \ DIV \ (NUMBER - ERROR);$$

Rerunning the program with this change produces the correct result. The use of strategically placed output statements within a program is the most systematic way to isolate and find logical errors.

In addition to the output statement, some computer systems also provide special debugging aids. However, since these aids are not really part of the PASCAL language, they may not be available on your specific computer system. You should check into the local availability of the aids described in the following paragraphs.

One of these useful debugging aids has already been mentioned—the postmortem dump. Whenever a PASCAL program terminates abnormally, output similar to that in Figure 6-4 will be produced. However, it is not always necessary to wait for an abnormal termination to get this potentially useful information. Some versions of PASCAL include a procedure named HALT that will terminate a program and produce a postmortem dump. During debugging, you may wish to use the HALT procedure to guarantee that even upon normal termination all variables have the correct values.

Another useful debugging aid available on some computer systems is a type of dump called a *snapshot dump*. A snapshot dump produces the same general information as the postmortem dump—the current values of all important variables—but does not cause program termination. Using some special "snap" procedure, you indicate in the program that you wish to produce a snapshot dump. Your program will be temporarily suspended, the dump produced, and the program continued at the point immediately following the request for a snap.

Finally, we should mention what is probably the most useful automatic debugging aid—an *automatic trace* feature. The automatic trace is a way to have the computer system produce a running commentary of exactly what the program is doing. In a way it is similar to inserting a WRITELN command after every statement in the program. The exact output produced by these automatic trace aids varies from system to system and depends on the type of statement currently being executed. Since a complete trace of an entire program would usually produce an excessive amount of output, an on/off switch is usually included. When you wish to investigate a specific portion of a program, you execute some type of a "TRACE ON" command [e.g., TRACE(TRUE)] prior to entering that portion. The full trace output will now be produced until the program encounters a "TRACE OFF" command [e.g., TRACE(FALSE)]. If the system you are using has a trace feature you should become acquainted with it. It is a quick and power-ful technique for helping to locate and correct programming errors. How-ever, if you do use it, use it wisely. Indiscriminate tracing can use an enor-mous amount of time and paper, which is both expensive and ecologically unsound. As a general rule, remember that it is almost never appropriate to trace either an entire program or a highly repetitive loop.

6.4 PROGRAM TESTING

The process of *program testing* is concerned with proving that a computer program produces correct and meaningful results for all possible input data. This goal, however, is generally impossible to achieve for any but the small-est programs. All we can actually determine is that a program is working incorrectly. Some computer scientists theorize that it should be possible to prove deductively that a program is correct, but their work is not yet com-plete enough to solve practical problems. We must still proceed by testing.

In a way, finding mistakes in a program is not unlike looking for someone in a haystack using a pitchfork. By shoving the fork into the haystack, we will know without a doubt when we have found someone! However, we can never be completely sure that the haystack is empty. What we do then is put the fork into the stack a sufficient number of times and places to satisfy our-selves that the probability that someone is inside the haystack is infinites-imally small. But a small, clever, lucky person might possibly escape detection.

In effect, we use a "pitchfork" made of data during the testing phase. Since we cannot guarantee correctness, we must convince ourselves that the probability of a program being correct is high. We do this by testing the pro-gram with a sufficient number of interesting data sets to see if the program produces correct answers in all cases. If it does, we tentatively say that it is correct, and we release it for general use. Obviously, there may be errors that went undetected because no data set tested for them. That is why *pro-gram maintenance* is important. Program maintenance involves the con-tinuing responsibility for monitoring a program's operation in the field, correcting any errors found through continued use, and issuing the appro-priate corrections to all users of the program. It is not at all unusual in the case of large, complex programs for an installation to be issuing *patches* (program updates to correct errors) 2, 3, or even 4 years after the program has entered general use.

Therefore the most important aspect of program testing is choosing the specific data sets with which to test the program. Too often, quantity of test data is accepted in place of quality of data. A program that worked on 1000 sample runs should not be accepted solely because 1000 may be considered by some to be a large number. If, in fact, all 1000 cases tested the same logical part of the program, all we would know is that that specific part does, indeed, work correctly. We would know nothing at all about the remainder of the program. Our objective in testing should be to create test data that exercise all aspects of our program. This requires a perception of the different logical paths that exist in the program. Of course, we know that the logical paths can be identified most readily in a program that uses clear control structures, and that is another reason for writing well-structured programs.

Test cases can be roughly broken up into four classes, and we must insure that we validate our program with a selection of data from all four.

The *valid* cases represent data sets that are logically meaningful to our program and for which the program should produce answers. Our first set of tests should be designed to insure that our program does indeed work correctly on the valid data sets, because these cases will probably represent most input. As mentioned before, we should attempt to test all possible alternatives.

For example, assume that we were developing a payroll program to produce employee paychecks from hourly time cards. We would initially test the program with a few data sets chosen from each of the following classes.

1. No overtime, standard deductions.
2. No overtime, special deductions (e.g., credit union).
3. Overtime pay.
4. Regular social security deduction.
5. Maximum social security deduction (pay exceeds the maximum wage base).
6. No dependents.
7. One or more dependents.

.

.

.

Other distinct cases.

(In actuality a program of this complexity would probably be developed and checked out in stages. It would not be tested only as a single large unit. However, the testing at each individual stage would still proceed along the lines discussed here. This will be discussed further in Chapter 9.)

As you can see, it may require a large number of test cases to check all valid alternatives. The creation of this test data can become a time-consuming task. An interesting approach for reducing the time involved in developing valid test cases is to use the computer itself to generate the data. This can be done quite easily by the use of random number generators—built-in routines for generating random numbers within any range and for any type. Assume we have the following built-in functions.

REALRANDOM(A,B)   Generate a random number of type
                         REAL in the range [A,B]

INTEGERRANDOM(A,B)   Generate a random number of type
                         INTEGER in the range [A,B]

We could test our payroll system in the following way.

```
READLN(CASECOUNT);   {The number of test cases to run}
FOR I := 1 TO CASECOUNT DO
   BEGIN
   HOURSWORKED := REALRANDOM(0.0, 50.0);
   PAYRATE := REALRANDOM(1.80, 10.00);
   DEPENDENTS := INTEGERRANDOM(0, 10);


       .
       .
       .
```

Payroll computations

These statements will cause our payroll computations to be tested
CASECOUNT times using random values for hours worked in the range
0.0 to 50.0, random pay rates between $1.80 per hour and $10 per hour, and
a random number of dependents from 0 to 10. We hope that because of the
large number of test cases being run there will be a very high probability that
a data set for every possible case will eventually be generated.

Another class of test cases actually represents just a subset of the valid
cases. However, it is such an important subset that it is usually treated separately. These arc called the *boundary* cases—the data sets that represent the
extremes of the valid problems that our program will accept. Many common
programming errors (e.g., the off-by-one error mentioned in Chapter 5) show
up only when tested with these boundary conditions. Examples of these
extremes might be working with a list as long or as short as the program
allows, working with the first or last item in a list, or setting a variable to its
largest or smallest allowable value.

In our payroll program we would want to make sure we had at least one
data case that tested each of the following conditions.

1. Gross pay exactly equal to the social security wage base maximum.
2. Hours worked equal to the maximum allowed by company policy.
3. Persons in the highest and lowest tax brackets.
4. A test on the first and last entries in the payroll file.
5. Deductions exactly equal to the total earnings, leaving a net of 0.

The previous two classes of test data represent all the valid, meaningful
conditions of the problem. However, as everyone is aware, errors do occur

—because of a misinterpretation of the problem, a misunderstanding of what was intended, or simply a manual error in reading and entering the data. It is imperative that our program perform meaningful operations for all data sets, even those that seemingly violate the conditions of the problem. The following two classes of data values are used in testing for these errors.

The *special* or *unusual* cases represent the conditions that are not necessarily invalid but for which normal processing cannot be done or for which some special or unusual handling may be required. When the program cannot produce the normal answers, it still should perform some meaningful recovery action. This may include sending an error message to the operator, making an entry in an error log, or having the computer drop the data card into a special hopper. In our payroll problems such special cases might, for example, include:

1. Hours worked equal to 0.0 (on vacation? sick? mispunched?).
2. Total deductions exceeding employee's gross pay (who makes up the difference?).
3. Pay rate of $108.50 per hour (highly improbable, could it be $10.85?).
4. Deductions claimed greater than 1 but an "individual" health plan. (Is the person unaware of this? Should we warn him or her?).

The final phase of testing should be on the *invalid* cases—those situations that are utterly meaningless and that violate physical reality or the statement of the problem. Although these cases should never normally occur when the program is operating, "Murphy's law" will usually prevail. Our program must be completely impervious to and insulated from the effects of bad data—no matter how pathological. The possibility of abnormal termination for any data set whatsoever is a sign of a poorly written program. To insure

STYLE CLINIC 6-5

Graceful Degradation

The invalid cases bring into play a characteristic that we might call *graceful degradation:* a program should "do nothing" in a reasonable way. Invalid data values should result in a meaningful error message and if at all possible an assumption that allows the program to continue. Perhaps the invalid data can be set to the minimum or maximum acceptable values or perhaps the data should be ignored. In any case, let the error message indicate clearly what action is being taken. Your program should be designed so that it will always behave gracefully—it should never "blow up" when it is faced with the unexpected.

that our program does indeed display these characteristics, we would conclude the testing phase of the payroll program with the following classes of data.

1. Hours worked < 0.0 or > 168.0
2. Dependents < 0.
3. Pay card for a nonexistent employee.
4. Two pay cards for the same employee.
5. Pay rate < 0.00.

When we have completed all this testing, what have we proved? As we stated at the beginning of this section, we have not proved the absolute correctness of our program. What we have done is to show that the program operates satisfactorily on a wide range of test cases. From this we extrapolate to the statement that the program will operate satisfactorily for all possible data sets. If we have designed and chosen the test data carefully, this extrapolation will, for the most part, be valid, and we can hope that further modifications to correct undetected errors will not be needed.

STYLE CLINIC 6-6

When Should Comments Be Written?

Instructors of introductory programming courses frequently see student programs that have few, if any, comments. A student will usually explain, "Don't worry, I'll put in the comments when I get the program working." That is a very bad policy.

Comments belong in your program from the very beginning. Meaningful comments should be included in your program as you begin to code in PASCAL (or any language). These comments should reflect your thinking as you code a program segment. What portion of the problem solution is being dealt with in this segment? Are there any special conditions under which this segment will or will not be executed? Commentary of this kind is invaluable if someone else is reading your program. Even you (the program's author) will find this information helpful during debugging. Comments inserted after the fact tend to be superficial and inadequate, because you can quickly forget why you wrote a segment in a particular way.

Of course, when comments are written with the initial program text, they may have to be changed as parts of the program are changed. Indeed, you must keep your comments up to date and accurate—incorrect comments are worse than no comments at all! But this is really a small price to pay, because your high-quality comments will aid you in debugging and they will contribute toward a more polished and professional finished product.

6.5 DOCUMENTATION AND MAINTENANCE

Documenting and maintaining programs are two very important aspects of the programming process. Unfortunately, these items usually receive scant attention in an introductory programming course, because they do not have direct relevance to the environment in which student programs are written. Nevertheless, we will discuss them because we believe that programmers who are aware of them will write better programs.

One of the mistaken ideas held by too many programmers is that the documentation for a program should be written only after the program is "finished." That is a very dangerous point of view! It will certainly lead to inadequate documentation and it might very well result in an incomplete or incorrect program. Documentation is an ongoing task. It starts when we first begin to formulate a clear problem statement and it continues as we devise a solution, express the solution algorithmically, and code the algorithm as a computer program. The proper point of view is that documentation is an inherent part of a program. It is meaningless to assert, therefore, that documentation should be written after the program is finished.

Most programs that are written by professional programmers are used in a production environment. This means that once a program is deemed operational, it is used on a regular basis, usually by people other than the author(s). For example, programs to process payrolls, maintain inventories, or handle hotel or airline reservations are invariably used by people who did not write them. Moreover, these people are usually not even programmers. In this sort of environment we can see the need for two different kinds of documentation: user documentation and technical documentation.

User documentation provides the information that one needs in order to use a program. This includes a number of different items.

1. A description of the application area of the program—what will this program do?
2. A description of the data that the program requires.
3. A description of the output produced by the program.
4. A description of the commands we need to issue to start the program.
5. If appropriate, a description of the kinds of interactions that are possible with the program.
6. An explanation of all the messages that the program can produce.
7. A discussion (in nontechnical terms) of the performance capabilities and limitations of the program.

Note that the user documentation is much more than a list of commands that are needed to invoke the program. A great deal of information must be provided to enable the potential user to determine if the program is suitable for him or her. Perhaps the program is not capable of handling certain special cases that happen to be of interest at this time, or perhaps the program is based on an algorithm that performs efficiently only when the number of data items does not exceed a certain value. These matters must be addressed in the user documentation.

When a person has determined that a particular program is the one that is needed, the user documentation will tell how to use it. Since a user may know very little about programming (perhaps nothing at all), there is no need for this part of the documentation to describe the internal workings of the program. The user wants (and needs) to know everything that must be done to use the program, but the user is not interested in the technical details of its implementation. The program is simply a tool that the user wishes to use.

However, we do want to maintain a description of the technical details, and we do this in the *technical documentation*. This documentation is addressed to programmers who might be faced with the task of modifying the program at some time. Perhaps a bug will become apparent after the program has been placed into use, or a decision may be made to enhance the program by adding a new feature. In either case, good technical documentation is a necessity.

This documentation is usually in two parts. First, the commentary that we wrote as we coded the program is part of the technical documentation. This information is addressed to someone who knows how to program and is interested in examining in detail what the program does. In extreme cases— when a program is small and not very sophisticated—this documentation (if done well) may be all the technical documentation that is needed. However, this will not often be the case. Most of the time it is appropriate to prepare a separate document that provides further technical documentation. This document usually includes program design information of a global nature. For example, there will usually be a list of procedures and functions (see Chapter 8) and a brief explanation of the purpose of each one. There will also be a description of the data items that are accessible from different program units (again, see Chapter 8), and often there is a chart that depicts the relationships among the program units.

This information provides a general outline, as well as a few specific details, of the overall program structure. Further details are obtained by reading the comments in the program and reading the text of the program itself. Needless to say, it is a tremendous aid if the program adheres to the rules for good style, such as the use of appropriate structured statements, well-placed and meaningful comments, meaningful names for identifiers, and a consistent and clear indentation scheme.

Now we are in a good position to see why documentation should take place throughout the programming process. Most, and in many cases all, of the user documentation should be written before any coding is done. The user documentation represents a functional description of a program, and it can serve as a set of specifications to the programmer. If the programmer has done a good job of problem analysis, these specifications can be very useful in keeping things on course during the coding phase. Of course, it is always possible that some changes will need to be made as the implementation proceeds, and these changes must be reflected in a revised user document. However, if the user document is undergoing a large number of changes once the implementation is under way, that should serve as a warning. It is quite likely that inadequate attention has been given to the analysis of the problem.

Once the problem has been analyzed and a user document has been prepared, the programmer can proceed with the development of algorithms. It is at this stage that much of the technical documentation can be written. Indeed, if more than one programmer is involved, it is essential to prepare a technical description of the proposed implementation. It is simply impossible to coordinate the activities of several programmers without such a document. Even if only one person will be doing the coding, a technical description prepared before the coding has started will be invaluable. The coding task will be much better organized and the technical documentation will be of a higher quality when the project is completed.

Changes to the technical documentation are apt to be somewhat more numerous than changes to the user documentation as implementation proceeds. But, again, if the technical documentation is undergoing a high degree of change, that is a bad sign. It is probable that too little time was devoted to the development of an algorithmic solution. Remember that it is always a bad practice to rush into the coding phase. The result will be an incorrect, inadequate, or incomprehensible program.

When the implementation is complete and the final full-scale testing has been done,* it is appropriate to review all the documentation and make certain that it is in order. If the documentation is to be of any value it must describe the program accurately. It may be appropriate to run some performance tests to obtain a measure of the speed and capabilities of the program. This information should be added to the user documentation, since it could have an important bearing on the suitability of the program for some users.

Why are we so concerned with documentation? There are several reasons, and they should now be apparent.

Good user documentation is essential if a program is to be a useful tool. We may have designed and coded an outstanding program, but what good is it if no one knows how to use it?

Good technical documentation is essential for maintaining a program. We may decide to add features to the program or we may have to find and

---

* In Chapter 9 we will discuss techniques for building and testing large programs. Each portion of a program is usually tested as it is developed and integrated into the existing program.

correct errors in the program. These things can be virtually impossible if the technical documentation is inadequate. There have been many instances of a program being thrown out entirely because it was too difficult to change.

Finally, good documentation can be educational. When we are faced with the task of designing and coding a program, we may be able to learn a great deal by studying the documentation of a similar project.

We began this section by observing that the topics of documentation and maintenance are not usually discussed in detail in an introductory programming course. That is because a student programming environment is somewhat artificial. Problems are usually presented in a form in which most of the analysis has been done. Of course, the problems must be of modest size and, when the programs are complete, they are executed once or twice and usually discarded. This means that there is little need for detailed documentation, and there is almost never any program maintenance.

Do not be shortsighted. Things will be different as you write larger and more complex programs (perhaps in more advanced courses, certainly in the "real world"). For now, you should keep in mind the ideas we have discussed in this section. If you begin applying them now (in a modest way for modest programs) your programs will be the better for it.

6.6 CONCLUSION

This chapter has discussed the overall transition from a potential solution written in PASCAL to a computer program that produces the desired results. This transition involves three distinct phases. Debugging involves locating and correcting all syntactic, run-time, and logical errors in the program. This

---

STYLE CLINIC 6-7

Overall Program Development

Although the operations described in this chapter may not be considered as creative or challenging as some of the earlier operations (e.g., algorithm development), they are, nevertheless, just as important in the overall solution of a problem. Too often, interest in a problem wanes once the "interesting" aspects are complete. The dirty work—debugging and testing—are poorly and sloppily done. This leads to poorly tested, poorly documented, and poorly maintained programs. Such programs are useless. A competent programmer must always view the problem solving process from start to finish and be willing to carry out all necessary operations, which were discussed in Chapter 1. The programming tools and techniques discussed in this chapter are critically important to the programmer.

requires a working knowledge of the debugging tools that are available. Next, there is the testing phase, which involves showing that the program does, indeed, produce correct results. This requires a knowledge of the specifications of the problem and the techniques for designing program test data. Finally, there is documentation and program maintenance, which simply acknowledges that it may be necessary to change a program either to fix a bug or add a feature. It involves the continuing responsibility for monitoring, correcting, and updating programs that have already been released for general use.

EXERCISES

*1. Using the syntax diagrams in Appendix A, state whether the following PASCAL statements would or would not cause a syntax error. Assume that all necessary variables have been correctly declared and defined.

    a. WHILE X < 1 AND Y <> 2 DO READLN(CH)

    b. FOR I := 1 DOWNTO N DO SUM := SUM + I

    c. IF TESTFLAG AND (I <= N)
        THEN
        ELSE WRITELN (' DONE')

    d. CIRCLEAREA := PI * R ** 2

    e. REPEAT
        BEGIN
        X := Y; Y := Z; Z := X + Y;
        END;
      UNTIL Z > 1000

    f. ROOT := −B + SQRT(DISC)/2A

    g. IF COUNT := 0
        THEN WRITELN (' EMPTY FILE ')

    h. WRITELN; WRITELN; WRITELN

    i. VAR I, J, K = INTEGER;

    j. CASE I OF
        BEGIN
           0, 1 :   J := J + 1; K := K + 1
              2 :   J := SQRT(J + K); K := 0
           3, 4 :   J := ABS(J + K); K := −1
        END

    k. IF COUNT < 15
        THEN   A := A + 1;
        ELSE   B := B + 1

*2. Find and correct all of the errors in the following program. Character-
ize each error as either a syntax, run-time or logical error.

```
Line
Number
   1        PROGARM SAMPLE(INPUT,OUTPUT);
   2        {This program computes the sum of the integers from
   3        1 to K. K is read as a data value}
   4        VAR   K, SUM : INTEGER;
   5            READLN(K);
   6            SUM := 1
   7            FOR I = 1 TO K DO
   8               SUM = K
   9            WRITELN(' THE SUM FROM 1 TO K IS', SUM)
  10        END.
```

*3. Assume that you have entered the following program.

```
00100  PROGRAM FIBONACCI(INPUT, OUTPUT);
00110  {    This is a first attempt at a program to
00120        generate the fibonacci sequence x(i) = x(i−1) +
00130        x(i−2), i=2,3, . . . ; x(0)=x(1)=1. We will stop when
00140        we come to some user specified upper limit }
00150  VAR I, X, Y, Z, LINIT: INTEGER;
00160  BEGIN
00170     READLN(LIMIT); WRITELN(' INDEX
           FIBONACCI NUMBER');
00180     I:=0; X:=1;     WRITELN('I:6, X:15);
00190     I:=1; Y:=1;     WRITELN(I:6, Y:15);
00200     WHILE (Z<LIMIT) DO
00210     Z:= X+Y  { This will determine the next number
00220                  in the fibonacci sequence       }
00230      I:=I+1;  WRITELN(I:6, Z:15);
00240      Y:=Z;
00250      X:=Y     { These last two statements set up for
00260                  the next iteration              }
00270      END;
00280     WRITELN(' END OF THE FIBONACCI SEQUENCE');
00290     WRITELN(' A TOTAL OF ', I,' NUMBERS WERE GENERATED)
00300  END. {Of fibonacci}
```

After giving the command to RUN the program, the computer produced the following error messages.

```
PASCAL    PROGRAM    FIBONACCI
00471  00170  READLN(LIMIT); WRITELN(' INDEX   FIBONACCI
***                       ^104                     NUMBER');
```

```
000035 00180  I:=0; X:=1;    WRITELN('I:6, X:15) ;
***                                           ^202
000037 00190  I:=1; Y:=1;    WRITELN(I:6, Y:15);
***           ^6  ^4
000056 00200  WHILE (Z<LIMIT) DO
***                      ^104
000057 00230     I:=I+1; WRITELN(I:6, Z:15);
***              ^59
000073 00270     END;
***              ^6
000117 00290  WRITELN(' A TOTAL OF ', I,' NUMBERS WERE
                         GENERATED)
***                                           ^202
***        PREMATURE END OF SOURCE FILE
COMPILER ERROR MESSAGES:
    4:  ")" EXPECTED
    6:  ILLEGAL SYMBOL
   59:  ERROR IN VARIABLE
  104:  IDENTIFIER NOT DECLARED
  202:  STRING CONSTANT MUST NOT EXCEED SOURCE LINE
ERROR(S) IN PASCAL PROGRAM
```

Locate and correct all the syntactic errors in the program.

4. Assume that after making all the appropriate changes to the program in problem 3, you attempted to run the program and got the following run-time error message.

```
?100
INDEX          FIBONACCI NUMBER
  0                    1
  1                    1

—PROGRAM TERMINATED AT: 00053 IN FIBONACCI
—ATTEMPT TO REFERENCE AN UNDEFINED VARIABLE

FIBONACCI
    I       =      1
    X       =      1
    Y       =      1
    Z       =      U
  LIMIT     =      100

END OF PROGRAM FIBONACCI
```

Discuss how you would go about determining what the error was. Discuss your use of hand simulation, the program output, the dump, and WRITELN commands in helping you to locate the problem.

5. Again, assume that you have corrected the run-time error which caused the error discussed in problem 4. Now when the program is run, it produces the following output.

```
? 100
INDEX           FIBONACCI NUMBER
  0                    1
  1                    1
  2                    2
  3                    4
  4                    8
  5                   16
  6                   32
  7                   64
  8                  128
END OF THE FIBONACCI SEQUENCE
A TOTAL OF             8 NUMBERS WERE GENERATED
```

a. Discuss how you would go about finding and correcting this logical error. In your answer discuss the role that hand-simulation, the program output, and additional WRITELN commands would play in helping you correct the mistake.

b. After correcting the error(s) from part a, test the program to see if it works properly under all possible conditions. If not, suggest necessary changes to make the program more secure against pathological conditions.

6. Suppose that the ROOTFINDER program at the end of Chapter 5 was executed with the following data.

$$F(X) = x^2 - 15x + 56$$
$$XSTART = 0.0$$
$$XFINAL = 50.0$$
$$DELTA = 3.0$$
$$EPSILON = 0.005$$

However, instead of producing the correct result,

ROOT = 7.0   (or ROOT = 8.0)

it produces:

CANNOT FIND A ROOT IN THIS INTERVAL

Discuss your approach in finding why ROOTFINDER is apparently not operating properly. You should discuss the roles of trace statements, additional output statements, and hand simulation in helping you find the problem.

7. Assume that the ROOTFINDER program needed to be modified in the following two ways.

   a. If the program could not find a root in the interval [XSTART, XFINAL] it would allow the user to provide another set of starting and ending points. This searching would continue until either a root is found or the user provided a pair of values in which XSTART = XFINAL = 0. This would mean he wished to terminate the search.

   b. After finding one root, the program would immediately begin looking for another from the point where it executed its first turnaround;

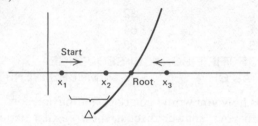

   that is, the point x_3 above. The stepsize should be reset to its original value and XFINAL should remain unchanged.
   When implementing these two changes, try to estimate the effort involved in modifying the existing program as compared to rewriting it from scratch. Are there any characteristics of the program that make it particularly easy or difficult to modify?

8. Write the user-level documentation for the program ROOTFINDER in Figure 5-15 so that a user will be able to use the program properly and intelligently by merely reading this documentation.

9. Suppose you are designing a program that will produce a graph of an equation. The program will accept the equation and other pertinent information as input data. You expect that your program will be widely used by both students and instructors in the engineering and mathematics departments, so good documentation is essential. Outline the information that you might include in the user documentation for your program.

10. Modify the averaging program AVERA in Figure 5-7 so that it does the following.

    a. Checks the value of HOWMANY and produces an error message if it is nonpositive. It may take any other recovery action you think appropriate for this situation.

    b. Accepts data values only in the range [LOW, HIGH] inclusive where LOW and HIGH are user specified parameters and HIGH > LOW.

    c. Prints the number of legal scores used in computing the average.

    d. After processing one set of data, repeats the process for another set and continues until end-of-file.

After making these modifications, design test data to test all possible paths through the program. State what type of case (valid, boundary, special, invalid) each data set is intended to represent. Write the user documentation for AVERA so that it could be used easily by others.

11. A good example of the difficulty that can be encountered with program maintenance is working with an unfamiliar program whose details are not fully understood. Exchange a program that you have written with a similar program written by someone else, and agree on some interesting, nontrivial modification which each of you will then make to the other's work. After completing the modification, write the necessary user documentation. Discuss the style and organizational characteristics of the program that aided (or hindered) the maintenance process.

CHAPTER 7

ADDITIONAL
PASCAL DATA TYPES

7.1 ADDITIONAL SCALAR TYPES

7.1.1 USER-DEFINED SCALAR DATA TYPES

The basic data types in PASCAL are the scalar types that we introduced in Chapter 3. These scalar types are composed of individual elements, called constants, and the relationship between any two constants of a type can be described by saying that one is less than, equal to, or greater than the other. Thus, each scalar data type in PASCAL is *ordered*. The total number of constants in the data type is termed the *cardinality* of the data type.

PASCAL automatically provides four standard scalar data types—INTEGER, REAL, BOOLEAN, and CHAR. Frequently, however, these standard data types are insufficient to describe a particular problem adequately. In some programming languages we may actually be forced to modify or constrain the problem to match one of the available data types. For example, if we wished to work with values that would range over the days of the week, it would be convenient to have a data type whose constants were 'sunday', 'monday', 'tuesday', 'wednesday', 'thursday', 'friday', and 'saturday', and that were ordered in just that sequence. We could declare variables to be of this data type and let them assume the values of any of those constants—exactly as we did with the standard PASCAL types. Statements such as

        X:= MONDAY

or

        IF (DAY=SATURDAY) OR (DAY=SUNDAY)
           THEN WRITELN(' WEEKEND')

would have a valid meaning in our language, and the intent of the statements would be quite clear to any reader.

If the ability to create this "days-of-the-week" data type were not a part of our language, we would be forced to modify the representation so that we might use an existing standard data type. Most probably this would be done by mapping the days of the week onto the integers 1 to 7. Although this would work adequately and the program could be written, we would have lost the readability inherent in using the day names themselves and would have diminished the clarity and understanding of the program.

Perhaps it has occurred to you that we could use a series of CONST declarations to provide meaningful names.

        CONST   SUNDAY=1;
                 MONDAY=2;
                 TUESDAY=3;

            .
            .
            .

This would allow us to refer to SUNDAY, MONDAY, . . . instead of the integers 1, 2, . . . , and the readability of our program would be enhanced. However, it is a bit awkward and inconvenient to write the sequence of CONST declarations, which constitutes the mapping of the names into the integers. It would be helpful if we could simply name the constants we wished to use without explicitly having to associate each constant with an integer.

To allow algorithms to be translated into the language most naturally, PASCAL permits users to define new scalar data types. To create these new data types, we need to provide two specific pieces of information: the constants contained in the data type and their ordering. This information is provided by the following PASCAL TYPE declaration.

TYPE type-name = (identifier, identifier, . . .);

The "identifiers" contained in the TYPE declaration are the constants of the data type, and "type-name" is the symbolic name associated with the new data type. The constants are assumed to have the ordering relationship specified by their left-to-right position in the TYPE declaration.

Examples of user-defined scalar types would include:

```
TYPE DAYSOFTHEWEEK = (SUN, MON, TUE, WED, THUR,
                      FRI, SAT);
     CLUBMEMBERS = (JOE, BILL, SUE, TOM, JANE,
                    JOHN);
     MONTHS = (JANUARY, FEBRUARY, MARCH, APRIL,
              MAY, JUNE, JULY, AUGUST,
              SEPTEMBER, OCTOBER, NOVEMBER,
              DECEMBER);
     FAMILY = (MOTHER, FATHER, SISTER, BROTHER);
```

The only restriction on enumerating the constants of a user-defined scalar type is that each identifier must appear in no more than one user-defined type. This restriction is necessary to guarantee that all operations on these data types are unambiguous. For example, given the following additional type declaration:

TYPE FRIENDS = (TOM, BILL, AL, KEN, DAVE);

the truth of the boolean relation:

BILL < TOM

is ambiguous, since it depends on which data type we are referring to—FRIENDS or CLUBMEMBERS.

We may now declare variables for these newly created data types using the same VAR declaration that we have been using all along. The only difference is in the data type field, where we use the name of our new scalar data type.

```
VAR DAY       :   DAYSOFTHEWEEK;
    FRIEND    :   CLUBMEMBERS;
    DATE      :   MONTHS;
    RELATION:     FAMILY;
```

One can also use a shorthand PASCAL notation by effectively compacting the functions of the TYPE and VAR declarations into a single declaration.

```
VAR DAY      :    (SUN, MON, TUE, WED, THUR, FRI, SAT);
    FRIEND   :    (JOE, BILL, SUE, TOM, JANE, JOHN);
    DATE     :    (JANUARY, FEBRUARY, MARCH, APRIL,
                   MAY, JUNE, JULY, AUGUST,
                   SEPTEMBER, OCTOBER, NOVEMBER,
                   DECEMBER);
    RELATION:    (MOTHER, FATHER, SISTER, BROTHER);
```

These declarations are virtually the same as the earlier ones. The only difference is that in these examples the new data types are not named explicitly. This format will be an acceptable alternative for all TYPE and VAR declarations used in this textbook.

We may now use these variables anywhere within our PASCAL program. If s_1, s_2, s_3, . . . are valid PASCAL statements, all of the following examples, based on the above declarations, are meaningful PASCAL statements.

IF DAY $<=$ FRI THEN s_1 ELSE s_2

(s_1 will be executed if DAY has the value SUN, MON, TUE, WED, THUR, or FRI; s_2 will be executed if DAY is SAT)

FOR FRIEND := JANE DOWNTO BILL DO s_3

(s_3 will be executed 4 times with FRIEND assuming the values JANE, TOM, SUE, and BILL.)

DATE:= SUCC(JUNE);
RELATION:= PRED(FATHER);
I:= ORD(JOHN)

(DATE will be JULY, the successor of JUNE; RELATION will be MOTHER, the predecessor of FATHER; and I, which must be declared integer, will be 5, the ordinal position of JOHN within the data type CLUBMEMBERS. Ordinal values of the constants of user-defined data types start with 0.)

The above examples show that in addition to the six relational operators we can apply the standard functions SUCC, PRED, and ORD to user-defined scalar types. However, the other arithmetic or boolean operators cannot be applied to user-defined data types.

To illustrate the use of user-defined scalar data types in a complete program, we will now write a program to produce a weekly payroll report. Assume that for each employee of the company we have eight data cards. The first card is the master payroll card, which contains the employee's social security number and base pay rate. The next seven cards are time cards and contain the number of hours worked by that employee each day of the week. Furthermore, assume it is company policy to pay the employee the standard base rate during the week and double for any weekend work.

Algorithmically, our solution might look something like the following.

```
START
    While we still have employees to process do
        Read the master payroll card for the next employee
        Check the card
        If incorrect Then Write an error message
                          Skip the remaining 7 cards for that employee
                     Else Repeat the following 7 times
                              Read a time card
                              Check for correctness
                              Compute the pay for this day
                              Add it to the weekly total
                          End of the repeat loop
                          Write the weekly total for this employee
    Stop
    End of the while loop
END OF THE ALGORITHM
```

When we translate this algorithm into PASCAL, what data type should we choose for the variable that will be used to count the seven time cards for each employee? The integers 1 to 7, 856 to 862, or the characters "a" to "g" would all work correctly. But these choices would not clearly illuminate what the code is doing and would certainly not help a user or maintainer determine our intent.

The most natural and lucid choice for this data structure would be the data type DAYSOFTHEWEEK. We will modify the ordering of the data type we defined earlier so that the weekend days (SAT and SUN) occur consecutively. This ordering is different from the normal calendar ordering, but it is more in keeping with the notion of a "work week" and it is more appropriate for payroll processing. Using this data type, our translation to PASCAL would look like Figure 7-1.

The use of the descriptive data type DAYSOFTHEWEEK has definitely enhanced the readability of the program and made the operations being performed much more obvious to anyone working with the program listing.

```
PROGRAM PAYROLL(INPUT,OUTPUT);
TYPE DAYSOFTHEWEEK=(MON, TUE, WED, THUR, FRI, SAT, SUN);
VAR DAY: DAYSOFTHEWEEK;
    SOCSECNUM: INTEGER;
    BASERATE, HOURS, TOTALPAY, PAYRATE: REAL;
BEGIN
{This program computes a paycheck (without regard to taxes or
  any other deductions) from an employee's master card and 7 daily
  time cards                                                      }
WHILE NOT EOF DO
  BEGIN
  READLN(SOCSECNUM, BASERATE); WRITELN(' SOC. SEC.
    NO.=', SOCSECNUM, ' BASERATE=', BASERATE);
  IF (BASERATE<0.0) OR (SOCSECNUM>999999999)
    THEN BEGIN
           WRITELN(' INVALID PAYROLL MASTER CARD');
           FOR DAY:=MON TO SUN DO READLN(HOURS)
         END
{We get here if the master card was legal and we are actually
  able to generate the paycheck                                  }
    ELSE BEGIN
           TOTALPAY:=0.0;
           FOR DAY:= MON TO SUN DO
             BEGIN
             READLN(HOURS);WRITELN (' HOURS=',HOURS);
             IF DAY <= FRI THEN PAYRATE:=BASERATE
                           ELSE PAYRATE:=2.0*BASERATE;
             TOTALPAY:=(PAYRATE*HOURS) + TOTALPAY
             END;
           WRITELN (' TOTAL WEEKLY PAY IS', TOTALPAY:8:2)
         END   {Employee's pay computation}
  END   {Of while loop}
END.   {Of program payroll}
```

FIGURE 7-1   Pay Computation Illustrating User-Defined Types.

7.1.2 SUBRANGE TYPES

Frequently, when choosing the data types we will be using in our program, we find that we really do not need a completely new data type but simply a portion of some existing type. A *scalar subrange* data type is a data type composed of a specified range of any of the other standard or user-defined scalar types, except type REAL.

We define a subrange type with a TYPE declaration of the following format.

TYPE type-name = lowerlimit . . upperlimit;

where "lowerlimit" and "upperlimit" are elements of the same standard or user-defined scalar type, termed the *base type,* and lowerlimit < upperlimit. The new type will be called type-name and will be composed of only those elements belonging to the base type that lie between lowerlimit and upperlimit inclusively.

Examples of subrange declarations are:

```
TYPE EXAMSCORES = 0 . . 100;
      LETTERS = 'A' . . 'Z';
      DIGITS = '0' . . '9';
      WEEKDAYS = MON . . FRI;
      SUMMER = JUNE . . SEPTEMBER;
      FALL = SEPTEMBER . . NOVEMBER;
```

An obvious question is why we really need subrange types. After all, if a portion of an already existing data type is needed, why not just use the entire data type? If, as in the example above, we required a variable called EXAMSCORES that would take on values only in the range 0 to 100, we could simply say:

VAR EXAMSCORES: INTEGER;

An important advantage of the subrange data type is that it helps make programs clear. The above declaration gives us some useful information. We know that the variable EXAMSCORES will be used for storing examination scores (by its name), and that these scores will be integers. However, the declaration

VAR EXAMSCORES: 0 . . 100;

gives the same information and at the same time tells us the valid range of the scores for that exam. We have made the statement more informative and made the purpose of the statement more obvious to someone reading the program listing. Likewise, the statement

VAR SPECIALCHAR: CHAR;

merely tells us that SPECIALCHAR will be a character variable, while

VAR SPECIALCHAR: 'A' . . 'Z';

tells us that this variable will range over the alphabetic characters.

In addition to the increased clarity that can be gained by utilizing a sub-range data type, there is another extremely useful feature that can be provided to the user—execution-time error checking. A subrange data type provides information about the valid range of constants that can be assigned to a variable. This information can be used to check the validity of all assignments made while the program is being run. This validity checking cannot all be done at compile time. Although a statement such as

EXAMSCORES:=101

can be immediately categorized as invalid, the statement

EXAMSCORES:=N

cannot be analyzed for correctness until it is actually executed. If a PASCAL program is being run in *debug mode,* PASCAL will check all assignments of values to variables declared to be of subrange type. Any attempt to assign an out-of-range value to such a variable will cause an execution-time error and program termination. Entering debug mode is usually done with a control card command. Since the exact format of this control card will vary from machine to machine, this information will have to be provided by your instructor. The execution of a program in debug mode will naturally increase the computer time needed to execute the program. This is due to the additional run-time checking being performed. This increase may be quite significant. However, in many cases, the extra time can be considered well spent because of its help in locating and correcting errors.

7.2 STRUCTURED DATA TYPES

The scalar data types introduced so far could be called *simple* data types. This is because variables of these data types are limited to assuming the values of constants of that data type. No higher-level relationships or structures are possible. The declaration

VAR X, Y: INTEGER ;

simply implies that the scalar variables X and Y will take on integer values in the range −MAXINT . . MAXINT. It implies nothing at all about a possible relationship between X and Y. For example:

1. Is X logically related to Y? If so, how is it related?
2. Does X come "before" or "after" Y in any sense?
3. Is X in any way subservient to Y?
4. Does the value of X limit the value of Y in any way?

Structured data types are higher-level types built up (ultimately) from collections of simple scalar data types and contain or imply some additional relationships among the various elements of that scalar type. These relationships, together with the rules for constructing elements of a higher-level type from the simple scalar types, are how we categorize the various structured data types available in PASCAL.

As we mentioned when discussing control statements and scalar data types, the provision for higher-level data types is another example of PASCAL's extraordinary range of power. There are four distinct varieties of structured data types available in PASCAL.

1. Arrays.
2. Records.
3. Sets.
4. Files.

In addition to the four basic structured types listed above, we can also create a number of additional structured data types. Instead of constructing our higher-level data types only from scalar building blocks, we can build them out of other high-level types. This leads to sophisticated and complex structures such as:

1. Arrays of arrays of arrays.
2. Arrays of records.
3. Records containing array components.
4. Files of records.
5. Arrays of sets.

　·
　·
　·

However, ultimately, all of these complex higher-level data types can be viewed as being constructed from the simple PASCAL scalar data types.

An understanding of the enormous data structuring capabilities available in PASCAL is essential for taking advantage of the full power of the language.

7.2.1 ARRAYS

With the scalar data types that we have been limited to so far, we are required to give each variable a unique name. There are times when this is extremely cumbersome. For example, to read in 10 character values at once would require something like this.

> VAR A, B, C, D, E, F, G, H, I, J: CHAR;{The names are hor-
> rible, but so is the
> technique!}

> .
> .
> .

> READLN(A, B, C, D, E, F, G, H, I, J)

To find out if any of the values just read had the value ';' we would need to write something along these lines.

> IF (A=';') OR (B=';') OR (C=';') OR . . .

If the above operations are a cumbersome way of handling 10 items, imagine the problems of working with 100 or 1000! What we need is a data structure in which we can refer to a collection of data objects of identical type by the same name. In PASCAL this type of data structure is called an *array*.

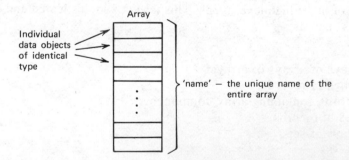

However, since a single "name" now refers to many objects, we must be careful to avoid ambiguous operations such as:

> NAME:=NAME + 1;

> IF NAME =   3   THEN X:=X+1;

In these two examples, which particular element or elements of the array NAME we are referring to is unclear—the first, the third, all of them? Therefore, in a reference to an element of an array, the name will always be composed of two distinct parts—the array name itself and the *array index* (which is frequently termed a *subscript*). This subscript specifies the particular element of the array we are referring to. Syntactically the subscript is represented by enclosing it in square brackets immediately after the array name.

name [subscript]

To create an array data type, we use the following TYPE declaration.

TYPE type-name = ARRAY[t_1] OF t_2;

t_1 specifies the data type to be used in the subscript field. It must be a scalar data type other than REAL. (In many cases it will be a subrange of the data type INTEGER.) This field indicates how we are going to be accessing the individual elements of an array and it specifies how many objects will be contained in the array (i.e., how big the array is). t_2 specifies the data type of the objects stored in the array. We cannot store elements of different data types (e.g., REAL and BOOLEAN) in the same array.

Example 1
        TYPE SAMPLE1 = ARRAY [1 . . 100] OF INTEGER;
        VAR X: SAMPLE1;

These declarations state that X will be a 100-element array of integers. The first element will be accessed by X[1], the second by X[2], . . . , and the hundreth by X[100].

Example 2

        TYPE SAMPLE2 = ARRAY [−5 . . 5] OF CHAR;
        VAR Y: SAMPLE2;

Y will be an 11-element array of characters. The first element will be accessed by Y[−5], the second by Y[−4], . . . , and the eleventh by Y[5].

Example 3

        TYPE SAMPLE3 = ARRAY[DAYSOFTHEWEEK] OF INTEGER;
        VAR Z: SAMPLE3;

If DAYSOFTHEWEEK is the user-defined scalar type we created in the program in Figure 7-1, then Z will be a 7-element integer array. The first element will be referenced by Z[MON], the second by Z[TUE], . . . , and the seventh by Z[SUN].

Example 4

```
TYPE SAMPLE4 = ARRAY[CHAR] OF 'A' . . 'Z';
VAR W: SAMPLE4;
```

The exact length of W will depend on the size of the character set of the computer you are using. For example, if you are using a computer in the IBM/360 or /370 series, W will contain 256 elements. The first element can be accessed as W[CHR(0)], the second as W[CHR(1)], . . . , and the 256th can be accessed as W[CHR(255)]. The value of any array element will be one of the characters between 'A' and 'Z' in the character set.

Now that we know how to create an array, how can we utilize it to avoid the cumbersome constructs that we wrote at the beginning of this section? Assume that we have the following declarations,

```
TYPE STRING = ARRAY[1 . . 10] OF CHAR;
VAR ALPHA: STRING;
```

and we wish to read 10 values into the array ALPHA. If we say

```
READ(ALPHA[1], ALPHA[2], ALPHA[3], . . .)
```

we are no better off than we were before, and the use of an array has gained us nothing. However, if we say instead,

```
READ(ALPHA[I])
```

and we iteratively execute the statement with the value of I ranging from 1 to 10, then we have gained enormously. By using a variable subscript, we can operate successively on all elements of the array merely by changing the current value of the subscript. All that is necessary is to decide how best to assign the necessary values 1, 2, 3, . . , 10 to I. In Section 5.3.3 we introduced the FOR statement, which automatically initializes, increments, and tests a scalar variable. The FOR loop is an ideal method for controlling the index of an array—especially when we know exactly how many elements it has. The above example of reading in an array could now be written:

```
FOR I:=1 TO 10 DO READ(ALPHA[I])
```

The FOR loop will cause the READ statement to be executed 10 times, each time reading one character and putting it into the next slot of the array. If the next 10 characters on the current data card were

```
HELLO BILL
```

the array ALPHA would look like:

H	ALPHA[1]
E	ALPHA[2]
L	ALPHA[3]
L	ALPHA[4]
O	ALPHA[5]
⊔	ALPHA[6]
B	ALPHA[7]
I	ALPHA[8]
L	ALPHA[9]
L	ALPHA[10]

If we wished to count the number of times the letter 'L' occurred any-where within ALPHA, we could again use the FOR construct and a variable subscript to search through the entire array.

```
COUNT:=0;
FOR I:= 1 TO 10 DO
    IF ALPHA[I]='L' THEN COUNT:=COUNT+1
```

The use of a variable in the subscript field of an array reference is actually a special case. Any expression is allowed in the subscript field as long as it has a scalar value of the proper type. To search only the even number elements of ALPHA in reverse order, we could say:

```
COUNT:=0;
FOR I:=5   DOWNTO 1   DO
    IF ALPHA[2* I]='L' THEN COUNT:=COUNT+1
```

In some cases control of the subscript may better be handled by either a REPEAT/UNTIL or a WHILE statement. This is especially true in cases where we do not know exactly how many elements of the array we will be processing. For example, suppose that instead of automatically reading in 10 characters, we wish to keep reading characters into the array until we come to the end of the sentence—denoted by a period. We could write the following.

```
I:=0;
REPEAT
    I:=I+1;
    READ(ALPHA[I])
UNTIL ALPHA[I]='.'
```

The REPEAT loop will now read characters into the array ALPHA one at a time until the last character read is a '.' . When we leave the loop, the variable I will contain the total number of characters that were read in.

There is a problem, however, in this last example. If you look back to the original VAR declaration for ALPHA you will see that it is a 10-element character array. In the previous example, if we have not encountered a period in the first 10 characters, the subscript I would become 11 and we would attempt to execute READ(ALPHA[11]). There is no such element, since the subscript falls outside the bounds of the array. This is an error. In some systems this type of error terminates a program immediately. In others the program continues processing with unpredictable results. Regardless of what your local system does, however, this situation should be avoided. It is always invalid to attempt to access an array element that is outside of the defined limits. Your programs should be constructed so as to prevent this from occurring. This is just another example of the concept of foolproof programming we have stressed repeatedly.

In our second example it would have been much better to write:

```
I:=0;
REPEAT
  I:=I+1;
  READ(ALPHA[I])
UNTIL (ALPHA[I]='.') OR (I=10)
```

There may appear to be another solution to the problem of overrunning arrays. If we do not know how long to make an array when we write the program, we could simply postpone the decision until we do know. For example, if the number of elements to be put into an array were contained on the first data card, it would be nice if we were able to write:

```
TYPE LIST = ARRAY [1 . . N] OF INTEGER;  {This is not
                                                allowable}
VAR  TABLE: LIST;  {An N element array}
     I, N: INTEGER;  {N is the length of the list}
BEGIN
READ(N);  {Determine the length of the list}
FOR I:=1 TO N DO
        READ(TABLE[I]);  {Read in the list itself}
        .
        .
```

What we are trying to do here is say that the size of the array will become known when the program is run. However, declarations like the above are not possible in PASCAL. When an array is declared in PASCAL, the necessary memory space is reserved immediately. Therefore, the PASCAL compiler must know exactly how much space is needed when it processes the TYPE declaration. In the above example the value of N will not be known until the program is actually executed and a data value is read. All array declarations must be given in terms of scalar constants (which may be symbolic constants defined using a CONST declaration).

What do we do if we wish to set up an array whose exact length is unknown? We can plan for the worst case by setting up an array large enough to handle the longest list the program will ever encounter. Although it is invalid to attempt to access more of an array than we declared, it is acceptable to leave part of an array unused. In Figure 7-2, which finds and prints

```
PROGRAM FINDEXTREMES(INPUT, OUTPUT);
{Program to find the largest and smallest numeric
 values in a list of no more than 64 values. An array
 structure will be used to hold the values}
CONST UPPERBOUND=64;  {The maximum length of the array}
TYPE LIST=ARRAY [1. .UPPERBOUND]OF INTEGER;
VAR  TABLE: LIST;
        I: 1. .UPPERBOUND;
        NUM, BIG, SMALL: INTEGER;
BEGIN
        READLN(NUM);   {The number of elements actually needed}
        IF NUM > UPPERBOUND   {Check if the array would
                                      overflow}
            THEN BEGIN
                    WRITELN (' ERROR—LIST LENGTH GREATER THAN
                        LIMIT. WILL RESET TO', UPPERBOUND);
                    NUM:=UPPERBOUND   {Reset so it is a valid value}
                    END;
        {The main algorithm begins here}
            BIG:= −MAXINT; SMALL:=MAXINT;
            FOR I:=1 TO NUM DO
                BEGIN
                READLN(TABLE[I]);
                IF TABLE[I] > BIG THEN BIG:=TABLE[I];
                IF TABLE[I] < SMALL THEN SMALL:=TABLE[I]
                END;
        {If list was not empty print the results of our search}
            IF NUM<=0 THEN  WRITELN (' NO RESULTS—LIST WAS
                                    EMPTY ')
                        ELSE WRITELN (' LARGEST VALUE WAS', BIG,
                                    ' SMALLEST VALUE WAS', SMALL)
        END.   {Of Findextremes}
```

FIGURE 7-2 Program to Find Extreme Values.

the largest and smallest elements within an array, we have declared the array to be 64 elements. If the actual list size is not more than 64, the program will run correctly. If we wish to run the program for a list that has a length greater than 64, we would need to make a single change to the CONST declaration in line 5 of the program.

This example raises an interesting and fundamental question about using arrays—when and why do we need them? This program can be written without the use of arrays. The inner FOR loop of the program could be replaced by this.

```
FOR I:=1 TO NUM DO
    BEGIN
    READLN(X);
    IF X>BIG THEN BIG:=X;
    IF X<SMALL THEN SMALL:=X
    END
```

One major difference, however, becomes obvious. In the first example, which uses arrays, when we have completed the program the original data is still available in the array called TABLE. In the second example, the original data, except for the last item, has been destroyed. Each new value brought in has overwritten the previous value. One of the primary considerations used in determining the need for an array (or some other structure) is: is it necessary to retain the original data for use in later operations? So, while the previous example may have been a poor choice to illustrate the need for the array structure, a slightly different version makes this need quite obvious. Assume we wish to scan a list to find the largest value. We then wish to scan it again to find the second largest, and so on until we have found all items in numerical order. This is basically the sorting problem that we have discussed several times and whose algorithms are outlined in Section 2.3. Now the need for an array becomes quite obvious, since we will be making numerous passes over the original list to put it into numerical sequence. If we lose the data after the first pass we will be unable to complete the sorting process. The insertion sort algorithm of Section 2.3, when translated into PASCAL, would look like the program in Figure 7-3.

7.2.2 MULTIDIMENSIONAL ARRAYS

In the previous section we defined an array as a collection of identical elements known by a single name. For those identical elements we have so far limited ourselves to the scalar data types—INTEGER, REAL, CHAR, and BOOLEAN. We now generalize this to say that the elements of an array can be any data type—including another array. A *multidimensional array* is,

```
PROGRAM INSERTIONSORT(INPUT, OUTPUT);
{Program to sort a list of values into descending numerical sequence
  using the insertion sort algorithm shown in section 2.3          }
LABEL 99;  { For error termination }
CONST MAXSIZE=100;  { We will sort a list of up to 100 elements }
TYPE LISTRANGE=1 . . MAXSIZE;
VAR  LIST: ARRAY[LISTRANGE] OF REAL;
     LOCATION, POINTER, I: LISTRANGE;
     LENGTH: 0 . . MAXSIZE;
     BIG, TEMP: REAL;
BEGIN
   LENGTH:=0;
   WHILE (NOT EOF) AND (LENGTH<MAXSIZE) DO
         BEGIN
         LENGTH:=LENGTH+1;
         READLN(LIST[LENGTH])
         END;
   {See if there was anything to sort}
   IF LENGTH=0 THEN BEGIN
                    WRITELN (' EMPTY LIST—CANNOT SORT');
                    GOTO 99   {Branch to end of program and
                                    terminate}
                    END;
   {The actual sorting algorithm begins here}
   FOR POINTER:= 1 TO LENGTH−1   DO
         BEGIN
         BIG:= LIST[POINTER]; LOCATION:= POINTER;
         FOR I:= POINTER+1 TO LENGTH DO
             IF LIST[I]>BIG THEN
                    BEGIN
                    BIG:=LIST[I];
                    LOCATION:=I
                    END;
         {Now interchange the largest value just found with the
           value at position POINTER                            }
         TEMP:=LIST[POINTER];
         LIST[POINTER]:=LIST[LOCATION];
         LIST[LOCATION]:=TEMP
         END;  { Of outer FOR loop }
   WRITELN ('  THE SORTED LIST');
   FOR I:=1 TO LENGTH DO WRITELN(LIST[I]);
99: END.  {Of insertion sort}
```

FIGURE 7-3   An Insertion Sort Program.

therefore, not a new data type. We have separated it only for pedagogical purposes.

As an example of a multidimensional array, suppose we wished to create a five-element array called SCORE. Each element would itself be a three-element integer array containing integer values in the range 0 to 100. This type of structure is usually called a *two-dimensional array*. Graphically it would look like Figure 7-4.

To create this structure in PASCAL, we would say:

$$\text{VAR SCORE: ARRAY[1 . . 5] OF ARRAY[1 . . 3] OF INTEGER;}$$

This type of declaration is quite cumbersome, so PASCAL provides a shorthand notation.

$$\text{VAR SCORE: ARRAY[1 . . 5, 1 . . 3] OF INTEGER;}$$

In general a two-dimensional array is created using the following TYPE declaration.

$$\text{TYPE type-name} = \text{ARRAY[}t_1, t_2\text{] OF } t_3;$$

where t_1 is a finite scalar type that gives the subscript range of the first dimension (whose size is termed the number of *rows*), t_2 is a finite scalar data type specifying the subscript range of each row (whose size is termed the number of *columns*), and t_3 is the *base type*—the data type of each identical scalar object in the array.

To refer to an element stored in a two-dimensional array we must, as before, use both an array name and a subscript. However, a single subscript is

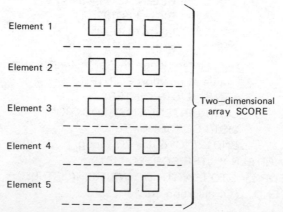

FIGURE 7-4 A Two-Dimensional Array.

now insufficient. Looking at the previous diagram, we can see that if we write SCORE[3] we are not referring to a single object but to three. To locate a single object uniquely within the array, we must identify it by its row and its position within that row. To work with the second element of the third row, we would refer to SCORE[3,2]. The elements of the fourth row would be termed SCORE[4,1], SCORE[4,2], and SCORE[4,3].

The enumeration of the elements of a two-dimensional M by N array is shown in Figure 7-5.

As with the one-dimensional arrays discussed in the previous section, the real power of a two-dimensional array comes from our being able to use expressions in place of constants as subscripts. Since we now have two subscripts, however, we will be required to initialize and increment each one explicitly. This can be done by using a FOR loop or a REPEAT/UNTIL loop, as was done in the previous examples. We have the additional problem, however, of determining the order in which to change the two subscripts. The sequence in which we change subscript values determines the order in which we will process elements in the array. Assume, for example, that the array called SCORE holds examination scores for a class. Each row of SCORE corresponds to three exams for a single student. If we want the average score for each student on the three exams, we will need to process the array by rows. This implies holding the row subscript fixed while the column subscript varies from 1 to the total number of scores (in this case 3). This can be accomplished by the following PASCAL statements.

```
FOR I:=1 TO NUMBEROFSTUDENTS DO
    BEGIN
    SUM:=0;
    FOR J:=1 TO NUMBEROFEXAMS DO
        SUM:=SUM+SCORE[I,J];
    AVERAGE:=SUM DIV NUMBEROFEXAMS;
    WRITELN(' AVERAGE OF STUDENT NO.', I, ' IS',
            AVERAGE)
    END
```

SCORE[1,1]	SCORE[1,2]	SCORE[1,3]	...	SCORE[1,N]
SCORE[2,1]	SCORE[2,2]	SCORE[2,3]	...	SCORE[2,N]
.				.
.				.
.				.
SCORE[M,1]	SCORE[M,2]	SCORE[M,3]	...	SCORE[M,N]

FIGURE 7-5 Element Enumeration in a Two-Dimensional Array.

Since the inner FOR loop will be executed to completion for each value of I in the outer FOR loop, we will handle one complete row and then deal with the next one. If we wanted a class average for each examination, we would process the array by columns. This would involve holding the column subscript fixed while the row subscript ranged from 1 to the total number of students in the class.

```
FOR I:=1 TO NUMBEROFEXAMS DO
    BEGIN
    SUM:=0;
    FOR J:=1 TO NUMBEROFSTUDENTS DO
        SUM:=SUM+SCORE[J,I];
    AVERAGE:=SUM DIV NUMBEROFSTUDENTS;
    WRITELN(' AVERAGE OF EXAM NO.', I, ' IS', AVERAGE)
    END
```

These examples illustrate two important principles to remember when working with multidimensional arrays.

1. Use an appropriate control structure (e.g., FOR, WHILE, or REPEAT/UNTIL) to control the values assigned to each subscript expression.
2. Insure that the order in which the subscripts are modified is correct for the problem being solved.

We have illustrated the concepts of multidimensional arrays by using the specific example of a two-dimensional array. As you might expect, however, all of our comments generalize completely to arrays of arbitrarily high dimension—bounded only by the limitations imposed at your particular installation. These higher-dimensional arrays allow a greater representation of interrelationships between data objects. For example, assume that we wished to store examination scores on students in a number of different classes. We could make SCORE an array of two-dimensional arrays—in effect a *three-dimensional array*. Each array element would represent a single class and would be an array of student scores on a number of exams. There would be as many elements as there are different classes.

```
CONST   NUMOFCLASSES  = 5;   {5 distinct classes}
        NUMOFSTUDENTS=30;    {At most 30 students
                               to a class}
        NUMOFEXAMS    = 3;   {Each student took 3
                               exams}

TYPE    SCORE = ARRAY[1 . . NUMOFCLASSES, 1 . .
        NUMOFSTUDENTS, 1 . . NUMOFEXAMS] OF
        INTEGER;
```

The array would look like the one in Figure 7-6. When we refer to SCORE[2,5,1] we would mean the first examination of the fifth student in class number two.

We could continue this process by adding a "fourth dimension" to the data structure. Then the entire diagram in Figure 7-6 would simply be the first three-dimensional subarray of a four-dimensional array. There would be as many of these three-dimensional array elements as we declared in the TYPE statement for this array. A reference to SCORE[3,2,5,1] might refer to the first examination of the fifth student in the second class of the third school!

7.2.3 RECORDS

We have seen that an array can be a useful data structure because it allows us to form a structure in which all of the items have the same type. There are times, however, when we want to deal with a structure that contains

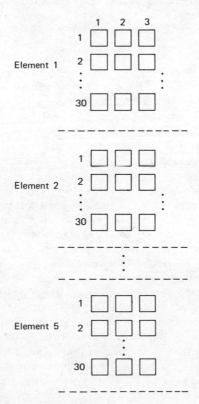

FIGURE 7-6   A Three-Dimensional Array.

elements of different types. For example, we might want to maintain inventory information in the following form.

Part number: 43754
Part name: brake shoe
Price: 15.75
Quantity: 12

We want to keep track of four different pieces of information, and there are three different data types involved: integer, real, and char (actually an array of characters). A multidimensional array will not be helpful in this case, because the individual objects have different types.

STYLE CLINIC 7-1

Efficiency and Multidimensional Arrays

Multidimensional arrays allow you to create interesting data structures describing a fairly complex set of relationships. But one word of caution is in order—they can quickly use up an enormous amount of memory space. The seemingly innocuous declaration

    VAR X: ARRAY[0 . . 50, 0 . . 50, 0 . . 50] OF INTEGER ;

will require an allocation of more than 125,000 memory locations. That may be more memory locations than are available in your computer.

Before creating a very large multidimensional array, be particularly sure that the entire array is really needed. If it is, and you begin getting squeezed for space, some of the space-saving alternatives you should consider are:

1. *Sharing the same space*. If two arrays of the same type are used at different times, that is, if you finish using the first array before you need the second, then consider simply using a single array for both purposes. However, we caution against doing this unless absolutely necessary. It can lead to types of errors that are extremely difficult to find and correct.
2. *Overlays*. If it is impossible to fit the entire array structure in memory at once, consider bringing in a portion of it at a time and working with just that portion. Each new segment will overwrite, or *overlay,* the previous segment when it is brought in. (This is not a PASCAL programming technique. Instead, it is a facility that may be provided by the *operating system* of your computer. Ask your instructor or computer center for details.)
3. *Packing*. When storing information in a memory location, it is not uncommon for much of the memory space to be unused. For example, most computers allow anywhere from two to six constants of type CHAR to be stored in a single location. However, the normal storage of array elements is one element per memory location. Thus, if a particular computer permits

four characters per location, the word PASCAL would internally look like the following.

			P

			A

			S

			C

			A

			L

This has wasted 75% of the available space. To avoid this waste, PASCAL allows you to create *packed arrays*—arrays that try to minimize wasted space by packing information as tightly as possible. If the above were a packed array it would be stored internally as:

P	A	S	C

A	L		

To create a packed array structure, simply add the optional reserved word PACKED to the TYPE declaration:

TYPE type-name = PACKED ARRAY [t_1, t_2 . . .] OF basetype;

Alternatively, arrays can be packed or unpacked dynamically in the program by using the standard PASCAL functions PACK and UNPACK described in Appendix B.

The use of a packed array will have no logical effect on a program. You work with and manipulate the array in exactly the same fashion. It is PASCAL's job to access the individual array elements properly. Be aware, however, that when you use packed arrays you gain *space*—a reduction in the total amount of memory space needed to contain the program—at the expense of *time* efficiency—an increase in the computer time required to execute the program. It takes additional time to isolate and fetch an array element from a packed array, and that makes the program run slower. Whether or not the time lost invalidates the savings in space will depend on the particular problem and the particular computer.

PASCAL includes a structured type called a *record* in which the elements can have different types. A record has a fixed number of components, and each component has a name, called the *field identifier*. We declare a record structure by using a type declaration of this form:

```
TYPE record-identifier = RECORD
                    field-identifier–1: data type;
                    field-identifier–2: data type;
                              .
                              .
                    field-identifier–n: data type
              END;
```

In this definition, "record-identifier" represents the name we are giving to the entire structure. Each "field-identifier" and its associated data type is listed between the reserved identifiers RECORD and END.

Example 1.   Inventory information

```
TYPE INVENTORY = RECORD
                    PARTNUMBER:  INTEGER;
                    PARTNAME  :  PACKED ARRAY
                                 [1 . . 20] OF CHAR;
                    PRICE     :  REAL;
                    QUANTITY  :  INTEGER
              END;
```

Example 2.   Calendar date

```
TYPE      DATE = RECORD
                    DAYOFWEEK :  (SUN, MON, TUE,
                                 WED, THUR, FRI,
                                 SAT);
                    MONTH     :  (JAN, FEB, MAR,
                                 APR, MAY, JUN,
                                 JUL, AUG, SEP,
                                 OCT, NOV, DEC);
                    DAYOFMONTH:  1 . . 31;
                    YEAR      :  INTEGER
              END;
```

Example 3.   Employee information

```
TYPE EMPLOYEEINFO = RECORD
                    NAME      :  PACKED ARRAY
                                 [1 . . 30] OF CHAR;
```

```
                    IDNUMBER:   INTEGER;
                    SEX      :  (MALE, FEMALE);
                    WAGE     :  REAL;
                    DEPT     :  (SALES, LEGAL,
                                PRODUCTION,
                                ACCOUNTING)
                    END;
```

Example 4. Mailing Labels

The individual elements of a record structure can be of any type, including another record. So, to represent the following information,

1. Name.
2. Address.
    a. Street number.
    b. Street name.
    c. City.
    d. State.
    e. Zip code.

we might use the following PASCAL type declaration.

```
TYPE MAILRECORD = RECORD
                NAME       : PACKED ARRAY[1 . . 20] OF
                             CHAR;
                ADDRESS  : RECORD
                             STREETNUM   : INTEGER;
                             STREETNAME,
                             CITY,
                             STATE         : PACKED
                                             ARRAY
                                             [1 . . 20]
                                             OF CHAR;
                             ZIP           : 0 . . 99999
                           END {Of the address record}
                END; {Of the mailrecord}
```

Each of these examples has made use of the fact that a record need not be homogeneous—the components of a record do not have to be all of one type. Note that a component can be any data type whatsoever, including the standard scalar types, user-defined scalar types, or structured types.

Once a record structure has been declared, we can use a VAR declaration to designate that one or more variables are instances of that data type. For example, if we write

```
        VAR DATE1, DATE2 : DATE;
```

then the two variables DATE1 and DATE2 each have the structure indicated in the TYPE declaration for DATE.

To access a particular record component, we write the name of the variable, a period, and the name of the component:

```
        record-variable.field-identifier
```

For example, if DATE1 is to contain the date

```
        Sunday, June 6, 1982
```

we would write:

```
        DATE1.DAYOFWEEK   :=SAT;
        DATE1.MONTH       :=JUN;
        DATE1.DAYOFMONTH:=  6;
        DATE1.YEAR        :=1982
```

This notation illustrates one of the restrictions we face when we use records. When we refer to a record variable, we must explicitly name the component we are interested in—we cannot use a variable name to designate the component. To see what this means, consider the following declarations.

```
        VAR   LIST :   ARRAY[1 . . 50] OF INTEGER;
              SUM,I:   INTEGER;
              PART :   INVENTORY; {INVENTORY is the record
                                     structure defined previously}
```

We know that it is often convenient to use a variable as a subscript when we refer to an array element, as in SUM:=SUM + LIST[I]. Each time this statement is executed, an element of the array will be added to the sum; the particular value added depends on the value of I.

We cannot apply this concept to record components. This is, we cannot write something like "PART.variable-name" where "variable-name" might represent PARTNUMBER at one time and QUANTITY at another time. We must make an explicit reference to the component by using its name.

```
        PART.PARTNUMBER:=43754;
        PART.QUANTITY    :=12
```

Thus, in comparing records to arrays we see that the method of access is more restrictive for records. On the other hand, records provide a richer structure because their components can be of different types.

Earlier we used a VAR declaration to indicate that PART was to have the structure of the record we called INVENTORY. This would allow us to keep track of the inventory information for one part. Of course, if we were actually maintaining inventory information, we would have many parts and we would want more than one data object with this structure. We could write

VAR   PART1, PART2, PART3, PART4: INVENTORY;

but this will obviously be cumbersome when the number of data items is large.

We want a way to state conveniently that a number of data objects all have the same structure. This leads us back to the idea of an array. To set up a data structure for inventory control, we might want to declare an *array of records*. Each element of the array will be a record structure (of type INVENTORY). The number of elements in the array will be equal to the number of different parts we have. For example, if we have 500 parts and we have already declared a record structure for INVENTORY, we might write:

VAR   PARTS :   ARRAY[1 . . 500] OF INVENTORY;

To access some particular item, we use a subscript to indicate which of the 500 parts we are interested in and a field identifier to indicate the record component. For example, the quantity on hand of the fifth part in the list is PARTS[5].QUANTITY. The price of the last item in the list is PARTS [500].PRICE.

If J is an integer variable we can set each of the quantity-on-hand fields to a given value (e.g., 50) quite simply:

FOR J:= 1 TO 500 DO PARTS[J].QUANTITY:= 50

An array of records is a convenient, useful data structure. For example, suppose that personnel records for 100 employees are kept in the EMPLOYEEINFO structure that we defined earlier. We will use these variables.

VAR   WORKER: ARRAY[1 . . 100] OF EMPLOYEEINFO;
      J, COUNT: INTEGER;

If we want to find out how many of the employees in the accounting department are females, we can write:

```
COUNT:=0;
FOR  J:=1 TO 100 DO
    IF  (WORKER[J].DEPT=ACCOUNTING)
    AND  (WORKER[J].SEX=FEMALE)
        THEN     COUNT:=COUNT+1;
WRITELN(COUNT, ' EMPLOYEES IN ACCOUNTING ARE
        FEMALE')
```

In this example we have referred to two of the components of each element in the record structure. There may be times when we want to refer to many of the components, and it can be bothersome to have to repeat the name of the structure in each reference. In these cases we can use the WITH statement to name the structure once. Then, within the scope of the WITH statement, we use the names of the record components as if they were variable names—we omit the name of the structure and the period that separates the structure name from the component name. We could rewrite the previous example as:

```
COUNT:=0;
FOR  J:=1 TO 100 DO
    WITH WORKER[J] DO
        IF  (DEPT=ACCOUNTING) AND (SEX=FEMALE)
        THEN     COUNT := COUNT+1;
WRITELN(COUNT, ' EMPLOYEES IN ACCOUNTING ARE
        FEMALE')
```

The general form of the WITH statements is:

```
WITH record-variable-1, record-variable-2, . . . DO
statement
```

The scope of the WITH statement is the statement that follows DO. As usual, this can be a compound statement. If we have record structures within record structures, we can list all of the record names to allow direct access to the component names within the scope of the WITH statement.

There is one other area of interest in the PASCAL record structure. *Record variants* allow us to set up a record whose precise structure may be slightly different for different variables. For example, suppose we want to set up an array of records that contains student enrollment information for a university. The record components might be:

Name
Student number
Number of credits completed

Grade point average
Year started
Received financial aid? (If so, how much this year and how much on a cumulative basis?)

The last component is of particular interest. If a student has received financial aid, we want to record this year's amount and a cumulative total. Of course, there is no need for entries in these areas if a student has never received aid, so these fields need not be present for all students. We say that these are record variant fields.

We can set up a record structure with variant fields by using a case clause to specify the circumstances in which each variant is used. Each variant has associated with it a list of components, and each component has a type. The components and their types are enclosed in parentheses, and all of the variants are listed after the invariant portions of the record structure. Component names cannot be duplicated,even in different variants.

We can set up our student enrollment structure as follows.

```
TYPE STUDENTRECORD = RECORD
                    NAME: PACKED ARRAY[1 . . 30] OF CHAR;
                    NUMBER: INTEGER;
                    CREDITS: INTEGER;
                    GRADEAVG: REAL;
                    YEARSTARTED: INTEGER;
                    FINANCIALAID: BOOLEAN;
                    CASE BOOLEAN OF
                        TRUE: ( CURRENT:  REAL;
                                      TOTAL: REAL);
                        FALSE:( )   {No variant fields for
                                        this case}
                    END;
VAR   STUDENT :ARRAY[1 . . 5000] OF STUDENTRECORD;
```

If a student has received financial aid, field FINANCIALAID will be TRUE, and two additional fields will exist: CURRENT and TOTAL. These fields will not exist if FINANCIALAID is FALSE.

Because the variant part depends on the component FINANCIALAID, which is defined in the same record structure, we can achieve a slight economy of notation by combining the declaration of FINANCIALAID with the CASE clause:

```
        CASE FINANCIALAID: BOOLEAN OF
             TRUE:    (CURRENT: REAL;
                           TOTAL: REAL);
             FALSE : ( )
```

We conclude our discussion of records with a more detailed example than the ones we have used up to now (Figure 7-7). We will consider the initial part of a large inventory control program—we will illustrate the portion of the program that reads data values to initialize the data structure. Subsequent parts of the program would process data about transactions that indicates that some stock has been depleted or augmented. The processing of these data involves updating the appropriate fields of the record structure. We will not pursue these details at this time, since the principles of setting up and accessing the data structure will be illustrated by the initial part of the program.

We will utilize the record structure that we used to illustrate inventory information in Example 1 at the beginning of this section. Our program will initialize the data structure by reading a line of data that contains the following information for each part.

Part number. A five-digit integer (numbers range from 10000 to 99999).
Part name. Always 20 characters (blanks used if necessary).
Price. A real number with two positions to the right of the decimal point and one to three positions to the left of the decimal point.
Quantity. An integer (must be nonnegative).

We will echo-print and validate the data.

```
PROGRAM INVDATA(INPUT,OUTPUT);
{
Establish a data structure for inventory information. Initialize the structure
by reading in the data values
                                                                    }
CONST SIZE = 500; NAMELENGTH =20;
TYPE  NAMERANGE=1 . . NAMELENGTH;
      PARTRANGE= 1 . . SIZE;
   INVENTORY = RECORD
                    PARTNUMBER: INTEGER;
                    PARTNAME   : PACKED ARRAY[NAMERANGE]
                                 OF CHAR;
                PRICE      : REAL;
                QUANTITY   : INTEGER
              END;
VAR PARTS       : ARRAY [PARTRANGE] OF INVENTORY;
    NUMITEMS  : PARTRANGE;
    K               : NAMERANGE;
    CHARACTER: CHAR;
{Initialize the structure}
BEGIN
```

```
NUMITEMS:=1;
WHILE (NOT EOF) AND (NUMITEMS<=SIZE) DO
    BEGIN
    WITH PARTS[NUMITEMS] DO
        BEGIN
        READ(PARTNUMBER); WRITE(' PART NUMBER = ', PARTNUMBER);
        IF (PARTNUMBER < 10000) OR (PARTNUMBER > 99999)
            THEN BEGIN
                    WRITE(' *INVALID PART NUMBER; ZERO USED*'); WRITELN;
                    PARTNUMBER := 0
                    END;
        WRITE(' NAME = ');
        FOR K := 1 TO NAMELENGTH DO
            BEGIN
            READ(CHARACTER); WRITE(CHARACTER);
            PARTNAME[K] := CHARACTER
            END;
        READ(PRICE); WRITE(' PRICE = ', PRICE:8:2);
        IF (PRICE < 0.0) OR (PRICE > 999.99)
            THEN BEGIN
                    WRITE(' *INVALID PRICE; 0.00 USED* '); WRITELN;
                    PRICE := 0.0
                    END;
        READLN(QUANTITY); WRITE(' QUANTITY = ', QUANTITY);
        IF QUANTITY < 0
            THEN BEGIN
                    WRITE(' *INVALID QUANTITY;   ZERO USED* ');
                    QUANTITY := 0
                    END;
        WRITELN;
        NUMITEMS := NUMITEMS + 1
        END { Of the WITH }
    END; {Of the WHILE}
NUMITEMS := NUMITEMS - 1; { The number of items in the inventory }
        .
        .
        .

    { The remainder of the program will go here. It will read transaction data
    and update the inventory information                                    }

        .
        .
        .

END. { Of the program INVDATA }
```

FIGURE 7-7 Portion of an Inventory Management Program.

7.2.4 SETS

When we worked with array and record data types we did so primarily by manipulating the individual elements of the structure. We never worked with the entire array or record as a single unit. If we wanted to search an array we had to write code that checked each array element individually.

A *set* is a PASCAL structured data type that, like the array and record, is a collection of elements. However, unlike the array or record, we do not index and access the indivdual elements which comprise the set. Instead, we work with it as a single unit.

The elements that comprise any particular set are chosen from a collection of objects termed the *base type*. To create a set data type in PASCAL, we use the following declaration.

TYPE type-name = SET OF basetype;

Variables of type "type-name" will be sets whose *members* are chosen from the specified basetype. To indicate set constants, we use the square brackets, [ ], to enclose the set elements.

For example, consider the following declarations.

TYPE LETTERSETS = SET OF 'A' . . 'Z';
VAR V, W, X, Y, Z: LETTERSETS;

V, W, X, and Z are variables that can be assigned values of set constants. In this example the members of these sets will be chosen from the alphabetic characters 'A' to 'Z'. We could say, for example:

W := ['A', 'E', 'I', 'O', 'U'];
X := ['A', 'B', 'C'];
Y := [ ];   {The *empty set*}
Z := ['I' . . 'N']

There are three binary operators that specifically operate on sets to produce new sets.

+	Set union.	An element is contained in the *union* of two sets, denoted A+B, if and only if it is an element of set A or set B or both.
−	Set difference.	An element is contained in the *difference* of two sets, denoted A−B, if and only if it is an element of set A but not an element of the set B.
*	Set intersection.	An element is contained in the *intersection* of two sets, denoted A*B, if and only if it is an element of both set A and set B.

```
V:= W+X;     {V will be the set ['A', 'B', 'C', 'E', 'I', 'O', 'U']}
V:= X+Y;     {V is ['A', 'B', 'C']}
V:= W−X;     {V is ['E', 'I', 'O', 'U']}
V:= W*X      {V is ['A']}
```

There are three important relational operators which apply to the set data type. They produce a boolean result.

=   Set equality.   If A and B are sets, the relation A=B is TRUE if and only if every member of set A is a member of set B and every member of set B is a member of set A.

<>   Set inequality. The relation A<>B is TRUE if and only if A=B is FALSE.

<=   Set inclusion.   The relation A<=B is TRUE if and only if every member of set A is also a member of set B. In effect, this relationship says that the set A is included in or contained within the set B.

For example:

```
W = ['A', 'I', 'O', 'U', 'E']  is TRUE  {Notice that order is
                                         unimportant.}
W <> Y  is TRUE
X <= W  is FALSE
['B', 'C'] = X − (W*X)  is TRUE
```

There is one more set operator that is particularly useful—set membership.

IN   Set membership. If A is an element of type t, and B is a set over the basetype t, the relation A IN B is TRUE if and only if the element A is contained in the set B.

Consider the following declaration.

```
VAR C: CHAR;
```

Then the expression C IN W is TRUE if C currently has any of the character values 'A', 'E', 'I', 'O', or 'U'.

The set membership operation can be a very quick way to perform a series of disjoint tests that would otherwise be very cumbersome. Suppose that we want to write a program to count the number of punctuation marks used in a given text. The 10 specific punctuations marks that we are looking for are

. , ; : ' - ( ) [ ] . The entire text is terminated by the special symbol '*'. Without using sets and set operations, we would write something like Figure 7-8.

```
PROGRAM COUNTPUNCTUATION(INPUT, OUTPUT);
{Program to count the frequency of occurrence of the 10 punctua-
  tion symbols . , ; = ' - ( ) [ ] on a single card}
VAR CH: CHAR;
    COUNT: INTEGER;
BEGIN
    COUNT:=0;
    REPEAT
      READ(CH); WRITE(CH);
      IF  (CH='.') OR (CH=',') OR (CH=';') OR
          (CH=':') OR (CH='''') OR (CH='-') OR
          (CH='(') OR (CH=')') OR (CH='[') OR
          (CH=']')
              THEN COUNT:=COUNT+1
    UNTIL (CH = '*') OR EOLN;
    WRITELN;
    WRITELN(' NUMBER OF PUNCTUATION MARKS IS ', COUNT)
END.   {Of countpunctuation}
```
FIGURE 7-8   Counting Punctuation Characters (Without Sets).

This awkward construction can be greatly simplified by the use of sets. Instead of performing the test with a number of disjunctive clauses, we can
perform the entire operation at once using a single set inclusion test (Figure 7-9).

```
PROGRAM COUNTPUNCTUATION(INPUT, OUTPUT);
{Program to count the frequency of occurrence of the same 10 punc-
  tuation symbols but now using sets}
VAR PUNCTUATION: SET OF CHAR;
    CH: CHAR;
    COUNT: INTEGER;
BEGIN
    COUNT:=0;
    PUNCTUATION:=['.', ',', ';', '''', '-', '(', ')', '[', ']', ':'];
    REPEAT
      READ(CH); WRITE(CH);
      IF CH IN PUNCTUATION THEN COUNT:=COUNT+1
    UNTIL (CH= '*') OR EOLN;
    WRITELN;
    WRITELN(' NUMBER OF PUNCTUATION MARKS IS ', COUNT)
END.   {Of countpunctuation}
```
FIGURE 7-9   Counting Punctuation Characters (Using Sets).

One final word about sets. Because of the way that sets are generally implemented, many implementations of PASCAL limit the maximum number of elements allowed in the basetype. This limit may be fairly small, and it could possibly prohibit you from performing some meaningful and useful set operations. In this section we utilized set declarations in the following way.

```
TYPE LETTERSETS = SET OF 'A' . . 'Z';
VAR PUNCTUATION : SET OF CHAR;
```

In the first case the basetype 'A' . . 'Z' probably contains 26 elements. In the second case the number of elements depends on the size of the character set for your machine and would typically be 64, 128, or 256. Whether either of the above declarations would actually be valid, then, depends on the limitation on the size of set base types at a particular installation. This information will have to be provided by your instructor. As a specific example of these limits, one current implementation of PASCAL on a Control Data 6000 series computer accepts base types with no more than 59 elements. However, the 6000 series has a 64-element character set. So the second example above would not be accepted, and we would get an error message—even though the statement is, at least syntactically, perfectly correct. Since we cannot increase this upper bound, we are limited to only two courses of action—either reduce the size of the base type in our set declaration or use an array of sets.

7.2.5 FILES

In PASCAL a *file* is a structured data type containing a sequence of elements of identical type. Although this definition sounds exactly like the definition of the array given in Section 7.2.1, there are a number of significant differences. Unlike an array, the entire file is not accessible all at once. With the array we merely index the desired element, A[1] or A[1000], and it is immediately available. With a file only a single element, sometimes termed the *window,* is available. The remainder of the file is assumed to exist on some external or secondary storage device, although the specific details of that device need not be known. To access an element of a file not currently in the window, we must read sequentially through the entire file until we come to the desired element. A second major difference between file and array data types is that the length of an array must be known at the time it is declared. However, a file can be of arbitrary and unlimited size, since we never look at more than a single item of the file at a time.

To declare a file type, we use the following declaration.

```
TYPE type-name = FILE OF basetype;
```

where "basetype" indicates the data type of each individual element of the file. For example:

```
TYPE    DATAFILE = FILE OF INTEGER;
        CHARFILE = FILE OF CHAR;
        ARRAYFILE = FILE OF ARRAY [1 . . 10] OF REAL;

VAR          X: DATAFILE;
             Y: CHARFILE;
             Z: ARRAYFILE;
```

The declaration of a file variable will automatically create a window into that file. This window, more formally called a *buffer variable,* is indicated by the special character '↑'. For example, the VAR declaration above would create three buffer variables X↑, Y↑, and Z↑. A buffer variable can be thought of as the position where we are currently reading from or writing into a file. The file and the buffer variable are controlled and tested by five standard functions or procedures.

1. EOF(file).   If the buffer variable has moved beyond the end of a file the value of this function is true. Otherwise it is false. We have already used EOF quite extensively with the standard file INPUT, but we see now that it may be used with any arbitrary file.

2. RESET(file).   Initializes a file for reading by setting the buffer variable, file↑, to the first element of the file and setting EOF(file) to false if the file is not empty. All input files (except INPUT) must be reset before reading.

3. REWRITE(file).   Initializes a file for writing by clearing it completely and setting EOF(file) to true. All output files (except OUTPUT) must be cleared before use.

4. GET(file).   Reads the next element of the file into file↑ and leaves EOF(file) false. If nothing else was on the file, EOF(file) becomes true and file↑ is undefined.

5. PUT(file).   Writes the contents of file↑ onto the end of the file. EOF(file) remains true.

To illustrate the use of these functions, we will write a sample program to "launder" a data file (Figure 7-10). This is a common operation in which we take one data file, remove all invalid, improper, or unwanted values, and create a second data file containing only the desired values. Assume that we have a file of integers called INFILE and we wish to create a second file called OUTFILE that contains only those input values in the range 200 to 800.

```
PROGRAM LAUNDER(OUTPUT, INFILE, OUTFILE);
{Program to launder a data file by removing
 all values outside the range 200 to 800}
VAR   INFILE, OUTFILE : FILE OF INTEGER;
      SIZE            : INTEGER;
BEGIN
      RESET(INFILE); REWRITE(OUTFILE);
      SIZE:= 0;
      WHILE NOT EOF(INFILE) DO
        BEGIN
        IF (INFILE↑ >=200) AND (INFILE↑<=800)
          THEN      BEGIN
                    OUTFILE↑:=INFILE↑;
                    PUT(OUTFILE);
                    SIZE:=SIZE+1
                    END;
        GET(INFILE)
        END;  {Of the WHILE loop}
      WRITELN(' NEW OUTPUT FILE NOW CREATED.   TOTAL
              SIZE IS ', SIZE, ' ELEMENTS')
END.  {Of launder}
```

FIGURE 7-10   Program Using File Data Types.

Figure 7-10 illustrates one additional requirement for using files. Any file that is either created outside the program and passed into it (e.g., INFILE above) or that is created by the program and needs to be passed out (e.g., OUTFILE above) is called an *external file*. All external files must be declared in the program heading, as shown in line 1 of Figure 7-10. The standard files INPUT and OUTPUT (if needed), along with all other external file names, are listed immediately following the program name. In addition to this requirement, it is frequently the case that special control cards are needed to allow the use of external files. However, since this information is not part of PASCAL but is specific to each computer installation, the necessary details will have to be provided locally.

There is one particular file type that is so important that it deserves special mention. A *textfile* is a file of characters. PASCAL contains a standard file type, called TEXT, which is defined as follows.

TYPE TEXT = FILE OF CHAR;

A textfile can be thought of as a file of variable length units, called lines, composed of just the printable characters. Each line in the file is separated from the next by a special *line separator* character. If c represents any printable character, LS represents the line separator, and EOF the end of file, then a textfile can be represented as in Figure 7-11.

cccc ... c LS cc ... c LS ccccc ... c LS ... EOF

　　Line 1　　　　Line 2　　　　Line 3　　　　. . .

FIGURE 7-11　Organization of a textfile.

The standard procedures READ, READLN, WRITE, and WRITELN, and the boolean predicate EOLN can now be described more accurately than was possible in Chapter 4. These standard procedures operate on text-files in the following way (assume F has been declared as a textfile and CH as a character variable).

EOLN(F)	EOLN(F) is true if F↑ currently points at a line separator character and false otherwise.
READ(F, CH)	CH:= F↑;　GET(F)
READLN(F, CH)	CH:= F↑; WHILE NOT EOLN(F) DO 　GET(F); GET(F)
WRITE(F, CH)	F↑:= CH; PUT(F)
WRITELN(F, CH)	F↑:= CH; PUT(F); F↑:= "LS"; PUT(F) {LS is the line separator}

Notice that when the above procedures are applied to files other than the standard textfiles INPUT and OUTPUT, the file name must be the first parameter. If the file name is omitted the default name INPUT is assumed for reading, and the name OUTPUT is assumed for writing.

As an example of the use of textfiles, consider the problem of creating a textfile of fixed length 80 character lines from a file containing variable sized lines 1 to 80 characters in length. We will pad the lines with blanks as necessary (Figure 7-12).

```
PROGRAM FIXEDLENGTH(TEXTIN, TEXTOUT, OUTPUT);
{This is a program to read lines of 1 to 80 characters
 in length from one textfile and produce a second
 textfile with fixed length 80 character lines}
CONST MAXLINE = 80;
          BLANK = ' ';
VAR   TEXTIN, TEXTOUT: TEXT;
          CURRENTSIZE: 0 . . MAXLINE;
                    I: 1 . . MAXLINE;
                  CH: CHAR;
BEGIN
      RESET(TEXTIN); REWRITE(TEXTOUT);
      WHILE  NOT  EOF(TEXTIN)  DO
          BEGIN
          CURRENTSIZE := 0;
          WHILE NOT  EOLN(TEXTIN) AND (CURRENTSIZE
                    <= MAXLINE) DO
              BEGIN READ(TEXTIN,CH);
                    CURRENTSIZE:=CURRENTSIZE+1;
                    WRITE(TEXTOUT,CH)
              END;
          FOR I:=(CURRENTSIZE+1) TO MAXLINE DO
              WRITE(TEXTOUT,BLANK);
          READLN(TEXTIN);
          WRITELN(TEXTOUT)
          END  {Of the WHILE loop};
WRITELN(' COPY OPERATION HAS BEEN SUCCESSFULLY
COMPLETED')
END.  {Of program fixedlength}
```

FIGURE 7-12   Program to Illustrate Use of Textfiles.

A final comment should be made about textfiles and extensions to the standard procedures READ, READLN, WRITE, and WRITELN. If F is any textfile (including INPUT or OUTPUT), then the following operations are also valid if the sequence of characters in the textfile corresponds to the proper syntax of an integer or real constant in PASCAL.

```
VAR   I: INTEGER;
       R:  REAL;

      .
      .
      .

READ(F,I)  ; READLN(F,I);
READ(F,R)  ; READLN(F,R)
```

```
WRITE(F,I) ; WRITELN(F,I);
WRITE(F,R); WRITELN(F,R)
```

The procedures above will either assemble the required number of characters from the textfile into an integer or real decimal value, or disassemble the decimal value into the appropriate sequence of characters. The procedures READ and READLN will skip leading blanks and line separators when looking for integers and reals. The procedures WRITE and WRITELN will also allow strings (packed arrays of characters) and booleans to be written. Some installations will possibly extend the READ and WRITE procedures even further to include the input and output of data types such as user-defined scalars, arrays, records, and sets. Some of these operations are nonstandard and thus availability will have to be determined locally.

7.3 POINTER TYPES

All the variables discussed so far, whether simple or structured, share a common characteristic—they are *static* entities. This means that all necessary memory is allocated for that variable at the time the program containing the variable declaration is about to begin execution. It remains in existence as long as the program is executing.* This approach contrasts sharply with the class of variables we will look at next—the dynamic variables.

A *dynamic variable* is created and destroyed dynamically during the execution of a program. Unlike static variables, dynamic variables are not referenced by a user-specified name. Instead, they are referenced indirectly by *pointers* to the newly created variable. For example:

p ⟶ | V |

The dynamic variable "V" would be referenced not by name, but by its associated pointer variable p, which "points to" V.

PASCAL provides dynamic variables through the following TYPE declaration.

TYPE type-name = ↑ base-type;

The "type-name" defined above is now a dynamic data type whose pointers will point to objects of the indicated "basetype." We say that the type-name is *bound* to the basetype. For example:

---

* The variant record type may superficially seem to be a contradiction, but actually is not. Enough memory is initially allocated for the largest variant form regardless of how much memory is eventually required.

TYPE INTPOINTER = ↑ INTEGER;

VAR IP: INTPOINTER;

IP is now a *reference variable* or a *pointer variable* that may be bound to an integer value, while IP↑ will be the actual integer value being pointed to.

There are two standard PASCAL procedures that create and destroy dynamic variables.

NEW(p)   NEW will create a dynamic variable of the basetype. A pointer to this new variable is assigned to the variable p.

DISPOSE(p)   DISPOSE will destroy the variable pointed at by p and return the space just released to some "available space list" for future use. p is then undefined.

As an example, the statement

NEW(IP)

will create an unnamed integer variable and store the pointer to it in IP. To use this newly created variable, we reference it as IP↑.

Either of the following statements would correctly assign the new variable an initial integer value.

IP↑ := 1

READ(IP↑)

The statement

DISPOSE(IP)

will destroy the variable. Any future reference to IP↑ will result in a run-time error.

As a more meaningful example, we look back at the binary tree discussed in Section 2.4. As described there, a binary tree can be viewed as a collection of nodes. Each node contains three values—a left pointer, a right pointer, and a name. This structure could be created in PASCAL by the following declarations.

```
TYPE    POINTER = ↑NODE;

        NODE =      RECORD
                        LEFTPOINTER : POINTER;
                        NAME : CHAR;
                        RIGHTPOINTER : POINTER
                    END;
        VAR    P, ROOT : POINTER;
```

Each node is now comprised of three fields—a one-character name and two pointer variables. Each pointer refers to another element of type node. The nodes themselves are never referred to directly by name (notice there is no variable declared of type NODE). Instead, we make indirect references through the pointers.

For example, to create the following one node tree:

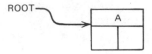

we would write the following:

NEW(ROOT);   {This allocates the space for a new node}

ROOT↑.NAME := 'A'   {Defines the name field of the new node}

However, what should we do with the left and right pointer fields of this new node? As the diagram above shows, they are not being used. So what should we put there? In PASCAL there is a special *pointer constant* that is used to indicate that a pointer variable is not pointing to anything! This constant is termed NIL and is sometimes indicated on diagrams by the symbol Λ. Thus, to complete the creation of the one-node tree above would require these two commands.

ROOT↑.LEFTPOINTER:=NIL;

ROOT↑.RIGHTPOINTER:=NIL

If we wished to build on the existing tree to create the following:

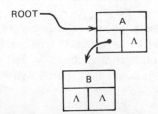

we would require these five statements (assume that P is also a pointer type bound to type NODE).

> NEW(P);   {Create the space for the second node}
>
> ROOT↑.LEFTPOINTER:=P;   {Set the left pointer of A to point to this new node}
>
> P↑.NAME:= 'B';
>
> P↑.LEFTPOINTER:= NIL;
>
> P↑.RIGHTPOINTER:= NIL

If we wished to remove the node just added, we merely write:

> ROOT↑.LEFTPOINTER:= NIL;
> DISPOSE (P)   {Remove the node just added}

As a final example, consider the diagram in Style Clinic 7-2. It indicates why a linked list structure can sometimes be a very efficient way to represent a sorted list, especially if we frequently need to insert a new element into the list. The pointer mechanism we have been discussing now gives us a way to create and use this linked list structure.

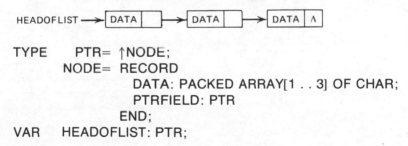

```
TYPE    PTR= ↑NODE;
        NODE= RECORD
                DATA: PACKED ARRAY[1 . . 3] OF CHAR;
                PTRFIELD: PTR
              END;
        VAR   HEADOFLIST: PTR;
```

If we assume that the string values in the data field of each node above are ordered by increasing magnitude, then inserting a new string into the list involves finding where it belongs, creating a new node, and adjusting the pointers accordingly. Let us assume that the list has been searched and a pointer variable called NEWPTR currently points to the element prior to the one being inserted. The following statements will correctly insert the string value 'ABC' into the list (assume that P is a pointer bound to type NODE).

> NEW(P);   {Get space for a new node}
> P↑.DATA:= 'ABC';   {Set data field of new node}
> P↑.PTRFIELD:= NEWPTR↑.PTRFIELD;   {Set pointer field of new node}
> NEWPTR↑.PTRFIELD:= P   {Adjust pointer of the item in the list just before the new one}

Figure 7-13 shows the situation just before and after the execution of the above four commands.

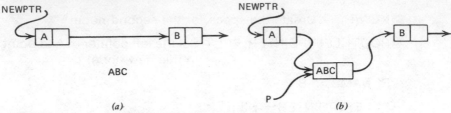

FIGURE 7-13   List Insertion Using Pointers. (*a*) Before. (*b*) After.

We began our discussion of structured data types in Section 7.2 by saying that they are built up from simple scalar types. Likewise, the examples in this section should indicate that the best way to view the pointer data type is as a building block for creating complex and powerful linked data structures. Figure 7-14 shows a number of different linked structures. They all occur quite frequently in computer applications and can all be created and manipulated by the PASCAL pointer type. The meaning and purpose of these complex structures is beyond our discussion. Our purpose here is merely to show

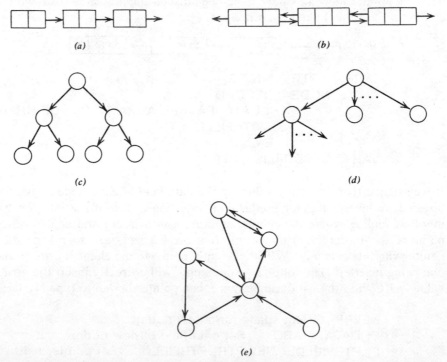

FIGURE 7-14   Some Common Linked Data Structures. (*a*) Singly Linked List. (*b*) Doubly Linked List. (*c*) Binary Tree. (*d*) General Tree. (*e*) Directed Graph.

the wide range of structures that can ultimately be created from the simple pointer building blocks. This dynamic data structuring ability gives a programmer enormous flexibility in choosing the most appropriate data structure for the problem being solved.

STYLE CLINIC 7-2

A Passing Comment About Data Structures

The last few sections have introduced you to an enormous variety of data structures. The last type discussed, the pointer, is actually just a building block for other interesting structures—lists, queues, trees, and graphs, to name a few. It is the job of the programmer to wade through this maze of potential data structures and select the one most appropriate and most efficient for the problem being solved. Choosing the right one can greatly simplify and speed up the task.

For example, if we had a sorted array of integers, the addition of one new element would require us to resort the entire array. If, however, the integers were stored as a linked list, the problem would be solved by merely changing two pointers.

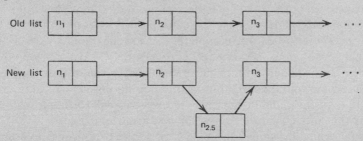

For this example the linked list would be a far superior structure if the list of values were updated frequently.

Just as a programmer must be able to work with and evaluate alternate algorithms, so must he or she be able to work with and evaluate alternate data structures. The two topics are inextricably related.

7.4 CASE STUDY—THE GAME OF LIFE

The Game of Life is a fascinating simulation game developed by the mathematician John Horton Conway of Cambridge University.* It is intended both as a diversion and as a model for the life cycle of societies of

---

* See "Mathematical Games," *Scientific American, 223* (4), October 1970, pp. 120–123 for complete details.

living organisms. Conway's game is played on a very large (assumed infinite) checkerboard. Each square, or cell, on the board represents the possible location of a living organism. Each cell has eight adjacent cells.

```
1   2   3
8   *   4
7   6   5
```

Conway's three basic rules, or "genetic laws" as he calls them, are quite simple.

1. *Birth*. Each empty cell adjacent to exactly three neighbors will have a birth in the next generation.
2. *Death*. Each occupied cell with exactly 0 or 1 neighbors dies of isolation and loneliness. Each occupied cell with 4 or more neighbors dies of overpopulation.
3. *Survival*. Each occupied cell with exactly 2 or 3 neighbors survives to the next generation.

All births and deaths occur simultaneously, and the application of these genetic laws to an entire board position to produce a new board position is called a *generation*. The game is typically played until one of three things happens: the society dies out completely; it reaches some "steady-state" pattern that either does not change or oscillates forever; or, finally, we voluntarily halt the generations because we have run out of time (or interest). Depending on the initial configuration, the population growth may undergo startling, unexpected, and fascinating changes and will form interesting configurations that move, mutate, grow, or disappear entirely.

The game is ideally suited to being programmed on a digital computer. In fact, Conway himself used a computer in his early studies of the game to study very complex patterns. The basic outline of the algorithm is quite simple (Figure 7-15).

However, this "solution" is much too simplistic because it does not take into account the pragmatic limitation of finite time and finite space. This solution is not even an algorithm, since it violates the criterion of termination

```
Read the initial board position
Repeat the following forever
    Compute births, deaths, survivors
    Produce the new board
    Write the new board
End of the loop
```

FIGURE 7-15   Initial Game of Life Representation.

in finite time. We need a way to halt the program. Our discussion listed three criteria for termination.

1. Population dies out (that is, an empty board)
2. Steady state (i.e., generation [n+1] = generation [n]; we will ignore the problem of oscillations.
3. Reaching a user-specified upper bound on the number of generations.

All three of these should be included in the algorithm.

Another question is how should we represent the playing surface? Theoretically it is viewed as an infinite two-dimensional checkerboard. Obviously, we cannot make that assumption when writing the program. We will be limited to a finite-size, two-dimensional array. If we make the board a character array we can use two distinct characters (e.g., '*', ' ') to indicate that a cell is occupied or empty. With these two refinements our algorithm might now look something like Figure 7-16.


```
Set the generation counter to 0
Read the upper limit on new generations
Read the initial board position
Repeat the following until the new generation is empty, the new generation
    is the same as the old generation or generation counter > maximum
        Compute births in this generation
        Compute deaths in this generation
        Compute survivals in this generation
        Produce the new generation
        Write new generation
        Increment generation counter
    End of the loop
```

FIGURE 7-16   Game of Life Algorithm.

Before we translate this into PASCAL, we have a few more decisions to make.

1. How shall we input the initial board positions? Instead of forcing the user to specify the initial state of every cell on the board, it would be much more convenient to specify only the cells that are initially occupied. These cells represent only a small fraction of the overall board and will greatly reduce the amount of input data required. We can do this by specifying the subscripts of the cells that initially contain organisms. To describe the following initial board position for a 5 × 5 game of life:

		*		
	*	*	*	
		*		

we would say (if our subscripts begin at 1):

$$
\begin{array}{cc}
2 & 3 \\
3 & 2 \\
3 & 3 \\
3 & 4 \\
4 & 3 \\
\end{array}
$$

To indicate the end of a set of data, we could use the end-of-file condition described earlier. However, that would limit our program to processing a single set of data per run. A more generalized approach would be to use a signal card, for example, 0 0 (again assuming we index our arrays beginning at 1), to indicate the end of each data set except the last and the end of file to indicate the end of all data. This allows us to handle numerous data sets per run. Now the input phase of our algorithm, which was simply "Read the initial board position," can be expanded and refined (Figure 7-17).

```
While we have not reached end of file do
    Initialize all board positions to ' '
    Read board coordinates X, Y
    While X and Y are both not 0 do
        If (X, Y) is a legal board position, place an '*' there
        Read the next board coordinates X, Y
    End of loop
          .

          .

          .
            process this data set
          .

          .

          .
    End of the loop
```

FIGURE 7-17   Refinement of the Input Phase.

2. How many arrays should we use? It would be difficult to use only a single array for this problem. This is because all births and deaths occur simultaneously. We cannot change the contents of a cell until its effect on all its neighbors has been determined. Then, at the end of a generation, we must change all cells. If we assume that space is not critical the most straightforward way to approach the problem is to have two arrays—OLD-BOARD and NEW-BOARD. The births, deaths, and survivals from OLD-BOARD will be recorded in NEW-BOARD. When that generation is finished, what was the NEW-BOARD will become the OLD-BOARD and the process will continue. To produce a new generation, see Figure 7-18.

> Copy NEW-BOARD into OLD-BOARD
> Clear NEW-BOARD
> Repeat for every element in OLD-BOARD
>> Determine if there has been a birth in this element of OLD-BOARD and store that fact in the corresponding NEW-BOARD element
>> Determine if there has been a death in this element of OLD-BOARD and store that fact in the corresponding NEW-BOARD element
>> Determine if this element of OLD-BOARD has survived and store that fact in the corresponding NEW-BOARD element
> End of the loop
> Write the NEW-BOARD
> Increment the generation-counter

FIGURE 7-18   Refinement of the Processing Loop.

3. How should we handle the boundary phenomena? In the Game of Life the board is viewed as an infinite space. In our version of the game the organisms, of necessity, must be "caged" and strictly limited to the bounds of the array. An attempt to wander outside this environment is strictly prohibited. So while a center cell (Figure a) has 8 neighbors, an edge cell (Figure b) has 5, and a corner cell (Figure c) has only 3.

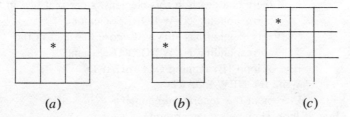

(a)   (b)   (c)

We must be very careful to avoid generating subscript expressions that are invalid and that would terminate the program abnormally. There are several approaches we can take in handling this boundary. For this case study we will assume that the spaces immediately beyond the edge of our board are always empty. Thus, in the diagram above, the organism in Figure *b* could never have more than 5 neighboring occupied cells while the organism in Figure *c* will be limited to a maximum of 3 occupied neighbors.

At this point, we ought to consolidate the pieces of our algorithm to see where we stand. If we combine Figures 7-16, 7-17, and 7-18 we have Figure 7-19.

This is a fairly detailed algorithmic structure, but we will probably want to perform another level of refinement before we begin to code in PASCAL.

```
ALGORITHM  GAME OF LIFE
    While we have not reached end of file do
        {Start a new game}
        Read the upper limit on new generations
        Set the generation counter to 0
        Initialize all board positions to ' ' in OLD-BOARD and NEW-BOARD
        Read board coordinates X,Y
        While X and Y are both not 0  do
            {Read an initial board position}
            IF (X,Y) is a legal board position, place an '*' at that position of
                NEW-BOARD
            Read the next board coordinates X,Y
        End of loop {For initializing the board}
        Repeat until (the new generation is empty) or (the new generation is the
                                                       same as the old genera-
                                                       tion)
              or (generation counter > upper limit)
            Copy NEW-BOARD into OLD-BOARD
            Clear NEW-BOARD
            Repeat for every element in OLD-BOARD
                If there is a birth in this element, store that fact in the
                    corresponding NEW-BOARD element
                If there is a death in this element, store that fact in the
                    corresponding NEW-BOARD element
                If this element has survived, store that fact in the
                    corresponding NEW-BOARD element
            End of loop {Examining OLD-BOARD}
            Write the NEW-BOARD
            Increment the generation counter
        End of loop {For a new generation}
    End of loop {One game is complete}
END OF THE ALGORITHM {All games are complete}
```

FIGURE 7-19   The Game of Life Algorithm (Consolidated).

We will illustrate the refinement for determining if a birth has occurred; the refinements for death and survival will be analogous (Figure 7-20).

ALGORITHM CHECK FOR BIRTH
    Check all neighbors of this cell (with proper care if the cell is at an edge)
    Tally occupied cells
    If (tally=3) and the cell is currently empty then there is a birth
END OF THE ALGORITHM

FIGURE 7-20   Checking for a Birth.

When we perform similar refinements to check for death and survival and place these refinements in Figure 7-19, we will probably be in a position where it is worthwhile to begin coding. We have now developed a reasonable algorithm, refined it a number of times so that the basic operations are fairly well understood, chosen the necessary data structures and, finally, made certain necessary assumptions where alternatives were available. It is important to realize that the coding phase should begin only now, after we have completed all of these operations to our complete satisfaction.

The following program represents one possible PASCAL translation of the Game-of-Life algorithm developed in this case study (Figure 7-21).

```
PROGRAM GAMEOFLIFE(INPUT, OUTPUT);
{ Program to play the Game of Life as developed by H. L. Conway
  at the University of Cambridge }
CONST   MAXBOARDSIZE = 50;  { Maximum board size }
TYPE    STATE = (DEAD, STABLE, GROWING);
        NEIGHBOR = SET OF 0 . . 8;
        BOARDS = PACKED ARRAY [1 . . MAXBOARDSIZE,
                               1 . . MAXBOARDSIZE] OF CHAR;
VAR     SURVIVEPOPULATION : NEIGHBOR;
        BOARDSTATE : STATE;
        NEWBOARD, OLDBOARD : BOARDS;
        I, J : 0 . . MAXBOARDSIZE;
        NUMBEROFNEIGHBORS : 0 . . 8;
        GENERATION, MAXGENERATION, BOARDSIZE : INTEGER;
        ALIVECOUNT, CHANGECOUNT : INTEGER;
        LEFT, RIGHT, UP, DOWN, HORIZOFFSET, VERTOFFSET : −1 . . +1;
BEGIN   { Game of Life }
SURVIVEPOPULATION := [2,3];
WHILE NOT EOF DO
    BEGIN
    { Here is the input section. It initializes all necessary parameters and
      creates the initial board }
    GENERATION := 0;
```

```
READLN(MAXGENERATION);
READLN(BOARDSIZE);
IF BOARDSIZE > MAXBOARDSIZE
    THEN BEGIN
            WRITELN(' BOARD SIZE TOO BIG—WILL BE RESET TO ',
                    MAXBOARDSIZE);
            BOARDSIZE := MAXBOARDSIZE
            END;
FOR I := 1 TO BOARDSIZE DO
    FOR J := 1 TO BOARDSIZE DO
        OLDBOARD[I,J] := ' ';
READLN(I,J);  {Read location of initial organism}
WHILE (I<>0) AND (J<>0) DO
    BEGIN
    IF (I<1) OR (I>BOARDSIZE) OR (J<1) OR (J>BOARDSIZE)
        THEN  WRITELN(' ATTEMPT TO INSERT ELEMENT IN ',
                      'NONEXISTENT CELL AT LOCATION', I, J,
                      ' VALUE DISREGARDED')
        ELSE   OLDBOARD[I,J] := '*';
    READLN(I,J)  { Read location of next organism }
    END;
{ The actual board processing begins here }
REPEAT
    ALIVECOUNT := 0; CHANGECOUNT := 0;
    FOR I := 1 TO BOARDSIZE DO
        FOR J := 1 TO BOARDSIZE DO
            BEGIN
            { First we must compute the number of neighbors for
              a cell at coordinate I,J. We must make sure that the
              cell is not on an edge }
            IF I>1          THEN LEFT := -1   ELSE LEFT := 0;
            IF I<BOARDSIZE THEN RIGHT := +1  ELSE RIGHT := 0;
            IF J>1          THEN UP := -1     ELSE UP := 0;
            IF J<BOARDSIZE THEN DOWN := +1   ELSE DOWN := 0;
            NUMBEROFNEIGHBORS := 0;
            FOR HORIZOFFSET := LEFT TO RIGHT DO
                FOR VERTOFFSET := UP TO DOWN DO
                    IF (OLDBOARD[I+HORIZOFFSET,J+
                        VERTOFFSET] = '*') AND
                        ((HORIZOFFSET <> 0) OR
                        (VERTOFFSET <> 0))
                        THEN NUMBEROFNEIGHBORS :=
                            NUMBEROFNEIGHBORS + 1;
                        { That last test is to insure we do not
                          count the cell as a neighbor of itself }
```

```
                { Now see which cells should be alive next
                  generation }
                NEWBOARD[I,J] := ' ';
                IF ((OLDBOARD[I,J] = ' ') AND
                  (NUMBEROFNEIGHBORS = 3)) OR ((OLDBOARD
                  [I,J] = '*') AND (NUMBEROFNEIGHBORS IN
                  SURVIVEPOPULATION))
                    THEN BEGIN
                        NEWBOARD[I,J] := '*';
                        ALIVECOUNT := ALIVECOUNT + 1
                        END
            END;  { Of the processing of each individual cell }
        { We have now completed a new generation. Print it out and
          copy it back into the OLDBOARD to get ready for the next
          cycle }
        GENERATION := GENERATION + 1;
        WRITELN;
        WRITELN(' GENERATION # ', GENERATION:3,
                ', POPULATION = ', ALIVECOUNT:3);
        FOR I := 1 TO BOARDSIZE DO
            BEGIN
            FOR J := 1 TO BOARDSIZE DO
                BEGIN
                WRITE (NEWBOARD[I,J]);
                { See if anything has changed during this
                  generation }
                IF NEWBOARD[I,J] <> OLDBOARD[I,J]
                    THEN BEGIN
                        CHANGECOUNT :=
                        CHANGECOUNT + 1;
                        OLDBOARD[I,J] := NEWBOARD[I,J]
                        END
                END;
            WRITELN  { Begin a new line }
            END;
        { Set a flag indicating the state of the board at the end of this
          generation }
        IF ALIVECOUNT = 0
            THEN BOARDSTATE := DEAD
            ELSE IF CHANGECOUNT = 0
                THEN BOARDSTATE := STABLE
                ELSE BOARDSTATE := GROWING
    UNTIL (BOARDSTATE = DEAD) OR
        (BOARDSTATE = STABLE) OR
        (GENERATION >= MAXGENERATION);
```

```
                { Print out why we stopped }
                CASE BOARDSTATE OF
                    DEAD     : WRITELN(' COLONY DIED.');
                    STABLE   : WRITELN(' COLONY IS STABLE.');
                    GROWING  : WRITELN(' MAXIMUM GENERATION NUMBER
                               EXCEEDED.')
                END   { Of case statement}
            END   { Of a single data set }
        END   { Of all data sets }   { GAMEOFLIFE }.
```
FIGURE 7-21   Program for the Game of Life.

As an example of the output from this program, we assume that we provided the following input data.

```
        5     (the maximum number of generations)
        6     (the board will be 6 × 6)
    3   4
    4   3
    4   4
    4   5
    5   4
    0   0 (end of the data set)
```

The output of the program would be the following.

```
        *
      ***          The original input data
        *


      ***
      * *          Generation 1
      ***


        *
      * *
    *   *          Generation 2
      * *
        *


        *
      ***
    ** **          Generation 3
      ***
        *
```

```
       ***
      *   *
      *   *        Generation 4
      *   *
       ***


        *
       ***
      * * *
      *** **       Generation 5
      * * *
       ***
```

(The run terminates because we have reached the maximum number of generations.)

This case study was significantly more complex than any of the programs we have done so far. The development of such a large program was aided significantly by our use of algorithmic notation and the step-by-step refinement of each piece of the algorithm. All of these operations preceded the coding phase and greatly simplified that step—essentially making it not much more than a mechanical translation. The next two chapters will say a great deal more about the methods for developing large, complex programs. Chapter 8 will introduce an extremely important PASCAL concept—the subprogram. Chapter 9 will utilize this subprogram concept to describe formally a number of useful techniques for developing and managing large programming projects.

EXERCISES

*1.   Define a new scalar data type for each of the following situations.

    a. The crops wheat, barley, rye, corn, and soybeans.
    b. The New England states.
    c. The authors of this book.
    d. The time zones in the continental United States.
    e. The possible classes of solutions to a quadratic equation.

*2.   Create a scalar subrange type for each of the following situations.

    a. All the nonnegative integers.
    b. The letters of the alphabet (*Note.* State any assumption that you make.)
    c. The crops soybeans and corn from problem 1a.
    d. The numbers -40 to $+2$ inclusive.

3. Which of the following sets of declarations are valid? Make corrections to the invalid declarations.

   a. TYPE COLOR = (RED, BLUE, GREEN, YELLOW);
      VAR ITEM: ARRAY [COLOR] OF INTEGER;
   b. VAR SAMPLE: ARRAY [100] OF BOOLEAN;
         REC1:   RECORD
                    NAME: ARRAY [1 . . 10] OF CHAR;
                    NUMBER: 0 . . 50
                 END;
   c. TYPE   SET1 = SET OF 5 . . 10;
              RANGE = 0 . . 100;
              FAMILY = (MOTHER, FATHER, SON);

      VAR   ARRAY1:   ARRAY [RANGE] OF RANGE;
             ARRAY2:   ARRAY [SET1] OF FAMILY;
             ARRAY3:   ARRAY [RANGE, RANGE] OF SET1;

4. For each of the structures described below, provide the required declarations and code needed to perform the specified initialization.

   a. An array named PRICE is to contain the prices for each of 300 items stocked by a small store. Initialize all entries to zero.
   b. A 10 × 10 matrix, initialized to one's on the diagonal and zero elsewhere.
   c. An array of 26 integers, indexed by the characters 'A' to 'Z' and initialized to all zeroes.
   d. A set of the integers [0 . . 1000] initialized to contain only those values that are not multiples of 2 or 3. Assume that the limit to the size of a set is 50 elements so that an array of sets is needed.

*5. Provide the necessary declarations and program statements needed to define a standard deck of playing cards. Begin by defining user data types for suits and for values. A card may then be represented as a record containing a suit and a face value, and a deck is an array of cards.

*6. Assume that you are given a 10-element array of characters. The values in the array are limited to '+', '−', and the characters '0' to '9'. The characters represent a signed PASCAL integer in valid syntactic format. Write a PASCAL fragment that converts the characters in the array into the correct integer value. The character string is terminated by the end of the array or the first blank character.

7. a. Write a RECORD declaration that might be used by a library for

maintaining information about a book. The information needed includes:

1. Title—a string of characters.
2. Author(s)
   a. Number of authors—an integer.
   b. Names of authors—a string of characters.
3. Publication information.
   a. Name of publisher—a string of characters.
   b. Year of publication—an integer.
4. Catalog number—a string of characters.

b. Using the RECORD description just developed, write a complete program that reads information about a variable number of books (not exceeding 20); sorts the books based on year of publication (oldest book first); and prints all the information about each book in a readable format.

*8. Assume that

$$A = [1,3,5,7,9]$$
$$B = [2,4,6,8,10]$$
$$C = [1,2,3,4,5]$$
$$D = [5]$$
$$E = [\ ]$$

What is the value of each of the following set operations?

a. $(A+B)-C$
b. $(A*C)=D$
c. $(A+E) * (B+D)$
d. $7 \ IN \ (((A-B)-C)-D)$
e. $C <= (A+B)$

9. Read in a file of characters and develop a frequency count of all alphabetic characters contained in the file. The output of the program should be a report in the following format.

LETTER	FREQUENCY COUNT	PERCENT
A	XX	XX.X
B	XX	XX.X
.	.	.
.	.	.
.	.	.
Z	XX	XX.X
Total alphabetic characters	XXX	100.0

10. FILE1 and FILE2 each contain a list of names in alphabetical order. Each name consists of no more than 20 characters. The number of names in each list is unknown.

    a. Write suitable declarations for FILE1 and FILE2.
    b. Write a complete program that produces FILE3 that is formed by merging FILE1 and FILE2 in such a way that FILE3 will contain all the elements of FILE1 and FILE2, ordered alphabetically, with duplicates eliminated.

11. Items A, B, C, D, and E exist in the following tree structure.

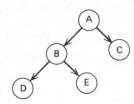

Provide the necessary declarations and assignment statements to establish this structure with the use of pointers.

12. Write a PASCAL program that first reads, row by row, an N × N two-dimensional array, where N is an input parameter. The program should then determine whether the array just read falls into any of the following special classes.

    a. Symmetric.
        $A_{ij} = A_{ji}$ for all i, j
    b. Upper triangular.
        $A_{ij} = 0$ for j = 2, 3, . . . , N
                   i = 1, 2, . . . , (j−1)
    c. Diagonal.
        $A_{ij} = 0$ whenever $i \neq j$

Print out the array and state whether it is or is not in any of the above classes.

13. A *sparse matrix* is defined to be a two-dimensional array in which the great majority of elements are 0. It is very wasteful to store these sparse matrices as arrays, since so few of the elements actually contain meaningful information. A more efficient way to represent an M × N sparse matrix is as a K × 3 array in which we store the row index, the column index, and value of only the nonzero elements of the original array. This is called a *reduced representation*. For example, the matrix

$$
\begin{array}{cccccc}
0 & 0 & 7 & 0 & 0 & 0 \\
0 & 0 & 0 & 0 & -8 & 0 \\
0 & 0 & 0 & 0 & 0 & 0 \\
2 & 0 & 0 & 0 & 0 & 0 \\
0 & 0 & 0 & 0 & 0 & 0
\end{array}
$$

could be efficiently stored as the following reduced representation.

$$
\begin{array}{rrr}
1 & 3 & 7 \\
2 & 5 & -8 \\
4 & 1 & 2
\end{array}
$$

Write a PASCAL program that reads, one row at a time, a sparse two-dimensional M × N matrix and produces and prints the reduced representation of that matrix. At what percentage of nonzero elements does this reduced representation actually become more inefficient than a regular array representation?

*14. Assume that we have a linked list structure of the following form.

Each node will be a two-element record structure with an integer DATA field and a pointer P to another node.
Write a PASCAL fragment that searches the entire list looking for a special value called KEY. If the value is found, return a pointer to that node in a variable called PTR. If it is not found, return a value of NIL in PTR.

15. Assume that we have an N × 2 table set up in the following format.

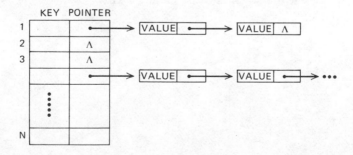

The table contains a key field and a pointer field. The pointer field is either NIL or the head of a chain of all the values associated with that key. For example, the key could be a student ID number and the values could represent all the classes taken by that student.

Write a complete PASCAL program that reads data cards and builds a table of the format just described. Assume that the data cards all contain two integer values—the KEY and the VALUE to enter in the table. There may be any number of cards containing the same KEY, and they do not have to be in sequence in the data. Assume that there exists a standard function called PLACE (KEY) that returns a value in the range [1 . . N]. This represents the location in the table to enter both the KEY and the VALUE. Enter KEY in the key field if it is not already there and add value to the end of the chain pointed to by the pointer field.

*16. A *stack* is a data structure in which the last element inserted is always the first one removed. Associated with the stack is a *stack pointer* that points to the top element of the stack. For example, if X, Y, and Z were placed on a stack in that order, the stack would look like this.

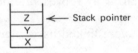

a. Write the TYPE and VAR declaration to construct a 32-element stack data structure from each of the following.
   (1) A one-dimensional array.
   (2) A record.
   (3) Pointers.
b. For each of the three declarations from part a, write a PASCAL fragment to do a "PUSH" and "POP" operation. A PUSH means to put a new value on top of the stack if there is room. A POP means to remove the top element of the stack if the stack is not empty. In all examples, assume the value we are putting on or taking off the stack is to be called VAL.

CHAPTER 8

FUNCTIONS AND PROCEDURES

8.1 INTRODUCTION

In the case study at the end of Chapter 5, we developed a program called ROOTFINDER to find roots of arbitrary equations. This program required the evaluation of a formula, which we called F(X), at three different places within the algorithm. This fact was not belabored since, at the time, it was only incidental to the development of the example. However, we now wish to examine this aspect of ROOTFINDER in depth, because it will serve to lead us into a rich and beautiful concept in computer programming—the *subprogram*.

Observe first that, as it is currently written, ROOTFINDER is not ready to be run on a computer because the three statements

```
NEWVAL:= F(X);
            .
            .
            .
NEWVAL:= F(X);
            .
            .
            .
NEWVAL:= F(X);
```

will produce errors when the program is compiled, since the symbol F has not been defined. Of course, the problem is easily solved. To handle the example worked out in the chapter, we simply change the above statements to read:

```
NEWVAL:= X*X− 3.5;
            .
            .
            .
NEWVAL:= X*X− 3.5;
            .
            .
            .
NEWVAL:= X*X− 3.5;
```

But what happens if F(X) is more complicated? F(X) could be, for example, an enormously complex computation arising out of a problem in engineering design, statistical analysis, or economic optimization. The specifics are not really important here. The point is that the function F(X) could easily require hundreds or thousands of lines of code. Now the value of a subprogram facility becomes evident. In the first place, the sheer tedium of replicating this much program text several times makes us wish to write the code just once and use it wherever we need it. We can not use a simple GOTO statement to jump to the code that will evaluate the function, because we also need to keep track of where to resume processing after computing the function. To be sure, we could keep track if we really wanted, but the result would be clumsy. Suppose, for example, that we have a very complicated formula F and wish to determine whether F(X) (i.e., the value of the formula at the point X) is larger than F(Y) for two numbers X and Y that are to be read in. We could use the program COMPARE in Figure 8-1.

The program in Figure 8-1 would be quite tedious to write out. However, the most significant problem with this program is not actually the labor required to produce all that code. The major problem is one of clarity.

```
PROGRAM COMPARE(INPUT, OUTPUT);
{Read two numbers, X and Y, and determine whether F(X)
 is larger than F(Y)}
VAR X, Y, FX, FY: REAL;
BEGIN
    READLN(X,Y);
        .
        .
        .

    {Several hundred statements which compute F(X).
     The variable X appears in some of them, and
     finally the result is assigned to FX}
    FX:= {Final expression}
        .
        .
        .

    {The same several hundred statements as above
     which compute F(Y).
     This time the variable Y appears instead of X
     in those statements that contained X. Finally
     the result is assigned to FY}
    FY:= {Final expression}
    IF FX > FY THEN
        WRITELN(' F(', X, ') IS LARGER THAN F(', Y, ')')
    ELSE
        WRITELN(' F(', X, ') IS NOT LARGER THAN F(', Y, ')')
END.
```

FIGURE 8-1   COMPARE Using Replicated Code.

The abstract algorithm for compare is quite simple.

Read X and Y
Set the variable FX to the value of F(X)
Set the variable FY to the value of F(Y)
Write a message telling whether FX is greater than FY

Four statements in the PASCAL program represent that algorithm.

```
READLN(X,Y);
FX:= . . .
FY:= . . .
IF FX > FY THEN . . .
```

In Figure 8-1, however, these statements are separated from each other by hundreds of lines of code whose purpose is to compute the function F. In a full program listing, the statements that reflect the important and fundamental steps of the algorithm would each be separated by several pages, and the main theme of the program would be obscured by the large volume of code that is, in fact, subservient to these four statements. Figuratively, we have lost the melody in the orchestration.

In Figure 8-2 we have eliminated both the replicated code and the separation of the important statements by using GOTO statements to transfer control. The code needed to compute the function F appears just once, and the statements that drive the algorithm are localized at the end of the program. However, we are still far from an acceptable situation. In the first place, we could do without the confusion caused by the many labels and jumps. Keep in mind that if all of the several hundred statements used to compute the function F were listed, it would not be so easy to follow the logical flow of the program. The destinations of some of the GOTO statements would be separated by several pages from the GOTO statements themselves. A

```
PROGRAM COMPARE(INPUT, OUTPUT);
{Read two numbers, X and Y, and determine whether F(X)
 is larger than F(Y)}
LABEL 1, 2, 11, 12;
VAR X, Y, FX, FY, INPUTVALUE, RESULTVALUE: REAL;
                            RETURNVALUE: INTEGER;
BEGIN
    GOTO 1;
  2: {Compute F}
           .
           .
           .
    {Several hundred statements to compute F(INPUTVALUE)
     The variable INPUTVALUE appears in some of them,
     and finally the result is assigned to RESULTVALUE}
    RESULTVALUE:= {Final expression}
    {Now figure out how to get back to the correct spot}
    IF RETURNVALUE = 11 THEN GOTO 11
    ELSE GOTO 12;
  1: READLN(X,Y);
    INPUTVALUE:= X; RETURNVALUE:= 11; GOTO 2;
 11: FX:=RESULTVALUE;
    INPUTVALUE:= Y; RETURNVALUE:= 12; GOTO 2;
 12: FY:= RESULTVALUE;
    IF FX > FY THEN
        WRITELN(' F(', X, ') IS LARGER THAN F(', Y, ')')
    ELSE
        WRITELN(' F(', X, ') IS NOT LARGER THAN F(', Y, ')')
END.
```
FIGURE 8-2 COMPARE Using GOTO Statements.

second problem is that if we wished to modify the program to handle three input variables and three function evaluations, we would have to add still more labels and jumps and elaborate on the code that returns control to the proper place in the program after each evaluation. We would be adding code not only in the section that evaluates the function, but also in the driving portion at the end. The approach pictured in Figure 8-2 will lead only to confusion and an illegible, unreadable program.

A third and greatly superior alternative for writing the COMPARE program is available. The PASCAL language (indeed, almost every computer language) lets us define independent program units called *subprograms*. As we will see, this mechanism permits the construction of programs consisting of thousands or even tens of thousands of lines of code that are nevertheless clear and quite comprehensible. We do this by successively dividing the problem into smaller, simpler, and more manageable subproblems. We will quickly find that the most compelling reason for defining a subprogram is neither to avoid the repetitious code of Figure 8-1 nor to avoid the unnecessary GOTO statements of Figure 8-2, but to group sequences of closely related statements into conceptual entities that can subsequently be dealt with as single units.

These units are often referred to as program *modules,* and the process of breaking a large, complex algorithm into modules is called *modularization.* The advantage to such an approach in the COMPARE program, for example, is that once the function F is defined and verified to be correct, it is no longer necessary to be concerned with how it works. The higher-level portion of the COMPARE program can be written to compare the values of any function, F, at two points without regard for how F itself operates. In fact, because F is viewed at this level in an abstract sense, it is possible and, as we will see later, quite desirable to code these higher-level, or more general, parts of the program first. This process of developing a program module in terms of other, lower-level modules is the key point in the development technique called *top-down program design,* which was mentioned in Chapter 2. The subprogram facility in PASCAL is fundamental to the effective use of the top-down design method.

In PASCAL there are two types of subprogram—*procedures* and *functions*. In the next section we will look at an example of a function. Most of the treatment, however, will apply to both types of subprogram, and we will discuss the differences between them later.

8.2 FUNCTIONS

8.2.1 FUNCTION DECLARATION

A *function* is an independent program unit in PASCAL. Unlike a WHILE or FOR loop, which are merely parts of a larger program, a function has its own declarations for labels, constants, types, variables, and even other subprograms. Here is an example of the function F that would be needed to make the ROOTFINDER program acceptable to the PASCAL compiler.

```
FUNCTION F(POINT: REAL): REAL;
{This is an example of a function F(X) supplied
  by the user of ROOTFINDER to evaluate his own formula}
BEGIN
    F:=SQR(POINT) − 3.5
END {Of the function F};
```

This is called a *function declaration,* because it defines the name that is to denote the function. It should appear immediately after the VAR declarations of the program. Let us examine the function declaration for F in detail. Following the reserved word FUNCTION is an identifier that names the function. In this case the one-character name F is used. Any valid user identifier may be chosen. Following the name is a list of identifiers called *formal parameters.* These parameters describe both the variables that constitute input data to the function and their type. This list is enclosed in parentheses. In this example, there is only one parameter, called POINT, of type REAL. In general, there can be any number of parameters of any type, including none at all, and we will see many examples to come. Finally, we have the data type of the result that will be computed by the function. In this case, the result is of type REAL. The result of a function may be any scalar type. The entire line beginning with the word FUNCTION and ending with the semicolon is called the *function heading*.

Following this heading is a sequence of statements that describes the operations to be performed on the input data when the function is executed. These statements may contain any valid PASCAL construct and, like a program, must have a BEGIN-END pair. However, somewhere within these statements, a value must be assigned to the function name itself. This is the means by which the result of the computation is communicated back to the main or driving program. A similar effect was achieved in Figure 8-2 by using the variable RESULTVALUE to pass information between different parts of the program. In our example above, the assignment of a value to the function name is the only statement present.

8.2.2 INVOKING A FUNCTION

The purpose of a function subprogram is to describe a computation to be performed on a set of input data. It is very important to note that no actual computation is done as a result of merely writing out the function itself. The actual execution of statements in the function takes place only when the function is invoked, that is, when it is referenced within the main program. In ROOTFINDER the statement:

NEWVAL:= F(X);

is an invocation. In the following program the single line

IF F(X) > F(Y) THEN . . .

actually contains two invocations of the function F. Figure 8-3 shows the COMPARE program implemented using a function declaration and invocation.

```
PROGRAM COMPARE(INPUT, OUTPUT);
{Read two numbers, X and Y, and determine whether F(X)
  is larger than F(Y)}
VAR X, Y: REAL;
FUNCTION F(POINT: REAL): REAL;
    .
    .
    .
BEGIN
    .
    .
    .
{Here there will be several hundred statements to compute
  the value F(POINT). The variable POINT appears in some
  of them, and finally the result is assigned to F}
F:= {Final expression}
END {Of the declaration for the function F};

{The main program begins right here}

BEGIN
    READLN(X,Y);
    IF F(X) > F(Y) THEN
        WRITELN(' F(', X, ') IS LARGER THAN F(', Y, ')')
    ELSE
        WRITELN(' F(', X, ') IS NOT LARGER THAN F(', Y, ')')
END.
```

FIGURE 8-3   COMPARE Using a Function.

Although the programs in Figures 8-2 and 8-3 look considerably different, their behavior with respect to the computer itself is remarkably similar. The first statement executed in Figure 8-3 is the READLN statement. When the boolean expression

$$F(X) > F(Y)$$

is evaluated, the following events occur.

1. The value of X is transferred to POINT and control jumps to the function F.
2. The value of F(X) is computed and stored and control passes back to the boolean expression.
3. The value of Y is transferred to POINT and control again goes to the function F.
4. The value of F(Y) is computed and saved and control again returns to the boolean expression where the two values F(X) and F(Y) are then compared.

The variables FX, FY, and RETURNVALUE as well as all the labels declared in Figure 8-2 are not needed in Figure 8-3. In fact, they still exist in some sense at the machine level, but their roles are handled automatically. As PASCAL programmers, we are now free to think in terms of the construction of algorithms from subalgorithms without having to burden ourselves very much with considerations of subprogram linkage, transfer of data, or return techniques.

Returning to our example subprogram for ROOTFINDER, we note that the formal parameter POINT is quite different from any other variable we have dealt with before. Although it appears within an executable statement just as any other variable might, there is no VAR declaration for it. Nor does it appear to have been initialized. In every example program presented so far, each variable that has occurred within an expression on the righthand side of an assignment statement must have previously had a value assigned to it, usually by means of an assignment statement or a READ statement. In this case, however, POINT acquires a value when the function F is invoked, and the value it assumes is the value of the actual parameter used in the call to the function. In the statement

$$\text{NEWVAL} := F(X);$$

the variable X is termed the *actual parameter*. Here, X is a variable of type REAL, and it has acquired a value before it is used as an actual parameter in the function invocation. The actual parameter—X, in this case—in the function invocation corresponds to a formal parameter—here, POINT—in the function declaration. Formal parameters are used merely as placeholders to indicate where the actual parameters will be placed when the subprogram is called. We distinguish between formal and actual parameters to make clear this notion of placeholding. Until now, we have been able to trace the logical flow and execution of a program by reading it from beginning to end. When we come upon a function declaration, however, we are looking at lines of code that we cannot think of as being executed in place (i.e., just after the VAR declaration). Its execution will be deferred until the function is invoked. Only then do the formal parameters become associated with values, those values being obtained from the actual parameters.

The correspondence between formal and actual parameters is established solely on the basis of position. The first actual parameter in the invocation replaces the first formal parameter in the function heading, the second actual parameter replaces the second formal parameter, and so on.

The total number of formal and actual parameters must match. For example, the main program in Figure 8-4 utilizes a function that checks

```
PROGRAM CHECKORDER(INPUT, OUTPUT);
{Read three characters and report whether they are in
 alphabetic order. Loop until reading '***'}
VAR C1, C2, C3: CHAR;
    WORKING: BOOLEAN;

FUNCTION CHKORDER(X: CHAR; Y: CHAR; Z: CHAR): BOOLEAN;
{The function CHKORDER returns true if and only if X ≤ Y ≤ Z}
BEGIN
    IF X <= Y THEN
        CHKORDER:= Y <=Z
    ELSE
        CHKORDER:= FALSE
END   {CHKORDER};
{The main program starts here}
BEGIN
    WORKING:=TRUE;
    WHILE WORKING DO
       BEGIN
         READLN(C1,C2,C3);
         WRITE(C1,C2,C3);
         IF (C1='*') AND (C2='*') AND (C3='*') THEN
            WORKING:=FALSE
         ELSE
            IF CHKORDER(C1,C2,C3) THEN
              WRITELN(' ARE IN ORDER')
            ELSE
              IF CHKORDER(C3,C2,C1) THEN
                WRITELN(' ARE IN REVERSE ORDER')
              ELSE
                WRITELN(' ARE NOT IN ORDER')
       END {WHILE loop}
    END.
```

FIGURE 8-4 Positional Dependence of Formal and Actual Parameters.

whether the three characters provided as actual parameters are in alphabetical order. When the order of the actual parameters is changed, however,
the same function can be used to check for reverse order.

An alternative way of writing the function heading for CHKORDER is:

FUNCTION CHKORDER(X, Y, Z: CHAR): BOOLEAN;

Formal parameters of the same type need only be separated by commas and
have their type specified once. Semicolons are used to separate the typefield
from the parameter that follows it. For example, we might write:

FUNCTION OFMANYPARAMS(X, Y, Z: REAL; I, J: INTEGER;
FYLE: TEXTTYPE): CHAR;

As a matter of syntax, it is also required that subprogram declarations must
follow all variable declarations. Finally, an invocation of a function may
appear anywhere in a program that a variable of the same type may appear.

8.3 PROCEDURES

Frequently, we wish to use a subprogram not to compute and return a
value, but to perform a set of operations. For example, a substantial portion
of a program might serve the purpose of printing the results of a computation. The development of the necessary code rests on considerations for the
formats to be used for titles, headings, and result values. However, these
detailed decisions are not needed in order to deal with the more general
notion of output. Just as the main portion of the COMPARE program could
be written without explicit knowledge of the function F, so the main portion
of any program can invoke the printing of a report without explicit information about the format of that report.

In PASCAL a *procedure* is also an independent program unit. In general,
procedures and not functions are more often used to create program
modules. One reason for this is that a procedure invocation is a statement
in itself. Thus, for example, with appropriate declarations, the following is
a valid main program.

```
BEGIN
    INPUTDATA;
    COMPUTERESULTS;
    WRITEREPORT
END.
```

The body of the program consists solely of calls to three procedures called
INPUTDATA, COMPUTERESULTS, and WRITEREPORT.

To understand the required syntax for PASCAL procedures, let us look at a simple example. The WRITEREPORT procedure mentioned above might be used to print the average distances that the students live from school. The following procedure declaration could be used.

```
PROCEDURE WRITEREPORT(R: REAL);
{Procedure to print out the average distance to school}
    BEGIN
    WRITELN('  AVERAGE DISTANCE TO SCHOOL IS ', R)
    END;
```

An invocation of this procedure might be simply:

```
WRITEREPORT(AVG);
```

The differences between a procedure declaration and a function declaration are: first, we do not specify a type for the procedure itself, since there is no explicit value returned; and second, it is not necessary (or even allowed, for that matter) to assign a value to the procedure name within the associated block. The name of the procedure is used only for identification. Finally, the reserved word PROCEDURE is used instead of FUNCTION. The association between formal and actual parameters is exactly the same as for functions.

Again, remember that a function call is always a component of an expression, but a procedure call is a statement in itself.

8.4 PARAMETERS

A subprogram may be thought of as a program within a program. As such, it may do all the things that any program can do, such as input, output, declare variables, and even define and invoke subprograms of its own. This property, along with a capability known as pass-by-reference parameters, which will be described shortly, enables us to define a program structure that is the crux of the modularization process used to write large, complicated programs. We will first describe the pass-by-reference mechanism and then study the concept of block structure. In the next chapter we will see how this block structure can be used.

The point of *pass-by-reference*, or simply *reference*, parameters is that a means is provided by which a subprogram can both obtain the initial value of an actual parameter and change its value as well. The importance of this to program structure is that it opens the communication lines back to the calling program. Without pass-by-reference, the only piece of information that could be returned is a function value. With pass-by-reference parameters, any amount of information can move both into and out of the subprogram through powerful data types such as arrays or records.

STYLE CLINIC 8-1

A Note on Writing Readable Programs

Names chosen for subprograms should indicate very clearly what the subprogram does. A reader should be able to get a clear idea of what a program does just by looking at its main, or driving, portion. A reader should be required to look at the subprogram declarations themselves only to learn how these subprograms work.

For example, the following program is quite meaningless because the code for the functions is not shown.

```
PROGRAM DOSOMETHING(INPUT, OUTPUT);
{An appropriate comment here would also be helpful}
VAR      AVG: REAL;
         THEDATA: ARRAY[1 . . 100] OF REAL;
         .
         .
         .
{Declarations for STEP1, STEP2, STEP3, and STEP4 would go here}
BEGIN
   STEP1(THEDATA);
   STEP2(THEDATA);
   AVG:= STEP3(THEDATA);
   STEP4(AVG)
END.
```

However, if we were just to change the names of the four functions so that the main program reads as follows, it is quite obvious what the program is doing.

```
PROGRAM AVGDISTTOSCHOOL(INPUT, OUTPUT)
{A comment should be here, but the point is that subprogram
  names should be informative, too}
      .
      .
      .
BEGIN
   READIN(THEDATA);
   CHECKALLVALUESPOSITIVE(THEDATA);
   AVG:= AVERAGE(THEDATA);
   WRITEREPORT(AVG)
END.
```

```
PROGRAM PARENCHECK(INPUT, OUTPUT);
{This is a program to check for proper parenthesizing of
 arithmetic expressions}
CONST    LEFTPAREN  = '(';
         RIGHTPAREN = ')';
         MAXLENGTH  = 72;
TYPE     EXPRESSION = ARRAY [1 . . MAXLENGTH] OF CHAR;
VAR      PARCOUNT, I, NESTDEPTH, SIZE : INTEGER;
         INSTRING, OUTSTRING          : EXPRESSION;
         WORKING, OK                  : BOOLEAN;

PROCEDURE PARENCNT(VAR INST, OUTST: EXPRESSION; VAR NUMBER,
                       DEPTH: INTEGER; STRLENGTH: INTEGER;
                       VAR VALID: BOOLEAN);
   {Left and right parentheses within the input string, INST, are scanned
    and checked for proper form. The nesting structure is left in OUTST.
    Upon return, NUMBER holds the number of parentheses found, DEPTH
    holds the maximum nesting depth encountered, and VALID
    will be TRUE if the structure is valid and FALSE otherwise}

   VAR I, J, CURRENTDEPTH: INTEGER;
   BEGIN
      I:=0; NUMBER:=0; DEPTH:=0; CURRENTDEPTH:=0;
      VALID:=TRUE;
      FOR J:= 1 TO STRLENGTH DO
          IF(INST[J] = LEFTPAREN) OR (INST[J] = RIGHTPAREN) THEN
                  BEGIN
                      I:=I+1;
                      OUTST[I]:=INST[J];
                      NUMBER:=NUMBER+1;
                      IF INST[J] = LEFTPAREN THEN
                          BEGIN
                          CURRENTDEPTH:= CURRENTDEPTH+1;
                          IF DEPTH < CURRENTDEPTH THEN
                              DEPTH:= CURRENTDEPTH
                          END
                  ELSE
                      BEGIN
                      CURRENTDEPTH:= CURRENTDEPTH-1;
                      IF CURRENTDEPTH < 0 THEN
                          VALID:=FALSE
                      END
                  END {Handling a paren};
      IF    CURRENTDEPTH <>0 THEN VALID:= FALSE
   END {PARENCNT};
```

```
{The main program begins here}
BEGIN
   WORKING:= TRUE;
   WHILE WORKING DO
      BEGIN
      I:=0;
      WHILE (I < MAXLENGTH) AND (NOT EOLN) DO
             BEGIN
             I:=I+1;
             READ(INSTRING[I])
             END;
      SIZE:=I;   READLN;
      IF INSTRING[1] = '*' THEN WORKING:= FALSE
      ELSE                        {  The * is used to terminate the program  }
             BEGIN
                FOR I:=1 TO SIZE DO WRITE (INSTRING[I]); WRITELN;
                PARENCNT(INSTRING, OUTSTRING, PARCOUNT,
                              NESTDEPTH, SIZE, OK);
                IF OK THEN
                   BEGIN
                   FOR I:=1 TO PARCOUNT DO WRITE(OUTSTRING[I]);
                   WRITELN(' IS VALID');
                   WRITELN(' MAXIMUM NESTING LEVEL IS', NESTDEPTH)
                   END
                ELSE
                   WRITELN(' NOT VALID')
                END {One string}
             END {The WHILE loop}
END.
```

FIGURE 8-5   A Function Using Pass-by-Reference.

The parameters we have seen until now are known as *value* parameters. To illustrate the difference and the way in which each kind works, we may think of a subprogram as a clerk at a desk with an IN basket and an OUT basket. Behind this clerk is a file cabinet (the computer memory) in which each file folder contains a single number. Whenever we provide a set of values in the IN basket (an invocation of the subprogram), the clerk performs a prescribed set of operations using those values. In the case of a function, the clerk places a single result value in the OUT basket. We may provide input to the clerk in either of two ways. In the value mode, we go to the file cabinet, look up the required input values, copy them onto a separate sheet of paper for the clerk to use, and drop them in the IN basket. We then lock the cabinet so that the numbers on file cannot be altered. The clerk may use only these values in supplying us with a result in the OUT basket.

In the reference mode, instead of placing the needed values in the IN basket, we specify which file folders contain these values and make these folders available to the clerk for the duration of the computation. Since the clerk has access to the folders themselves, the numbers currently stored there can be modified or deleted if the process being performed requires such changes. When the operation is finished, we may go to the file cabinet and examine the current contents of the folders we originally specified, thereby obtaining any results that may have been placed there.

The syntax for specifying pass-by-reference parameters requires the reserved word VAR to precede the parameters that are to be pass-by-reference. The program of Figure 8-5 contains a function that illustrates the use of reference parameters. The purpose of the procedure is to check whether the parentheses within an arithmetic expression are validly placed. A properly parenthesized expression in PASCAL must meet two conditions. The number of left '(', and right ')', parentheses must match and, if the expression is scanned left to right, the number of right parentheses can never exceed the number of left parentheses. The input parameters to the procedure are an array of characters that may or may not be a properly parenthesized expression, an output array into which the parentheses structure alone is placed, an integer that will be the deepest nesting level found in the expression, an integer that will be the number of parentheses found, and a Boolean variable that will be set TRUE if the input expression is properly parenthesized and FALSE otherwise.

If PARENCHECK were run with the following input:

$$(A + 3.0 * (1.0 - B) / (2.0 - C))$$

its output would be:

$$(A + 3.0 * (1.0 - B) / (2.0 - C))$$

(()()) IS VALID

MAXIMUM NESTING LEVEL IS 2

The general rule for choosing parameter types is to use value parameters to pass values into a subprogram and reference parameters to return them. Each mode has certain attributes associated with it, and the choice of which to use should be based on which attributes are needed. Value parameters do not allow the value of the actual parameter to be changed. Therefore, they should be used when the values of actual parameters must be protected, but this same feature means that results cannot be transferred back to the calling program through these parameters. On the other hand, reference parameters can be used to pass values in and must be used for returning results. However, because a return path is possible, the protection of actual parameters is lost when this calling mode is used. Changes to the formal parameters will cause corresponding changes to the actual parameters.

One might ask why the first parameter of PARENCNT, INST, is pass-by-reference when it is only used for input data. The reason is because large data structures should generally be passed by reference in order to save space and processing time. The value parameter entails the making of a duplicate copy of the input data in order to protect the value of the actual parameter. All subsequent changes are then only changes to this local copy, not to the actual parameter itself. This copying is cheap enough if the parameter is a scalar type, but copying large structured values, such as a 1000-element array, can be unnecessarily costly.

Another way of looking at the difference between parameter types is to understand that in the case of value parameters, only the value of the actual parameter is passed to the formal parameter, which then assumes that value. We are really dealing with two distinct variables, one within the subprogram and the other outside. In the case of pass-by-reference, the value exists in only one place. Even though the actual and formal parameters may be two different symbolic names, both refer to the same entity. In fact, this is true even if both formal and actual parameters have the same name.

If the formal parameter of a procedure is pass-by-reference, then the corresponding actual parameter must be a variable (i.e., an entity that refers to a value). If the formal parameter is pass-by-value, then the corresponding actual parameter may be any expression whose value has the appropriate type. In this regard, a variable is just a simple special case of an expression. For the procedure heading:

```
PROCEDURE F(VAL: REAL; VAR REF: REAL);
```

the following statements are valid invocations of the procedure F.

```
F(X, Y);
F(1, A[5]); {Assuming A is an array of REALS}
F(SIN(Y)+0.5, Z);
F(3.0*Z−2.0+SQRT(X), R);
```

The following are examples of invalid invocations for the reasons given.

```
F(X, 1); {Not valid because the second parameter does
            not reference a value—it simply is a value}
F(Z, SIN(Y)); {Expressions cannot be passed by reference}
```

With value parameters there is no need to introduce extra steps or temporary variables with code such as:

```
TEMP1:=  SIN(Y)+0.5;
TEMP2:=  3.0*Z-2.0;
F(TEMP1, Z);F(TEMP2, R);
```

8.5 BLOCK STRUCTURE

We now return to a discussion of the concept of block structure. A *block* is a sequence of declarations, a BEGIN, a sequence of statements that describes actions to be performed on the data structures described in the declarations, and an END. Pictorially a block can be represented by

```
        declaration;
          .

          .

          .
        declaration;
BEGIN
        statement;
          .

          .

          .
        statement
END
```

We can see from the above diagram that a PASCAL program consists of a program heading such as:

```
PROGRAM PROG(INPUT, OUTPUT);
```

followed by a block. Indeed, one of the purposes of a program heading is to give the following block a name. Furthermore, each subprogram declared within a block also contains a heading and a block, and so a PASCAL program becomes a construction of named blocks. The program itself is often referred to as the *outer block,* and each subprogram constitutes an *inner block.* Any program can have many levels of nesting of blocks within blocks, so even the terms *inner* and *outer* are sometimes used relative to a particular subprogram. The usefulness of this kind of structuring lies not just in the potential it provides for modularizing the computations, but in its ability to protect data that are the exclusive concern of one set of modules from encroachment or contamination by other modules. This is accomplished by the fundamental rule of block structuring—all data values declared at the beginning of a block are accessible to all executable statements that are part of that block, including statements belonging to inner blocks, but to no others. The program of Figure 8-6 demonstrates this mechanism.

```
PROGRAM BLOCKSTRUCTURE(INPUT, OUTPUT);
VAR A0, B0, C0: REAL;

    PROCEDURE BLOCK1;
    VAR A1, B1, C1: REAL;
        FUNCTION BLOCK11: REAL;
        VAR A11, B11, C11: REAL;
        BEGIN
            .
            .
            .
        END {Of block 11};
    BEGIN
        .
        .
        .
    END {Of block 1};

    PROCEDURE BLOCK2;
    VAR A2, B2, C2: REAL;
    BEGIN
        .
        .
        .
    END {Of block 2};

BEGIN
    .
    . {Here is the main program}
    .
END.
```

FIGURE 8-6   Block Structure.

The identifiers A0, B0, and C0 are declared in the outer block of the program called BLOCKSTRUCTURE. They are therefore accessible at all levels of the program and are termed *global*. The variables A1, B1, and C1 are declared in BLOCK1, so they are available only within that block. They would be available in BLOCK1, but could not be referenced from BLOCK2 nor from the statements of the program outer block. The variables A11, B11, and C11 can be referenced by statements within BLOCK11 but no others. An identifier declared in a block is said to be *local* to that block, while an identifier that is valid in an inner block by virtue of its having been declared in an outer block is said to be global to the inner block. In Figure 8-6 the variables A1, B1, and C1 are local to BLOCK1, global to BLOCK11, and not defined in BLOCK2 nor in the program outer block.

We also refer to the block in which an identifier is declared as the *scope* of that identifier. In the example above, the scope of A0, B0, and C0 is the entire program, the scope of A1, B1, and C1 is BLOCK1, and the scope of A2, B2, and C2 is BLOCK2. In other words, the scope of an identifier is the portion of a program in which the definition of the identifier is valid.

Two very important points about block structure should be emphasized here. The first is that global variables as well as reference parameters provide a means for getting data into and out of a subprogram. The second point, whose importance bears further emphasis, is that local variables provide a means for protecting data from undesirable accessing. The value of this feature is that it allows us to write subprograms without undue concern

```
PROGRAM ARRAYMAX(INPUT, OUTPUT);
{This is a program to read in a 10 × 10 array of reals, locate the
  maximum value, as well as the row and column index of where
  that maximum was located}
    TYPE ARRAYROW = ARRAY [1 . . 10] OF REAL;
    VAR A: ARRAY [1 . . 10] OF ARRAYROW;
        MAX, BIGGESTSOFAR: REAL;
        K, INDEX, ROW, COLUMN: INTEGER;
    BEGIN
        FOR K:=1 TO 10 DO ROWREAD(A[K]);
        {ROWREAD will read in the array one row at a time}
        BIGGESTSOFAR :=A[1] [1]; ROW:=1; COLUMN:=1;
        FOR K:=1 TO 10 DO
            BEGIN
            ROWMAX(A[K], MAX, INDEX);
            {ROWMAX locates the maximum element in row K of
              the array and stores that value in MAX. The column
              index is returned in INDEX}
            IF MAX > BIGGESTSOFAR THEN
                {We have found a new largest item so we must
                  redefine our values}
                BEGIN
                BIGGESTSOFAR:=MAX;
                ROW:=K;
                COLUMN:=INDEX
                END;
            END; {Of the FOR loop}
        WRITELN(' MAXIMUM ELEMENT ', BIGGESTSOFAR, ' IS
                LOCATED AT ', ROW, ', ', COLUMN)
    END.
```
FIGURE 8-7 Main Program for ARRAYMAX.

for the program environment in which those subprograms will exist. We need only declare variables local to the subprogram to assure ourselves of control over the subprogram we are writing. Name conflicts, that is, the declaration of an identifier with the same name in an inner and outer block, are automatically resolved by a convention known as *name precedence*. The rule is that an identifier always refers to the variable of most limited scope. Any global variables represented by the same identifier become inaccessible and simply retain whatever values they had when the new variable was declared. To demonstrate this mechanism and its use, let us put together a program to read in a two-dimensional array and then find both the largest element it contains and the row and column subscripts that reference that element. We begin with the main program shown in Figure 8-7 and work inward.

We now need a procedure, ROWREAD, to read one row of the array and another procedure, ROWMAX, to find both the maximum element of a row and its location. Note that the use of ROWMAX requires that MAX and INDEX be reference parameters. Note also that the problem now consists of two smaller, independent subtasks. The two required procedures might be written as shown in Figure 8-8.

If the two modules were placed into the main program ARRAYMAX immediately after the variable declarations, we would have a complete and valid program. The most important aspect of this example is that the two procedures operate only on their own parameters and local variables. Therefore, while writing them, we need not be concerned with the variable names used in the rest of the program. We are thus able to concentrate entirely on the immediate subalgorithm.

Note, for example, that ROWREAD contains a FOR loop on the variable K, but the function itself is invoked in ARRAYMAX within another loop using the variable K. There is no problem here, because K is declared inside ROWREAD. So even though we have two variables referenced by the same identifier, the program works properly. The name precedence rule insures that neither variable will interfere with the other. If, on the other hand, K were not declared locally, the program would still compile without errors, but it would no longer execute properly. This is because both the outer loop and the inner loop would, indeed, be using the same variable.

The procedure ROWMAX demonstrates another aspect of name precedence. Outside the block for this function the name A refers to a two-dimensional array, but inside the block, it refers to a local REAL variable. Even though the function was called with the actual parameter A, inside the block the formal parameter V has assumed the role of the array row A. Again, there is really no confusion between the array A outside the block and the REAL variable A inside as far as the PASCAL language is concerned.

One final comment should be made about the example programs in Fig-

```
PROCEDURE ROWREAD(VAR A: ARRAYROW);
{Read one row of the array. We should also check here for
 error conditions arising during the input, but we leave
 that out at this time so that we do not cloud the example}
    VAR K: INTEGER;
    BEGIN
        FOR K:=1 TO 10 DO READ(A[K]);
        READLN;
        FOR K:=1 TO 10 DO WRITE(A[K], ' ');
        WRITELN
    END; {Of ROWREAD}

PROCEDURE ROWMAX(V: ARRAYROW; VAR MAX: REAL;
                        VAR INDEX: INTEGER);
{Find the maximum element in the array V. Return its value in the
 parameter MAX and its location in INDEX}
    VAR K: INTEGER;      {K is a local variable}
        A: REAL;         {A is a local value, and not the same as the
                          variable in the outer block}
    BEGIN
        A:=V[1]; INDEX:=1;
        FOR K:=2 TO 10 DO
            IF V[K] > A THEN
                BEGIN
                A:=V[K];
                INDEX:=K
                END;
        MAX:=A
    END; {Of ROWMAX}
```

FIGURE 8-8   Subprograms Needed for Program ARRAYMAX.

ures 8-7 and 8-8. We intentionally chose identical names for variables serving different roles to illustrate the concepts of name precedence with local and global variables. However, as is probably obvious, this is poor programming style and can lead to a great deal of confusion on the part of a reader. Even though the program will operate properly, its clarity and legibility could have been significantly improved by choosing more descriptive names that, whenever possible, do not conflict between modules.

8.6 FUNCTIONS AND PROCEDURES AS PARAMETERS

Besides value parameters and reference parameters, it is possible to pass procedure names and function names themselves into other subprograms. The method is to use the reserved word PROCEDURE or FUNCTION in

STYLE CLINIC 8-2

Side Effects

The alteration of a global variable by a subprogram is called a *side effect*. Although it is at times appropriate to let procedures act on global data, the practice should always be extremely well considered, and beginning programmers should probably avoid it altogether. It is too easy to build in unnecessary complications or even outright errors. Such problems tend to arise because the actual behavior of subprograms that have side effects can be quite different from what we surmise when we invoke them. Consider, for example, the program below. The problem is that the value returned by the function S depends not only on its parameter but on how many times the function itself has been called before. The output printed by this program is

```
0   1   2   3   4
```

yet the main program makes it appear that the same value would be printed five times.

```
PROGRAM SIDEEFFECT(INPUT, OUTPUT);
    {An illustration of side effects}
    VAR G: INTEGER;
    FUNCTION S(X: INTEGER): INTEGER;
      BEGIN
      S:=X+G;   {The global variable G is referenced here}
      G:=G+1   {and altered here. This is a side effect}
      END;   {Of function S}
BEGIN
    G:=0;
    WRITELN(S(0), S(0), S(0), S(0), S(0))
END.
```

We cannot caution too strongly about the dangers posed by functions or procedures that have side effects. Use them only with care and when you have a specific reason to do so. The accidental alteration of global values during the invocation of a subprogram can be an extremely difficult error to detect and correct.

the subprogram heading to specify the parameters appropriately, just as we use the reserved word VAR to indicate reference parameters. The type of each function parameter must also be stated. To illustrate, let us define a function that returns as a result the maximum value of two other functions.

STYLE CLINIC 8-3

Global Variables versus Formal Parameters

In the program ARRAYMAX the variable INDEX declared in the outer block and the formal parameter INDEX of the procedure ROWMAX are two distinct variables. In other words, the formal parameter might just as well have been called INX, COLUMNNUMBER, or most anything else. However, if the heading had been:

PROCEDURE ROWMAX (VAR V: ARRAYROW): REAL;

the procedure would still work because the identifier INDEX inside ROWMAX would now refer to the global variable INDEX declared in the outer block. The resulting simplified calling sequence makes the program a little more efficient, and we have a little less writing to do when we call the procedure. But we have introduced a side effect. In this case, the use of the global variable to pass information out is not entirely unacceptable, because the global variable INDEX is used only as a means of conveying information between ROWMAX and the program outer block. The danger now, however, is that an unsuspecting programmer who wishes to make a change to the program might use INDEX for his or her own purpose as well. If ARRAYMAX were a very large program, the cause of the subsequent troubles could be very difficult to trace. So, although global variables and formal parameters are both valid techniques for passing information into and out of a subprogram, formal parameters should probably be the method of choice unless there is a compelling reason to do otherwise.

```
FUNCTION FINDMAX(FUNCTION F, G: REAL; X: REAL):
                REAL;
{A function to test whether F(X) > G(X) for some arbitrary
   functions F and G}
VAR FVAL, GVAL: REAL;
BEGIN
    FVAL:= F(X); GVAL:= G(X);
    IF FVAL > GVAL THEN FINDMAX:= FVAL
       ELSE FINDMAX:= GVAL
END;
```

Similarly, we may pass the name of a procedure as a parameter to a subprogram. This facility might be used, for instance, when any one of several validity checks is to be performed on input data. The name of the appropriate check routine could be passed into the input subprogram, and a global flag set if the check fails.

```
PROGRAM SAMPLE(INPUT, OUTPUT);
{This program illustrates the use of procedure names as
 parameters to other procedures}
     .
     .
     .

VAR FLAG: BOOLEAN;   {Set by CHECK1 and CHECK2}

PROCEDURE CHECK1(X, Y, Z: REAL);
     {Performs some type of validity checking on X, Y, and Z
      and sets FLAG accordingly}
     BEGIN
        .
        .
        .

     FLAG:=TRUE
     END;

PROCEDURE CHECK2(X, Y, Z: REAL);
     {Performs a different type of validity check and sets
      FLAG accordingly}
     BEGIN
        .
        .
        .

     FLAG:=TRUE
     END;

PROCEDURE READDATA(PROCEDURE CHECK);
     {This procedure reads in data and validates it using a
      checking procedure passed in as a parameter}
     BEGIN
        .
        .
        .

     READLN(X, Y, Z);   {Input the data}
     CHECK(X, Y, Z);   {Check it for correctness}
     IF FLAG THEN . . .
        .
        .
        .

     END;
{The main program begins here}
```

```
BEGIN
    .
    .
    .
    IF DATAISFORMONTHEND THEN READDATA(CHECK1)
                        ELSE READDATA(CHECK2);
    .
    .
    .
END.
```

One constraint on passing procedure or function names as parameters is that the parameters of those subprograms must be scalar, value parameters. In particular, this means that the only way that one procedure passed as a parameter to another can communicate results back is through global variables.

8.7 RECURSION

PASCAL permits procedures or functions to invoke themselves, a technique mentioned in Chapter 2 and known as *recursion*. This capability offers an approach to problem solving not available in many programming languages. For the case of functions, recursion is indicated by the appearance of the function name as part of an expression. For example, the following function computes X^n using the recursive definition $X^n = X \cdot X^{n-1}$.

```
FUNCTION POWER(X: REAL; N: INTEGER): REAL;
{Compute X raised to the power N recursively. The function
  always returns 0 for X = 0}
BEGIN
    IF X = 0.0 THEN POWER:=0.0
    ELSE IF N = 0 THEN POWER:=1.0
        ELSE IF N < 0 THEN POWER:=POWER(X, N+1)/X
                ELSE POWER:=POWER(X, N-1)*X
END;   {Of POWER}
```

Each line of code contains a reference to POWER that serves to return a value. In addition, the last two lines contain recursive calls.

It is important to keep in mind that the value of recursion lies in the alternative approach that it offers. Recursion is sometimes relatively expensive in terms of storage requirements. We will pursue the above example a bit further. Since X^n can be computed very simply without recursion, we can write:

```
FUNCTION POWER(X: REAL; N: INTEGER): REAL;
{Compute X to the power N iteratively. The function
 always returns 0 for X=0}
VAR  I: INTEGER;
     R: REAL;
BEGIN
     R:=1.0;
     IF X=0.0 THEN R:=0.0
          ELSE  IF (X=1.0) OR (N=0) THEN  {Do nothing}
               ELSE IF N<0 THEN
                    FOR I:=1 TO −N DO R:=R/X
               ELSE
                    FOR I:=1 TO N DO R:=R*X;
     POWER:=R
END;  {Of power}
```

Both of these functions require N multiplications or divisions. We can do better by observing that $X^{2n} = X^n X^n$ and $X^{2n+1} = X^n X^n X$. To use this latter algorithm, we could write:

```
FUNCTION POWER(X: REAL; N: INTEGER): REAL;
{Computes X to the power N recursively but more efficiently.
 The function always return 0 for X = 0}
VAR T: REAL;
BEGIN
     IF X=0.0 THEN POWER:=0.0
     ELSE IF N=0 THEN POWER:=1.0
          ELSE IF N=1 THEN POWER:=X
               ELSE IF N<0 THEN
                    BEGIN
                    T:=POWER(1/X, (−N) DIV 2);
                    POWER:=T*T*POWER(1/X, (−N)
                      MOD 2)
                    END
               ELSE
                    BEGIN
                    T:=POWER(X, N DIV 2);
                    POWER:=T*T*POWER(X, N
                      MOD 2)
                    END
END;  {Of power}
```

This function could also be rewritten without using recursion. The point is that sometimes thinking in terms of recursion can help us to arrive at a superior algorithm, even though the resulting program might be written iteratively. The reason why recursion can be expensive can best be illustrated by walking through an example. If we were to call the first version of POWER with X having a value of 5 and N having a value of 3, we would ultimately perform the operation

POWER:= POWER(5.0, 2) * 5.0

Both 5s and the 2 are stored in the computer during the second call, which effectively produces

POWER:= (POWER(5.0, 1) * 5.0) * 5.0

At this point we have three 5s, a 1, and a 2. The next call to POWER does not produce any further recursion, since the value of N is 1, and the result of 5*5*5 is finally computed, but it is clear that we actually generated and saved three 5s and then multiplied them all together. The looping version of the function does not suffer this need for extra storage space, since it accumulates the product as soon as the factors are generated.

Although looping methods are often more efficient than recursive methods, there are times when recursion is preferable. Some problems that can be handled very simply with recursion would involve complicated data structures and control methods in order to avoid recursion. A typical situation is one in which the solution is easily done with N nested FOR loops, but N is a variable. For example, suppose we wish to generate all possible character strings of length N where only the characters 'A', 'B', and 'C' may be used. If N were fixed, we could write:

```
FOR CH1:= 'A' TO 'C' DO
FOR CH2:= 'A' TO 'C' DO
        .

        .

        .
FOR CHN:= 'A' TO 'C' DO
        WRITELN(CH1, CH2, . . . , CHN);
```

To do this recursively, we might write:

```
PROGRAM RECURSIVECALL(INPUT, OUTPUT);
CONST MAXLENGTH=5;
VAR STRING: ARRAY [1 . . MAXLENGTH] OF CHAR;
    N      : INTEGER;
    PROCEDURE GENERATESTRINGS(N, K: INTEGER);
        {Recursively generates all strings of length
```

```
                    N consisting of the characters A, B, and C}
                    VAR J: INTEGER; I: CHAR;
                    BEGIN
                    FOR I:= 'A' TO 'C' DO
                        BEGIN
                        STRING[K]:=I;
                        IF K=N THEN
                            BEGIN
                            FOR J:=1 TO N DO WRITE(STRING[J]);
                            WRITELN
                            END
                        ELSE GENERATESTRINGS(N, K+1)
                        END
                    END   {GENERATESTRINGS};
            {Main program begins here}
            BEGIN
                READLN(N);   {N must be no bigger than MAXLENGTH}
                IF N <= MAXLENGTH THEN GENERATESTRINGS(N, 1)
                ELSE WRITELN(' N IS TOO BIG')
            END.   {Of RECURSIVECALL}
```

In addition to the obvious recursion discussed so far, less direct forms are also possible. A procedure P1 might not call itself directly, but might instead invoke another procedure P2 that subsequently calls P1.

In general, if a procedure P1 references another P2, then P2 must be declared before P1 uses the name. Otherwise an unidentified symbol would occur. This is not a serious restriction; however, it does require a special construct to handle the situation where subprograms each call the other. It is called a *forward declaration,* and it is the same as any subprogram declaration with the body replaced by the single word FORWARD (Figure 8-9). The complete declaration occurs later on with the heading reduced to just the procedure or function name.

8.8 EXTERNAL SUBPROGRAMS

Two additional kinds of procedure and function declarations are available in some implementations of PASCAL. Because they depend to some degree on the particular computer installation, a detailed description of these features is not possible here. However, we can give a general discussion.

The idea is to provide a means whereby programmers can share subprograms. This facility allows the construction of *libraries* of general-purpose subroutines that can be conveniently made available to every user of

```
{The following line is the forward declaration of FN}
FUNCTION FN(X, Y: REAL; VAR FLAG: BOOLEAN): REAL; FORWARD;
PROCEDURE PR(VAR   R1, R2: REAL);
   BEGIN
      .
      .
      .

   R1:= FN(A, B, BOOL);   {This is the statement that requires the
                           forward declaration}
      .
      .
      .

   END;   {Procedure PR}
FUNCTION FN;   {Note the abbreviated heading}
   BEGIN
      .
      .
      .

   PR(U, V);
      .
      .
      .

   END;   {Function FN}
```

FIGURE 8-9 Skeleton of a Program Illustrating FORWARD Declaration.

the computer. Typical examples of the contents of such collections might include programming tools such as general purpose input/output programs, sorting programs, plotting packages, and a variety of mathematical and statistical functions and procedures.

In order to use a library routine written in PASCAL, we substitute an *external declaration* for the usual procedure or function declaration. The appearance is similar to a forward declaration, except that the symbol EXTERN is used instead of FORWARD.

```
PROGRAM GRAPHICS(INPUT, OUTPUT);
      .
      .
      .

PROCEDURE PLOT(X, Y: REAL; PEN: INTEGER);
         EXTERN;
{The main program begins immediately}
```

```
        BEGIN
            .
            .
        PLOT(X, Y, 0);
            .

            .

            .
```

No procedure body appears anywhere in the program. The PASCAL system will locate the procedure PLOT stored in a library and include it automatically. Some control cards, meaningful only to the individual computer system being used, may be required to specify which of several libraries is to be used. The method for adding subprograms to a library is also installation dependent.

Some installations also allow PASCAL programs to use subprograms written in the FORTRAN language (refer to Figure 1-1). They are no different from other external subroutines but, because of the characteristics of that computer language, it is necessary to specify that the external subprogram was, in fact, written in FORTRAN. We do this by using the symbol FORTRAN in the declaration instead of EXTERN.

```
        PROGRAM GRAPHICS(INPUT, OUTPUT);
            .
            .

            .
        PROCEDURE PLOT(X, Y: REAL; PEN: INTEGER);
                    FORTRAN;
        {The main program begins immediately}
        BEGIN
            .

            .

            .
        PLOT(X, Y, 0);
            .

            .

            .
```

All of the above, however, may or may not be available at any particular site. You should check with your instructor or local computing center to inquire about the availability of external procedures and program libraries.

It should also be mentioned that global variables are not an allowable method of communication between a main program and an external routine. The only means of communication are by formal parameters—either call-by-value or call-by-reference.

STYLE CLINIC 8-4

The Importance of Library Routines

The ability to incorporate external subprograms into a main program is one of the most valuable properties a programming language can have. Without it, sharing programming tools and ideas would be severely limited. Most computer installations maintain extensive libraries of generally useful routines such as mathematical operations, input/output routines, graphics packages, statistical analysis programs, and sorting and searching routines. Before undertaking the construction of any substantial program, it is a good idea to find out whether helpful library subroutines are available. There is no point in developing a routine that already exists.

Likewise, if you have developed a program that may possibly be of interest to a number of other people, consider putting it in a program library for general use. This will, of course, require that you produce good user documentation so people will know that the program exists, what it does, and how it may be used.

8.9 CASE STUDY

Computers are not limited simply to mathematical applications. In this case study, we will look at one aspect of text processing. The problem is to produce a frequency count of the words in a given piece of English text. This application has been used for evaluating writing style in cases of disputed authorship. Other examples of text processing include editing, word processing, and compiling computer programs.

The general idea will be to accept input in the form of a stream of words and to build a table containing the number of times each word appears in the text. The end of the input stream will be signified by an end-of-file condition, and the program will then print an alphabetical list of the words encountered together with the frequency of each.

A general algorithm can be sketched out as follows.

        START
            While there is a word available
                Get the next word.
                If it is in the table, then increment the count for that word
                Else put it in the table.
            End of the loop.
            Print the table in alphabetical order.
            Stop.
        END OF THE ALGORITHM

STYLE CLINIC 8-5

Signal Flags

After invoking a procedure, we must be careful to check that the procedure did indeed work properly before going ahead and using any values returned by the procedure. Therefore, a subprogram must always be able to inform the calling program of the outcome of any attempted operation. Merely writing an error message is insufficient.

```
IF X < 0.0 THEN WRITELN (' ILLEGAL VALUE FOR X')
           ELSE Y:= SQRT(X);
```

The user will be able to see the message, but the program that invoked this procedure will have no way of knowing whether the SQRT operation was successfully completed. An attempt to reference the variable Y could then lead to a run-time error.

One way to determine whether a subprogram execution was successful is to include a parameter whose sole purpose is to say, "Yes, the program produced results," or "No, it did not." These parameters are usually called *signal flags* and their use in subprograms is an extremely important concept.

Using the boolean signal value OK, we could write the above operations as follows.

```
PROCEDURE TAKEROOT (X: REAL; VAR Y: REAL; VAR OK:
                          BOOLEAN);
BEGIN
     IF X < 0.0 THEN   OK:=FALSE
               ELSE   BEGIN
                      OK:=TRUE; Y:=SQRT(X)
                      END
END;   {Of takeroot}
```

The main program can now use the signal flag to determine the appropriate action to take.

```
READLN(VAL); WRITELN(VAL);
TAKEROOT(VAL, RESULT, FLAG);
IF FLAG THEN WRITELN(' THE ANSWER IS ', RESULT)
         ELSE WRITELN(' ATTEMPT TO TAKE THE SQUARE
                       ROOT OF A NEGATIVE NUMBER')
```

The algorithm divides neatly into input, process, and output phases. For the input task, a subprogram will be used that makes the input appear to be a stream of words. Thus, if the mode of input is to be changed, only the input module would be affected. Processing and output, however, are both affected by the structure of the table, so careful consideration must be given to the stored data before we think much more about developing processes. The table should probably begin empty and be expanded as new words are encountered. However, since every word in the input stream must be sought in the table, the structure should lend itself to an efficient search. Finally, since the output must be alphabetical, the table must either be kept ordered or it must be in a form convenient for sorting. Ordering the table is also good for searching but requires a great deal of reshuffling whenever a new word must be added. Consequently, we elect a scheme in which 26 separate tables are maintained, one for each letter of the alphabet. The reordering required to add a new entry is now considerably reduced. A single entry in any of the table will be a (word, count) pair and, for now, we will not decide what the maximum word size or maximum table size should be. Nevertheless, a program already begins to take shape.

```
PROGRAM WORDCOUNT(INPUT, OUTPUT);
    CONST   MAXWORDSIZE =   {We have not decided
                                yet}
            TABLESIZE =
    TYPE    WORDTYPE = PACKED ARRAY [1 . .
            MAXWORDSIZE] OF CHAR;
            TABLEENTRY = RECORD
                            WORD: WORDTYPE;
                            FREQ: INTEGER
                         END;
    VAR     FREQTABLE: ARRAY ['A' . . 'Z',
            1 . . TABLESIZE] OF TABLEENTRY;
                        {The above declaration as-
                        sumes 'A' . . 'Z' includes all
                        26 characters}
BEGIN
    INITIALIZE;
    WHILE WEHAVEAWORD(WORD) DO
            PROCESS(WORD);
    {PROCESS looks for "word" in the FREQTABLE.
    If it is there, the count is incremented, otherwise
    WORD is added to the table. WEHAVEAWORD
    returns false when EOF comes up}
    REPORT
END.
```

Four subprograms have been defined. INITIALIZE will be put off until last because it is not yet clear what initialization entails, but the other three can now be developed simultaneously and independently. REPORT can be a procedure that simply prints the contents of FREQTABLE in some convenient format. Assuming this format has been decided, the programming can be assigned to another person.

Schematically, the program modularization can be represented by the following tree chart.

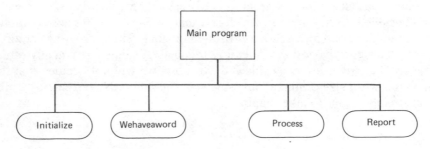

The only additional information needed is how many entries are in each row of the table. For this purpose, we will use another array, such as

ROWSIZE: ARRAY['A' . . 'Z'] OF INTEGER;

and we will initialize this array to all zeroes. The input routine requires the declaration of WORD and also needs a global string for holding one full line of input as well as current and final position markers. PROCESS needs nothing more, and the program can be fleshed out a bit. Temporary code is included so that the program may actually be compiled and executed for testing purposes, even though it does not yet perform as intended.

The inclusion of such "do-nothing" modules is very common and, indeed, quite necessary in top-down program design. Each high-level routine will typically make use of a number of lower-level routines for handling some details of the computation. However, in a well-organized project, many of these lower-level routines will not yet exist. In order to test the correctness of the high-level procedures, we must include declarations for all routines invoked by the subprogram being tested. Even if the body of these lower-level routines does nothing useful, it will allow program testing to proceed. These dummy program units are usually called *stubs*. They will eventually be replaced by meaningful code. In the following example we have included stubs for WEHAVEAWORD, INITIALIZE, PROCESS, and REPORT, so we could test the syntactic correctness of all declarations.

```
PROGRAM WORDCOUNT(INPUT, OUTPUT);
    CONST MAXWORDSIZE =  10;   {Only first 10 characters of word
                                used}
```

```
           TABLESIZE      =200;  {Capacity of each table row}
           MAXLINEWIDTH=  80;  {See WEHAVEAWORD}
  TYPE     WORDTYPE = PACKED ARRAY [1 . . MAXWORDSIZE]
              OF CHAR;
           TABLEENTRY = RECORD
                            WORD: WORDTYPE;
                            FREQ: INTEGER
                         END;
  VAR      FREQTABLE:    ARRAY ['A' . . 'Z', 1 . . TABLESIZE]
                            OF TABLEENTRY;
           ROWSIZE:      ARRAY ['A' . . 'Z'] OF INTEGER;
           INPUTLINE:    PACKED ARRAY [1 . . MAXLINEWIDTH]
                            OF CHAR;
           CURCHARPOS,   {Just for WEHAVEAWORD}
           LASTCHARPOS: INTEGER;
           WORD: WORDTYPE;
FUNCTION WEHAVEAWORD(VAR WORD: WORDTYPE): BOOLEAN;
        BEGIN
        WRITELN (' IN WEHAVEAWORD');
        WEHAVEAWORD:= NOT(WORD = ' AARDVARK '); {For
                                      testing purposes only}
        WORD:= ' AARDVARK '
        END; {Of WEHAVEAWORD}
PROCEDURE   INITIALIZE;
VAR C:CHAR;
        BEGIN
        WRITELN(' IN INITIALIZE ');  {for testing purposes only}
        FOR C:='A' TO 'Z' DO ROWSIZE[C]:=0
        END; {Of INITIALIZE}
PROCEDURE   PROCESS(WORD: WORDTYPE);
        BEGIN
        WRITELN(' IN PROCESS ')  {For  testing  purposes  only}
        END; {Of process}
PROCEDURE   REPORT;
        BEGIN
        WRITELN(' IN REPORT')   {For testing purposes only}
        END; {Of REPORT}
BEGIN
  INITIALIZE;
  WHILE WEHAVEAWORD(WORD) DO PROCESS(WORD);
     { PROCESS looks for "WORD" in the FREQTABLE. If it is there,
     the count is incremented, otherwise "WORD" is added to the
     table. WEHAVEAWORD returns false when EOF comes up}
  REPORT
END.
```

At this point, the CONST declarations have been completed so that the program will be complete in some sense. They could easily be changed at any time. The program itself is now a running program but, at the same time, it is little more than an expansion of the original algorithm.

The necessary subprograms may now be developed in turn, and the dummy code for each can then be replaced. We begin with WEHAVEA-WORD. This function must locate the next word in the current input line and, if the line is exhausted, a new line must be read. To locate a word, we assume that each word is preceded by a blank unless it is the first word of a line. Having located the first character of a word, we will assume that the word is terminated by any nonalphabetic character. Obviously, this is a simplification, but it serves our purpose here.

Our algorithm might look like this.

> Get the next character until a letter is found.
> If the process fails, return an end condition.
> Get up to MAXWORDSIZE letters, and assemble them into WORD.
> If necessary, fill out WORD with blanks.
> If necessary, skip input characters until a blank is found.

It seems that we really want to view the input as a stream of characters, not words, so we will have an inner subroutine called GETACHAR that actually handles the physical input. The function can be laid out thus.

```
FUNCTION WEHAVEAWORD(VAR WORD: WORDTYPE):
                        BOOLEAN;
        {  Returns the next word of text in the input stream.
           Function value is false on end-of-file  }
LABEL 99;
VAR CH: CHAR;
    I, J: INTEGER;
FUNCTION GETACHAR (VAR CH: CHAR): BOOLEAN;
BEGIN   {Do it later}   CH:= 'A'; GETACHAR:=TRUE END;

BEGIN
{Find beginning of a word}
CH:=' ';
WHILE NOT (CH IN LETTERS) DO
    IF NOT GETACHAR(CH) THEN
        BEGIN
        WEHAVEAWORD:=FALSE; GOTO 99   {Transfer    to
                                       the end of
                                       routine}
        END;
```

```
{Assemble the word }
I:=1;
WHILE (CH IN LETTERS) AND (I <= MAXWORDSIZE) DO
    BEGIN
    WORD[I]:=CH;
    IF  NOT GETACHAR(CH) THEN
        BEGIN
        WEHAVEAWORD:= FALSE; GOTO 99 {Transfer to
                                            the end of
                                            the routine}
        END;
    I:=I+1
    END;   {WHILE loop}
FOR J:=I TO MAXWORDSIZE DO WORD[J]:=' ';   {Pad out
                                the word with blanks}
WHILE CH IN LETTERS DO      {Skip tail of long word}
    IF  NOT GETACHAR(CH) THEN
        BEGIN
        WEHAVEAWORD:=FALSE
        END;
WEHAVEAWORD := TRUE;
99: END;   {WEHAVEAWORD}
```

This procedure needs a set of letters as well as the function GETACHAR, so we add:

```
LETTERS : SET OF ['A' . . 'Z'];
```

to the VAR declarations of the main program, and we also add code to initialize this set in the INITIALIZE procedure. Next we turn our attention to GETACHAR. It might look something like this.

```
FUNCTION GETACHAR( VAR CH: CHAR): BOOLEAN;
{ Treat input as a character stream. Return next character }
LABEL 99;
VAR I: INTEGER;
BEGIN
    IF CURCHARPOS >= LASTCHARPOS THEN
        BEGIN   {Need new line}
        IF EOF THEN
            BEGIN
            GETACHAR:=FALSE; GOTO 99
            END;
        I:=1;
        WHILE (I<=MAXLINEWIDTH) AND
```

```
                    (NOT EOLN) DO
                    BEGIN
                    READ (INPUTLINE[I]); I:=I+1
                    END;
                READLN;
                LASTCHARPOS:=I-2;
                CURCHARPOS :=0;
                {Echo-print   input }
                FOR I:= 1 TO LASTCHARPOS DO
                       WRITE (INPUTLINE[I]); WRITELN
                END; {Need new line}
             CURCHARPOS:=CURCHARPOS+1;
             CH:= INPUTLINE[CURCHARPOS];
             GETACHAR:=TRUE;
         99: END  {GETACHAR};
```

This procedure is self-contained, so WEHAVEAWORD is now complete. We need only note that in order to have the first input line read, CURCHARPOS and LASTCHARPOS must initially be set equal. Accordingly, we might go back to the INITIALIZE procedure before continuing with the PROCESS subroutine.

```
         PROCEDURE INITIALIZE;
         VAR CH: CHAR;
         BEGIN
             WRITELN(' IN INITIALIZE ');
             LETTERS:= [ ];   {Initialize the letters set}
             FOR CH:= 'A' TO 'Z' DO
                    BEGIN
                    ROWSIZE[CH]:=0;   {FREQTABLE empty}
                    LETTERS:= LETTERS + [CH]
                    END;
             CURCHARPOS:=0;   LASTCHARPOS:=0
                                    {INPUTLINE empty}
         END   {INITIALIZE};
```

The PROCESS subprogram deals with each WORD passed into it. The algorithm can be written:

> Search for WORD in the FREQTABLE
> If it is there, Increment the count
>   Else Add WORD to FREQTABLE
>   Initialize its count to 1

We have already decided what FREQTABLE will look like, so we can go ahead and express the algorithm in PASCAL.

```
PROCEDURE PROCESS(WORD: WORDTYPE);
{Search FREQTABLE for word. Update proper count
 or add word to table}
VAR INDEX : INTEGER;
FIRSTCHAR: CHAR;
{Subprogram declarations needed here}   {Testing}
BEGIN
        FIRSTCHAR:= WORD[1];
        IF TABLESEARCH(WORD, FIRSTCHAR,INDEX) THEN
                FREQTABLE[FIRSTCHAR, INDEX].FREQ:=
                FREQTABLE[FIRSTCHAR, INDEX].FREQ+1
        ELSE
                ADDTOTABLE(WORD, FIRSTCHAR, INDEX)
END;   {PROCESS}
```

PROCESS needs two subprograms of its own, TABLESEARCH and ADDTOTABLE. The former will begin:

```
FUNCTION TABLESEARCH(WORD: WORDTYPE;
        FIRSTCHAR: CHAR; VAR INDEX:
        INTEGER): BOOLEAN;
```

Its purpose will be to search the row of FREQTABLE indicated by FIRST-CHAR for the word WORD. If successful, the reference parameter INDEX will have the location within the row of that word, and the function value will be TRUE. If not successful, INDEX will hold the position within the row where WORD should be added, and the function itself will be FALSE. The completion of this procedure is left to the reader. It could use a binary search process that incorporates a BOOLEAN function that determines, for example, whether the first of its two WORDTYPE arguments occurs earlier in the alphabet than the other.

The procedure ADDTOTABLE is much simpler. It is nothing more than a utility to ripple down the entries in a row. An error-handling routine will be called if a table row is already full. This routine will also be left unfinished here, but it might simply list the word that could not be added, terminate the program or, if the program is interactive, it might ask for instructions.

```
PROCEDURE ADDTOTABLE(WORD: WORDTYPE;
                FIRSTCHAR: CHAR; INDEX: INTEGER);
{Add WORD to row FIRSTCHAR of FREQTABLE}
PROCEDURE TABLEFULL;
        BEGIN   {We will write it later. It is included}
        END;   {Now for testing purposes only}
BEGIN
        IF ROWSIZE[FIRSTCHAR]=TABLESIZE THEN
        TABLEFULL
```

```
            ELSE
              BEGIN
              ROWSIZE[FIRSTCHAR]:=ROWSIZE
                [FIRSTCHAR]+1;
              FOR I:=ROWSIZE[FIRSTCHAR] DOWNTO
                INDEX+1 DO
                BEGIN   {Make room for new entry}
                FREQTABLE[FIRSTCHAR,I].WORD:=
                  FREQTABLE[FIRSTCHAR,I-1].WORD;
                FREQTABLE[FIRSTCHAR,I].FREQ :=
                  FREQTABLE[FIRSTCHAR,I-1].FREQ
                END;
              FREQTABLE[FIRSTCHAR,INDEX].WORD:=
                WORD;
              FREQTABLE[FIRSTCHAR,INDEX].FREQ :=1
              END
        END;  {ADDTOTABLE}
```

The whole program continues to be developed downward through a tree of subprograms. Since the completed program has become somewhat lengthy, we conclude this case study with a diagram of the program's structure (Figure 8-10). An asterisk indicates a module that we did not complete here.

8.10 CONCLUSION

The case study just developed is the most complex program we have yet done. However, except for a few intimations on programming technique, we have dealt mainly with how to write subprograms and with the various

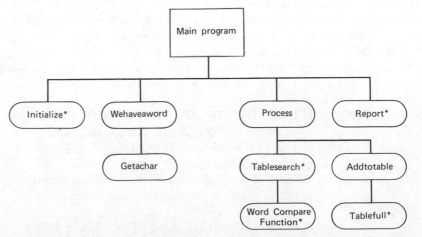

FIGURE 8-10   Modularization of the Word Processing Case Study.

methods of communicating between subprograms such as parameters and global variables. The important techniques of program modularization and top-down development we utilized in the case study were not stressed heavily. Without these development aids, however, the case study would have been significantly more difficult. In the next chapter we will look at the questions of what makes a good subprogram and how we can go about using subprograms to decompose a complex program into several simpler ones.

EXERCISES

*1. Describe the scope of all the variables used in the following program fragment.

```
PROGRAM OUTER;
VAR A, B : INTEGER;
      .
      .
      .
      PROCEDURE P1;
      VAR B, C : INTEGER;
          .
          .
          .
      END;  {Of P1}

      PROCEDURE P2;
      VAR C, D : INTEGER;
          .
          .
          .
          PROCEDURE P3;
          VAR E : INTEGER;
              .
              .
              .
          END;  {Of P3}
          .
          .
          .
      END;  {Of P2}
BEGIN
      .
      .
      .
END.  {Of OUTER}
```

2. Consider the following two procedures:

```
PROCEDURE SWAP1          PROCEDURE SWAP2
(X, Y: REAL);            (VAR X, Y: REAL);
   VAR T: REAL;             VAR T: REAL;
   BEGIN                    BEGIN
   T := X; X := Y; Y := T   T := X; X := Y; Y := T
   END;                     END;
```

If A has the value 1.2 and B has the value 1.5, what is the result of each of the following invocations?

```
SWAP1(A, B);          SWAP2(A, B);
```

*3. Given the following procedure:

```
PROCEDURE SILLY(X: INTEGER; VAR Y: INTEGER);
VAR Z: INTEGER;
BEGIN
     X := 5; Y := 6; Z := 7
END;  {Of silly}
```

what is the output produced by the following three lines?

```
X := 1; Y := 2; Z := 3;
SILLY(Y, X);
WRITELN(X, Y, Z)
```

*4. Given the following program:

```
PROGRAM MAINLINE(INPUT, OUTPUT);
VAR A, B, C: INTEGER;
PROCEDURE PROC1;
    VAR A, C: INTEGER;
    PROCEDURE PROC2;
        VAR B: INTEGER;
        BEGIN A:=4; B:=5;
            WRITELN (' INSIDE PROC2, VALUES FOR
                A, B, AND C ARE CURRENTLY',
                A, B, C)
        END;  {Of PROC2}
    BEGIN
        C:=6;
        WRITELN(' INSIDE PROC1, VALUES FOR A, B, C
                ARE CURRENTLY', A, B, C);
        PROC2;
```

```
                WRITELN(' STILL INSIDE PROC1 VALUES FOR
                        A, B, C ARE CURRENTLY', A, B, C)
        END  {Of PROC1};
    {Main program begins here}
    BEGIN
    A:=1; B:=2; C:=3;
    PROC1;
    WRITELN(' INSIDE MAIN PROGRAM, VALUES FOR A, B, C
            ARE CURRENTLY', A, B, C)
    END.  {Of main program}
```

what would be the exact output of the program if it were executed? (If any of the WRITELN commands would attempt to print an undefined quantity, just indicate that with the symbol '***' and keep tracing.)

5. What is the output that will result from the execution of the following program? Denote undefined variables by ***.

```
PROGRAM  BLOCK(OUTPUT);
    VAR A, B, C: INTEGER;
    PROCEDURE P1(VAR X: INTEGER; Y: INTEGER);
        VAR B, C, D: CHAR;
        PROCEDURE P2;
            VAR X, Y: INTEGER;
            BEGIN
            WRITELN(' IN P2:', X:3, Y:3, A:3, B:3,
                        C:3, D:3);
            A:=ORD(B)
            END;  {Of P2}
        BEGIN
        D:='X';
        WRITELN(' IN P1: ', X:3, Y:3, A:3, B:3, C:3, D:3);
        X:=Y; Y:=0; B:=CHR(A); C:=CHR(X);
        P2;
        WRITELN(' OUT P1: ', X:3, Y:3, A:3, B:3, C:3, D:3)
        END;  {Of P1}
    BEGIN
        A:=1; B:=2; C:=3;
        P1(A, B);
        P1(B, C);
        P1(C, A)
    END.  {Of BLOCK}
```

*6. Given the following recursive function:

```
FUNCTION DUNNO (M: INTEGER): INTEGER;
VAR VALUE: INTEGER;
BEGIN
    IF M = 0 THEN VALUE := 3
            ELSE VALUE := DUNNO(M − 1) + 5;
    DUNNO := VALUE;
    WRITELN(' CURRENT VALUES OF M AND VALUE ARE ',
            M, VALUE)
END;  {Of DUNNO}
```

what output is produced by the following statement?

```
WRITELN(DUNNO(3));
```

7. What is the output produced by the following program?

```
PROGRAM   REC(OUTPUT);
        FUNCTION   P(X: REAL; N: INTEGER): REAL;
        BEGIN
                WRITELN(' IN P: ', X:6:1, N:3);
                IF N = 0 THEN P:=1.0
                ELSE
                        IF ODD(N) THEN P:= X*SQR(P(X, N
                                        DIV 2))
                                ELSE P:= SQR(P(X, N
                                        DIV 2));
                WRITELN( END OF P')
        END;  {Of function P}
BEGIN
    WRITELN(P(2.0, 13))
END.  {Of PROGRAM REC}
```

8. Consider the following function.

```
FUNCTION   F(VAR X: INTEGER): INTEGER;
BEGIN
        F:=X;
        X:=X+1
END;
```

Are the values of the boolean expressions

```
X=F(X)
F(X)=X
```

the same?
What is the trouble?

*9. Write a subprogram that computes the value of an investment, P, after N years of interest at a rate R compounded quarterly. Should your subprogram be a procedure or a function? Should the parameters be passed by value or by reference?

10. Write a procedure that accepts a character string and returns the same character string with all blanks deleted, along with an integer that indicates how many blanks existed in the input string. What will be the parameters of the procedure and what will be their form?

11. Write a complete PASCAL function that computes SIN(X) using the approximation formula

$$SIN(X) \cong \frac{X}{1!} - \frac{x^3}{3!} + \frac{x^5}{5!} - \frac{x^7}{7!} + \cdots$$

The number of terms of the series to be used should be a parameter of the function. For example, SIN(Y, 3) should compute the SIN(Y) using the first three terms of the series.

12. Write a complete PASCAL function which *integrates* another function F(x) between two points a and b. To integrate a function means to determine the total area contained under its curve.

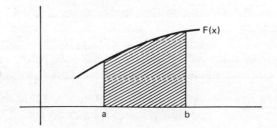

One way to do this is to approximate the area using a number of rectangles.

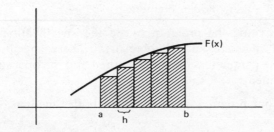

Obviously, the more rectangles used, the better the approximation. If we assume that there are N rectangles then the approximation to the integral I can be written as

$$I = h(F(a) + F(a + h) + F(a + 2h) + \ldots + F(a + [N - 1]h))$$

where h is the width of each rectangle and is defined as

$$h = \frac{b - a}{N}$$

Your function should be able to integrate an arbitrary function F between any limits a and b.

*13. In Section 2.4 we presented an algorithmic representation of a recursive search of a binary tree. Code this algorithm as a PASCAL procedure.

14. Write a PASCAL program to solve the following problem.

Read in a list of integer values from data cards. Each data card may contain one or more integer values and the end of the entire data set will be indicated by an end of file. Every value read should be in the range 200 to 800. Print out the following two pieces of information.

a. The list in ascending order
b. The first, second, and third quartiles. The first quartile is the score that has 25% lower scores and 75% higher scores, the second quartile (median) is the score that has 50% below and 50% above. The third quartile is the score that has 75% lower and 25% above.

In order to write this program you may assume that there will exist a procedure called "bubblesort" and a function called "median" with the following capabilities.

Bubblesort. This procedure will sort an integer array into ascending order using a technique called the bubble sort.
Median. This function will accept an integer array in ascending order and return, as a result, the value of the median, or middle, element.

After writing the program, write the specifications for the two modules "median" and "bubblesort." These specifications should include the parameters that are required and the operations that must be performed.

Test your program using stubs for both "median" and "bubblesort."

15. a. Write the PASCAL procedure called "bubblesort" that was described in problem 14. The bubble sort technique sorts a list by comparing the first and second items in the list and exchanging their position if they are out of order. It then compares the second and third items, the third and fourth, and so on, until we have compared all items in the list. This entire operation is called a single *pass*. This is repeated until the list is eventually in order. Here is a simple example.

10	10	10
30	25	25
25	30	26
78	26	30
26	78	78
Exchanges during pass 1	Exchanges during pass 2	Sorted list

Your procedure should work for any integer array up to a limit of 200 elements.

b. Write the PASCAL function "median" that was described in the previous question.

*16. A student was given the job of writing a PASCAL procedure to find the average of a list of up to 200 examination scores in the range 0 to 150. Here is what was produced.

```
PROCEDURE AVG;
BEGIN
    TOTAL:=0.0; AVERAGE:=0.0; BAD:=0;
    IF (NUMBER < 1) OR (NUMBER > 200)
        THEN WRITELN(' IMPROPER NUMBER OF SCORES ')
        ELSE BEGIN
            I:=1;
            WHILE I <= NUMBER DO
                BEGIN
                IF (LIST[I] < 0.0) OR
                (LIST[I] > 150.0)
                THEN BAD:=BAD+1
                ELSE TOTAL:=TOTAL+LIST[I];
                I:=I+1
                END;
            AVERAGE:=TOTAL/(NUMBER-BAD);
            WRITELN(' THE AVERAGE IS ', AVERAGE)
            END
END;   {Of AVG}
```

a. Assume that the procedure AVG was going to be put into a program library and used by different people. Within this context discuss the poor programming habits and poor style displayed by the procedure as it is currently written.
b. Rewrite AVG to remedy these problems.
c. Write the documentation needed for AVG so that it can be intelligently and properly utilized.

17. In Section 7.4 we developed a complete program for the Game of Life How might that program be reorganized with the use of subprograms? Write the function or procedure heading as well as the declarations for each subprogram you would use.

CHAPTER 9

BUILDING QUALITY PROGRAMS

9.1 INTRODUCTION

The programs presented so far have been small ones, because each was intended to illustrate a point about programming in PASCAL. We are now ready to consider how to develop larger programs. Why give large programs such special treatment? Isn't a large program just like a small program, only longer? Definitely not! As an analogy, consider how a small business grows into a large one. At first, the proprietor alone tends customers, keeps records, maintains the shop, and does everything else that a successful enterprise requires. As the business grows, however, the proprietor can no longer keep up with the volume of work, so he or she hires a salesperson, an accountant, an inventory clerk, a truck driver, and a maintenance person. With further growth, the company may require eight salespeople, two accountants, two buyers, five people to handle inventory, a fleet of three delivery trucks, and a maintenance crew of three. The business is no different than it was at the last stage except for size, yet the owner, who had no trouble supervising a staff of five, finds that he or she cannot adequately manage the 23 people who now work for him or her. Furthermore, the problem is not only a matter of insufficient time but of one person's inability to keep track of the various activities of each member of such a large group. In order to control the operation, the owner must now establish a staff of managers so that he or she can direct about five distinct activities.

Although the only aspect of the business that has changed is its size, the concerns of the owner have varied radically. In the beginning he or she dealt with everything from customers to the preparation of tax returns. Later, with five employees handling routine functions, the owner was probably still aware of daily operations, but got involved only with exceptional situations such as a dissatisfied customer wanting a refund, procuring a security system for the stockroom, or providing a fill-in for the delivery person who was home sick with the flu. Now, with an organization of over 20 people, the owner can no longer remain aware of everything that happened from day to day. His or her own view of the company has shifted to general considerations such as the overall effectiveness of the sales force, the amount of capital tied up in the physical plant, and the company's policy on sick leave.

Regarding a large program in the same way as a small one is similar to attempting to manage a staff of 20 (or 100 or 1000) without establishing intermediate levels of management. The limited ability of the human mind to deal with independent entities makes the situation impossible. Therefore, just as organizational hierarchies are established for coordinating large groups of people, a structural hierarchy needs to be built in order to keep the many detailed operations of a large program understandable.

9.2 PROGRAMMING FOR PEOPLE

It is not enough for a machine to be able to execute the programs we construct. People must also understand them. In the early days of electronic computing, the machines were so expensive with respect to the work that they could perform that programming always favored run-time efficiency at the expense of program clarity. Since then, the cost of computer hardware has decreased phenomenally, while the value of a good programmer has continued to rise. Today, the most expensive component of a new computer is the "people costs" associated with program development and maintenance, yet the habit of coding for run-time efficiency instead of for clarity is still difficult to break.

In order to write programs that are easy for people to comprehend, we must approach programming from a psychological point of view. We must consider the abilities and limitations of the human mind to see why certain presentations of a given concept are readily understood while others are not. Analyzing the psychology of good programming may seem impossible, or at least too difficult, for beginning programmers. However, we can have considerable success by making some simple, intuitive observations about ourselves.

The first of these observations is that humans cannot cope with two independent concepts simultaneously. For example, it is not possible to read a novel and add a column of figures at the same time. At best we might alternately read a sentence and then add a few numbers, but even that would be hopelessly confusing for most of us. As a second example, we cannot carry on two simultaneous independent conversations. Recognizing this, our society forbids us to interrupt a conversation. If we could handle two unrelated conversations at once, speaking while someone else is speaking would not be discourteous; it would not even constitute an interruption!

Our next observation is that human short-term memory has a very limited capacity. Remembering seven or eight items is the upper limit for most of us. For example, we have to write down a grocery list of more than eight items lest we forget some of them. Furthermore, even if we memorized such a list, it would fade very rapidly. Within a few days it is unlikely that we could recall more than a few items, and after two weeks and several more trips to the store, we probably could not remember any of them. We are very good at "unlearning" things that have lost their importance.

Despite these limitations, the human brain has some remarkable abilities. One of these is an apparently unlimited capacity for abstracting and generalizing. For example, even though short-term memory is limited to about seven items, the nature of those items is of no consequence whatsoever. It is no more difficult to remember a list of seven cities than it is to remember a list of seven streets, even though a city might be comprised of thousands of streets. In both cases the items on the list are treated simply as names without regard for the specific objects associated with those names. The concept of a city is understood abstractly. It is not necessary to know the names of all the streets or the relationships among the streets in order to accept the idea that a city is composed of many streets. It is not even essential to know what a city is in order to remember the names of a few. The ability to work with generalizations is what allows a single individual to control a large entity, such as a corporate organization or a military unit, by establishing a hierarchy of control centers. In fact, the restrictions already discussed necessitate this kind of structure.

Two other mechanisms that help us compensate for the severe limits on our ability to recall unrelated items are our vast capacities to perceive relationships and to form associations. The two often work together; therefore, without being too rigorous about which one is involved, we will look at some examples. One of the most notable is our ability to count. Although a sequence of random integers becomes more and more difficult to recall as it increases in length, we would have no trouble reciting the integers from 10 to 20,000, given enough time. And we could recite them by ones, by fives, by tens, by omitting every other odd number, or by applying any of many other clearly defined exclusionary processes. The reason we can recall the integers but not the random numbers seems to be that we can form a meaningful relationship between the successive integers in the sequence. In effect, long sequences are committed to memory not in any absolute sense, but by forming associations between each member and its successor. Most of us, for example, could not name the sixteenth letter of the alphabet without mentally reciting the first fifteen.

Again, suppose we must remember the outcomes of as many successive coin-tosses as possible. It is very easy to surpass the usual seven- or eight-item limit by thinking not in terms of heads or tails, but in run lengths. Thus, the sequence heads, heads, heads, tails, heads, tails, tails, tails becomes three, one, one, three. The sequence of eight items has been reduced to another sequence that is shorter and therefore easier to remember.

In order to write computer programs that are as clear and understandable as possible, we must avoid practices that exceed the limits of humans to understand or recall in favor of techniques that take advantage of the capacities for generalization, modularization, abstraction, and association. There is never much problem with programs that are small enough to stay within the fundamental bounds of comprehension. Unfortunately, a sample program that is good for illustrating a point about a programming language is usually of this small variety. Consequently, it is easy to lose sight of the fact that learning a programming language is only the beginning of learning programming. To make matters worse, a sample program large enough to provide an appreciation for the complexities of size would be prohibitively large for any other illustrative purpose. A version of a PASCAL compiler might be appropriate to illustrate a large program, but it seems wasteful to print such a large piece of code just to discuss its size while ignoring its content. Nevertheless, we will attempt to convey the idea of large size later by means of examples.

9.3 HOW BIG IS BIG?

We have said a great deal regarding the difference between a small program and a large one without really discussing what we mean by small or large. There are, of course, no standard definitions available, and no great amount of formality is necessary. So, just to be definite, we will stipulate that a program is small if it consists of less than 60 lines of code and the role of each line is immediately related to the overall purpose of the program. This definition is motivated by an underlying notion that a program is small only if it can be easily grasped in its entirety. The seemingly arbitrary number 60 is chosen because it is the maximum number of lines that will fit on one page of many common printer listings, and a program that cannot be laid out from beginning to end before the reader's eye can hardly qualify as readily comprehensible. The second condition is based on the idea that a program is small only if it does not require any kind of hierarchic structure in order to be clearly understood.

The definition of large, however, is not simply the opposite of small. We will regard a program as large if it is too big to be intrinsically understood, and if it lacks the hierarchical structure necessary to make it comprehensible. Thus, from here on, the term "large" will take on a very special meaning.

To illustrate the difference between large and small, consider the role of a single variable within a program. Possibly, it is an integer named K and, while reading the program, we encounter a statement that begins

$$\text{IF } K < 0 \text{ THEN} \ldots$$

If the program is small, then we have probably not lost track of the value of K, and it is easy to continue following the flow of control. At worst, even if we forget the value assigned to K, the statements that set the value are in sight to serve as an instant reminder. Furthermore, the total number of variables in the program is sufficiently small that we can keep track of all of them in the same ways. On the other hand, if the program is not small, the statements that assign a value to K may not be in sight. In fact, the typical case is that the program is so big that the statements of interest are not only out of sight, but are not even easy to find. For example, the operating system program for the Burroughs B6700 computer consists of about 130,000 lines of code written in a language very similar to PASCAL, and the PASCAL compiler that runs on the CDC 6600 contains about 7000 lines of PASCAL code. The various IBM operating systems, written in a low-level language called BAL, range in size to upward of 3 million lines, and the New York Times bibliographic project, which is a milestone in the development of program construction techniques, resulted in about 80,000 lines of COBOL.

Understanding programs of this magnitude can be something like finding the way through a labyrinth. At each turn only the local situation is apparent, and many points will be revisited more than once before the main path is clear. Similarly, while developing an understanding of a large program, we may read the code on any given page not just once but over and over as the relation among pages becomes clear.

9.4 PROGRAMMING FOR READABILITY

We will soon discover that one of the most important aspects of a good program is readability. In fact, nearly every attribute of a good program is linked in some way to how easily people can deal with it, and that generally depends on how easy the program is to read. It is, therefore, well worthwhile to devise some guidelines and methods for writing readily readable programs.

The immediate observation that can be drawn from our discussion so far is that small programs are readable and large ones are not. Therefore, our first fundamental rule is never write a large program! This statement may seem absurd at first, but it is really quite profound because it is the essence of top-down design. Presented with a problem whose solution requires a large amount of code, a programmer might produce a large program and claim that the problem was too big to do otherwise. The programmer fails to realize that it is not the fault of the problem for being so large but, instead, that the degree of modularization is too small! However, if the subprogram definition facility is regarded as a way to extend the language itself, then no problem's solution need be expressed as anything other than a small program written in a sufficiently extended language.

A program to produce a table of compound interest, for example, would be no more complex than a program to generate a table of sines and cosines if the language had predefined functions, similar to SIN and COS, built in, for compound interest. But the absence of these functions does not preclude our writing the program as if they did exist. It only means that after the program to generate the table is finished, we must still write function subprograms that will compute the values for the desired table entries.

This kind of approach to program design has a number of nice features. In the first place, the outer block is quite readable, since it is written in a sufficiently high-level language (PASCAL), extended by compound interest functions. Second, if PASCAL is, by itself, not sufficient for writing small programs to evaluate the required functions, then the same approach can be used again without concern for the role each submodule has in the overall structure. Ultimately, a natural control structure emerges in which every module is small (and thereby readable), since it is expressed in terms of sufficiently powerful submodules, and the relative power of each module affects the level of that module within the structure but not its size. Thus the method provides a straightforward way of constructing the hierarchy that has already been recognized as necessary if the resulting program is to be managed by human beings. In fact, modularization is probably the most important intellectual tool that allows us to tackle and solve large, complex problems.

To illustrate the development process, Figure 9-1 presents a program that will generate a compound interest table provided the function COMPOUNDINT exists. Furthermore, the program as written is quite easy to change in order to print, for example, a different number of columns. At the next level, Figure 9-2 shows a function, COMPOUNDINT, that could be used in Figure 9-1. It, too, is very simple to understand because it relies on

```
PROGRAM COMPINTTAB(INPUT, OUTPUT);
      {Computes and prints a table of compound interest for four
      rates and any number of years}
VAR  RATE, AMT          : ARRAY[1 . . 4] OF REAL;
     PRINCIPAL          : REAL;
     MAXYEARS,
     PERIODSPERYEAR,
     YEAR, I            : INTEGER;


FUNCTION COMPOUNDINT(PRINCIPAL, RATE: REAL;
                        PERIODNBR: INTEGER): REAL;
     {Computes the accumulated total amount when 'PRINCIPAL'
     dollars is left in the bank at 'RATE' interest rate for
     'PERIODNBR' interest periods}
     BEGIN  {Deferred—for now, assume it exists}
     END;


BEGIN
     {Input}
     READ(PRINCIPAL, MAXYEARS, PERIODSPERYEAR);
     FOR I:= 1 TO 4 DO READ(RATE[I]);
     WRITELN(' ACCUMULATED INTEREST OVER', MAXYEARS :5,
             'YEARS');
     WRITELN(' FOR AN INITIAL AMOUNT OF $', PRINCIPAL:10:2);
     WRITELN; WRITELN;
     WRITE('   YEAR');
     FOR I:= 1 TO 4 DO WRITE('    AT ', RATE[I]:5:2, '%');
     WRITELN; WRITELN:
     {Process and output}
     FOR I:= 1 TO 4 DO AMT[I]:= PRINCIPAL;
     FOR YEAR:= 1 TO MAXYEARS DO
        BEGIN
        FOR I:= 1 TO 4 DO
           AMT[I]:= COMPOUNDINT(AMT[I], RATE[I]/
                                PERIODSPERYEAR,
                                PERIODSPERYEAR);
        WRITE(YEAR:7);
        FOR I:= 1 TO 4 DO WRITE(AMT[I]:13:2);
        WRITELN
        END
  END.   { Of COMPINTTAB }
```

FIGURE 9-1   Generation of a Table of Compound Interest.

```
FUNCTION COMPOUNDINT(PRINCIPAL, RATE: REAL; PERIODNBR:
                          INTEGER): REAL;
     {The function needed for program COMPINTTAB}
     FUNCTION POWER(X: REAL; N: INTEGER): REAL;
        {Computes X raised to the nth power}
        BEGIN   {Deferred—assume it exists for now}
        END;
  BEGIN
     COMPOUNDINT:= PRINCIPAL * POWER (1.0+RATE,
                                         PERIODNBR)
  END;   {Of COMPOUNDINT}
```

FIGURE 9-2   A Function for Computing Compound Interest.

yet another function, POWER. At the third level, POWER is just the function described in Chapter 8. The outer level is easy to read because the inner workings of COMPOUNDINT do not cloud the issue of how the table is formatted, and the computation of the interest rates within COMPOUND-INT is not complicated by the complexities of computing a power function. If anything, we have carried the hierarchy one level too far, but the point is to demonstrate hierarchical development.

9.5 INTRODUCTION TO STRUCTURED PROGRAMMING

Module size, although unquestionably very important, is not the only aspect of good programming practice that has a bearing on readability. Even a small program or subprogram can be comprehensible to a greater or lesser degree, depending on various other factors. Among these are the design of logical flow, the names chosen for variables, the appropriateness of comments, and the style of indentation used. All of these topics have already been discussed to some extent, but the emphasis here is going to be not so

STYLE CLINIC 9-1

Never Write a Large Program!

While designing the algorithm for the solution of a problem, think in terms of processes that are sufficiently general so that the resulting program, expressed in an algorithmic language (not necessarily PASCAL) is small. These general processes can later be realized as subprogram modules. Conversely, if a program (or program module) becomes so big that it is not easy to read, it needs to have some additional subprograms defined.

much on what the good programming techniques are, but on what makes them good.

Of the four items mentioned, the design of logical flow is the most interesting. The power of a computer lies not only in its speed, but in its ability to take either of two distinct courses of action, depending on conditions that can be sensed and, as a natural outgrowth of this, its ability to repeat a process many times. The branching and looping capabilities of the machine give rise to the development of algorithms that are in a very real sense two-dimensional. The development of flowcharts as a means of describing algorithms is graphic evidence of their two-dimensionality. Yet the physical computer program, which is always a linear sequence of statements, is decidedly one-dimensional. So the immediate problem that arises is how to express a two-dimensional concept with a one-dimensional medium. To make matters worse, computer programs look physically very much like books. Both consist of pages, and the pages of each consist of lines of text. The similarity is even greater if the statements of the program are thought of as the sentences of a book. Most books are not only physically linear but logically linear as well. In other words, they are best understood if they are read from front to back. Most computer programs, on the other hand, are not logically linear, since they represent loops and branches. Thus, our natural tendency to read them from front to back is often counterproductive.

How can programmers deal with these problems? We could discourage people from trying to read programs like books, or we could, to make our programs as readable as possible, cater to people's inclination to read from front to back. In fact, we must do both, but we should strive hardest to do the latter. At present, to follow the execution sequence of a typical large program, a reader will likely flip back and forth through the pages of the listing. A procedure is invoked on page 426. The declaration begins on page 203, but the first executable statement does not appear until page 260 because of local, lower-level submodule definitions. On page 261 a global variable called TABLESTATE is referenced, and the current value is unknown. The reader puts an old punched card in the listing to mark where he or she left off and begins tracing down the logic that set TABLESTATE. After more page flipping, the reader discovers that it was set to 0 on the bottom of page 425. With the question about TABLESTATE settled, the reader returns to page 261 and encounters a GOTO statement that transfers control to page 264, where another procedure is invoked whose code is to be found on page 227. This procedure ends on page 228, and the reader returns to page 264. Another exit occurs on the top of page 265, and the reader finally returns to page 426 where the next statement involves a call on a function declared on page 119.

To have readable programs, we must minimize this kind of page flipping. Proper modularization goes a long way toward this end. Even if a program is 500 pages long, it should be written so that the outer block occupies only one page and the procedure and function calls are commented clearly so that it is not necessary to read the actual subprogram declarations in order to understand the outer block. Each subprogram should be similarly written. Read "from the top down" instead of front to back, the program—its basic logic—can be understood relatively quickly, and further reading increases the depth of that understanding.

Within a submodule, transferring control from one section to another should also be minimized. In fact, because submodules are the basic building blocks of every program, the logic within each one should be linearized as much as possible in order to make reading easier. High-level control structures like those of PASCAL are precisely what is needed to do this. For example, the five program fragments shown in Figure 9-3 are logically equivalent, yet the WHILE form is conceptually easier because the transfer of control is implicit and because it is more natural for a person to repeat an operation while some condition is true than it is to interrupt the operation constantly in order to check whether or not the condition is still true. Examples of this kind of behavior are numerous. Consider, for instance, a recipe that instructs a baker to "beat egg whites until stiff." The baker does exactly that. He or she does not stop beating in order to ask whether the egg whites are stiff. Similarly, if the instructions for going to a friend's house say

```
WHILE boolean expression DO        10: IF boolean expression THEN
    statement;                            BEGIN
                                          statement;
                                          GOTO 10
                                          END;
```

                    (a)   (b)

```
10: IF boolean expression THEN     10: IF NOT boolean expression THEN
        statement                           GOTO 20;
    ELSE GOTO 20;                      statement;
    GOTO 10;                          GOTO 10;
20:                                20:
```

                    (c)   (d)

```
            10: IF boolean expression THEN GOTO 11;
                    GOTO 20;
            11: statement;
                    GOTO 10;
            20:
```

                                       (e)

FIGURE 9-3   Five Ways to Express a Loop.

to "continue along the road until the pavement ends," it is not necessary to stop moving in order to check whether the pavement has ended yet. Only Figure 9.3a describes the intended operation in such a manner that a person can internalize the stopping condition and concentrate on the operation to be performed. The IF-THEN construct that appears in each of the other four fragments actually obscures the intent of the code because the attendant GOTO must be regarded as an instruction in itself. Conscious consideration of the stopping condition is forced at each iteration, and the reader who, as we have already observed, is not very good at concentrating on two things at once, must switch attention back and forth between the loop operation and the stopping condition. Many persons who read program fragments like these will mentally translate Figures 9-3b to 9-3e into Figure 9-3a in order to conceptualize what is happening. It is a way of using generalization and abstraction to aid understanding, much like the conversion of a long string of coin tosses from heads and tails to run lengths.

It is fairly clear that a primitive instruction set for a machine is too primitive for a person. Whereas a machine operates at a decision-making level of

IF boolean expression THEN GOTO label

a person requires more abstract instructions for easy comprehension. Note that in Figure 9-3 there is an inverse relationship between the readability of the program sections and the level of the constructions used. Indeed, this relationship might well be taken as the basis for a definition of "level" as we use it when we say that one syntactic construct is of a higher level than another. Figure 9-3a is the most general expression of the loop. Figure 9-3b eliminates the explicit WHILE and uses a compound statement with a single GOTO in order to achieve the desired looping. Figure 9-3c no longer requires the compound statement, but instead uses an IF-THEN-ELSE construct and two labels. Figure 9-3d is the first one in which the loop control instructions are machine primitive. It is also interesting to note that if the statement comprising the body of the loop were itself a compound statement, this is the first time that the BEGIN-END brackets could be dropped off. However, in order to reduce the number of labels required, the boolean expression had to be negated. Finally in Figure 9-3e, the boolean expression is expressed as it was in Figure 9-3a, and the loop control instructions are all machine primitives, but the loop now requires three labels. The flow of control has become so convoluted that it is difficult to understand the fragment by reading it from front to back. One must instead follow the logic through twice in order to understand what effect the value of the boolean expression has on the behavior of the code.

It is just this kind of complicated control that must be avoided when coding individual submodules of a program. Just as subprogram modularization is used to reduce a big program to manageable pieces, high-level control structures are used to keep the flow within each subprogram as linear as possible. In fact, the hierarchy that was developed for program modularization reappears here in the form of nested control structures.

9.6 THE DISCIPLINE OF COMPUTER PROGRAMMING

It is one thing to write programs for readability and quite another to read someone else's work. A programmer who is very good at writing readable code may nevertheless be at a loss when required to read a poorly written program. Consequently, we need (or at least desire) to develop programming languages in which it is not possible to write code that is hard to read. The extent to which this can be done remains to be seen, but the movement away from the use of the GOTO statement can be viewed as a move in this direction. Another step is the establishment of a uniform discipline for programming so that all programmers will have a conceptual basis for communicating algorithms. Resistance to such a discipline has ranged from well-considered arguments to the defense of freedom of expression but, in the long run, most of the objections seem to be rooted either in the notion that producing complicated code is a source of pride or in the fact that it is easier to work in a situation where no constraints are imposed. Nevertheless, in the sciences and engineering, adhering to proven techniques insures the quality of the result, and computer programming need be no different. The problem up to now has been that programming is so new that often a program that merely worked was considered adequate, and any programmer who could write a large program that worked reasonably efficiently was regarded as a good programmer. Now, however, the criteria for what constitutes a good program encompass much more than correctness and efficiency. Furthermore, the development of programming languages with high-level control structures can make the writing of correct programs relatively easy, regardless of the size of the program. It is precisely the fact that it is easier to write programs that work well that has allowed programmers to concern themselves with things such as readability. In the early days, it was hard enough to write a program that worked at all, let alone one that was readable as well.

One of the reasons why correctness has always been difficult to attain is that the programming languages available have forced the programmer to translate personal thought processes into simpler ones expressible in the language being used. The translation itself can produce errors, and even a correct translation, like Figure 9-3e, is difficult to follow compared to the original concept because it is so nonlinear.

The programming discipline that has emerged from the desire for clarity, efficiency, and correctness can be summarized in three basic principles.

1. Every subprogram is constructed in such a manner that the corresponding flowchart can be reduced to a linear sequence of *elementary forms*

each of which has exactly one entry point and one exit. A flowchart that has this form will be referred to as a *segmented flowchart*.

2. Each elementary form has at least one segment box, and every segment box has exactly one entry point and one exit and may itself contain any segmented flowchart.

3. The elementary forms include:

   a. A simple segment box.

   b. A decision facility such as IF-THEN-ELSE.

   c. A looping facility such as WHILE-DO.

They may also include constructs of the same or higher levels but not constructs of lower levels.

Each of these concepts will be discussed in detail.

Figures 9-4 and 9-5 illustrate a set of elementary forms for programming in PASCAL. Figure 9-4 shows the three forms required by point 3, and Figure 9-5 shows some additional constructs that, although not essential, are convenient to have. Note first of all that all of the structures illustrated conform to the requirements of point 2. The structures of Figure 9-5 are regarded as inessential because they can all be derived from those of Figure 9-4. The IF-THEN is the same as the IF-THEN-ELSE if one of the two segment boxes of the latter is regarded as null. The CASE statement can be constructed by means of a sequence of IF-THEN-ELSE statements. For example,

```
CASE COMPASSPOINT OF
NORTH, SOUTH: statement1;
        EAST: statement2;
        WEST: statement3
END
```

is equivalent to

```
IF (COMPASSPOINT=NORTH) OR (COMPASSPOINT=SOUTH)
    THEN statement1
    ELSE IF COMPASSPOINT=EAST
            THEN statement2
            ELSE IF COMPASSPOINT=WEST
                    THEN statement3
```

A loop controlled by REPEAT can be converted into a loop controlled by WHILE by changing

```
REPEAT
    statement
UNTIL boolean expression
```

into

       statement;
       WHILE NOT boolean expression DO
           statement

Because of the repeated statement in the WHILE form, using it could be very cumbersome if the body of the loop consists of a sizeable compound statement, so the equivalence of the REPEAT and WHILE forms is of both academic and practical interest. Finally, a FOR loop such as

Simple segment

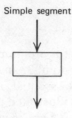

       BEGIN
       statement;
       .
       .
       .
       statement
       END

Decision using IF—THEN—ELSE

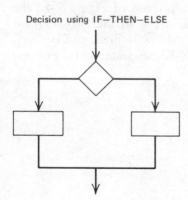

       IF boolean expression THEN
           statement1
       ELSE
           statement2

Loop using WHILE—DO

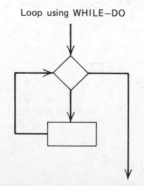

       WHILE boolean expression DO
           statement

FIGURE 9-4   The Three Required Elementary Forms.

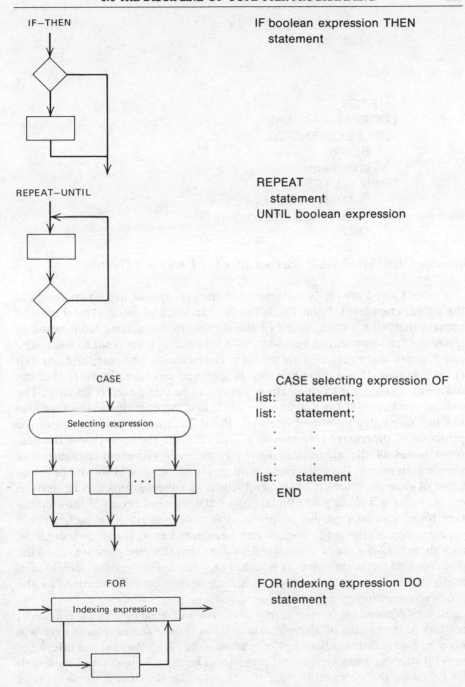

FIGURE 9-5   Additional Elementary Forms for PASCAL.

```
FOR I:= FIRST TO LAST DO
    statement
```

can be realized as

```
I:=FIRST;
LOOPING:= I<=LAST;
WHILE LOOPING DO
    BEGIN
    statement;
    IF I<LAST
        THEN I:=SUCC(I)
        ELSE LOOPING:=FALSE
    END
```

provided that "statement" does not alter I or LAST or LOOPING.

Points 1 and 2 are really statements of the precepts of top-down design at the subprogram level. Point 1 calls for the existence of an outermost level of control that, like a cake recipe or the directions for getting from home to grandmother's house, can be understood by reading from front to back. The requirement that every elementary form have exactly one entry and one exit is no accident. It is a condition that is imposed in order to insure that the only way a sequence of elementary forms can be composed is linearly. The exit of one becomes the entry to the next, and the combined structure also has just one entry point and one exit. Point 2 is another expression of the principle of successive refinement. It will often be the case that if the segment boxes of the elementary forms could only represent sequences of simple statements, the discipline would prove inconvenient for the development of clear programs. Consequently, just as subprograms can be used as components of a more powerful language, the segment boxes of the elementary forms can be regarded as being arbitrarily powerful. In fact, since a segment box is allowed to contain any segmented flow, it can be thought of as a subprogram. One of the major decisions that the discipline leaves to the discretion of the programmer is whether any particular segment should contain a call to a separately defined submodule or the actual instructions for the required operation.

Before proceeding further with a discussion of how to make this choice, a study of the coding of a single module is in order. The emphasis here will be on the successive refinement of a segmented flow. We will see afterward several ways to improve the final program. The most important of these will be based on the observation that the result is bigger than a single module should be.

9.7 A STUDY IN STRUCTURED CODING

The problem to be solved is the construction of a program that determines all ways to place N nonattacking queens on an N × N chess board, where the number N will be provided as a data value. Since the queen can move any number of squares forward, backward, and along either diagonal, as illustrated in Figure 9-6, a solution will have exactly one piece in each column, exactly one in each row, and at most one on each diagonal. Before getting into a method for generating solutions, however, we already have enough information to lay out a rough outer block. Figure 9-7 illustrates this first step. Note that very little is precise at this stage. The decision to limit N to 15 is arbitrary, but this is placed in a CONST declaration so that it can be easily changed. The major portion of the program will be concerned with generating and printing solutions. A backtracking algorithm will be used for this purpose. Since a solution is characterized in part by the placement of exactly one piece in each column, and each column has N squares in it, the placement of queens on the board can be represented by an array, COL, of length N. In this structure, COL[K]=J means that a queen has been placed on row J of column K. The columns and rows of the board will be numbered 1 to N, as shown in Figure 9-8, which also illustrates the use of the array COL. A value of 0 in any column position will be taken to mean that the column is empty.

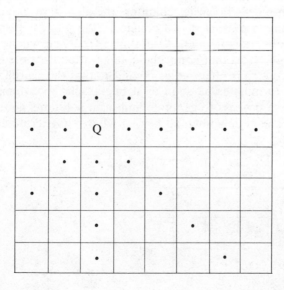

FIGURE 9-6   The Squares of an 8 × 8 Board that Are "Attacked" by the Queen.

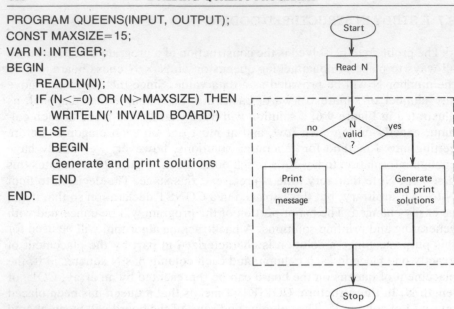

```
PROGRAM QUEENS(INPUT, OUTPUT);
CONST MAXSIZE=15;
VAR N: INTEGER;
BEGIN
    READLN(N);
    IF (N<=0) OR (N>MAXSIZE) THEN
        WRITELN(' INVALID BOARD')
    ELSE
        BEGIN
        Generate and print solutions
        END
END.
```

FIGURE 9-7   First Stage of the QUEENS Program.

Backtracking is just an orderly way of proceeding through all possible configurations. In each column, in turn, a piece will be placed in the smallest numbered allowable square. If no square in the column is allowable because of placement of pieces in earlier columns, the algorithm moves back to the previous column (backtracks) and considers the current placement of the piece in that column as invalid. A solution is reached whenever a piece is placed in column N. At that point, the configuration is printed and the position of the last queen is regarded as invalid so that the search can continue. The algorithm terminates as soon as it backtracks to column 0. The first refinement of the process to generate and print solutions appears as shown in Figure 9-9. The code shown all belong where "Generate and print solu-

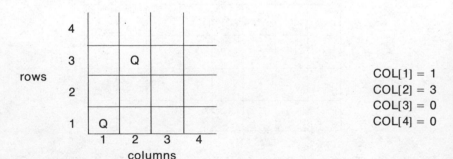

FIGURE 9-8   The Representation of the Board for the QUEENS Program.

tions'' appears in Figure 9-7. In addition, this section implies the need for more declarations in the outer block:

```
VAR COL          : ARRAY[1 . . MAXSIZE] OF INTEGER;
    I, CURCOLNBR  : INTEGER;
    PLACEDAQUEEN: BOOLEAN;
```

Several more remarks should be made here. First, the flowchart conforms to the structured discipline. The outer linear sequence is just a simple segment, followed by a WHILE loop, followed by another simple segment. The segment box of the WHILE loop is composed of a segment box, followed by an IF-THEN-ELSE, and one of the branches of the IF-THEN-ELSE is itself another IF-THEN-ELSE. Observe also the very close parallel between the code on the left side of the figure and the flowchart on the right. Finally, note that we have come this far with very little thought about how to decide whether a prospective placement of a queen is valid. At this point, the program only has a vague comment regarding the computation of the boolean variable PLACEDAQUEEN. The inner WHILE loop, which depends on this variable, places a queen at successive positions within the current column and exits if either a valid square is found or the column is exhausted. In the latter case, the value of PLACEDAQUEEN indicates whether to backtrack to the previous column.

The computation of PLACEDAQUEEN and the coding of the output complete the program. The output section is easily finished off with a sequence

```
WRITE(' SOLUTION: ');
FOR I:= 1 TO N DO WRITE(COL[I]:4);
WRITELN
```

The validation of a prospective placement requires a little effort, however. The search algorithm itself insures no other pieces in the same column, so it is only necessary to check the row and the two diagonals. Furthermore, if we are working in column CURCOLNBR, then we know that only columns 1 to CURCOLNBR−1 need to be checked. As coded so far, the variable PLACEDAQUEEN must be set to TRUE if square I of column CURCOLNBR is valid and FALSE otherwise, so the row can be validated by

```
J:=1; PLACEDAQUEEN:=TRUE;
WHILE PLACEDAQUEEN AND (J<CURCOLNBR) DO
    BEGIN
    PLACEDAQUEEN:= COL[J]<>I;
    J:=J+1
    END
```

To check the diagonals, notice from Figure 9-8 that the lower-left to upper-right diagonals are characterized by the fact that the row number minus the

```
FOR CURCOLNBR:=1 TO N DO COL[CURCOLNBR]:=0;
CURCOLNBR:=1;
WHILE CURCOLNBR>0 DO
    BEGIN   {Place a queen or backtrack}
    PLACEDAQUEEN:=FALSE;
    I:=COL[CURCOLNBR]+1;   {Next available row}
    {Attempt to put a queen on column CURCOLNBR}
    WHILE (I<=N) AND (NOT PLACEDAQUEEN) DO
        BEGIN
        {Compute PLACEDAQUEEN for row 1}
        IF NOT PLACEDAQUEEN THEN I:=I+1
        ELSE COL[CURCOLNBR]:=I
        END;
    {If PLACEDAQUEEN is false then attempt failed}
    IF   NOT PLACEDAQUEEN THEN
        BEGIN
        COL[CURCOLNBR]:=0;   {Mark column empty}
        CURCOLNBR:=CURCOLNBR-1   {And backtrack}
        END
    ELSE
        IF CURCOLNBR=N THEN   {Search complete}
            {Output the solution}
        ELSE CURCOLNBR:=CURCOLNBR+1
    END;
WRITELN(' SEARCH COMPLETE')
```

FIGURE 9-9   First Refinement of the QUEENS Program.

column number is constant, while the upper-left to lower-right diagonals have the property that the row number plus the column number is constant. Therefore, the code shown in Figure 9-10 can be used where "Compute PLACEDAQUEEN" appears in Figure 9-9. The final program is shown in Figure 9-11. Notice in particular that even though there are no functions or procedures declared in the program, it would still be quite easy to make modifications such as improving the code that validates positions (which could indeed be done) or changing the format of the output. The code is

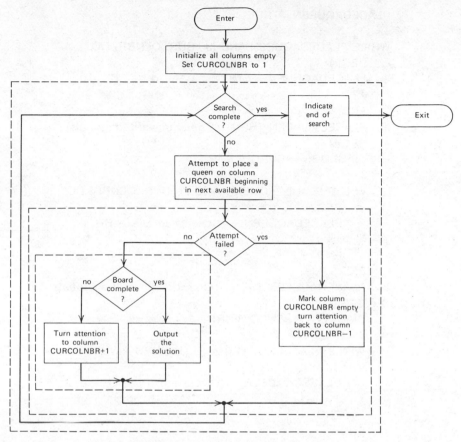

FIGURE 9-9a   Segmented Flow of First Refinement.

modular by virtue of the nested control structures, and most of the comments that appear are taken directly from the intermediate stages used to define the inner forms.

Consisting of 66 lines, the complete program taxes the limits of readability. It is certainly far less readable than the code in Figure 9-9, even though the latter is quite close to being complete. In retrospect, it can be seen that the placement checking should be done with a boolean function instead of in-line because it interrupts the reader's train of thought as he or she at-

```
PLACEDAQUEEN:=TRUE;
J:=1;
WHILE PLACEDAQUEEN AND (J<CURCOLNBR) DO
    BEGIN
    PLACEDAQUEEN:= COL[J]<>I;
    J:=J+1
    END;
IF   PLACEDAQUEEN THEN   {Check upward diagonals}
    BEGIN
    DIAGNBR:=I+CURCOLNBR;
    J:=1;
    WHILE PLACEDAQUEEN AND (J<CURCOLNBR) DO
        BEGIN
        PLACEDAQUEEN:= (COL[J]+J)=DIAGNBR;
        J:=J+1
        END
    END;
IF   PLACEDAQUEEN THEN   {Check downward diagonals}
    BEGIN
    DIAGNBR:=I-CURCOLNBR;
    J:=1;
    WHILE PLACEDAQUEEN AND (J<CURCOLNBR) DO
        BEGIN
        PLACEDAQUEEN:= (COL[J]-J)=DIAGNBR;
        J:=J+1
        END
    END
```

FIGURE 9-10   Validation of Prospective Placement for QUEENS.

tempts to understand the mechanism of the backtrack search. As it stands, however, the example illustrates that the arbitrary number of 60 lines chosen for the limit of a small program is, if anything, on the high side.

Having built the QUEENS program in accordance with the discipline put forth earlier, we may now take a critical look at the result. In so doing, we will consider both our intuition and our remarks about limitations to understanding. Two points stand out immediately. The first, as already mentioned,

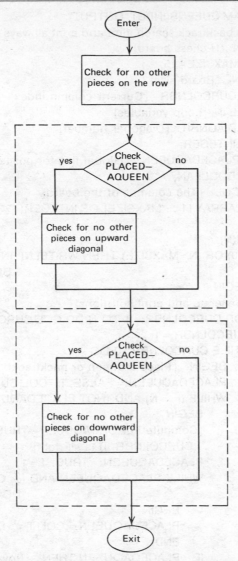

FIGURE 9-10a Segmented Flow of Placement Validation.

is that the placement validation routine belongs in a function subprogram of its own; the second is that the nesting level is so deep in places that reading becomes difficult.

The development of program modules in a top-down fashion is the primary tool for managing large, complex programs. However, there are no hard and fast rules that specify whether a particular module should be included directly in the program (in-line code) or put into a separate sub-

```
PROGRAM QUEENS(INPUT, OUTPUT);
{Using a backtrack search, find and print all ways to place N queens
 on an N ×N chess board}
CONST MAXSIZE=15;
VAR    N  {Board size}
          ,CURCOLNBR  {Current column index}
          ,I, J  {Loop variables}
          ,DIAGNBR  {Diagonal number}
          :INTEGER;
          PLACEDAQUEEN  {Global flag for position checking}
          :BOOLEAN;
          COL  {The columns of the board}
          :ARRAY [1 . . MAXSIZE] OF INTEGER;
BEGIN
READLN(N);
IF (N<=0) OR (N>MAXSIZE) THEN WRITELN(' INVALID
                                       BOARD SIZE')
ELSE BEGIN
      {Generate and print solutions}
      FOR CURCOLNBR:=1 TO N DO COL[CURCOLNBR]:=0;
      CURCOLNBR:=1;
      WHILE CURCOLNBR>0 DO
          BEGIN  {Place a queen or backtrack}
          PLACEDAQUEEN:=FALSE; I:=COL[CURCOLNBR]+1;
          WHILE (I<=N) AND (NOT PLACEDAQUEEN) DO
              BEGIN
              {Compute PLACEDAQUEEN—TRUE if piece at
               (CURCOLNBR, I) is all right}
              PLACEDAQUEEN:=TRUE; J:=1;
              WHILE PLACEDAQUEEN AND (J<CURCOLNBR)
                                      DO  {Check row}
                  BEGIN
                  PLACEDAQUEEN:=COL[J]<>I; J:=J+1
                  END;
              IF  PLACEDAQUEEN THEN  {Row is ok}
                  BEGIN  {Check upward diagonal}
                  DIAGNBR:=I+CURCOLNBR; J:=1;
                  WHILE PLACEDAQUEEN AND (J<CURCOLNBR) DO
                      BEGIN
                      PLACEDAQUEEN:=(COL[J]+J) <>
                         DIAGNBR; J:=J+1
                      END
                  END;
              IF  PLACEDAQUEEN THEN  {Upward diagonal is ok}
```

```
                    BEGIN  {Check downward diagonal}
                    DIAGNBR:=I-CURCOLNBR; J:=1;
                    WHILE PLACEDAQUEEN AND (J<CURCOLNBR)
                                            DO
                        BEGIN
                        PLACEDAQUEEN=(COL[J]-J)<> DIAGNBR;
                        J:=J+1
                        END
                    END;
                    {Piece at I is now known to be valid or not}
                    IF NOT PLACEDAQUEEN THEN I:=I+1
                    ELSE COL[CURCOLNBR]:=I
                    END;
                IF  NOT PLACEDAQUEEN THEN   {Column is exhausted
                                            so backtrack}
                    BEGIN
                    COL[CURCOLNBR]:=0; CURCOLNBR:=CURCOLNBR-1
                    END
                ELSE
                    IF  CURCOLNBR=N THEN   {We have a solution}
                    BEGIN  {Output the solution}
                    WRITE(' SOLUTION:');
                    FOR I:=1 TO N DO WRITE(COL[I]:4);
                    WRITELN
                    END
                    ELSE CURCOLNBR:=CURCOLNBR+1
                END;  {Of place a queen loop}
            WRITELN(' SEARCH COMPLETE')
            END
        END.
```

FIGURE 9-11 The Final QUEENS Program.

program and then invoked. This decision is essentially a value judgment and should be based on the following two considerations.

1. *Length*. The inclusion of too much in-line code within a module can create a program containing hundreds or thousands of lines of code. As we mentioned earlier, modules of this size can significantly increase the difficulty of understanding a program. A single module should contain no more than about 50 to 75 lines of code. If it has much more, consider placing some of the code into separate, lower-level subprograms.

2. *Readability*. When reading a module, we should immediately be able to grasp what the module is doing without worrying about how it is being done. If a particular section of code is becoming more and more con-

cerned with unimportant lower-level details, it should also be considered a prime candidate for a separate subprogram. This will allow the reader of the higher-level module to concentrate on the more important aspects of the program without worrying about specific implementation details. In this respect the readability of the QUEENS program would probably have been enhanced by procedures called:

CHECKCOLUMN
CHECKDIAGONAL

This would allow the outer block to concentrate on the backtracking algorithm while the details of placing queens on the board would be shunted into these two lower-level procedures.

The matter of nesting level is based partly on direct observation and partly on human limitations. When instructions are given sequentially, it is not necessary to remember much about previous steps as each instruction is carried out. However, the deeper one goes into a nested structure, the harder it becomes to keep track of what is happening because it is critical to keep in mind not only what instructions are at hand, but also the path that led to them. Actually, this calls for concentrating on several things at once and, as we have observed several times already, the less of that the better. Thus we arrive at another general guideline: within a subprogram, nested structures are to be avoided wherever possible. This may, at first, seem to be at odds with the concept of successive refinement, but it really is not. It merely says that linear sequence is to be preferred, and it lays down another consideration for when the use of additional submodules might be appropriate.

The QUEENS program suffers from the condition of being almost wholly contained within an ELSE branch, and as we mentioned in Chapter 5, the situation is easily remedied with a GOTO statement. In this instance, however, the use of the GOTO is not a departure from the discipline because the flow structure stays intact. This is because the construct

---

STYLE CLINIC 9-2

Always Read Your Own Code

It is a good idea to read your own code, preferably a day or two after it was written, just to get a feel for its comprehensibility. The reason for the delay is so that the mechanisms employed will not be fresh in your mind. If the program is not then immediately understandable, it needs alteration for the sake of clarity. If you cannot readily understand your own program, it is certainly not reasonable to expect anyone else to be able to read it easily.

```
        IF boolean expression THEN
            statement-1
        ELSE
            BEGIN
            statement-2;
                .

                .

                .

            statement-n
            END
```

is equivalent to

```
            IF boolean expression THEN
                BEGIN
                statement-1;
                GOTO 10
                END;
            statement-2;

                    .

                    .

                    .

            statement-n;
        10:
```

The latter form has the advantage of eliminating one level of nesting. The discipline as presented has no place in it for the GOTO statement, since that construct is too primitive. But the real point of the discipline is not to adhere to prescribed code constructs, but to prescribed control structures as implied by the segmented flowchart. It is of utmost importance to note in the example above that because the process block

```
        BEGIN
        statement-2;
            .

            .

            .

        statement-n
        END
```

has only one exit (through statement-n), there cannot be a GOTO statement within the block that will transfer control past the label 10. Thus, the segmented flow is preserved despite the existence of the GOTO.

This discussion shows that it is possible to adhere to structural discipline in any language at all no matter how primitive and, for PASCAL in particular, it is as much an error to avoid using GOTO statements when they are appropriate as it is to use them unnecessarily. The truly well-considered objection to the use of the GOTO statement is not in programming but in language design. Some languages are so primitive that a conditional branch is the only form of control available. One could hardly be expected to write a program in such a language without using that structure. Unfortunately, although it is possible to follow structural discipline in any programming language, it is also possible to deviate from it in any language that has a GOTO facility. If the GOTO statement were to be disallowed in order to force structuring, it is the duty of the language designer to provide enough replacements so that programs written are not only operationally correct, but readable as well. For example, the GOTO statement could be removed from PASCAL without impairing the ability to write correct, structured programs. However, they would likely suffer the same problems as the QUEENS program with regard to nesting level. A syntactic construct that would help in this case is an EXIT statement that would have the effect of GOTO (A label at the end of the current subprogram). Then the code

```
        IF (N<0) OR (N>MAXSIZE) THEN WRITELN(' INVALID
                                            BOARD SIZE')
        ELSE BEGIN
             statement-1;
               .
               .
               .

             END
```

becomes

```
        IF (N<0) OR (N>MAXSIZE) THEN
             BEGIN
             WRITELN(' INVALID BOARD SIZE');
             EXIT   {This is not a valid PASCAL command. It is for
                      illustration only}
             END;
        statement-1
          .
          .
          .
```

In the design of a number of programming languages, many constructs have been suggested (and implemented) to replace the GOTO statement with higher-level facilities. We do not wish to delve deeply into language design; therefore, suffice it to say that PASCAL retains the GOTO statement but that we should take care to use it appropriately to enhance readability.

Although subprogram modularization and linearized logical flow are the major tools for building readable programs, well-chosen variable names, appropriate comments, and consistent indentation serve as valuable back-ups. We have already noted that deep nesting of control structures can be confusing, but sometimes it may be necessary. This is just the case where a clear indentation style becomes essential and a few comments such as

BEGIN   {Place a queen or backtrack}
  .
  .
  .
END   {Of place a queen loop}

are a tremendous aid. This point is graphically illustrated by Figure 9-12, which is just the QUEENS program all over again with all commenting and indentation removed. The program as it appears in Figure 9-12 is no less comprehensible to a machine than the one in Figure 9-11, but that only points out once again the importance of programming for people as well as for machines. It is also interesting that the program of Figure 9-12 does conform to the structure discipline, so it is evident that structure alone is not enough. Good indentation is actually a requirement for readability.

In attempting to read the code in Figure 9-12, most people discover that the troubles encountered all revolve around the difficulty in matching cor-

```
PROGRAM QUEENS(INPUT,OUTPUT); CONST MAXSIZE=15; VAR N,
CURCOLNBR,I,J,DIAGNBR:INTEGER;PLACEDAQUEEN:BOOLEAN;COL:ARRAY
[1 . . MAXSIZE] OF INTEGER; BEGIN READLN(N); IF (N<0) OR (N>MAXSIZE)
THEN WRITELN(' INVALID BOARD SIZE') ELSE BEGIN FOR CURCOLNBR:=1
TO N DO COL[CURCOLNBR]:=0; CURCOLNBR:=1; WHILE CURCOLNBR>0
DO BEGIN PLACEDAQUEEN:=FALSE; I:=COL[CURCOLNBR]+1; WHILE
(I<N) AND (NOT PLACEDAQUEEN)       DO BEGIN PLACEDAQUEEN:=TRUE;
J:=1; WHILE PLACEDAQUEEN AND (J<CURCOLNBR) DO BEGIN
PLACEDAQUEEN:=COL[J]<>I; J:=J+1 END; IF PLACEDAQUEEN THEN
BEGIN DIAGNBR:=I+CURCOLNBR; J:=1; WHILE PLACEDAQUEEN AND
(J<CURCOLNBR) DO BEGIN PLACEDAQUEEN:=COL[J]+J<>DIAGNBR;
J:=J+1 END END; IF PLACEDAQUEEN THEN BEGIN DIAGNBR:=I−
CURCOLNBR; J:=1; WHILE PLACEDAQUEEN AND (J<CURCOLNBR) DO
BEGIN PLACEDAQUEEN:=COL[J]−J<>DIAGNBR; J:=J+1 END END; IF NOT
PLACEDAQUEEN THEN I:=I+1 ELSE COL[CURCOLNBR]:=J END; IF NOT
PLACEDAQUEEN THEN BEGIN COL[CURCOLNBR]:=0;     CURCOLNBR:=
CURCOLNBR−1 END ELSE IF CURCOLNBR=N THEN BEGIN WRITE('SOLU',
'TION: '); FOR I:=1 TO N DO WRITE(COL[I]:4); WRITELN END ELSE
CURCOLNBR:=CURCOLNBR+1 END; WRITELN('SEARCH COMPLETE')
END END.
```
FIGURE 9-12 The QUEENS Program Without Indentation or Comments.

responding syntactic pairs such as BEGIN-END and IF-ELSE. The reader's very limited short-term memory plagues him or her again, this time while trying to recall the position of the third or fourth previous BEGIN. Aligning corresponding BEGIN-END pairs serves as an aid in that it allows the reader to locate a BEGIN by association with the position of the matching END.

STYLE CLINIC 9-3

Another Note on Indentation Practices

Certain syntactic items in PASCAL come in pairs and, whatever the details of your style, you should always make the matching of dual items as easy as possible. Many programmers find it helpful to place the reserved words BEGIN-END, IF-ELSE, REPEAT-UNTIL, and CASE-END {Case} as the first item of a line and to keep the paired words aligned in the same columns.

These four pairs are the ones to watch because they can be separated by dozens of lines in between. Note that WHILE-DO is not included here; nor is IF-THEN. Since these pairs are separated only by a boolean expression, it is unlikely that they would be physically very far apart. The short comment included in the CASE-END{Case} pair is a good practice to avoid the possibility of confusing the END of a case statement with the END of a compound statement.

9.8 THE ROLE OF DATA STRUCTURE

The orderly development of program logic is extremely important; careful consideration for data structuring is equally essential. In fact, it is often the case that the method used for representing data is central to the processing algorithm itself. The QUEENS program is a good example. One of the first decisions made during the solution of the problem was the choice of a backtrack procedure. This led to the representation of the chesssboard as an array with one entry for each column. This seemed quite natural at the time, and the importance of this decision was not emphasized then, but there were other options available. For example, the board might have been symbolized as an N × N array of characters, each having the value "Q" or blank, depending on whether a queen occupied a given position. Alternatively, an N-element array of coordinate pairs might have been used with each entry describing the board position of one queen. Clearly, either of these data structures would have resulted in a quite different algorithm. Adopting a process that cycles through the columns of the board and representing the board itself as an array of columns are so closely connected that it is even difficult to tell which choice came first.

The parallel between data structure and computational algorithm is so close that the two can often be developed together and, just as logic is developed by successive refinement, the representation of data can be defined top-down also. For the QUEENS program, the refinement process is very simple and closely follows the program development. The decision to use an array of columns to represent the board was sufficient to permit the construction of the backtracking process itself. At this level, the operation of placing a queen on a column and the implied check for placement validity are still abstract concepts, even though the movement from one column to another is explicitly specified. It is not until the actual processing for a single column is being considered that it becomes necessary to decide exactly how the placement of a queen on a column will be represented. At this point, the major concern is to make validation easy, and it is precisely because the data structure has not already been specified in its entirety that we are still free to choose a convenient representation.

Some problems, such as root finding, are predominately computational in nature and require minimal concern about structuring data. Many others are concerned much more with the organization and structuring of large amounts of data. Most business applications are of this latter form. So are list processing, text editing, and even compiler construction. For example, the maintenance of a large inventory file or a set of financial records involves no more computation than integer addition and subtraction. Nevertheless, these functions are not entirely trivial, because they present a very real problem of locating the proper quantities to increment or decrement among thousands of entries on file. Text editing generally requires even less arithmetic, yet considerable processing could be needed to produce a final document. Among the many interesting data-handling problems with which a compiler must deal is maintaining a table of identifiers that appear in the program being compiled. This table must be designed for both rapid access and rapid update, and it must be constructed anew for each program that is compiled. There are, in fact, so many nonnumerical applications for computers that the use of the term "computer" has become unfortunate to the extent that it implies numerical computation. The alternative, "data processor," is far more descriptive.

9.9 THE ULTIMATE MEANING OF GOODNESS

The main point of this chapter has been an investigation into what makes a program readable and how to write readable programs. Yet, in the final analysis, readability is not an end in itself, but only a means to an end. The real concern is with the question of what constitutes a good program.

The obvious criteria for program goodness are correctness and cost effectiveness, and we will see that many of the attributes of a program that contribute to the achievement of these goals are themselves facilitated by readability. Since programs are written by people and people are expensive, costs are minimized when programmers can readily understand the programs they are building. Similarly, it goes without saying that the likelihood of producing a correct program is higher if the program itself is kept simple. In fact, it might even be stipulated that simplicity is directly related to cost effectiveness.

Increasing the likelihood of correctness is actually linked intimately to the foundations of structured programming. Although an in-depth discussion is beyond the scope of this textbook, one of the important properties of a sufficiently structured program is that its correctness can, in principle, be deduced logically. In other words, the absence of errors can be formally demonstrated. A program that could be proved to be correct contrasts sharply with a program that has been tested to locate and eliminate errors. With the latter, we can hope, but we can never be sure, that there are no errors left. To illustrate the basic idea, suppose that a table of values for some function is to be computed. The first step might be an algorithm of the form:

```
set table empty;
WHILE table not full DO
    compute next value and include it in the table;
```

As it stands, there is no possibility of quitting too soon, because the stopping condition will not permit it. Furthermore, that same stopping condition guarantees that whenever the body of the loop is entered, there is room in the table to hold the value to be computed. In practice, it is still prohibitively tedious to prove that a substantial program is correct, but even the possibility of doing it indicates what the future trends in program development practices will be.

Despite the move toward proving correctness mathematically, it is still the case that correctness is not an absolute property. It is possible for two programs to be correct and yet one can, in a sense, be "more correct" than another. One measure of a good program is its ability to handle all possible situations. The issue then becomes a matter of measuring how well each case is handled. This aspect of program goodness is called *robustness*. For example, consider a program that accepts a set of input data, performs some well-defined process, and subsequently generates appropriate output. The required input data might be a single number, a sequence of numbers, a character string of arbitrary, finite length, or virtually any other structure. In fact, a character string can be regarded as a general case. Some strings will be defined as valid and the rest will be considered invalid. Ideally, the program will always differentiate between valid and invalid input, and it will always produce the right output for valid input. For that matter, a message such as "INVALID INPUT DATA" is the right output for invalid data.

STYLE CLINIC 9-4

Don't Make Mountains Out of Molehills
or
Keep It Simple

If the cost of program development is to be minimized, it is important that the program does no more than necessary. The distinction between a production program with a 5-year expected life span and a special purpose, "one-shot" program must not be forgotten. It does not make sense, for example, to write a generalized statistics package in order to compute the mean and standard deviation of a single set of numbers. Furthermore, if the cost in time, effort, or dollars for the development of a program exceeds the savings to be gained by the existence of that program, the approach to the problem is clearly wrong.

Unfortunately, perfect behavior is too much to expect, and so robustness is just one measure of how close we are.

Given two programs with identical intent, it may be that one is more robust than the other. In other words, both programs produce correct results most of the time, but one is correct more often than the other. This does not imply, however, that one is correct and the other is not. In all likelihood, neither is perfect, and if the cost of a program malfunction is sufficiently small and the frequency of error is also small, then it may be that either program is "correct enough."

When a program moves into a production environment, errors that arise during regular operation must be corrected. The program becomes more and more robust as these problems are fixed, since the set of input sequences properly handled is increased. However, such maintenance activity is really run-time testing, and it can be quite time consuming and therefore expensive. This makes *maintainability* an important attribute of every good program, and since maintenance is seldom done by the people who developed the program originally, readability becomes paramount.

Along with maintenance that deals with routine bug fixing, there is also maintenance for the purpose of keeping a program current. For example, changing prices might affect the rate tables built into an invoicing program, or new reporting needs might require changes to the output portion of a report-generating program. The ease with which such changes can be made is a measure of the program's *adaptability*. This aspect of program goodness depends not only on clarity, but also on modularity and initial planning. A structured approach to program development is very often tremendously valuable here. Modularity falls naturally out of a structured design, and a high level of adaptability tends to result from appropriately delayed decisions.

Consider, for example, the concurrent development of a complex data structure and the attendant processing algorithms. Initially, a decision might have been made that the data would be organized as a file of records. A general algorithm might have been laid out next, followed by the specification of records containing 15 items, and then a refinement of the algorithm. Near the final stages, the allocation of item 12 of each record to an identification number might have been made and only then some process that needed that information designed. At some later date, when the identification number must be reassigned to the fourteenth item of each record, only the process developed toward the end has to be altered. Since the earlier design work did not rely on the precise location of the identification number, the resulting code can be left intact. The change is made easier by virtue of the delayed decision.

Finally, we must not overlook performance efficiency as another measure of goodness. A program that does a job in 10 minutes is certainly more desirable, it would seem, than another that requires 30 minutes to do the same work. However, execution time is not the last word. The real concern is, as always, the cost. A program that costs $10 to run is more efficient than another that costs $30 to do the same work. But now we must be very careful. The cost of running a program is not the end of the matter.

Suppose a program is needed to perform a function that requires processing once a week and that the life expectancy of the system is 3 years. The program will be run about 150 times and then be scrapped. Program A runs for $10 but cost $4000 in programmers' salaries to develop. Program B runs for $25 because less time and effort was spent in making it operationally efficient, but it cost only $1000 to develop. Which of the two is more cost effective?

The numbers in the preceding example were contrived to make a point, of course. We do not intend to imply that operational efficiency should be sacrificed for minimal development costs. On the other hand, because hardware costs are decreasing and the personnel costs of program development are rising, the desirable trend is indeed toward smaller development efforts. Certainly it is no longer worthwhile to spend hours trying to cut microseconds from the execution time of a program. Cost-effective data processing is beginning to rest more and more on the efficient development of readily comprehensible programs.

9.10 CONCLUSION

This chapter completes our discussion of programming and problem solving. We have accomplished our original goals as stated in the Preface and Chapter 1—to introduce and motivate all aspects of the programming process, to develop guidelines for producing good, reliable programs, and to teach PASCAL. However, as we mentioned earlier, programming, in this fullest sense, cannot be passively taught but must be actively learned and experienced. Hopefully, you will apply the principles presented here to every programming task, regardless of whether it is in a classroom or industrial environment, or whether it is for practice or profit. This experience is the only real way to gain insight into the programming process and to develop true programming ability.

STYLE CLINIC 9-5

Beware of Degradation Caused by Change

Working programs need to be changed from time to time in order to correct minor errors and to adapt to changing circumstances. While making such changes, one must be very careful. It is easy to introduce major problems while fixing small ones or while adding an enhancement.

This is especially true of programs that have not been properly modularized. One of the keys to writing adaptable and maintainable programs is to ensure throughout that local changes have only local consequences. In other words, to achieve an alteration in program behavior, it should always be possible to isolate a module in which a coding change has become necessary and to change thereby only the behavior of that module.

EXERCISES

1. Working with a team of three to five people, complete the text processing program at the end of Chapter 8. In order to do this, the following must be accomplished.

   a. Write up a complete set of design specifications for the program, including a maintenance document.
   b. Write a user document.
   c. Program each module described. Design and carry out adequate tests on each one as it is completed.
   d. Program the remaining modules described in the specifications developed in part a and test them also.

2. Design a document processor that accepts character strings and formatting commands as input and produces a properly formatted document as output. All input commands begin with a period in column 1. No text (except for the command itself) can appear on such a line. Commands consist of the following:

.LEFT n	Set left margin to column n
.RIGHT n	Set right margin to column n
.INDENT n	Terminate the current line of text and begin a new line after indenting n spaces
.CENTER	Center the next line of text between the left and right margins
.SPACING n	Set the line spacing to n (1 = single spacing, 2 = double spacing, etc.)
.BLANK n	Terminate the current line and leave n blank lines before starting the next line

Any line that does not begin with a period is to be considered a line of text. Text should be filled with an appropriate number of spaces between words so that the resulting text is flush with the left and right margins. If the current line of text does not contain enough characters, continue accumulating input text until the line is full (subject to any formatting commands that might be encountered). In general, there will not be a one-to-one relationship between lines of input and output text. Example:

Input data
.LEFT 20
.RIGHT 50
.CENTER
AN EXAMPLE
.SPACING 1
.INDENT 3
THIS IS AN EXAMPLE OF TEXT THAT WILL BE FILLED AND JUSTIFIED.
.BLANK 1
END OF EXAMPLE
Output text

```
                  AN EXAMPLE
          THIS   IS   AN   EXAMPLE   OF
          TEXT WILL BE FILLED AND
          JUSTIFIED.


          END OF EXAMPLE
```

In your design of the program, specify the modules you will use, the function of each module, and the interfaces between modules.

3. You are to work in teams of three to five persons to design and implement a *picture drawing system*. Basically this is a set of programs that allows you to input picture drawing commands that create points, lines,

circles, triangles, and other geometric shapes. These pictures may then be displayed on a computer terminal or line printer.

The programs will be creating the picture by inserting characters within a data structure to approximate the shapes you request. For example:

| Line | Triangle | Circle |

There are four basic classes of commands that can be provided to your system. The following are intended only as examples of these classes. The decisions on exactly which commands to implement will be part of the system design process.

I. Basic routines

   A. INITIALIZE M, N

      Clear a picture of size 1 . . M by 1 . . N. The value of M, N will depend on the output device being used.

   B. DISPLAYCHAR C

      Use the character 'C' when displaying pictures.

   C. PRINT X_1, Y_1, X_2, Y_2

      Print that portion of the picture lying within the rectangle $[X_1, Y_1]$, $[X_1, Y_2]$, $[X_2, Y_2]$, $[X_2, Y_1]$.

   D. SAVE NAME

      Save this picture under the designated name. Naturally we will need some command that retrieves it later.

II. Simple drawing commands

   A. POINT X_1, Y_1

      Place a character at location $[X_1, Y_1]$.

   B. LINE X_1, Y_1, X_2, Y_2

      Draw a line connecting point $[X_1, Y_1]$ and point $[X_2, Y_2]$.

   C. CIRCLE X_1, Y_1, R

      Draw a circle with center at $[X_1, Y_1]$ and radius R.

III. More complex drawing commands

   A. DOTTEDLINE X_1, Y_1, X_2, Y_2, S

      Draw a line connecting point $[X_1, Y_1]$ and point $[X_2, Y_2]$ alternately using line segments and spaces of length S.

   B. FACE

      Draw the following figure.

IV. Manipulation routines
 A. MOVE direction, units
  Move the entire picture (up, down, left, right) the indicated number of units.
 B. ROTATE
 C. ENLARGE
 D. ERASE

The goal of this assignment is twofold:
 1. To design the specifications of a good picture drawing system.
 2. To use teams of programmers to efficiently implement the system you have designed.

The former will require that you address the following problems:

 1. What is the optimal data structure for representing a picture?
 2. What are the most important picture drawing commands to provide to the user?
 3. What are the necessary parameters for each command?
 4. What is the most convenient command format?

The latter goal will require that you determine how to partition the work among the available people and how to monitor the progress of each individual. This will probably involve discussing and solving the following problems.

 1. How to modularize the picture drawing problem so that programmers can be given responsibility for specific modules.
 2. How each person can individually test the modules they are developing.
 3. How to interface the modules being developed by different people. For example, the FACE routine mentioned earlier will probably make 7 calls to LINE, 2 calls to CIRCLE, and 1 to POINT. It is necessary that the writer of FACE and the writers of these other routines make the same assumptions when developing their programs. Otherwise the pieces that work properly alone will not work when brought together.
 4. How to maintain correct and current documentation.

This assignment, probably more than any other in this textbook, will give you an accurate picture of what real-world programming projects are actually like.

APPENDIX A

Syntax of the PASCAL Language*

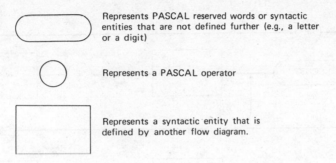

Represents PASCAL reserved words or syntactic entities that are not defined further (e.g., a letter or a digit)

Represents a PASCAL operator

Represents a syntactic entity that is defined by another flow diagram.

Program

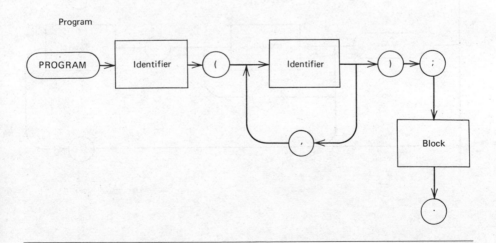

* This appendix is taken from Appendix D, p. 116–118 of Jensen and Wirth, *PASCAL Users Manual and Report,* Springer-Verlag, 1974, with their permission.

Block

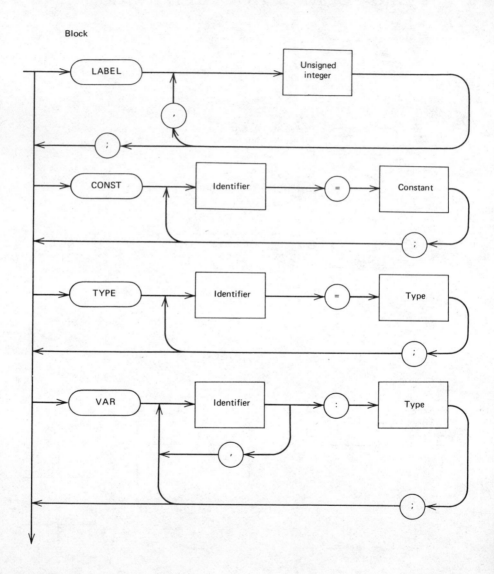

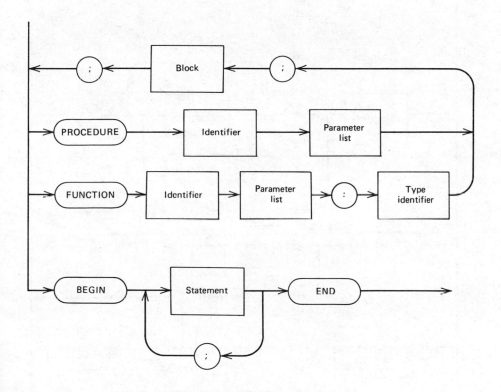

Statement

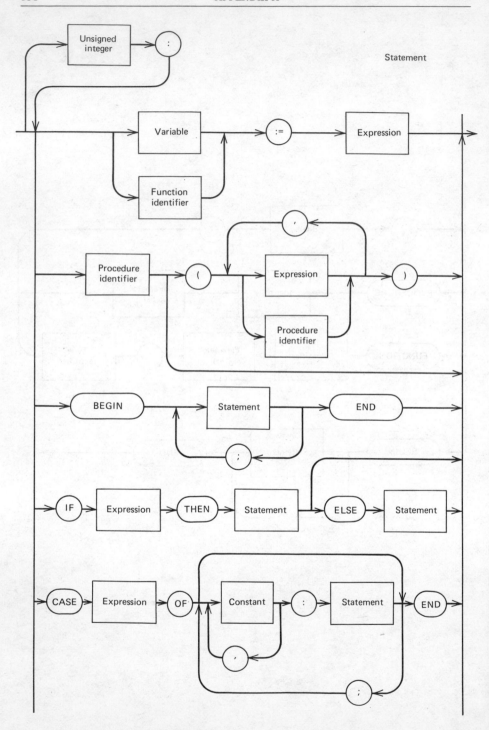

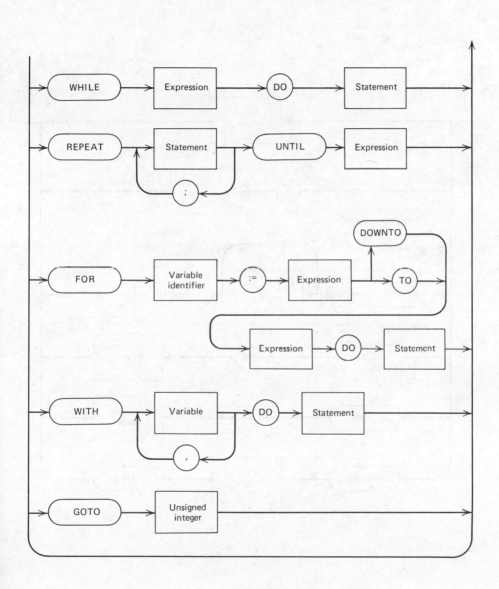

Type

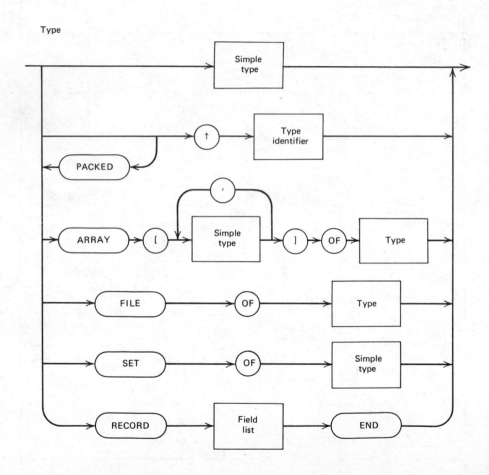

Simple type

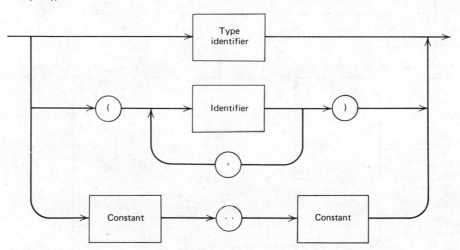

Parameter list

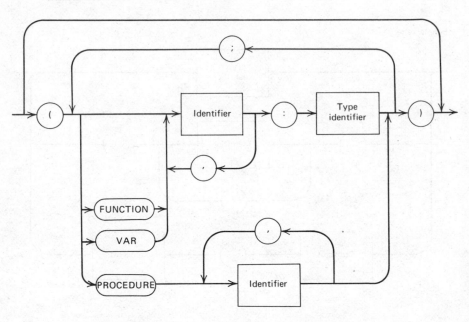

Field list

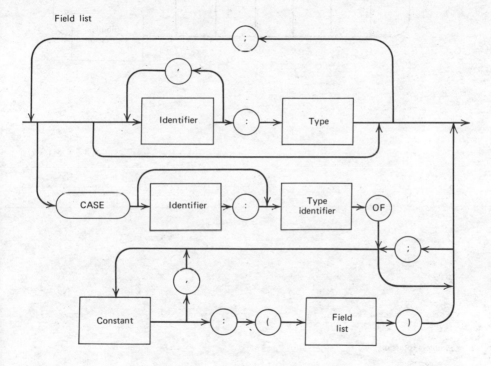

Expression

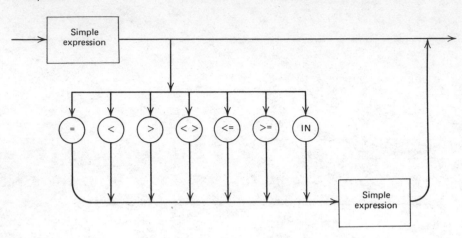

Simple expression

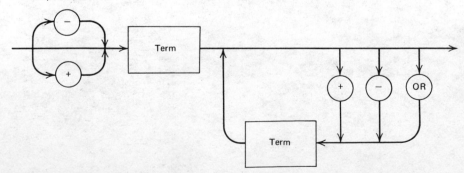

Term

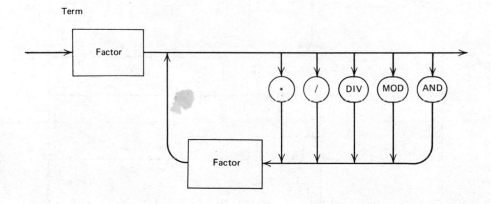

Factor

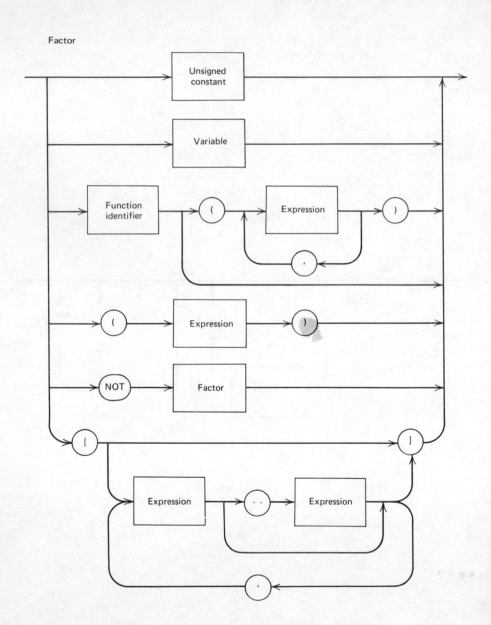

Variable

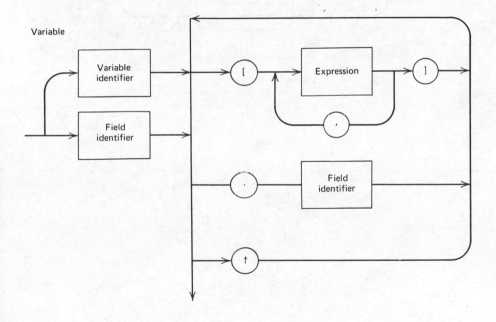

Unsigned constant

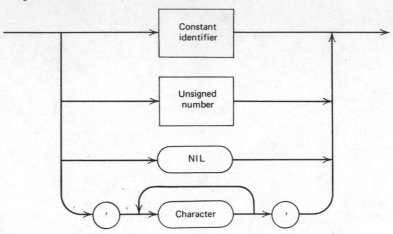

Constant

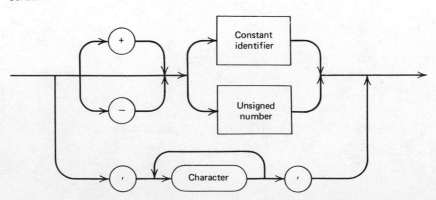

Identifier

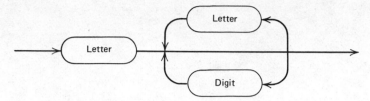

Unsigned integer

Unsigned number

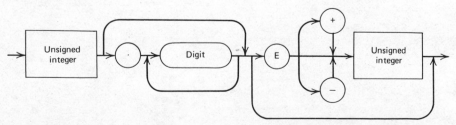

APPENDIX B
Standardized **PASCAL** Identifiers

B.1 RESERVED WORDS

AND	END	NIL	SET
ARRAY	FILE	NOT	THEN
BEGIN	FOR	OF	TO
CASE	FUNCTION	OR	TYPE
CONST	GOTO	PACKED	UNTIL
DIV	IF	PROCEDURE	VAR
DO	IN	PROGRAM	WHILE
DOWNTO	LABEL	RECORD	WITH
ELSE	MOD	REPEAT	

B.2 STANDARD IDENTIFIERS

Constants

FALSE   TRUE   MAXINT

Types

INTEGER   BOOLEAN   REAL   CHAR   TEXT

Files

INPUT   OUTPUT

Functions

Name	Parameters	Types Result	Description
ABS(X)	INTEGER or REAL	Same as parameter	Absolute value
ARCTAN(X)	INTEGER or REAL	REAL	Inverse tangent
CHR(X)	INTEGER	CHAR	Character whose ordinal number is X
COS(X)	INTEGER or REAL	REAL	Cosine
EOF(F)	FILE	BOOLEAN	End-of-file indicator
EOLN(F)	FILE	BOOLEAN	End-of-line indicator
EXP(X)	REAL or INTEGER	REAL	e^x
LN(X)	REAL or INTEGER	REAL	Natural logarithm

ODD(X)	INTEGER	BOOLEAN	True if X is odd False otherwise
ORD(X)	User-defined scalar, CHAR, BOOLEAN	INTEGER	Ordinal number of X in the scalar data type of which X is a member
PRED(X)	Scalar, but not REAL	Same as parameter	Predecessor of X
ROUND(X)	REAL	INTEGER	X rounded
SIN(X)	REAL or INTEGER	REAL	Sine
SQR(X)	REAL or INTEGER	Same as parameter	Square of X
SQRT(X)	REAL or INTEGER	REAL	Square root
SUCC(X)	Scalar, but not REAL	Same as parameter	Successor of X
TRUNC(X)	REAL	INTEGER	X truncated

Procedures

Name (parameters)	*Description*
DISPOSE(P)	Returns the dynamic variable referenced by pointer P to the available space list
GET(F)	Advances file F to the next component and places the value of the component in F↑
NEW(P)	Allocates a new variable that is accessed through pointer P
PACK(A, I, Z)	Takes the elements beginning at subscript position I of array A and copies them into packed array Z beginning at the first subscript position
PAGE(F)	Causes the printer to skip to the top of a new page before printing the next line of text file F
PUT(F)	Appends the value of the buffer variable F↑ to the file F
READ(. . .) READLN(. . .)	Reads information from text files. See Section 4.5.1
RESET(F)	Positions file F at its beginning for reading
REWRITE(F)	Empties file F and allows it to be written into
UNPACK(Z, A, I)	Takes the elements beginning at the first subscript position of packed array Z and copies them into array A beginning at subscript position I
WRITE(. . .) WRITELN(. . .)	Writes information to text files. See Section 4.5.2

B.3 SUMMARY OF OPERATORS

		Types	
Operator	*Description*	*Operand(s)*	*Results*
:=	Assignment	Any, except FILE	—
+	Addition	INTEGER or REAL	INTEGER or REAL
	Set union	Any SET type	Same as operand
−	Subtraction	INTEGER or REAL	INTEGER or REAL
	Set difference	Any SET type	Same as operand
*	Multiplication	INTEGER or REAL	INTEGER or REAL
	Set intersection	Any SET type	Same as operand
DIV	Integer division	INTEGER	INTEGER
/	Real division	INTEGER or REAL	REAL
MOD	Modulus	INTEGER	INTEGER
NOT	Logical negation	BOOLEAN	BOOLEAN
OR	Disjunction	BOOLEAN	BOOLEAN
AND	Conjunction	BOOLEAN	BOOLEAN
<=	Implication	BOOLEAN	BOOLEAN
	Set inclusion	Any SET type	BOOLEAN
	Less than or equal	Any scalar type	BOOLEAN
=	Equivalence	BOOLEAN	BOOLEAN
	Equality	Scalar, SET, or POINTER	BOOLEAN
<>	Exclusive OR	BOOLEAN	BOOLEAN
	Inequality	Scalar, SET, or POINTER	BOOLEAN
>=	Set inclusion	Any SET type	BOOLEAN
	Greater than or equal	Any scalar type	BOOLEAN
<	Less than	Any scalar type	BOOLEAN
>	Greater than	Any scalar type	BOOLEAN
IN	Set membership	Left operand: scalar Right operand: set with base type the type of the left operand	BOOLEAN

APPENDIX C
Character Sets

The charts in this appendix depict the ordering for several commonly used character sets. Numbers are base 10 and only printable characters are shown.

Many other character sets and collating sequences not included here are in current use.

C.1 CDC SCIENTIFIC, WITH 64 CHARACTERS

Left Digit \ Right Digit	0	1	2	3	4	5	6	7	8	9
0	:	A	B	C	D	E	F	G	H	I
1	J	K	L	M	N	O	P	Q	R	S
2	T	U	V	W	X	Y	Z	0	1	2
3	3	4	5	6	7	8	9	+	−	*
4	/	(	)	$	=		,	.	≡	[
5	]	%	≠	↱	∨	∧	↑	↓	<	>
6	≤	≥	¬	;						

C.2 ASCII (AMERICAN STANDARD CODE FOR INFORMATION INTERCHANGE)

Left Digit(s) \ Right Digit	0	1	2	3	4	5	6	7	8	9
3				!	"	#	$	%	&	'
4	(	)	*	+	,	—	.	/	0	1
5	2	3	4	5	6	7	8	9	:	;
6	<	=	>	?	@	A	B	C	D	E
7	F	G	H	I	J	K	L	M	N	O
8	P	Q	R	S	T	U	V	W	X	Y
9	Z	[	1/8	]	∧	—	`	a	b	c
10	d	e	f	g	h	i	j	k	l	m
11	n	o	p	q	r	s	t	u	v	w
12	x	y	z	{			}	~			

Codes 00 to 31 and 127 (decimal) represent special control characters that are not printable.

C.3 EBCDIC (EXTENDED BINARY CODED DECIMAL INTERCHANGE CODE)

Left Digit(s) \ Right Digit	0	1	2	3	4	5	6	7	8	9
6										
7					¢	.	<	(	+	|
8	&									
9	!	$	*	)	;	¬	–	/		
10							^	,	%	—
11	>	?								
12			:	#	@	'	=	"		a
13	b	c	d	e	f	g	h	i		
14						j	k	l	m	n
15	o	p	q	r						
16			s	t	u	v	w	x	y	z
17								\	{	}
18	[	]								
19				A	B	C	D	E	F	G
20	H	I								J
21	K	L	M	N	O	P	Q	R		
22							S	T	U	V
23	W	X	Y	Z						
24	0	1	2	3	4	5	6	7	8	9

Codes 00 to 63 and 250 to 255 represent nonprintable control characters.

BIBLIOGRAPHY

General Surveys

Dijkstra, E. W., *A Discipline of Programming*, Prentice-Hall, 1976.
Weinberg, G. M., *The Psychology of Computer Programming*, Van Nostrand, 1971.
Wirth, N., *Systematic Programming*, Prentice-Hall, 1973.
Yohe, J. M., "An Overview of Programming Practices," *ACM Computing Surveys*, December 1974.

Algorithms and Problem Solving

Aho, A. V., J. E. Hopcroft, and J. D. Ullman, *The Design and Analysis of Computer Algorithms*, Addison-Wesley, 1974.
Calter, P., *Problem Solving with Computers*, McGraw-Hill, 1973.
Horowitz, E., and S. Sahni, *The Analysis of Algorithms*, Computer Science Press, 1978 (in preparation).
Knuth, D., *The Art of Computer Programming*, Vol. 1, "Fundamental Algorithms," Addison-Wesley, 1968.
Polya, G., *How to Solve It*, Princton Press, 1971.
Watkins, R. P., *Computer Problem Solving*, McGraw-Hill, 1973.
Wirth, N., *Algorithms + Data Structures = Programs*, Prentice-Hall, 1976.

The PASCAL Language

Conway, R., D. Gries, and E. C. Zimmerman, *A Primer on PASCAL*, Winthrop, 1976.
Hoare, C. A. R., and N. Wirth, "An Axiomatic Definition of the Programming Language PASCAL," *Acta Informatica*, Vol. 2, 1973.
Jensen, K., and N. Wirth, *PASCAL—User Manual and Report*, Springer-Verlag, 1974.
Webster, C. A. G., *Introduction to PASCAL*, Hayden and Sons, 1976.
Wirth, N., "The Programming Language PASCAL," *Acta Informatica*, Vol. 1, 1971.

Programming Style

Kernighan, B. W., and P. J. Plauger, *Elements of Programming Style*, McGraw-Hill, 1974.
Kernighan, B. W., and P. J. Plauger, "Programming Style: Examples and Counter-examples," *ACM Computing Surveys*, December 1974.
Krietzberg, C. B., and B. Shneiderman, *The Elements of FORTRAN Style*, Harcourt Brace Jovanovich, 1972.
Ledgard, H., *Programming Proverbs*, Hayden, 1975.

Van Tassel, D., *Programming Style, Design, Efficiency, Debugging, and Testing,* Prentice-Hall, 1974.

Structured Programming and Program Design

Basili, V., and T. Baker, *Structured Programming: A Tutorial,* IEEE Publications, Catalog No. 75CH1049-6, 1975.

Dahl, O. J., E. W. Dijkstra, and C. A. R. Hoarse, *Structured Programming,* Academic Press, 1972.

Hughes, J. K., and J. Michtom, *A Structured Approach to Programming,* Prentice-Hall, 1977.

Knuth, D., "Structured Programming with GOTO Statements," *ACM Computing Surveys,* December 1974.

McGowan, C. L., and J. R. Kelly, *Top-Down Structured Programming Techniques,* Petrocelli-Charter, 1975.

Wirth, N., "Program Development by Stepwise Refinement," *Communications of the ACM,* April 1971.

Wirth, N., "On the Composition of Well Structured Programs," *ACM Computing Surveys,* December 1974.

Yourdon, E., *Techniques of Program Structure and Design,* Prentice-Hall, 1975.

ANSWERS TO SELECTED EXERCISES

Chapter 1

QUESTIONS TO BE ANSWERED

1. a. What is a prime number?
   Do we treat the "first" prime number as 1 or 2?
   Where are we getting the value for N?
   What do we do if N <= 0?
   What do we want the output to look like?
   When we are done, should we stop or read another value for N and produce another set of N primes?

PROBLEM SPECIFICATIONS

A *prime number* is a number $P \geq 1$ that is evenly divisible only by itself and one. (For example, 7 is prime while 9 is not, since it is evenly divisible by 3.)

Write a program that reads a data card containing an integer value N and produces as output the first N prime numbers in the following format.

THE FIRST nnnnn PRIMES ARE

nnnnnn nnnnnn .....   nnnnnn ⎱   10 values
                                        ⎰   per line
nnnnnn nnnnnn ......   nnnnnn ⎱   to conserve
                                             paper

If N is not an even multiple of 10, the last line should contain only the correct number of entries.
If N ≤ 0 then print an error message "INCORRECT NUMBER PROVIDED FOR N". In either case the program should terminate after producing the output.

Chapter 2

1. a. START "shampooing algorithm"
        Wet hair
        Set counter to 1
        While counter <= 2 do
            Lather
            Rinse
            Increment counter
        End of while loop
     END OF ALGORITHM

    b. START "shampooing algorithm"
        Wet hair
        Repeat the following 2 times
           Lather
           Rinse
        End of repeat loop
      END OF ALGORITHM

4. a. i. This is a poor algorithm because the length of the solution is proportional to the size of the problem being solved. This algorithm's approach might be acceptable for trivial problems, but it is not useful for problems of general interest.

      ii. The fifth line of the algorithm:

          see if $n > 0$

      is ambiguous as to what to do if the test is true or false. The sixth line of the algorithm:

          Go back and repeat

      is ambiguous about what statements are to be repeated.

      iii. The algorithm is wrong! It will produce a value of 0. We never incremented i, the value we are adding to the sum.

      iv. Superficially this may seem to be the same problem as in iii. However, there is an important difference. The solution in iii will stop and produce an incorrect answer. This version will *never* stop. The test, $i <= 10$, will never become false and the algorithm will repeat indefinitely.

    b. START
        Set I to 1 and SUM to 0
        While I $<=$ 10 do the following
           Add I to SUM
           Increment I
        End of the while loop
        Write SUM
      END OF THE ALGORITHM

    c. START
        Read in a value for K
        If K $\leq$ 0 Then Write out an appropriate error message
               Else⌈Set I to 1 and Sum to 0
                  │While I $<=$ K do the following
                  │   Add I to SUM
                  │   Increment I
                  │End of the while loop
                  ⌊Write SUM
      END OF THE ALGORITHM

7. START
   Read K {K is the number of characters in the word or phrase}
   Read $C_1, C_2, \ldots, C_k$
   Write $C_1, C_2, \ldots, C_k$
   Set FWD to 1
   Set BWD to K
   While FWD < BWD do
      If C_{FWD} = ' '
        Then Increment FWD
        Else If C_{BWD} = ' '
          Then Decrement BWD
          Else If $C_{FWD} = C_{BWD}$
            Then ⌈Increment FWD
               ⌊Decrement BWD
            Else ⌈Write "Not a palindrome"
               ⌊Stop
   End of the loop
   Write "This string is a palindrome"
   Stop
   END OF ALGORITHM

12. A recursive algorithm can be used if we assume that we begin with a
    string of length L and a set of K-L distinct letters. The problem is then
    to construct all possible strings whose first L characters are the ones
    given.

    START Generate (STRING, L, characters available)
    If L equals K Then Write STRING
    Else
       For each of the K-L characters left, do the following
         ⌈Append the current character to STRING
         ⌊Generate (STRING, L+1, characters available with current
               character deleted)
    END OF THE ALGORITHM

    We start the algorithm with an empty current STRING, L = 0, and all
    characters available.

14. Start BINARYSEARCH(FIRST, LAST, ITEM)
       If FIRST > LAST Then ⌈Write ITEM, "is not in the list"
                    ⌊Stop
       Set MIDDLE to (FIRST + LAST)/2
       If ITEM = $LIST_{MIDDLE}$ Then ⌈Write ITEM, "is at position",
                              MIDDLE
                           ⌊Stop

If ITEM $<$ LIST$_{\text{MIDDLE}}$ Then   BINARYSEARCH (FIRST,
                                     MIDDLE-1, ITEM)
                    Else   BINARYSEARCH (MIDDLE+1,
                                     LAST, ITEM)

END OF ALGORITHM

We start the algorithm by invoking:

        BINARYSEARCH (1, N, KEY)

where N is the number of items in the list and KEY is the value we are searching for.

15.   START
      Read N
      Read $X_1 \ldots, X_N$ and $Y_1, \ldots, Y_N$
      Rank(X, A) {an algorithm for ranking raw scores}
      Rank(Y, B)
      Set I to 1, SUM to 0 and BAD-SCORES to 0
      Repeat N times
         If either A_I or B_I is a -1
           Then Increment BAD-SCORES by 1
               Write the RAW-SCORES into the error log
           Else Compute $(A_I - B_I)^2$ and add it to SUM
               Write the RAW-SCORES into the correlation report
        Increment I
      End of the repeat loop
      Set N to (N $-$ BAD-SCORES)

      Set R to $1 - \left(\dfrac{6 * \text{SUM}}{N * (N^2 - 1)} \right)$

      Write "The rank correlation coefficient is", R
   END OF ALGORITHM

Chapter 3

1. a. 3.14159
    b. 2.71828
    c. 0.5 (the leading 0 is necessary!)
    d. 6.02E+23   602E21   0.602E+24
       60.2E+22   602.0E+21   0.060200E25
    e. 7 (as an integer)
       7.0 (as a real)
    f. '7'

2. a. Valid.

    b. Invalid—only one value is permitted.
    c. Invalid—the ':' should be '='.
    d. Valid.

3.   CONST   TERMINATOR = '.';
                MAXLINELENGTH = 80;
                LOWPERCENTAGE = 0.0;
                HIGHPERCENTAGE = 100.0;

4.   a. Invalid—all three names are invalid identifers.
    b. Invalid—the identifier A3 is declared twice.
    c. Valid.
    d. Valid.

5.   VAR   A, B, C : REAL;
          ROOT1, ROOT2 : REAL;
             SOLUTION : BOOLEAN;
          SETNUMBER : INTEGER;

8.   a. Reserved keyword.
    b. Standard keyword.
    c. User identifier.
    d. Standard keyword.
    e. Standard keyword that represents a constant value.
    f. User identifier.
    g. User identifier.
    h. Real constant.
    i. Invalid
    j. Integer constant.
    k. User identifier.
    l. User identifier.
    m. Invalid.
    n. Invalid.

10.   a. p = q
     b. p <> q
     c. p > q

Chapter 4

1.   a. −2
    b. 5
    c. −13
    d. 2

2. a. 10
   c. (Assume the ASCII character set, in which ORD('*') is 42.)
      $\sqrt{56} \approx 7.49$
   e. False.

4. a. Incorrect. The PASCAL expressions represents $\sqrt{A} + (B/C)$. The
      correct translation is

$$SQRT((A + B)/C)$$

   b. Correct.

5. a. TAXABLEPAY:= GROSSPAY − (11.00 * DEPENDENTS) − 14.00
   c. CAPACITY:= W * T * LN(1.0 + S/N)
   f. TEST:= (VALUE >= 1) AND (VALUE <= 10)

6. a.   X will be 53
         Y will be 78
         CH will be '*'
   c.   X will be 53
         Y will be 110
         CH will be ' '
         Z will be 59

8. WRITELN (' WHOLESALE PRICE IS', WPRICE:10:2);
      WRITELN (' RETAIL PRICE IS   ', RPRICE:10:2);
      WRITELN;
      WRITELN (' MARKUP IS   ', MARKUP:10:2, '%')

10. a. WRITELN('   GROSS PAY $', GROSS:6:2);
          WRITELN('   DEDUCTIONS $', DEDUC:6:2);
          WRITELN('   −−−−−−−');
          WRITELN('   NET $', NETPAY:6:2)

11. PROGRAM ROOTS(INPUT, OUTPUT);
      {This is a program to compute and print the two real roots of a
        quadratic equation $ax^2 + bx + c = 0$. It does not test for a negative
        discriminant or division by 0   }
      VAR A, B, C, DISCRIMINANT, ROOT1, ROOT2: REAL;

      BEGIN
          READLN(A, B, C);
          WRITELN(' THE THREE COEFFICIENTS ARE', A, B, C);
          {Now compute the two real roots using the quadratic
            formula}

```
        DISCRIMINANT:= SQR(B) − 4.0*A*C;
        ROOT1:= (−B + SQRT(DISCRIMINANT))/(2.0 * A);
        ROOT2:= (−B − SQRT(DISCRIMINANT))/(2.0 * A);
        WRITELN(' THE TWO REAL ROOTS ARE', ROOT1, ROOT2)
    END.
```

Chapter 5

1. a.
```
    REPEAT
        READ(CH)
    UNTIL (CH = '*') OR EOLN

    READ(CH);
    WHILE NOT ((CH = '*') OR EOLN) DO
        READ(CH)
```

Note that the boolean expression could also be written as

```
        (CH <> '*') AND NOT EOLN
```

3. FOR CURRENTVALUE: = 150 DOWNTO 15 DO S_1

5.
```
    IF V₁
        THEN IF V₂
                THEN S₁
                ELSE S₂
        ELSE S₃
```

8.
```
    PROGRAM CELSIUS(OUTPUT);
    VAR FTEMP:   INTEGER;
        CTEMP:   REAL;

    BEGIN
    FOR FTEMP: = −40 TO 120 DO
        BEGIN
        CTEMP: = 5 *(FTEMP−32)/9;
        WRITELN(' FAHRENHEIT TEMP = ', FTEMP:5, ' CELSIUS
                TEMP =', CTEMP:7:1)
        END
    END.
```

12.
```
    PROGRAM PIBYRAND(OUTPUT);
        CONST NN = 10000;
        VAR I, COUNT: INTEGER;
            X, Y: REAL;
        BEGIN
        COUNT: = 0;
```

```
    FOR I: = 1 TO NN DO
        BEGIN
        X: = RANDOM;
        Y: = RANDOM;
        IF SQR(X) + SQR(Y) < 1.0 THEN COUNT: = COUNT + 1
        END;
    WRITELN(' PI IS APPROXIMATELY', (COUNT/NN) * 4.0)
    END.
```

13.
```
    PROGRAM ONE (OUTPUT);
    CONST NN = 100000;
    VAR K2, K3, K4, K5, K6, K7, K8, K9, K10, K11, K12, I, ROLL:
        INTEGER;
    BEGIN
    K2: = 0; K3: = 0; K4: = 0; K5: = 0; K6: = 0;
    K7: = 0; K8: = 0; K9: = 0; K10: = 0; K11: = 0; K12: = 0;
    FOR I: = 1 TO NN DO
        BEGIN
        ROLL: = TRUNC(RANDOM*6) + 1 + TRUNC(RANDOM*6) + 1;
        {TRUNC(RANDOM*6) produces a random integer in
        the range 0 .. 5}
        CASE ROLL OF
            2: K2:= K2+1;
            3: K3:= K3+1;
            4: K4:= K4+1;
            5: K5:= K5+1;
            6: K6:= K6+1;
            7: K7:= K7+1;
            8: K8:= K8+1;
            9: K9:= K9+1;
           10: K10:= K10+1;
           11: K11:= K11+1;
           12: K12:= K12+1
        END {Case}
        END {For};
    WRITELN(' THE PROBABILITY DISTRIBUTION IS');
    WRITELN(K2/NN:6:3, K3/NN:6:3, K4/NN:6:3, K5/NN:6:3,
            K6/NN:6:3, K7/NN:6:3, K8/NN:6:3, K9/NN:6:3,
            K10/NN:6:3, K11/NN:6:3, K12/NN:6:3)
    END.
```

Chapter 6

1. a. Invalid. Parentheses will be required around both boolean conditions.

b. Valid.

c. Valid. The THEN clause is empty. Syntactically that is perfectly acceptable.

d. Invalid. PASCAL has no operator notation for exponentiation. ** is from other computer languages. Note the 10-character name CIRCLEAREA is perfectly acceptable.

e. Valid. There are numerous redundancies, but no actual syntactic errors. The BEGIN-END pair are not needed, but will not cause problems. The semicolons after Z := X + Y and END are also unnecessary, but the "empty statement" will allow things to work out correctly.

f. Invalid. There can be no implied multiplication in PASCAL. We must say 2 * A or 2.0 * A.

g. Invalid. := is the assignment operator
   = is the comparison operator

h. Valid. The WRITELN command does not require parameters.

i. Invalid. The VAR declaration uses the colon to separate the name field from the type field.

j. Invalid. The CASE statement allows only a single statement following each case label. If we wish to perform more than one operation we must enclose it in a compound statement. Also, the BEGIN is not used in a CASE statement.

k. Invalid. Illegal semicolon before the ELSE.

2.

Line Number	Error
1	PROGRAM is mispelled (syntax error)
4	The variable "I" is not declared as an integer (syntax error)
4–5	The reserved word BEGIN should appear after the VAR declaration (syntax error)
6	a. Initializing SUM to 1 will produce the wrong answer (1 will be counted twice) (logical error)
	b. Semicolon is missing after the assignment statement (syntax error)
7	= should be := (syntax error)
8	a. = should be := (syntax error)
	b. The assignment statement should be SUM := SUM + K (logical error)
	c. Semicolon is missing after the assignment statement (syntax error)
9	The text printed will be this: THE SUM FROM 1 TO K IS. 'K' should not appear as a character in the string; rather, its value should be printed. WRITELN(' THE SUM FROM 1 TO ', K, ' IS ', SUM) (logical error)

3. Line 150. The variable LIMIT is misspelled.
   Line 180. There is an unmatched quote mark in the WRITELN statement.
   Line 205. A BEGIN is needed.
   Line 210. There is a missing ';' after the assigment statement.
   Line 290. Same error as in line 180.

Chapter 7

1. TYPE CROP = (WHEAT, BARLEY, RYE, CORN, SOYBEANS);
         NEWENGLAND = (MAINE, NH, VT, MASS, CONN, RI);
         AUTHORS = (SCHNEIDER, WEINGART, PERLMAN);
         ZONES = (PACIFIC, MOUNTAIN, CENTRAL, EASTERN);
         SOLUTION = (REAL, DOUBLE, COMPLEX);

2. TYPE POSINT = 0 . . MAXINT;
         LETTERS = 'A' . . 'Z';
             {The above declaration assumes that the 26 letters of
               the alphabet are in proper collating sequence from
               A to Z}
         CASHCROPS = CORN . . SOYBEANS;
         NUMBERS = −40 . . 2;

5. TYPE SUITTYPE = (CLUBS, DIAMONDS, HEARTS, SPADES);
         VAULESTYPE = (ACE, TWO, THREE, FOUR, FIVE, SIX,
                         SEVEN, EIGHT, NINE, TEN, JACK,
                         QUEEN, KING);
          CARD = RECORD
                         SUIT : SUITTYPE;
                         VALUES : VALUESTYPE
                 END;
   VAR   SUITX : SUITTYPE;
          VALUES : VALUESTYPE;
          DECK : ARRAY [SUITTYPE, VALUESTYPE] OF CARD;

   FOR   SUITX := CLUBS TO SPADES DO
   FOR VALUEX := ACE TO KING DO
        WITH DECK [SUITX, VALUEX] DO
             BEGIN
             SUIT := SUITX;
             VALUES := VALUEX
             END;

6. VAR STRING : ARRAY [1 . . 10] OF CHAR;
       I, NUMBER : INTEGER;

```
SIGN : (POS, NEG, NONE);
    .
    .
    .
    .
    .
```

{Note that this fragment does not check for a value larger than MAXINT or check for illegal syntax}

```
NUMBER := .0; SIGN := NONE; I := 1;
WHILE (I <= 10) AND (STRING[I] <> ' ') DO
        BEGIN
        IF (STRING[I] = '+')
              THEN SIGN := POS
              ELSE IF (STRING [I] ='-')
                          THEN SIGN := NEG
                          ELSE NUMBER:= (NUMBER*10)+
                                    (STRING[I] - ORD('0'));
        I := I+1
        END;
IF (SIGN = NEG) THEN NUMBER := -(NUMBER)
```

8. a. [6, 7, 8, 9, 10]
    b. FALSE (A*C is [1, 3, 5])
    c. [5]
    d. TRUE
    e. TRUE

14.
```
DONE := FALSE;
PTR := HEAD;
WHILE (PTR <> NIL) AND (NOT DONE) DO
            IF PTR↑.DATA = KEY
                  THEN DONE := TRUE
                  ELSE PTR := PTR↑.P
```

16. a. 1. TYPE STACKTYPE = ARRAY [1 .. 32] OF INTEGER;
            VAR   STACK : STACKTYPE;
                      STACKPTR : INTEGER;
         2. TYPE STACKTYPE = RECORD
                                  STRUCTURE : ARRAY [1 .. 32]
                                      OF INTEGER;
                                  POINTER : INTEGER;
                              END;
            VAR STACK : STACKTYPE;

```
3. TYPE PTR = ↑STACKELEMENT;
      STACKELEMENT = RECORD
                          STRUCTURE : INTEGER;
                          POINTER : PTR
                     END;
      VAR STACKPOINTER : PTR;
```

Chapter 8

1. Variable A is global to the entire program.
   The variable B declared in OUTER is available to OUTER, P2, and P3.
   The variables B and C declared in P1 are available only in P1.
   The variables C and D declared in P2 are available in P2 and P3.
   The variable E declared in P3 is local to P3.

3. $X = 6, Y = 2, Z = 3$

4. Inside proc1, values for a, b, c are currently   *** 2 6
   Inside proc2, values for a, b, c are currently   4 5 6
   Still inside proc1, values for a, b, c are currently   4 2 6
   Inside main program, values for a, b, c are   1 2 3

6. Current values of M and VALUE are 0 3
   Current values of M and VALUE are 1   8
   Current values of M and VALUE are 2 13
   Current values of M and VALUE are 3 18
   18

9. The subprogram should be a function. Parameters should be passed by value.

```
FUNCTION INVEST(P: REAL; N: INTEGER; R: REAL): REAL;

CONST FREQ = 4;
VAR    VALUE, RATE  : REAL;
       YEAR, I      : INTEGER;

BEGIN
   VALUE:=P;
   RATE := R/FREQ;   {Interest rates per compounding period}
   FOR YEAR := 1 TO N DO
      FOR I := 1 TO FREQ DO
            VALUE := VALUE * (1.0 + RATE);
   INVEST := VALUE;
   WRITELN(P:10:2, ' WILL GROW TO ', VALUE:14:2, ' IN ', N:3,
            ' YEARS AT ', 100.0 * R, '% INTEREST')
```

END; {Of INVEST}

Possible function invocation:
    RESULT := INVEST(1000.0, 4, 0.06)

13. Assume each node of the tree is a record of the following form.

```
TYPE      NODEPTR = ↑NODE;
          NODE    = RECORD
                       LEFT  : NODEPTR;
                       NAME : CHAR;
                       RIGHT : NODEPTR
                    END;

PROCEDURE  SEARCHATREE(ROOT: NODEPTR);
BEGIN
    IF   ROOT <> NIL
      THEN   BEGIN
                SEARCHATREE(ROOT↑.LEFT);
                WRITELN(ROOT↑.NAME);
                SEARCHATREE(ROOT↑.RIGHT)
             END
    END;  {Of SEARCHATREE}
```

16. 1. The procedure uses global variables for passing information. However, global variables are not an acceptable way of passing information to an external procedure. We would need to make the following values parameters to the procedure.

    LIST   (value parameter)
    NUMBER   (value parameter)
    AVERAGE   (reference parameter)
    BAD   (reference parameter)

   2. The constant values for the legal range of scores and the upper bound for the number of scores should be variables passed in as call by value parameters. Or, alternatively, the range checking should be eliminated from the procedure altogether and placed in the read routine. As it now stands, the procedure is too specific for general use.
   3. I and TOTAL should be local variables.
   4. If range checking is left in the procedure, it should return a signal flag indicating that illegal values were encountered.
   5. The procedure should not write out the result but should return the result to the calling program. Note that this could mean that AVG might be better written as a FUNCTION.

INDEX